"SECRET SOCIETIES" RECONSIDERED

"This book is unprecedented in the analytical breadth of its interpretations of Chinese secret societies, the critical awareness it has of past treatments of its subject and their weaknesses, and the wisdom of its geographical balance which transcends national boundaries, so that we can see the phenomenon as a whole. It achieves the rare feat of making a major contribution to both Chinese and Southeast Asian history."

Alexander Woodside,
University of British Columbia

"This is a breakthrough volume. It offers a new paradigm for under-standing 'secret societies'—one in which their secrecy and alleged socio-political deviance are not their most important characteristics. Instead, they are to be understood as one version of a general type—the Chinese brotherhood—a characteristic organization of ordinary, non-elite male Chinese. It is the identification of the brotherhood as a major organizational type—one with several subcategories that include the 'secret society'—that opens up a new approach to the understand-ing of Chinese society at home and abroad. By showing us how the brotherhood was found in both early modern China and early modern Southeast Asian Chinese societies, the authors document the transfer-ence of Chinese institutions overseas. They also encourage us to apply their model to Chinese in more recent times and more distant places."

Edgar Wickberg,
University of British Columbia

History/China/Southeast Asia

Studies on Modern China

Studies on Modern China

"SECRET SOCIETIES" RECONSIDERED

PERSPECTIVES ON THE SOCIAL HISTORY OF EARLY MODERN SOUTH CHINA AND SOUTHEAST ASIA

DAVID OWNBY
MARY SOMERS HEIDHUES

editors

ROBERT J. ANTONY
JEAN DeBERNARDI
SHARON CARSTENS
DIAN H. MURRAY
BAREND J. ter HAAR
CARL A. TROCKI

An East Gate Book

M.E. Sharpe
Armonk, New York
London, England

An East Gate Book

Copyright © 1993 by M. E. Sharpe, Inc.

Library of Congress Cataloging-in-Publication Data

"Secret societies" reconsidered: perspectives on the social history of early modern South
China and Southeast Asia / edited by David Ownby and Mary Somers Heidhues.
p. cm. — (Studies on modern China)
Includes bibliographical references and index.
ISBN 1–56324–198–6. — ISBN 1–56324–199–4 (pbk.)
1. Secret societies—China.
2. Secret societies—Asia, Southeastern.
3. Hung men (Society)—History.
I. Ownby, David, 1958– .
II. Somers Heidhues, Mary F.
III. Series.
HS310.S43 1993
366—dc20
93–26121
CIP

Printed in the United States of America

The first printing of this work contained
an error on the cover and title page.
The word "Early" was left out of the subtitle.

BM (c) 10 9 8 7 6 5 4 3 2 1
BM (p) 10 9 8 7 6 5 4 3 2 1

Contents

Contributors

Robert J. Antony received his Ph.D. from the University of Hawaii in 1988 and is currently Assistant Professor of History at Western Kentucky University. He has published articles on Qing archives and legal history, and is preparing a book called *Bandits, Brotherhoods, and Qing Law in Guangdong, South China, 1760–1840*.

Sharon Carstens received her Ph.D. from Cornell University in 1980 and is now Associate Professor of Anthropology at Portland State University. Her research and writing have focused on Chinese culture in Singapore and Malaysia from both historic and ethnographic perspectives. She is editor of *Cultural Identities in Northern Peninsular Malaysia* (1986), and is currently working on an ethnography of the Chinese Malaysian community of Pulai.

Jean DeBernardi is a socio-cultural anthropologist who received her Ph.D. from the University of Chicago (1986) and currently teaches linguistic and cultural anthropology at the University of Alberta in Canada. Her research interests include Chinese popular religious culture (in particular spirit mediumship), the social history of the Straits Chinese, and social aspects of language use in Hokkien communities in Malaysia and Taiwan. She is completing a book titled *Empire over Imagination: Chinese Popular Religion in Colonial and Post-Colonial Malaysia*.

Barend J. ter Haar received his doctorate from Leiden University in 1990 and is currently a Research Fellow of the Royal Dutch Academy of Arts and Sciences. His general research focus is on the social history of religion and non-elite culture. He has published *The White Lotus Teachings in Chinese Religious History* (1992), and is currently completing a book on the ritual and mythology of the Triads, as well as shorter studies of Chinese cannibalism and the religious cult of Guan Yu.

Mary Somers Heidhues received her Ph.D. from Cornell University (1965) and currently teaches at the University of Göttingen and the University of Hamburg in Germany. Among her many publications are *Southeast Asia's Chinese Minorities* (1974), and *Banka Tin and Mentok Pepper: Chinese Settlement on an Indonesian Island* (1991). In connection with her general interest in Chinese minorities in Southeast Asia, she is presently conducting research on the history of the Chinese of West Kalimantan, Indonesia.

Dian Murray is Associate Professor of History and Associate Dean at the University of Notre Dame. She received her Ph.D. from Cornell University (1979) and began her teaching career at Linfield College in McMinnville, Oregon. She was the recipient of a Mellon Faculty Fellowship in the Humanities at Harvard University during the 1981–82 academic year. Murray is the author of *Pirates of the South China Coast, 1790–1810* (1987), and a second book, *The Origin of the Tiandihui (Heaven and Earth Society)* is in press.

David Ownby received his Ph.D. from Harvard University (1989) and now teaches at Southern Methodist University. His research focuses on the social history and popular culture of China's Southeast Coast. The chief results of this research will appear in a forthcoming volume titled *Not Quite Bandits: Brotherhoods, Secret Societies and the State in Early Modern Southeast China.*

Carl A. Trocki, who received his Ph.D. from Cornell University (1975), is the Professor of Asian Studies at Queensland University of Technology in Brisbane, Australia. He has also been the Jacobson Visiting Associate Professor of Southeast Asian History at Georgetown University. He is the author of *Opium and Empire: Chinese Society in Colonial Singapore, 1800–1910* (1990). His current research interests include the opium trade in the nineteenth century and the development of a global economy, as well as the history of Southeast Asia in the eighteenth century.

Preface

Providing a forum for interdisciplinary, inter-area, and international exchange among Asianists is a prime goal of the annual meetings of the Association for Asian Studies. When, however, Mary Somers Heidhues proposed bringing China and Southeast Asia specialists together to discuss recent research on "secret societies," neither she nor Carl Trocki, who helped conceive and assemble the panel, suspected where the dialogue might lead.

Entitled "Early Modern Socioeconomic Organizations: Kongsis, Triads, and *Hui*," the session brought together specialists on the early modern histories of both China and Southeast Asia, focusing on the *social* and *economic* functions of these organizations, as well as their better-known criminal and political activities. Ambitious in a number of ways, the panel included participants from both North America and Europe (Asian invitees, unable to attend for other reasons, are well represented in the bibliographies) and from the disciplines of history, sinology, anthropology, and political science, and offered papers which covered Mainland China, Taiwan, Malaysia, and Indonesia. Many of us met for the first time immediately before the presentation of the panel and some skepticism was evident: could it have been that participants were drawn by the venue of the conference—New Orleans—as much as by the intellectual agenda?

Whatever the authors' motivations, the papers meshed surprisingly well. Ownby recalls feeling that the Southeast Asian perspective answered many questions posed by his research in Fujian and Taiwan, and that Barend J. ter Haar's focus on messianism in the early Heaven and Earth Society added a cultural dimension which had been missing from recent studies of Chinese secret societies. At the dinner which followed the panel, we discovered that all panelists shared the feeling that the panel had been unexpectedly intellectually rewarding, and that the collection of the individual papers into a book might be worthy of consideration. Heidhues, who first proposed the idea, shared editorial responsibility with Ownby, whose North American location expedited the production process.

As the months proceeded and the original panel participants—Jean

DeBernardi, Barend ter Haar, Mary Somers Heidhues, Dian Murray, and David Ownby—revised and expanded their initial contributions, they were joined by Robert Antony, Sharon Carstens, and Carl Trocki, whose chapters add depth to the volume. We made a genuine effort to involve all contributors in the production of the book, and as editors, insisted that all chapter authors take one another's findings seriously. Consequently, the original panel became something of a scholarly workshop as the volume took shape, linked by technology (phone, electronic mail, fax) and common interests, even if separated by geographic distance.

Despite the inevitable difficulties and occasional tedium of producing a collection of essays, the editing of this volume has been a genuine pleasure, both intellectual and personal. We hope that our readers share some of this pleasure.

We are grateful for the editorial expertise of M. E. Sharpe and especially of Doug Merwin, Angela Piliouras, and Debra Soled. In addition, without the support of the History Department of Southern Methodist University, this book would hardly have been possible. Some of the research for Ownby's contributions was underwritten by a grant from the Undergraduate Research Council of Southern Methodist University, which allowed Ownby to assume a position as Associate in Research at Harvard University's John King Fairbank Center for East Asian Research during the summer of 1991. Much of the writing of Ownby's contributions was completed during his research sabbatical during the fall of 1992. In addition, Department Chair Daniel T. Orlovsky never raised an eyebrow (or at least Ownby never *saw* him raise one) at the cost of the many faxes, trans-Atlantic phone calls, and bulky mailings incurred during the production of this volume—no small statement in these days when many universities find themselves unable to provide their faculties with even basic services. The speedy completion of this volume reflects SMU's generosity and trust in the value of research, and Ownby wishes to thank Dan Orlovsky and all of his colleagues for creating an atmosphere conducive to research and writing.

Keeping in touch with a widely scattered and exceedingly mobile group of contributors and co-editing from across the Atlantic has not always been easy. Co-editor Heidhues, having participated in most of the process at the University of Göttingen, in the Seminar for Political Science, is grateful for the award, in late summer 1993, of a Luce Visiting Scholar grant at Ohio University's Southeast Asia Studies Program. Being at the Southeast Asia Collection of Ohio University's Alden Library made it possible to overcome distance, check references easily, and expedite the final editing chores.

The tedious task of proofreading has been cheerfully undertaken by Ken Larish and Karen Potje, as well as by the chapter authors, and (less cheerfully) by the editors.

David Ownby, Dallas, Texas
Mary Somers Heidhues, Athens, Ohio
September 1993

"SECRET SOCIETIES" RECONSIDERED

1

Secret Societies Reconsidered

David Ownby

Why *another* book about Chinese secret societies? Scores of Chinese scholars have written thousands of pages on the topic since the Republican period, focusing largely on the question of secret society origins. Western academics produced a spate of studies of secret societies in the 1960s and 1970s, probing their roles in the rebellions and revolutions of the nineteenth and twentieth centuries. Journalists in the 1980s and 1990s continue to link the societies to worldwide narcotics smuggling rings. Sociologists scrutinize their structure and membership. Novelists and film-makers exploit their violent exoticism. At present, an impressive (some might say *op*pressive) bibliography treats the origins, social significance, and contemporary relevance of Chinese secret societies. One might be forgiven for thinking that there is little left to add.

The contributors to this volume believe that there is. Many of the chapters present evidence from a new source: the historical archives of the People's Republic of China, closed to most foreign scholars until after the Cultural Revolution (1966–76). This evidence is placed alongside studies of secret societies and their analogues (brotherhoods, *hui*, kongsi) in the Chinese communities of Southeast Asia, affording a broader perspective on the topic. Taken together, the evidence and viewpoints permit us to offer a new interpretation of the early history of secret societies, one that grounds them in the non-elite social organization and popular culture of South China and Southeast Asia, rather than in national politics or ethnic consciousness.

This interpretation relies on a methodology that embeds secret societies in their local settings and examines the relationships between the societies and other institutions in these settings. In fact, many of the contributors concentrate as much on the local social context as on the secret societies themselves. Applying this approach to different settings helps to avoid reducing "secret societies" and their members to any single definitive characterization—not "primitive rebels," not "criminal gangs," not even "innocent practitioners of mutual aid." Instead, taken together, the chapters in this volume identify a continuum of organizational forms—brotherhood, *hui*, secret society, kongsi—and a corpus of

3

cultural symbols—clustering around the notion of fictive kinship—that could be drawn on by groups of non-elite Chinese in a variety of contexts and used for a variety of purposes. From this perspective, secret societies, with their complex rituals and professed political agendas, were only one manifestation of a broader set of non-elite social practices. The interpretation of these social practices employed in this book is spelled out in more detail later in this introductory chapter, but the following paragraphs introduce our approach and our most important findings.

We focus on South China and Southeast Asia. South China (for present purposes, chiefly Fujian and Guangdong provinces) teemed with brotherhoods, *hui*, and secret societies earlier than other parts of China, as evidenced by the greater number of cases from this area in the Qing archives, the chief source for most of our contributors working on China. The Chinese communities of Southeast Asia were composed almost entirely of immigrants from this South China region, and it is not inappropriate that these areas be considered part of a common culture. Our essays also concentrate on the early history of the societies, the eighteenth and early nineteenth centuries in the case of South China, the late eighteenth and mid-nineteenth centuries in the case of Southeast Asia. Focus on this early period is important because in both South China and Southeast Asia, the periods examined predate the full criminalization of secret societies and provide evidence of brotherhoods and secret societies dedicated to a wide range of activities.

The impulse to organize these associations grew out of circumstances somewhat unique to the regions under examination. In Taiwan and Southeast Asia, settlement of genuine frontiers by young, single men without the protection of lineage, village, or state prompted organization along the principles of brotherhood. In mainland South China, a complex of factors, including the protracted and disruptive dynastic transition in the late seventeenth century, followed in the eighteenth century by rapid population growth in a violent region already pressed for arable land, produced significant numbers of marginal young men who found organization by fictive kinship equally useful.

In some cases, these organizations were little more than ad hoc survival strategies—some protective, some predatory, some both (Perry 1980, 1–9)—but in other instances the associations facilitated cooperation and organization on a remarkable scale. Particularly in Southeast Asia, where Chinese brotherhood associations were not constrained by a jealous state and a local elite that owed much of its legitimacy to that state, brotherhood associations blossomed into shareholding corporations that mined gold in Borneo and organized plantation agriculture in the environs of what came to be Singapore (see chapters 3 and 4). In nineteenth-century Malaya, secret societies were accepted by Chinese, Malays, and British alike as social institutions that, among other functions, produced political leadership in the Chinese community (see chapters 4, 5, and 9). In South China, although fictive kinship in a somewhat different sense did play an important role in the settlement of Taiwan, facilitating the organization of surname groups where lineages were slow to grow (Hsu 1980, 88; Jordan 1972, 12–26), brotherhoods per se did not achieve the same size and influence as in Southeast Asia. Nonetheless, the early history of what we have heretofore taken to be "secret societies" might be as fruitfully linked with non-elite associational behavior such as funeral societies and rotating credit societies as with criminal entrepreneurship and rebellion.

In sum, this volume seeks to broaden our understanding of secret societies by grouping them together with other associations founded by similar types of people in similar contexts, employing similar organizational principles and cultural symbols. We are not rejecting the characterization of the secret society as a clandestine association with its own particular set of rituals and beliefs and a written tradition to pass on these rituals and beliefs—indeed ter Haar's chapter in this volume illustrates what can be done when scholars take seriously the documents and rituals of the Heaven and Earth Society (Tiandihui). Nor are we denying the frequent link between secret societies and rebellion. We are, however, asserting that preoccupation with exotica, violence, and rebellion has obscured important aspects of the social history of early modern South China and Southeast Asia. In the brotherhoods, *hui*, kongsis, and secret societies of South China and Southeast Asia, we see a flexible, non-elite response to the challenges of the mobile, commercial, competitive order of the early modern period, a complex of popular corporate activity with broad implications for our understanding of the evolution of the social histories of South China and Southeast Asia.

Historiography of Secret Societies

A brief overview of the imposing historiography of Chinese secret societies will bring our approach and findings into sharper focus. This overview can only skim the surface; a forthcoming study of the historiography of the Heaven and Earth Society alone includes nearly 350 bibliographic entries (Murray 1993). A comprehensive treatment of the literature on brotherhoods, *hui*, and secret societies in China and Southeast Asia would begin with commentary by Qing officials and lawmakers (which Antony discusses in his chapter in this volume), and include at least comparisons between Triads and Freemasons by nineteenth-century treaty port "sinologists," reports of colonial officials in Southeast Asia, and even popular journalism on Triads and gangs in Chinatowns throughout the contemporary world. For our immediate purposes, we narrow the relevant scholarship to four schools: Republican-period Chinese scholarship; Western scholarship of the 1960s and 1970s, often associated with French scholar Jean Chesneaux; recent archival scholarship in China and Taiwan; and the investigation by social scientists of secret societies and their analogues in Southeast Asia.

Republican-Period Chinese Scholarship

Several Republican-period Chinese scholars undertook the first attempts at genuine scholarly research into the origins and history of secret societies. Consistent with the statist orientation of Chinese historians throughout the ages, these scholars, of whom Xiao Yishan and Luo Ergang are the best known, pledged their energies to the consolidation of the new Chinese Republican government (for representative works, see Luo 1943; Xiao 1935).

The link between an academic history of secret societies and the consolidation of the Republican government lay in founding father Sun Yat-sen's political activities before the establishment of the Republic of China in 1912. Exiled from China, Sun traveled the world in the late nineteenth and early twentieth centuries, visiting communities of ethnic Chinese and asking for their help in toppling the Manchu regime and establishing a modern republic (Ma 1990; Schiffrin 1968; Wilbur 1976, ch. 2). Frequently, he found that courting—and even joining—local secret societies was essential to mobilizing the resources of the communities. These resources might range from financial contributions to concrete assistance in planning uprisings in China proper, if local Chinese societies had maintained active links with societies on the mainland. To encourage such financial and organizational aid, Sun praised the nationalist, anti-Manchu origins of secret societies, hoping to rally the latent patriotism of North American and Southeast Asian societies, which had historically been closer to mutual benefit societies than cabals of rebels-in-waiting. In his contacts with mainland secret societies, Sun again found it useful to stress the societies' early anti-Manchu history; by so doing, he hoped to redirect the activities of the frequently xenophobic societies away from foreigners and toward the Manchu rulers. As part of this general mobilization, "scholar-revolutionaries" like Tao Chengzhang and Hirayama Shu put together popular, journalistic histories of secret societies reflecting Sun's political intentions around the time of the 1911 revolution (Hirayama 1912; Tao n.d.) , but it fell to the postrevolution scholars to comb the historical record for genuine evidence to substantiate Sun's claims (Murray 1993, ch. 4).

The central mission of the Republican-period scholars thus came to be the location of evidence to prove that secret societies were founded in the early Qing period out of anti-Manchu sentiment. They focused their efforts on the Heaven and Earth Society, the earliest and most influential of the southern Chinese societies. The scholars quickly discovered that the standard court-produced historical works contained little information on the society and turned to other, society-generated sources. These sources, many of which the scholars themselves unearthed in the course of their research, consisted largely of various versions of the Heaven and Earth Society origin myth, generally called the *Xiluxu* (Preface on the Xilu), part of the written tradition of the society in circulation since the early nineteenth century, as well as poems and songs also recorded in Tiandihui handbooks.

The seemingly simple task of tracing the Heaven and Earth Society's historical origins produced decidedly complex results. Not only were there several versions of the origin myths (most of which were similar in narrative structure and iconography, revolving around the tale of the monks of the Shaolin temple; Murray 1993, appendix B, offers translations of several key versions of the myth), but it proved extremely difficult to match up the "facts" revealed in the origin myths with what the scholars knew about early Qing history. Mysterious people and places remained mysterious, even after extensive research. Dates of important events made no sense. Important places and events that *should* have been mentioned in any history of popular anti-Manchu resistance in the early Qing (Jiading and Yangzhou, for example, sites of notorious Manchu massacres of Ming loyalists) were omitted. Eventually, the historians decided that the language of the origin myths, as part of the esoteric cant of the secret societies, must be veiled in secrecy as well, and that the specific names, dates, and places discussed in the *Xiluxu* "reflected" (*yingshe*) their actual historic equivalents rather than recording them directly.

This prudent decision to view the origin myths as "coded" allegories—which they undoubtedly are, as ter Haar illustrates below—was unfortunately accompanied by imprudent use of the methodology of "reflection." Since it was difficult to determine the principles by which the symbolic elements in the origin myths reflected their authentic historical referents, scholars found themselves free to speculate—in ways that often strike the current reader as fanciful and unsubstantiated. As a result, the Republican-period scholars were unable to demonstrate conclusively the early Qing anti-Manchu origins of the Heaven and Earth Society. Even though they remained personally convinced of this interpretation, the ongoing debates concerning the concrete time and place of the society's founding, and the nature of the "reflected" material revealed by the origin myths, demonstrate a lack of scholarly consensus. The interpretations of this branch of scholarship thus have not stood the test of time, most of its assertions crumbling under the evidence produced by more recent archival historians.

Even if much of this scholarship seems flawed by today's standards, it remains nonetheless influential. Scholars in post-1949 Taiwan have continued to elaborate on the themes discussed above, supported in their efforts by the Kuomintang, which on occasion likened its position on Taiwan to that of the Ming loyalists who fled south in the seventeenth century to avoid the Manchus—and supposedly founded the Heaven and Earth Society. In addition, although some Western texts adopt an interpretation of Tiandihui origins closer to that arrived at by Chinese archival scholars in the 1970s and 1980s (Fairbank and Reischauer 1989, 290–91; Fairbank, Reischauer, and Craig 1973, 467–68; Michael and Taylor 1975, 43; Spence 1990, 113–14), others are clearly indebted to the Republican-period scholarship (Hsü 1990, 127–29; Hucker 1975, 338). Finally, we should not forget that the Republican-period scholars performed an invaluable service in locating and reprinting large numbers of documents that continue to enrich current studies of secret society origins and practices (see chapter 6).

Jean Chesneaux and the Radicalization of Secret Societies

Despite frequent mention in nineteenth-century treaty port writings and occasional articles in twentieth-century scholarly publications, secret societies did not become the central focus of any sustained body of Western academic scholarship until the 1960s and 1970s, when a series of publications associated with the French scholar Jean Chesneaux produced a new interpretation (Chesneaux 1965, 1972). This interpretation reflected the general radicalization of much of Western scholarship in the 1960s and portrayed secret societies as "primitive revolutionaries" (Davis 1977) rather than mere nationalist rebels.

Chesneaux himself largely ignored Republican-period Chinese historiography, though many of his contributors paid more careful attention; his introduction to *Popular Movements*, for example, includes only one cursory reference to this scholarship (Chesneaux 1972, 5, n. 8). From Chesneaux's point of view, the works of Xiao, Luo, and their school must have seemed unduly focused on the question of the early Qing origin of one particular society—the Heaven and Earth Society. By contrast, Chesneaux and many of those associated with him were more interested in the general topic of the impact of popular movements on dynasties throughout Chinese history, and the specific topic of the linkages between popular movements and the rebellions and revolutions of the nineteenth and twentieth centuries.

In this context, Chesneaux argued that secret societies constituted the major organized force of opposition to Confucian, imperial China and that secret societies had led the popular revolts that toppled decaying dynasties throughout the imperial period. While acknowledging the complexity of China's long history and richly textured social fabric, Chesneaux adopted a broad interpretation of "secret societies," treating White Lotus sectarians, Heaven and Earth Society members, and adherents of a wide array of popular organizations as part of the same general phenomenon—popular opposition to oppression—at the hands of either the state or the wealthy and powerful gentry. As Chesneaux wrote in the introduction to the English translation of the original edited volume, *Popular Movements and Secret Societies,*

> Chinese secret societies were an essential component of the "anti-society." . . .
> Throughout Chinese history they constituted an opposition force whose dissent
> was better organized, more coherent, and better sustained than that of the
> bandits, the vagabonds, and the dissident literati. (Chesneaux 1972, 2)

Chesneaux's indebtedness to E. J. Hobsbawm, and indeed to the entire enterprise of "history from the bottom up," need hardly be noted (Hobsbawm 1959, 1969).

In contrast to Chesneaux's sweeping depiction of secret societies through the dynasties, most of the essays in Chesneaux's volumes concentrate on the late nineteenth and early twentieth centuries, and contain many important discoveries and insights. As this suggests, it is both unfair and inaccurate to speak of a single, unified "Chesneaux school" of interpretation. Chesneaux's personal contributions appear to have been confined chiefly to organization and coordination. Apart from the introductions to the conference volumes, he has written little analyzing secret societies themselves, except for the discussion of their role in his numerous textbooks (Chesneaux 1973, 1976, 1977, 1979). He has nonetheless given the field a strong impetus by collecting and publishing translations of Chinese source materials (Chesneaux 1971).

Many of his contributors, however, did pioneering work on the nineteenth- and twentieth-century history of secret societies. Frederic Wakeman mined local gazetteers and foreign archives for new information on secret societies and their local activities (Wakeman 1972). Ella Laffey added analysis of the autobiography of Liu Yongfu, a secret society leader active in Guangxi province in the 1860s, to gazetteers and other local sources, producing a detailed study of secret society activities in a particular region (Laffey 1972). Winston Hsieh convincingly applied G. William Skinner's work on the contrast between formal administrative centers and marketing centers to the secret society–led rebellions in Waizhou in 1911 (Hsieh 1972). Fei-ling Davis offered an excellent schema of the economic activities of late Qing secret societies (Davis 1970). These contributions merit special mention either because they brought new source material to bear on important questions relating to secret societies or because they developed new interpretations, closer to those of the archival school (see below) or to those found in this volume. In addition, Chesneaux's volumes should be seen as an early attempt to bring the assumptions and methods of social history to the China field and stand together with the works of Ho Ping-ti, Frederic Wakeman, and Philip Kuhn as influential efforts to shift the focus of the field away from elite, institutional, and diplomatic history (see Wasserstrom 1991, 4–5).

Despite these valuable achievements, when we review this scholarship from the post-Communist world of the 1990s, it is hard to resist the feeling that Chesneaux and some (but certainly not all) of his collaborators were guilty of a certain romanticism. Although their work was an important step toward the inclusion of popular and heterodox perspectives in the broader field of Chinese history, Chesneaux and some of those associated with him were on occasion too eager to locate revolutionary consciousness in every non-elite organization. Moreover, this eagerness to identify secret societies with radical themes often obscured the orthodox, loyalist slant of much of Triad "ideology," as well as the embeddedness of many secret societies in the surrounding social order. Although the Republican-period Chinese scholarship and the research associated with Chesneaux appear very different at first glance, both schools are similar in that much of their work was guided by an underlying contemporary political agenda: Luo Ergang and Xiao Yishan sought to bring secret societies to the service of the Chinese Republic; Jean Chesneaux sought to employ secret societies in the construction of a more genuinely democratic world by unearthing heretofore obscured traditions of popular radicalism.

Archival Scholarship in China and Taiwan

In 1964, a year before Chesneaux began preparations for the Leeds conference, which led to the publication of his first edited volume, Cai Shaoqing, a young Chinese historian, published an article that opened a third important chapter of secret society scholarship. His article, "On the Origins of the Tiandihui," used materials from a previously untapped source—the Qing archives, housed at what are now called the Number One Historical Archives in Beijing—to advance what came to be a significantly different interpretation of the origins of the Heaven and Earth Society, and, in fact, of the emergence and importance of secret societies in general (Cai 1964). Although the development of this interpretation was slowed by the Cultural Revolution, the current leaders of research on secret societies in the People's Republic remain Cai and his former student Qin Baoqi, and their methods and interpretations have in principle been confirmed by the leading Taiwanese scholar of secret societies, Zhuang Jifa, whose own archival work has proceeded independently of that of Cai and Qin.

The chief virtue of this new interpretation—outlined immediately below—was that it was grounded in what appeared to be more reliable sources than those employed either by the early Chinese scholars of the Republican period or the scholars of the Chesneaux school. The Qing archives used by Cai, Qin, and Zhuang include confessions of captured secret society members as well as extensive records of government investigation and suppression of specific instances of secret society activity. These sources are without doubt more concrete than the society-generated origin myths and other documents used by Xiao Yishan and Luo Ergang, the provenance and authorship of which were frequently in question. And when compared with the foreign archives and gazetteers exploited by Wakeman, Laffey, and other scholars associated with Chesneaux, the Qing archives again offer a richness of detail that can often supplement (if not supplant) the frequently terse information available in local gazetteers.

The interpretation produced by these archival historians constitutes a complete rejection of the work of their Republican-period predecessors and an important modification of that of Chesneaux. These historians argue that the Tiandihui was founded in 1761, thus refuting the idea that the secret society was established in the early Qing period. And they argue further that the roots of the Heaven and Earth Society—and secret societies in general—lie in organization for mutual aid, rather than national politics.

The impulse to organize for mutual aid receives slightly different interpretations. Cai Shaoqing and Qin Baoqi, working from a Marxist perspective, place mutual aid and secret societies in the context of the corrosive power of commerce on the communal village in South China (Cai 1987, 5–10; Liu and Qin 1982,

1029–34); Zhuang's interpretations have evolved over the years, at one point highlighting the utility of brotherhoods and secret societies in the context of violent feuds (Zhuang 1981, 11–18), more recently focusing on population growth, migration, and the resulting need for protection among young men at the margins of society (Zhuang 1988).

Neither of these interpretations denies the historical linkages between secret societies and rebellion, but the secret society in the archival reinterpretation is not given a central role in rebellion in the same way it was for the Republican-period historians, or for Chesneaux and his school. This lack of emphasis on the "dissident" nature of secret societies distinguishes the archival school from Chesneaux's scholarship. To the Chinese Marxists, peasants were already potentially revolutionary, and additional information concerning secret societies added little to their understanding of the nature of agrarian class relationships. Secret societies are but a step on the road to "peasant wars," the "motive force" in Chinese history for at least part of the era of Maoist historiography. By contrast, Chesneaux's "discovery" of secret societies was a significant part of what he hoped would be a fundamental redirection of research in Chinese history.

As this suggests, the valuable evidence unearthed by the Chinese scholars who have been part of the archival reinterpretation awaits linkage to a larger, compelling interpretation of late imperial Chinese society. Post-Mao historiography in the People's Republic promises important reinterpretations of significant aspects of Chinese history (Liu 1981), and papers presented at the First International Symposium on "Secret Societies in Modern Chinese History," held in Nanjing in June 1993, indicate that these reinterpretations now extend to secret societies. One would expect the increasingly open academic atmosphere of post-Jiang Taiwan to produce equally exciting reformulations.

Despite these hopeful developments, the chief accomplishment of Cai's and Qin's work remains the establishment of the precise date and venue of the founding of the Tiandihui, and the refutation of the claim that the Tiandihui was an anti-Manchu revolutionary organization from its origin.[1] Zhuang Jifa has been less tempted to trace the precise date and place of the Tiandihui founding,[2] and has perhaps been more adventurous than Cai or Qin in seeking to explain the emergence and popularity of brotherhoods and secret societies. Nonetheless, Zhuang's emphasis differs from the perspective developed in this volume in that he examines and categorizes large numbers of secret societies, often producing tables and maps that provide an important overview of the spread and incidence of secret society activity. This valuable macro-level research necessarily devotes less attention to particular local settings.

Scholarship on Secret Societies in Southeast Asia

An extensive scholarly record on secret societies and their analogues in Southeast Asia complements that just described for China.[3] In some ways, documentation on secret societies—particularly in nineteenth-century Nanyang—is both fuller and more accessible to Western scholars than that in China itself. Major caches of Chinese documents (such as those translated in Schlegel 1866) exist alongside the voluminous commentaries of European colonial officials who sought to comprehend and govern the rapidly growing Chinese settlements throughout Southeast Asia. European languages and European biases present less imposing obstacles to contemporary Western scholars than does the Qing archival record.

Much of the work of these colonial officials was pioneering, and some was brilliant, contributing to the larger field of sinology and still, like the works of Schlegel and de Groot, influential today (Groot 1885; Schlegel 1866). Furthermore, Jean DeBernardi's epilogue illustrates that even those officials who did not leave brilliant scholarship nonetheless made insightful observations concerning the local Chinese and their "combinations." Such observations were crucial to the maintenance of colonial control, for as Carstens, Trocki, and particularly DeBernardi show, the British in Malaya employed secret society headmen in a form of "indirect rule" until 1890, as if they were chiefs in a tribal society.

Unsurprisingly, virtually all the scholarship of the colonial period was concerned in one way or another with this problem of controlling the Chinese, an agenda that could not help but affect the resulting scholarship (even if "control" did not always mean "suppress," as it did in Qing China). Schlegel's translations of secret society documents helped colonial authorities develop policies to deal with local Chinese associations. J. S. M. Ward, coauthor with W. G. Stirling of the three-volume *The Hung Society*, noted in his preface to the work, "As an Assistant Protector of Chinese [in early twentieth-century Singapore] it is one of Mr. Stirling's duties to help in the suppression of the Hung . . . Society" (Ward and Stirling 1925, iv). Even de Groot's arguments equating mining kongsis with "village republics" were made in the context of a disagreement over the proper form of colonial control over the Chinese, de Groot arguing for the maintenance of indirect rule.

A similar focus is evident in the major twentieth-century works on the subject. M. L. Wynne (1941), Leon F. Comber (1959), and W. L. Blythe (1969), authors of major studies of secret societies in Malaya, all compiled significant portions of their data while serving in the colonial police force and government. Blythe in particular obtained much of his documentation as Secretary for Chinese Affairs in the Malayan Union during the anarchic postwar "Emergency," when a Communist insurgency, led and staffed almost wholly by Chinese, sought to prevent the reconsolidation of British power in the late 1940s. While preoccupation with control almost certainly increased the amount of data these authors unearthed, it might also have influenced their search for information and led to a one-sided view of Chinese society. As late as 1986, the eminent scholar Wang Gungwu felt compelled to introduce Yen Ching-hwang's *Social History of the Chinese in Singapore and Malaya* with the somewhat defensive (if nonetheless rather apt) comment that the "Chinese in South-East Asia have a reputation among colonial powers for being secretive. . . . [T]he tendency of early nineteenth century colonial officials to group most Chinese social organizations under the misleading label of 'secret societies' . . . has given the impression that most Chinese associations were sinister" (Yen 1986, vii). Wang's comments thus speak directly to the legacy of colonial commentary, as well as to the central themes of this volume.

The postwar era brought significant changes in scholarly emphasis, in part connected with the upheavals that led to the decolonization of Southeast Asia, but more directly linked to China's 1949 revolution. This revolution effectively closed China to Western social science research for some decades and, to quote the late Maurice Freedman, "promote[d] a spurt in studies of the Overseas Chinese, primarily in southeast Asia. Indeed, during most of the decade 1949–58 Chinese studies conducted by anthropologists were almost entirely confined to that region, and within it to Thailand, the Malay peninsula, Sarawak, and Indonesia" (Freedman 1979, 414). This "spurt" resulted in many important studies of the Chinese communities of Southeast Asia during the 1950s and 1960s (see discussion in Lockard 1985), before social scientists began to explore Taiwan, the Hong Kong New Territories, and eventually, the People's Republic of China. Both Maurice Freedman and G. William Skinner, whose anthropological work continues to influence various fields of Chinese studies, were drawn to the Chinese communities of Southeast Asia during this period.

Freedman's field work in Singapore in 1949–50 led to numerous publications on a wide variety of anthropological subjects, laying the groundwork for a career that for some decades largely dominated the field of Chinese social anthropology. His 1960 essay on "Immigrants and Associations: Chinese in Nineteenth-Century Singapore" broke new ground in the area under discussion in this volume by emphasizing the linkages between secret societies and community and political organizations such as speech groups and friendly societies. Freedman still viewed the historical South China Triads as rebellious, anti-Manchu conspiracies, an attitude he might have chosen to revise somewhat in light of recent archival findings. Nonetheless, his inclusion of secret societies among the larger body of associations clearly informs several of the analyses in this volume.

Alongside Freedman's work on Singapore is Skinner's treatment of the Chinese community in Thailand, which also considered the role of secret societies. While Freedman emphasized the role of secret societies as "an aspect of . . . [Chinese] unity against colonial claims to rule them" (Freedman 1979, 82), Skinner highlighted the divisiveness of the Chinese societies in Thailand. Throughout the nineteenth century, the societies were closely related to opium use, gambling, and prostitution among the Chinese, and these predacious activities, together with their organization by dialect, readily embroiled large numbers of Chinese in violence (Skinner 1957).

Neither Skinner nor Freedman, however, devoted central attention to secret societies, kongsis, or brotherhoods. Skinner was primarily interested in questions of cultural change and assimilation, making comparisons across national boundaries (in Thailand and Java) (Skinner 1960). Other community studies of Chinese in Southeast Asia also devoted attention to the Chinese in local Nanyang settings, especially to their leadership and organization (among many examples, see Wickberg 1965, and Willmott 1967, 1970). Although these studies did not neglect secret societies, by the same token the societies rarely figured prominently.

Freedman himself became increasingly focused on *Chinese* society—*not* the Chinese of the Nanyang. As he admitted

> I had never been able to take [the Singapore Chinese] simply for what they were, a highly urbanized group of immigrants and their descendants, and had striven to see beyond them to the society from which they had come. During the early 1950s . . . I began to play with the notion of reconstructing traditional Chinese society . . . with special reference . . . to its institutions of kinship and marriage. (Freedman 1979, 414–15)

We need hardly mention here Freedman's resulting work on family and lineage in Southeast China. Eventually, Skinner also turned his attention to traditional marketing practices in China proper, producing his path-breaking 1965 articles. In addition, with the "discovery" of Taiwan and Hong Kong as fruitful venues for anthropological and sociological China studies, the centrality of Southeast Asia to the various fields of China studies faded in the 1970s and 1980s.

Studies of secret societies among the Chinese of Southeast Asia have nonetheless continued. Among recent authors, Mak Lau Fong has applied sociology to past and present societies in Malaysia and Singapore, explaining the changing functions of secret societies and their criminalization in terms of "modernization" (Mak 1981). He finds, with Freedman, that societies have united communities riven by speech-group differences. Yen Ching-hwang, in his social history of the Chinese in Singapore and Malaya, describes societies as a pillar of the community, but believes that they "lost" their "original aims" (presumably overthrowing the Manchus) when they moved overseas (Yen 1986, 111).

Furthermore, we may be witnessing a renewed focus of scholarly attention to Southeast Asia. The University of California at Berkeley and Cornell University held major academic conferences on the Chinese abroad in the early 1990s,[4] and several valuable community studies on similar topics have recently appeared (Ackerman and Lee 1988; Cushman and Wang 1988; Gosling and Lim 1983; Lim and Gosling 1983; Salmon and Lombard 1977; Tan 1988). In addition, many parts of Southeast Asia unavailable for research since the Vietnam War are in the process of reopening. This work will undoubtedly generate new insights that will enrich studies of the history of secret societies.

Nonetheless, in the eyes of this China-centered editor, the "paradigmatic differences" between the studies of Southeast Asian Chinese in our volume and the scholarly tradition on which these studies build are less stark than in the case of China. One might speculate that this is because the scholarship on Southeast

Asia has not been invested with the same political (and even emotional) intensity as much of the work on Chinese secret societies and has not been directly linked to moral issues such as nationalism and revolution. Still, the essays in the present volume are distinguished by close attention to history and historical documentation (in particular, previously untapped archival sources); by focus on the content rather than the structure of social life; and by a willingness to treat Southeast Asian Chinese communities in relation to a larger Chinese society, without losing sight of local uniqueness and regional history.

Our Interpretation: Brotherhood Associations as Non-Elite Institutions

In summary, the depiction of secret societies by Republican-period scholars as politically conscious organizations is demonstrably wrong, at least for the early period. Chesneaux and his school at points seem to overemphasize the distance between secret societies and the rest of the social order. The archival reappraisal has perhaps failed to develop an interpretation of secret societies that does justice to the richness of documentation their energetic research has produced. And although sociologists and anthropologists working in Southeast Asia have been more sensitive to nuances of social structure, we hope to add a richer historical perspective, based on the availability of new sources and methodologies and the ongoing research of the last two decades.

This historiographical discussion leads naturally to presentation of our own interpretation, or, more accurately, the interpretation that can be extracted from the essays in this volume. In many ways, this book builds on the recent archival reappraisal, at the same time seeking to focus on the position and function of secret societies within local communities that the archival scholarship has neglected, through examination of the linkages between brotherhood associations and the social institutions around them. As noted earlier in this chapter, secret societies should be viewed not in isolation and not in hindsight, but as one expression of a broader range of social practices that played an important role in the non-elite world of early modern China and the Chinese communities of Southeast Asia. These social practices, which might be thought of as constituting an informal institution, were based on the custom, ideology, and symbolism of brotherhood formation and facilitated a wide range of activities in many contexts.

From this perspective, brotherhood associations—including secret societies—should perhaps be grouped with friendly societies (Godsden 1967), *compagnonnages* (Sewell 1980), and other early modern working-class European institutions, or with Chinese guilds and urban associations (Rowe 1984, 1989), rather than with explicitly dissident or "revolutionary" organizations that consciously challenged accepted norms. In fact, it is difficult to find any brotherhood associations—again including secret societies—that were explicitly and thoroughly anti-Confucian in their orientation. Of course, the idea of brotherhood can and frequently does suggest egalitarianism, which clearly clashes with the hierarchical orientation of Confucianism, but many examples of fraternity contain their own hierarchies (including those within biological families). Even small brotherhoods in South China generally chose "elder brothers" as well as "second elder" and sometimes "third elder" brothers, presumably to maintain discipline and facilitate common action, and the elaborate hierarchy within larger secret societies is well known. Indeed, anthropologist David Jordan notes that in modern Taiwan, brotherhoods are sometimes seen as superior to mere friendships in part because the built-in hierarchy of the brotherhood supposedly works to reduce conflict (Jordan 1985, 239–41). Even when secret societies were at their most oppositional, in rebellion, they often remained quite Confucian, their rhetoric attacking local officials from a conventional Mencian standpoint—an observation that applies to most uprisings *not* led by secret societies as well (see discussion in Muramatsu 1960, 252–53; examples in *Tiandihui* 1980, vol. 1, 154–62).

For the purposes of this volume, however, the point is not whether brotherhood associations were Confucian or anti-Confucian. The point is that the brotherhood associations examined in this volume achieved their fullest capacity in contexts where the Confucian state and Confucian local elite were either weak or absent.[5] In these contexts, brotherhoods provided a form of social organization and a language of social identity that facilitated the cooperation of unrelated individuals in achieving mutual goals. Therefore, these brotherhood associations serve as a window into the popular culture and the organizational capacity of non-elite Chinese of the early modern period, illustrating that this set of practices was instrumental not only in the organization of violence and rebellion, but also in flexible pursuit of economic and social goals.

The Range of Brotherhood Activities: Mutual Aid, Corporations, Criminals, and Rebels in South China and Southeast Asia

The forms of brotherhood associations in South China and Southeast Asia are best understood as ranging along a continuum, from small-scale mutual aid societies, little more than formalized versions of friendships, to large organizations of varying degrees of integration. All these forms utilized at least part of the corpus of rituals and symbols attached to the idea of brotherhood, although as organizations grew they often tended to become more explicitly hierarchical and more likely to exploit the language of brotherhood for purposes of maintaining control. The activities in which these groups engaged ranged from simple pursuit of mutual aid to complex examples of corporate behavior.

Violence often accompanied ostensibly peaceful pursuits, even those of small groups. Small-scale mutual aid in a frontier context frequently meant self-defense. Frequent exercises in self-defense could produce mercenaries, strongmen, and gangsters. Complex corporate activity in frontier environments frequently required armed might to protect the profits and the assets of the corporation. In addition, much "corporate" activity in these frontier environments was at least predacious if not criminal in many cases—for example, secret society involvement in drugs, smuggling, prostitution, and gambling in both South China and Southeast Asia—which made violence a frequent part of "corporate strategy" even if not all of these activities were technically illegal. Of course, we should bear in mind that in China and Southeast Asia, as in most of the premodern world, violence was a commonly accepted component of social relationships, accompanying landlords' rent extractions and magistrates' administration of the law.

When the state intruded in frontier environments or in ongoing criminal activities, the long association (both symbolic and real) of brotherhoods with chivalry (*haoxia*—the knights-errant of Chinese history and legend), the organizations founded on brotherhood ties, and the ready familiarity with violence all paved the way for the involvement of brotherhood associations in rebellion. During successful rebellions, brotherhood ideals provided at least part of the political agenda and political practices of upstart regimes. Brotherhood associations could also assume rudimentary political functions in frontier environments even without rebelling against the (nonexistent or distant) state. The paragraphs that follow explore this continuum in greater detail.

Examples from South China and Southeast Asia

At the simple end of the continuum are small-scale organizations that used the idea of brotherhood to promote mutual aid. In the early 1680s, Ji Qiguang, county magistrate of Zhuluo, Taiwan, described these organizations in the censorious tones characteristic of Qing officials:

> In recent years it has become an evil custom for two or three young no-goods, looking for trouble and striving to stand out, to burn incense and pour out libations, and call one another "brother," seeking to forget differences of nobility and baseness and to aid one another in poverty and wealth. [They pledge to] remain together in sadness and in joy, and to watch out for one another in life and in death. . . . [S]cholars and gentry scorn such practices, which are most prevalent among idlers who loiter around the market-places. There is no doubt that the root cause of this is a mentality of hunger for fame and power, . . . [and] there are many who have ruined their families and their reputations through disasters brought on through these pacts. (*Taiwan xianzhi* 1720, 230–32. Throughout this volume, all translations are by chapter authors unless otherwise noted.)

These same themes are echoed in confessions of secret society members. Lin Shuangwen, the leader of the first Heaven and Earth Society–led rebellion, noted in his deposition, "I had often heard that there was something called the Heaven and Earth Society . . . which gathered together many people who took oaths and formed bands, [pledging to] help one another in time of need" (cited in Liu and Miao 1984, 218). Other depositions were even more specific in linking the society to traditions of mutual aid. Yan Yan, the itinerant cloth peddler who brought the society to Taiwan in the 1780s, noted, "In the beginning, those who entered the *hui* did so to help finance marriages and funerals" (*Tiandihui* 1980, vol. 1, 110–12). Although ter Haar argues in this volume that Tiandihui ritual and symbolism possessed messianic overtones from the very beginning, evidence from the Lin Shuangwen uprising also suggests that to many members of the society, the Tiandihui prior to the rebellion was little more than a small, local organization devoted to mutual aid—albeit mutual aid of a sometimes rather predatory nature.

The idea of mutual aid in the context of weddings and funerals links the Tiandihui, and hence brotherhood associations and secret societies, with organizations such as funeral societies (*fumuhui*, lit. "father and mother societies"). Qing authorities arrested the members of two *fumuhui* set up in Taiwan in the late 1720s by poor villagers to facilitate the burial of their parents. These societies each contained slightly more than twenty members who had paid a fee to join, thus establishing a common fund on which each of them could draw (GZDYZ 1978, 68–69). Although the documents do not describe the financial mechanisms employed by funeral societies to achieve their goals, it would be surprising if such enterprises did not draw on some of the same traditions as rotating credit societies (see chapter 2 below), which have provided credit—as well as money-making opportunities—at least since the Ming.[6]

The precise linkages between brotherhoods and these economically oriented associations are difficult to determine. The archives do not discuss whether the early eighteenth-century Taiwanese funeral societies bound members together with a blood oath or whether notions of fictive kinship helped ensure commitment to the society. It is not customary for modern rotating credit societies on Taiwan to pledge brotherhood.[7] Some enterprises in Southeast Asia, however, clearly used brotherhood associations and ideology to facilitate economic undertakings of considerable magnitude. Early colonial commentators on Chinese communities in Malaya noted that secret societies played a crucial role in the organization of workers who exploited the tin mines in the interior of Malaya (Purcell 1965, 261). Chinese mining corporations (kongsis) in West Borneo and Bangka also functioned according to brotherhood principles and were surprisingly egalitarian (see chapter 3 below). Profits were determined by shares, obtained through either labor or purchase. Leadership was temporary and elected by the workers. The Ngee Heng society—an offshoot of the Southern Chinese Tiandihui—played a similar role in organizing plantation agriculture in what came to be Singapore, integrating young, single, migrant workers into an unfamiliar environment and playing a role in the actual organization of work; secret society leaders often enjoyed positions of responsibility in the workplace as well. As the size of these enterprises increased, or as they came under the control of colonial rulers, brotherhood ideology frequently faded as a genuine organizing principle, remaining only as a tool through which managers could manipulate workers. Nonetheless, in the early period, there seems to be little doubt of the economic achievements of the brotherhood associations in frontier Southeast Asia.

Many of the enterprises just described went by the name of kongsi. The small-scale mining enterprises in West Borneo and Bangka were known as kongsis. The federations which the smaller mining kongsis in Borneo formed to protect themselves against native and colonial regimes were also called kongsis. The Ngee Heng secret society in Singapore and Malaya was officially known as the Ngee Heng Kongsi, largely because of its corporate, economic functions, but no one doubted its links to the traditions and symbols of the Heaven and Earth Society of South China. However, kongsis carried other connotations as well, and the multiple meanings of the term suggest the flexibility of the organization and the linkages between and among various sorts of immigrant organizations.

Kongsis appear in the literature as "district and clan associations" (Purcell 1965, 272–73; Yen 1986, 44), which served the religious, social welfare, and political needs of émigré communities in Southeast Asia (Yen 1986, 44–56), although Purcell also concedes that the Chinese in Southeast Asia made no distinction between kongsi and *hui*. G. William Skinner at one point offers a translation of kongsi as "company, public organization, office" (Skinner 1957, 376, n. 68), but elsewhere equates kongsi with the branch of a secret society (Skinner 1957, 141), and yet again as a subdivision within a large mining enterprise (Skinner 1957, 110). Some early colonial commentators viewed kongsi as "public clubs" that functioned as something like what we would call voluntary associations (Trocki 1990, 13). Carl Trocki perhaps best captures the range of organizational phenomena to which the term could apply: "Kongsi is a generic Chinese term for a range of social and economic configurations that includes everything from business partnerships to clan and regional associations to secret triad societies" (Trocki 1990, 11). It is beyond the scope of this volume to trace the complex linkages between kongsis as corporate "economic brotherhoods," as "regional and clan associations," and as secret societies. But the use of the same term surely suggests considerable interpenetration between the three forms of activity, which in turn suggests a remarkably flexible social order, based loosely on notions of brotherhood and fictive kinship.

Alongside these more benign economic and social functions, secret societies also engaged in a wide range of what we generally think of as criminal activities. The involvement of secret societies in opium distribution and smuggling, gambling, prostitution, and protection rackets is well known, though not all these activities were illegal (particularly in Southeast Asia) until fairly late in the nineteenth century.[8] In both China and Southeast Asia, government decisions to criminalize secret societies had a significant impact on the scope and character of society activities, but these decisions were undoubtedly influenced by ongoing criminal practices. In parts of colonial Southeast Asia, secret societies were permitted to exist for some time as legal "voluntary associations" that assisted in the control of the Chinese population. In Singapore, for example, secret societies were recognized, legal organizations, registered with the government, until the end of the nineteenth century. Once outlawed, however, "the secret societies began to decline to the status of small-scale criminal organizations as we have known them in more recent times" (Freedman 1979, 68).

In China, formal hostility toward brotherhoods, *hui*, and secret societies existed from quite early in the Qing period. As Antony illustrates in chapter 8, Qing laws directed at "heterodox" brotherhoods preceded the proliferation of the *hui* or the formation of the complex of secret societies associated with the Tiandihui, perhaps because of the number of blood brotherhoods that flourished during the Ming-Qing transition (ter Haar, personal communication). Despite this early hostility, and despite examples of extremely harsh punishment of brotherhoods and *hui*, the laws were not vigorously and consistently enforced until the Tiandihui-led Lin Shuangwen rebellion of 1787–88 convinced the Qing court that the society might be as dangerous as the White Lotus sect, associated with a troubling rebellion in 1774 (Naquin 1981). The suppression of the Lin rebellion and the search for the founders of the society forced many society members, including many who had been coerced into joining, to flee their homes and take to the road as outlaws (Ownby forthcoming; Zhuang 1988). As the society spread across South China, newly recruited local members adapted the Tiandihui to serve the purposes demanded by their own particular environment, ranging from rebellion in Taiwan and coastal Southeast China in the period immediately following the suppression of Lin Shuangwen, to robbery in Guangdong province, and to a sort of popular religion in western Fujian and eastern Jiangxi provinces. The society, which had originally combined messianic symbolism, mutual aid, and petty criminality among marginal members of village society, became in some cases more clearly criminal and oppositional, and more physically separate from the lineages and villages of South China. The half-criminal, half-rebellious secret society of nineteenth-century China, described by some of the contributors to Chesneaux's volume, was largely created by the suppression of Lin, the rise of the opium trade, and the declining effectiveness of Qing rule beginning in the early nineteenth century.

The frequent participation of secret societies in rebellion is perhaps even better known than *hui* links with criminal activities. Some authors find "secret society" participation in most of the rebellions that brought down old dynasties and founded new ones (Chesneaux 1972; Ward 1967), and even those of us who use a narrower definition of secret societies acknowledge the frequent linkage between societies and rebellion in the eighteenth, nineteenth, and even twentieth centuries.[9] As rebellion is not a major focus of most of the chapters in this volume, we will keep our remarks on the subject brief, noting that in terms of organization and "ideology," there appears to be little difference between brotherhood associations as "economic brotherhoods" and brotherhood associations in rebellion. When Dutch authorities dismantled the relatively autonomous kongsi mining corporations in the mid- to late nineteenth century, secret societies, calling themselves *hui* and not kongsis, emerged to lead Chinese opposition to the Dutch (see chapter 3 below). The leaders of the two organizations differed, no doubt, but both kongsis and *hui* used the idea of brotherhood to distinguish insiders from outsiders and to establish a rudimentary division of labor or chain of command. They simply drew on different aspects of the brotherhood tradition, and their choices were governed largely by the larger context in which they found themselves.

In sum, our argument is that all these examples can be traced in whole or in part to the tradition of brotherhood association and that the violence and rebellion generally associated with brotherhoods and secret societies was as much a product of contextual factors as it was determined by the character of the organizations themselves. Although both brotherhoods and associations have deep roots in Chinese history (on brotherhoods, see Lewis 1990; on associations, Leboucq 1880; on religious associations, ter Haar 1992), a proliferation of these associations and a multiplication of their functions seems to have been a product of the social conditions of seventeenth- and eighteenth-century South China. The violence and dislocations of the dynastic transition; the rapid eighteenth-century population growth; the migration to new frontiers; the partial revival of commerce—all separately or in combination worked to loosen the controls imposed by lineage, village, and state, producing a mobile, entrepreneurial, fragmented, and competitive society. And while the evidence in this volume does not permit us to generalize, these conditions describe not only South China, but, to some degree, early modern Chinese society as a whole. Brotherhood associations did more than protest or "resist" this fragmentation and competition through violence and rebellion; they built new enterprises, corporations, and communities to replace or supplement those that had been weakened.

Brotherhoods, Hui, and Secret Societies in China

The fate of brotherhood associations in China proper underscores the crucial role of the state as part of the broader context that helped to determine the character of brotherhood associations and their activities.[10] Although we find analogues to most of the practices of Southeast Asian brotherhood associations in China, the activities of Chinese brotherhoods were unquestionably constrained by the Chinese state and local elites. Even in China, however, we still find a range of brotherhood practices, which we can divide into the following categories:

Simple brotherhoods, much like those described by Ji Qiguang above (see p. 17), involved relatively few people who were already acquainted by residence or profession. The activities of simple brotherhoods were generally confined to the pursuit of mutual aid, either in the context of self-protection or economic activities such as funeral societies or rotating-credit societies. According to Qing law, simple brotherhoods did not involve a blood oath (and generally received relatively light punishment), but we doubt that this was a hard and fast rule.

Secret societies in South China appear to have attracted the attention of Qing officials by the early 1760s, when memorials began to mention the "esoteric" and secret practices well known to us now (see discussion in chapter 8 below). These built on brotherhood practices, but combined elements from folk religion and messianic and millenarian traditions. The creators of the Heaven and Earth Society, to take one example, appear to have been itinerant monks, merchants, and healers, and the lore of the society seems to have functioned as equal parts prophecy, magic, and entrepreneurship.

Hui, or "named associations," proliferated in Southeast China before the creation of the Tiandihui. Most *hui* seem to have been slightly larger versions of simple brotherhoods and were often made up of young men marginally attached to existing institutions. Blood oaths frequently accompanied the formation of *hui*, but not always. Like many institutions at the margins of polite society, *hui* were frequently involved in violence or crime, but again we know of enough examples where this was not the case to reserve judgment on the nature of the institution and to keep it separate from the secret society. Nonetheless, organized groups of marginal young men offered a convenient target for secret society members seeking adherents to their cause, or marks for their con games.

Descriptions of Individual Chapters

The interpretation just offered reflects one editor's particular preoccupations and only begins to reflect the richness of the individual contributions making up this volume. One final editorial point before introducing these chapters: we have been unable to unify completely the language of all the chapter authors with regard to the brotherhood associations they discuss. This has proven unavoidable, given the range of activities engaged in by brotherhood associations and the flexibility of individual organizations, as well as the layers of historical and scholarly commentary that the authors have had to sift through in the composition of their essays. To someone working on secret societies in eighteenth-century South China, "Tiandihui" refers to a very specific organization and corpus of beliefs and symbols; to someone working on nineteenth-century Malaya, "Tiandihui" is equivalent to "Triad" and refers to secret societies in general. Instead of imposing a single language on all contributors—which risks committing the formalist error of substituting abstract definitions for concrete social practices —contributors were only asked to define and employ their terms with care.

In chapter 2, David Ownby combines sinology, archival research, and comparative history to arrive at new perspectives on non-elite associations in eighteenth-century Southeast China. Attempting to understand what, if anything, was new about *hui* in the early Qing, he traces the pre-Qing history of the defining features of much of this associational behavior—the blood oath and the form of organization called the *hui*—and finds that while both had deep roots in earlier Chinese history, the combination of the two in named associations bound by blood oaths began to proliferate during this period. The *hui*, which heretofore had designated organizations attached to and under the control of villages, sur-name groups, and other institutions, began in the early Qing to refer to groups that were at least partly outside the control of these groups.

Ownby goes on to examine in detail two instances of *hui* activity and seeks to illustrate the embeddedness of the *hui* and *hui* members in the mid- to late eighteenth century in the structures and routines of the everyday lives of those who found themselves at the margins of lineage or village life. Consistent with the findings of the archival scholarship, and in contrast to ter Haar's interpreta-tions (see chapter 6), Ownby emphasizes the appeal of mutual aid and protection rather than messianic or millenarian themes, although the fact that both instances of *hui* activity were eventually involved in violence against the state suggests that mutual aid and messianism are by no means mutually exclusive. Finally, Ownby tests the proposition that the proliferation of the *hui* in the eighteenth century is in some way related to changes associated with China's "early modern" social order.

Mary Somers Heidhues's examination of kongsis and *hui* in eighteenth- and nineteenth-century West Borneo and Bangka provides the fullest exploration (in this volume) of the potential and limitations of the brotherhood as an economic institution. She agrees with Carl Trocki that the brotherhood ideology of the kongsi/secret society could indeed facilitate profit-oriented economic activity—as well as help bring social cohesion to young, single immigrants in a frontier environment. Small mining kongsis in West Borneo and Bangka in the early, eighteenth-century, period appear to have exhibited an unusual degree of egali-tarianism: membership in the kongsi was based on shares; leadership was tempo-rary and by popular election. Moreover, to facilitate large-scale economic activity, or to provide protection from native or colonial military challengers, the kongsis readily came together to form large federations (also called kongsis), which organized substantial networks to keep the mines supplied with new labor, or fielded thousands of fighters to meet military opponents.

At the same time, Heidhues illustrates that the commitment of the kongsis to egalitarian ideals was limited. Considerations of ethnicity, dialect, and native place remained important: local-born Chinese were not admitted to mining kong-sis, and in some instances, kongsis composed primarily of Chinese from one particular region in China might admit new members from other areas, but not allow them to serve as leaders. Chinese who engaged in farming were not per-mitted to enlist in the kongsis. Furthermore, Heidhues found a consistent rela-tionship between the size of the kongsi and its adherence to egalitarianism: as kongsis expanded in size and scale of operation, leadership tended to become permanent, and shareholders hired coolies to work their shares. Finally, the imposition of colonial control in the Bangkan tin mines in the nineteenth century weakened the "democratic" nature of the earlier, smaller kongsis as some Chi-nese headmen made common cause with the Dutch colonial rulers.

Heidhues also finds that *hui*, or secret societies, frequently emerged as vehicles of protest or rebellion with the decline or destruction of the kongsis (democratic or otherwise). Although colonial authorities frequently depicted kongsis as healthy, profit-oriented economic organizations, and *hui* as vehicles of antisocial, violent conspiracies, Heidhues argues that *hui* and kongsis were in fact "two sides of the same coin." Both grew out of the brotherhood ideology that had been central to the settlement of frontier regions and represented responses to different sets of circumstances.

Carl Trocki's essay on "The Rise and Fall of the Ngee Heng Kongsi" in nineteenth-century Singapore brings another new perspective to the study of secret societies: a Marxist approach reminiscent of Immanuel Wallerstein's world systems theory. Trocki identifies several stages in the history of this influential society and relates its evolution to changes in the economic environment produced by the incorporation of the Chinese economy of Southeast Asia into the global capitalist system.

At the outset, the society was instrumental in developing the pepper and gambier plantation agriculture, in a fashion similar to that described by Heidhues in the mining corporations of Borneo. The brotherhood ideology of the society provided an element of social cohesion in a frontier community of new migrants and, at the same time, provided a structure on which to build larger economic organizations. As the economy was absorbed into the free trade capitalism of imperial Britain, however, leadership of the Ngee Heng came to be linked to the British through complex ties of opium farming and debt. The historical consequence was the creation of an entrenched mercantile-capitalist elite structure in the Chinese society of Southeast Asia.

Trocki argues that the "secret society riots" that plagued Singapore in the 1840s and 1870s were actually linked to this larger ideological and class struggle rather than simply to ethnic conflicts within the Chinese community, as previous interpretations have insisted. In sum, Trocki emphasizes the economic nature of the Ngee Heng—thus confirming the embeddedness of the society in local social order—but also helpfully illustrates the manner in which changes in the macroeconomy have affected the meaning of the society for individuals of different economic strata.

Sharon Carstens's study of "Chinese Culture and Polity in Nineteenth-Century Malaya: The Case of Yap Ah Loy" applies sophisticated anthropological analysis to the career of one influential Chinese in nineteenth-century Malaya. Focusing on Chinese leadership styles and on changing economic and political factors, Carstens suggests the complexity of the choices and strategies available to talented and ambitious Chinese of this period. She rejects the notion that social life was determined by ethnicity or secret society membership—or indeed any single focus of social identity—but instead illustrates that these spheres of social activity could be employed by individuals in creative ways for different purposes.

More specifically, Carstens shows how Yap Ah Loy used secret societies in the rough-and-tumble world of mid-nineteenth-century Malayan politics to make his way from impoverished immigrant to man of influence and illustrates that secret societies during this period were a recognized part of the political structure, playing an important role in the production of Chinese political leadership. Furthermore, Carstens's examination of Yap's later career shows how readily Yap employed other aspects of the larger Chinese cultural notion of leadership— including philanthropy, patronage—again illustrating that he was not destined by his early secret society ties to life as a strongman. Carstens's essay was not originally written for the Association for Asian Studies panel that produced this volume and thus is not directly focused on secret societies; nonetheless, by treating the secret society as but one complex of cultural, political, and economic institutions among several, she contextualizes the secret society in a way that is wholly appropriate for the purposes of this collection.

Barend ter Haar's chapter on messianism in the Heaven and Earth Society "tradition" in some ways stands apart from the other contributions, most of which are representative examples of social history, examining social and economic structures, crime and law. By contrast, ter Haar focuses on the culture of secret society rituals—the meanings embedded in the written tradition generated by the Heaven and Earth Society. Of course, this supposed distinction between social structure and culture has been the subject of considerable discussion in recent years (Esherick and Wasserstrom 1992; Hunt 1984, 1989; Perry 1992), and we believe that social history, properly understood, *must* include discussion of consciousness as well as the structures of social life.

Ter Haar's study concentrates on messianic elements within the early history of the Heaven and Earth Society, elements that he links to familiar popular religious and ritual practices (both orthodox and heterodox), showing how they were repackaged in the late eighteenth and early nineteenth centuries to form a unique tradition. Ter Haar's contribution is not limited to methodology. His reading of the Tiandihui written materials also challenges the interpretation of the archival school and some of the contributors to this volume. He argues that the Heaven and Earth Society absorbed—and presumably spread—messianic and millenarian themes from the very outset, thus at least complicating, if not rejecting, the idea that the Tiandihui grew out of mutual aid practices. He also traces the formation of the Tiandihui tradition through the Ma Chaozhu uprising in Hubei in 1752, again diverging from the prevailing archival interpretation. Ter Haar is engaged in a larger work to link the findings presented here with an analysis of the bandit tradition of the Southern Fujian–Eastern Guangdong region, thus combining the sinological approach employed here with the concerns of more mainstream social history.

Dian Murray outlines the general reinterpretation of Chinese "secret societies" based on archival work over the past several years, piecing together a synthetic interpretation from the works of Cai Shaoqing, Qin Baoqi, and Zhuang Jifa. She also offers examples of entrepreneurial activity linking extortion and profit-seeking with society membership. The emphasis on mutual aid and the close relationship between the associations and local social structures, which Ownby stresses in his contribution, are less apparent in the atmosphere of late eighteenth- and early nineteenth-century South China, as many adherents of the Heaven and Earth Society fled their home networks out of fear of arrest by Qing authorities, and founded new branches of the society in unfamiliar places, for reasons of both protection and criminal entrepreneurship.

Robert Antony's chapter brings in the essential perspective of the state—essential because much of our evidence (and virtually all our archival evidence) concerning brotherhoods, *hui*, and secret societies, in both China and Southeast Asia, was produced by government efforts to suppress secret societies and apprehend their members. Consequently, this evidence reflects the views of the state in direct and indirect ways. Even the depositions of secret societies members, which appear to be the voices of the non-elite, were nonetheless framed by the questions of the representatives of the state and in many instances were edited in the process of being forwarded to the central authorities. Antony traces the complex history of Qing laws against brotherhoods, *hui*, and secret societies from the early Qing through the early nineteenth century, finding both extreme hostility to certain forms of non-elite association and recognition on the part of Manchu policymakers of important differences in the size, structure, and orientation of these associations, which merited very different treatment. In general, however, Qing laws toward brotherhoods, *hui*, and secret societies moved from an early (late seventeenth-, early eighteenth-century) posture of opposition to the organizations as heterodox and seditious, to a later (late eighteenth-, early nineteenth-century) stance emphasizing the criminal nature of the associations.

Jean DeBernardi's epilogue echoes many of the themes sounded by the earlier chapters. Combining anthropological sensitivity to the significance of ritual with a close reading of the rich record of British colonial commentary on nineteenth-century Chinese secret societies in Malaya, DeBernardi convincingly recasts the evolution of British policy on secret societies as a "war of competing colonialisms." Both the Chinese and the British, she notes, were newcomers to the region and both sought to control certain resources for their own purposes. The British, as representatives of the Crown, did so through methods familiar to the Western reader: through governmental institutions and policies designed to facilitate the construction of a *laissez-faire* economy under the benign guidance of an educated, well-meaning elite. The Chinese, by contrast, sought dominion over their "subjects" (chiefly, of course, the Chinese immigrants) through the institution of the secret society and the rituals of initiation. Since the secret societies remained legally recognized institutions until late in the nineteenth century, the writ of the "secret societies" had as much or more authority than that of the colonial government, at least in the eyes of the large Chinese population.

From this perspective, DeBernardi interprets the initiation rituals of the secret societies as representations of authority, invested with the sanction of the gods, designed to integrate new arrivals into the power structure of the Chinese community. The rituals were neither anti-Manchu nor anti-British—in explicit intent. However, the elaboration of brotherhood ideology to construct a politico-religious structure to rival the competing claims of the British underscores in a highly relevant manner the potential significance of the role of the brotherhood association in the lives of the non-elite Chinese of Southeast Asia.

The Roads Not Taken

We have tried to express as clearly as possible what we believe is the contribution of this volume. Let us briefly note what the book does *not* do and in so doing suggest avenues for future research.

Our focus is on the early, eighteenth-century, history of secret societies (particularly in China), and many chapter authors have stressed the links between secret societies and non-elite, nonviolent associational practices such as mutual aid and rotating-credit societies. As a result, few of the contributors address directly the frequent involvement of secret societies in revolts and other types of collective violence in the nineteenth and twentieth centuries, or the links between early modern secret societies and anti-dynastic popular movements throughout Chinese history. Ter Haar's chapter does examine the messianic strains at the heart of Tiandihui ritual and iconography, and Ownby, Murray, and Antony give more than passing mention to crime, violence, and rebellion, but a comprehensive treatment of the complex relationship between mutual aid, violence, and rebellion, bringing together the findings of this volume with the work of the contributors to Chesneaux's volumes, remains to be done.[11] Thus even though we criticize Chesneaux for presenting an overly "romantic" view of "secret society dissidents" and believe that evidence presented in this volume paints a fuller portrait of these associations, we acknowledge that the present volume remains only a partial treatment of the early modern and modern history of secret societies. Nor does this collection attempt to address the concerns of recent journalistic treatments of secret societies (Booth 1991; Posner 1988).

In addition, since this volume emphasizes the connections between brotherhoods, *hui*, secret societies, and other mainstream social institutions, a fuller exploration of the themes developed here would have included an examination of a wide variety of social practices in different spheres. Had it been feasible to commission articles for inclusion, we might have requested studies of business organization in eighteenth- and early nineteenth-century Taiwan; fictive kinship practices in frontier Taiwan and in other parts of China; shareholding practices in various types of organization in China; and the comparative social organization of the Chinese societies of North America and Southeast Asia.[12] More information on these topics—and we could think of many more—would help us to filter out the biases inherent in Qing and colonial archival information on Chinese secret societies and might afford us a clearer perspective on non-elite Chinese society in the early modern period.

Conventions

Romanization

Chapters which treat primarily China render personal names, place names, and Chinese terms in pinyin. Chapters dealing primarily with Southeast Asia employ pinyin in some instances, but more often maintain the spellings of personal names, kongsis, and secret societies traditionally used in their field. Most Southeast Asian place names are given in their modern Malay/Indonesian spellings: Melaka (Malacca), Johor (Johore), Pinang (Penang), and so on. An appended glossary should remove whatever confusion this may cause.

Dates

Chinese dates are recorded following the Chinese calendar, with the equivalent Western year provided in parentheses. QL 35.3.7 (1770), for example, refers to the seventh day of the third lunar month of the thirty-fifth year of the reign of the Qianlong emperor, which fell within the year 1770 of the Western calendar. Translating Chinese dates into their Western equivalents obscures the possible relationship of the events with the Chinese ritual calendar, an important consideration in some of the chapters. The names of the Qing reign periods are abbreviated in the text. The full names and dates of the reign periods of the Qing emperors are as follows:

> Shunzhi (SZ), 1644–61
> Kangxi (KX), 1662–1722
> Yongzheng (YZ), 1723–35
> Qianlong (QL), 1736–95
> Jiaqing (JQ), 1796–1820
> Daoguang (DG), 1821–1850
> Xianfeng (XF), 1851–61
> Tongzhi (TZ), 1862–74
> Guangxu (GX), 1875–1908
> Xuantong (XT), 1909–11

Notes

The author would like to thank Timothy Cheek and particularly Evelyn S. Rawski for their many helpful comments on this chapter.

1. These emphases are understandable, given the many apparent imprecisions concerning the Tiandihui founding date on the part of their Republican-period predecessors and the nature of the information contained in the Qing archives. The first extensive archival information about the Heaven and Earth Society resulted from the Qianlong emperor's demands that his officials produce precisely the information for which the Republican-period scholars had searched—the date and place of the founding of the Tiandihui—in the wake of the Tiandihui-led Lin Shuangwen rebellion of 1787–88, when the Tiandihui first came to the attention of metropolitan officials. The officials uncovered

enough information to enable later historians, with access to larger bodies of information, to piece together a plausible narrative of the establishment of the Tiandihui (see *Tiandihui*, vols. 1–5), but the officials in general failed to find conclusive evidence that the Tiandihui was an explicitly rebellious or restorationist organization. Instead, the group appeared to have more direct links to mutual aid and perhaps criminal entrepreneurship than to insurrection; hence Cai's and Qin's emphasis on mutual aid (Ownby 1989, ch. 6). Of course, neither Cai's nor Qin's work is limited to this particular aspect of secret society history, and both have written widely on the topic (see Cai 1987 and Qin 1988).

2. At one point, Zhuang distinguished between "broad" and "narrow" Tiandihui traditions. The "broad tradition" was the larger set of circumstances and associational activities that gave rise to the general proliferation of secret societies, and the "narrow tradition" referred to the establishment of the Tiandihui itself. See Zhuang 1980.

3. The author gratefully acknowledges the assistance of Mary Somers Heidhues, Jean DeBernardi, and Sharon Carstens in the completion of this section.

4. "The Legal, Political, and Economic Status of the Chinese Diaspora," held at Berkeley, California, November 1992; "Symposium on the Role of the Indonesian Chinese in Shaping Modern Indonesian Life," held at Ithaca, New York, July 1990. For discussion of these and other conferences see Tan 1992.

5. David Jordan appends "Two Community Contracts in the Form of Sworn Brotherhoods" to his 1985 article, illustrating the function of brotherhood associations along the Russian-Chinese border in Manchuria. See Jordan 1985, 253–62.

6. Daniel H. Kulp confirms that the financial mechanisms used by funeral societies in early twentieth-century Guangdong did indeed resemble those of rotating credit societies (Kulp, 1925: 201–2).

7. Kulp does not mention blood oaths in his discussion of funeral societies in early twentieth-century Guangdong (Kulp 1925, 196–203). David Jordan notes that sworn brotherhoods can have economic functions (Jordan 1985, 244)

8. The literature on the criminal aspects of secret societies is too large to summarize here. In Southeast Asia, much of the early investigation into secret societies was carried out by colonial police charged with the suppression of the societies. For example, Comber (1959, 1) notes that Chinese secret societies' "activities in Malaya . . . have included the organisation of opposition to the government; the stirring up of anti-foreign feeling; the formation of self-protection units against robber gangs; the 'protection' and extortion of money from hawkers, shopkeepers, hotel-keepers, prostitutes, labourers, opium and gambling dens; kidnapping for ransom; and the operation of criminal rings and rackets." Such examples could easily be multiplied, for both China and Southeast Asia.

9. Nevertheless, Barend ter Haar's discovery that the "White Lotus Society" was in large measure a product of the imagination of Chinese officialdom counsels prudence in accepting the widespread role of "secret societies" in rebellions as well. See ter Haar 1992.

10. A similar point could, of course, be made for the fate of secret societies under the colonial regimes of Southeast Asia.

11. Perry (1980) and Ownby (forthcoming) attempt this kind of integration.

12. We are aware that much work has been done on these individual issues that we have been unable to incorporate into this introduction.

References

Ackerman, Susan A., and Raymond L. M. Lee. 1988. *Heaven in Transition: Non-Muslim Religious Innovation and Ethnic Identity in Malaysia*. Honolulu: University of Hawaii Press.

Blythe, W. L. 1969. *The Impact of Chinese Secret Societies in Malaya: A Historical Study*. London: Oxford University Press.

Booth, Martin. 1991. *The Triads: The Growing Global Threat from the Chinese Criminal Societies*. New York: St. Martin's Press.

Cai Shaoqing. 1964. "Guanyu Tiandihui de qiyuan wenti" [On the question of the origin of the Heaven and Earth Society]. *Beijing daxue xuebao* 1: 53–64.

———. 1987. *Zhongguo jindai huidangshi yanjiu* [Studies of the history of secret societies in modern China]. Beijing: Zhonghua shuju.

Chesneaux, Jean. 1965. *Les Sociétés secrètes en Chine (19e et 20e siècles)* [Secret societies in China (nineteenth and twentieth centuries)]. Paris: F. Maspero.

———. 1971. *Secret Societies in China in the Nineteenth and Twentieth Centuries*. Ann Arbor: University of Michigan Press.

———, ed. 1972. *Popular Movements and Secret Societies in China 1840–1950*. Stanford: Stanford University Press.

———. 1973. *Peasant Revolts in China 1840–1949*. London: Thames and Hudson.

———, Marianne Bastid, and Marie-Claire Bergère. 1976. *China from the Opium Wars to the 1911 Revolution*. New York: Pantheon Books.

———, Françoise le Barbier, and Marie-Claire Bergère. 1977. *China from the 1911 Revolution to Liberation*. New York: Pantheon Books.

——— 1979. *China: The People's Republic, 1949–76*. New York: Pantheon Books.

Comber, L. F. 1959. *Chinese Secret Societies in Malaya: A Survey of the Triad Society from 1800 to 1900*. Locust Valley, NY: J. J. Augustin Inc.

Cushman, Jennifer, and Wang Gungwu, eds. 1988. *Changing Identities of the Southeast Asian Chinese Since World War II*. Hong Kong: Hong Kong University Press.

Davis, Fei-ling. 1970. "Le Rôle économique et social des sociétés secrètes" [The economic and social role of secret societies]. In *Mouvements populaires et sociétés secrètes en Chine aux xixe et xxe siècles*, ed. Jean Chesneaux, Fei-ling Davis, and Nguyen Nguyet Ho, 44–64. Paris: François Maspero.

———. 1977. *Primitive Revolutionaries: A Study of Secret Societies in the Late Nineteenth Century*. Honolulu: University of Hawaii Press.

Esherick, Joseph W., and Jeffrey N. Wasserstrom. 1992. "Acting Out Democracy: Political Theater in Modern China." In *Popular Protest and Political Culture in Modern China: Learning from 1989*, ed. Jeffrey N. Wasserstrom and Elizabeth J. Perry, 28–66. Boulder, Colo.: Westview Press.

Fairbank, John K., and Edwin O. Reischauer. 1989. *East Asia: Tradition and Transformation*. Boston: Houghton-Mifflin.

———, Edwin O. Reischauer, and Albert M. Craig. 1973. *East Asia: Tradition and Transformation*. Boston: Houghton-Mifflin.

Freedman, Maurice. 1979. *The Study of Chinese Society*. Stanford: Stanford University Press.

Godsden, P. H. J. H. 1967. *The Friendly Societies in England, 1815–1875*. New York: Augustus M. Kelley.

Gosling, Peter L. A., and Linda Y. C. Lim, eds. 1983. *The Chinese in Southeast Asia, Volume 2: Identity, Culture, and Politics*. Singapore: Maruzen Asia.

Groot , J. J. M. de. 1885. *Het kongsiwezen van Borneo: eene verhandeling over den grondslag en den aard der chineesche politieke vereenigingen in de koloniën* [The organization of the kongsis of Borneo: a treatise on the basis and the character of Chinese political associations in the colonies]. The Hague: Nijhoff.

GZDYZ. 1978. *Gongzhongdang Yongzhengchao zouzhe* [Palace memorials of the Yongzheng reign]. Taipei: Palace Museum.

Hirayama Shu. 1912. *Zhongguo bimi shehuishi* [History of China's secret societies]. Shanghai: Shangwu yinshuguan.

Hobsbawm, E. J. 1959. *Primitive Rebels: Studies in Archaic Forms of Social Movement in the 19th and 20th Centuries*. Manchester: University of Manchester Press.

————. 1969. *Captain Swing*. London: Lawrence and Wishart.

Hsieh, Winston. 1972. "Triads, Salt Smugglers, and Local Uprisings: Observations on the Social and Economic Background of the Waichow Revolution of 1911." In Jean Chesneaux, ed. *Popular Movements and Secret Societies in China 1840–1950*, 145–64. Stanford: Stanford University Press.

Hsu, Wen-hsiung. 1980. "Social Organization and Social Disorder." In *China's Island Frontier: Studies in the Historical Geography of Taiwan*, ed. Ronald S. Knapp, 87–106. Honolulu: University of Hawaii Press.

Hsü, Immanuel C. Y. 1990. *The Rise of Modern China*. New York: Oxford University Press.

Hucker, Charles O. 1975. *China's Imperial Past*. Stanford: Stanford University Press.

Hunt, Lynn A. 1984. *Politics, Culture, and Class in the French Revolution*. Berkeley: University of California Press.

————, ed. 1989. *The New Cultural History*. Berkeley: University of California Press.

Jordan, David K. 1972. *Gods, Ghosts, and Ancestors*. Berkeley: University of California Press.

————. 1985. "Sworn Brothers: A Study in Chinese Ritual Kinship." In *The Chinese Family and Its Ritual Behavior*, ed. Hsieh Jih-chang and Chuang Ying-chang. Taipei: Institute of Ethnology.

Kulp, Daniel H. 1925. *Country Life in South China: The Sociology of Familism, Volume I, Phenix Village, Kwantung, China*. New York: Columbia University Press.

Laffey, Ella S. 1972. "The Making of a Rebel: Liu Yung-fu and the Formation of the Black Flag Army." In Jean Chesneaux, ed. *Popular Movements and Secret Societies in China 1840–1950*, 85–96. Stanford: Stanford University Press.

LeBoucq, P. 1880. *Associations de la Chine: Lettres du P. LeBoucq* [Chinese associations: Letters of Father LeBoucq]. Paris: F. Wattelier.

Lewis, Mark Edward. 1990. *Sanctioned Violence in Early China*. Albany: State University of New York Press.

Lim, Linda Y. C., and Peter L. A. Gosling, eds. 1983. *The Chinese in Southeast Asia, Volume 1: Ethnicity and Economic Identity*. Singapore: Maruzen Asia.

Liu Meizhen and Qin Baoqi. 1982. "Guanyu Tiandihui lishishang de ruogan wenti" [Some questions concerning the history of the Heaven and Earth Society]. In *Ming-Qing shi guoji xueshu taolunhui lunwenji*, pp. 1023–39. Tianjin: Tianjin People's Press.

Liu Ruzhong and Miao Xuemeng, eds. 1984. *Taiwan Lin Shuangwen qiyi ziliao xuanbian* [Selected materials on the Lin Shuangwen uprising on Taiwan]. Fuzhou: Fujian People's Press.

Liu, Kwang-Ching. 1981. "World View and Peasant Rebellion: Reflections on Post-Mao Historiography." *Journal of Asian Studies* 40, no. 2: 295–326.

Lockard, Craig A. 1985. Review of Linda Y. C. Lim and Peter L. A. Gosling, eds., *The Chinese in Southeast Asia*. In *Journal of Southeast Asian Studies* 16, no. 1: 171–74.

Luo Ergang. 1943. *Tiandihui wenxianlu* [Documents on the Heaven and Earth Society]. Shanghai: Zhengzhong shuju.

Ma, L. Eve Armentrout. 1990. *Revolutionaries, Monarchists, and Chinatowns: Chinese Politics in the Americas and the 1911 Revolution*. Honolulu: University of Hawaii Press.

Mak Lau Fong. 1981. *The Sociology of Secret Societies: A Study of Chinese Secret Societies in Singapore and Peninsular Malaysia*. Kuala Lumpur: Oxford University Press.

Michael, Franz H., and George E. Taylor. 1975. *The Far East in the Modern World*. Hinsdale, Ill.: Dryden Press. (1956 original.)

Muramatsu, Yuji. 1960. "Some Themes in Chinese Rebel Ideologies." In *The Confucian Persuasion*, ed. Arthur F. Wright, 240–67. Stanford: Stanford University Press.

Murray, Dian H. 1993. *The Origin of the Tiandihui (Heaven and Earth Society)*. Stanford: Stanford University Press.

Naquin, Susan. 1981. *Shantung Rebellion: The Wang Lun Uprising of 1774*. New Haven: Yale University Press.

Ownby, David. Forthcoming. *Brotherhoods, Secret Societies, and the State in Early Modern Southeast China.*

Perry, Elizabeth J. 1980. *Rebels and Revolutionaries in North China, 1845–1945*. Stanford: Stanford University Press.

———. 1992. "Introduction: Chinese Political Culture Revisited." In *Popular Protest and Political Culture in Modern China: Learning from 1989*, ed. Jeffrey N. Wasserstrom and Elizabeth J. Perry, 1–12. Boulder, Colo.: Westview Press.

Posner, Gerald L. 1988. *Warlords of Crime: Chinese Secret Societies—The New Mafia*. New York: McGraw-Hill.

Purcell, Victor. 1965. *The Chinese in Southeast Asia*. London: Oxford University Press.

Qin Baoqi. 1988. *Qing qianqi Tiandihui yanjiu* [A study of the early Qing Heaven and Earth Society]. Beijing: People's University Press.

Rowe, William T. 1984. *Hankow: Commerce and Society in a Chinese City 1796–1889*. Stanford: Stanford University Press.

———. 1989. *Hankow: Conflict and Community in a Chinese City 1796–1895*. Stanford: Stanford University Press.

Salmon, Claudine, and Denys Lombard. 1977. *Les Chinois de Jakarta: Temples et vie collective*. [The Chinese of Jakarta: Temples and Collective Life] Paris: Editions de la Maison des Sciences de l'Homme. Reprinted in 1980. Ann Arbor: University Microfilms International.

Schiffrin, Harold Z. 1968. *Sun Yat-sen and the Origins of the Chinese Revolution*. Berkeley: University of California Press.

Schlegel, Gustave. 1866. *Thian Ti Hwui: The Hung League or Heaven-Earth League*. Batavia: Lange and Co.

Sewell, William H. 1980. *Work and Revolution in France: The Language of Labor from the Old Regime to 1848*. Cambridge: Cambridge University Press.

Skinner, G. William. 1957. *Chinese Society in Thailand: An Analytical History*. Ithaca: Cornell University Press.

———. 1960. "Change and Persistence in Chinese Culture Overseas: A Comparison of Thailand and Java." *Journal of the South Seas Society* 16: 86–100.

Spence, Jonathan D. 1990. *The Search for Modern China*. New York: W. W. Norton.

Taiwan xianzhi [Gazetteer of Taiwan county]. 1720. Reprinted in *Taiwan congshu*, ed. Fang Hao.

Tan Chee Beng. 1988. *The Baba of Melaka: Culture and Identity of a Chinese Peranakan Community in Malaysia*. Selangor, Malaysia: Pelanduk Publications.

———. 1992. "International Conference on Changing Ethnic Identities and Relations in Southeast Asia: The Case of the Chinese Minority." *Archipel* 44: 3–14.

Tao Chengzhang. n.d. "Jiaohui yuanliukao" [Study of the origins of sects and societies]. Reprinted in *Xinhai geming* [The 1911 Revolution], vol. 3: 99–111. Shanghai: Renmin chubanshe, 1957.

Ter Haar, Barend J. 1992. *The White Lotus Teachings in Chinese Religious History*. Leiden: E.J. Brill.

Tiandihui [The Heaven and Earth Society]. 1980–88. Qing History Research Institute of People's University, and Number One Historical Archives of China, eds. Beijing: China People's University Press. Vols. 1–7.

Trocki, Carl A. 1990. *Opium and Empire: Chinese Society in Colonial Singapore, 1800–1910*. Ithaca: Cornell University Press.

Wakeman, Frederic, Jr. 1972. "The Secret Societies of Kwangtung, 1800–1856." In *Popular Movements and Secret Societies in China 1840–1950*, ed. Jean Chesneaux, 29–48. Stanford. Stanford University Press.

Ward, Barbara E. 1967. "Chinese Secret Societies." In *Secret Societies*, ed. Norman MacKenzie, 210–41. New York: Holt, Rinehart, and Winston.

Ward, J. S. M., and W. G. Stirling. 1925. *The Hung Society or The Society of Heaven and Earth*. London.

Wasserstrom, Jeffrey N. 1991. "Towards a Social History of the Chinese Revolution: A Review." *Social History* 16, no. 4: 1–44.

Wickberg, Edgar. 1968. *The Chinese in Philippine Life, 1850–1898*. New Haven: Yale University Press.

Wilbur, C. Martin. 1976. *Sun Yat-sen: Frustrated Patriot*. New York: Columbia University Press.

Willmott, William E. 1967. *The Chinese in Cambodia*. Vancouver: University of British Columbia Press.

———. 1970. *The Political Structure of the Chinese Community in Cambodia*. London: Athlone Press.

Wynne, M. L. 1941. *Triad and Tabut: A Survey of the Origin and Diffusion of Chinese and Mohamedan Secret Societies in the Malay Peninsula* A.D. 1800–1935. Singapore: Government Printing Office.

Xiao Yishan. 1935. *Jindai mimi shehui shiliao* [Historical materials on modern secret societies]. Beiping: Beiping yanjiuyuan.

Yen Ching-hwang. 1986. *A Social History of the Chinese in Singapore and Malaya, 1800–1911*. Singapore: Oxford University Press.

Zhuang Jifa. 1980. "Cong guoli gugong bowuyuan diancang Qingdai dang'an tan Tiandihui de yuanliu" [A discussion of the origins of the Heaven and Earth based on Qing archives held in the National Palace Museum]. *Gugong jikan* 14, no. 4: 63–91.

———. 1981. *Qingdai Tiandihui yuanliukao* [Studies of the origins of the Heaven and Earth Society of the Qing dynasty]. Taipei: Gugong congkan bianji weiyuanhui.

———. 1988. "Qingdai Min-Yue diqu de renkou liudong yu mimi huidang de fazhan" (Population mobility and the development of secret societies in Qing Fujian and Guangdong). In *Jindai Zhongguo chuqi lishi yantaohui lunwenji* [Collected essays from the conference on early modern Chinese history], ed. Academia Sinica, Institute of Modern History, 737–73. Taipei: Academia Sinica.

2

Chinese *Hui* and the Early Modern Social Order: Evidence from Eighteenth-Century Southeast China

David Ownby

Introduction

References to *hui*—widely translated as "secret society"—proliferate in eighteenth- and nineteenth-century Chinese sources, a fact that until recently has been explained in two complementary ways. Republican-period Chinese historians argued that secret societies emerged in the early Qing as popular "nationalistic" protests against the alien Manchu regime, anticipating Sun Yat-sen's republican revolution by some two centuries (Luo 1943; Murray 1993, ch. 4; Tao 1943; Xiao 1935). A few decades later, Western historians inspired by the radicalization of scholarship in the 1960s and 1970s rewrote the history of secret societies, adding their own Marxian convictions that secret society "rebels" were conscious or unconscious revolutionaries as well, responding to crises of immiseration and social injustice (Chesneaux 1972; Davis 1977; Murray 1993, ch. 3). The first wave of historians wrote secret societies into the history of the Republican Revolution of 1911; the second wave wrote secret societies into the Communist Revolution of 1949. This chapter seeks to write secret societies into the history of early modern China, arguing that most "secret societies" are better understood as associations created by young men who found themselves at the margins of settled society.

Scholars have long been aware of this corporate aspect of "secret society" history (Jones and Kuhn 1978, 134–36; Kuhn 1970, 168–69; Perry 1980, 254–56), and archival research by Chinese and Western scholars over the past 25 years has provided abundant proof of the accuracy of viewing *hui* as "mutual aid fraternities" rather than secret societies established to overthrow the Qing, particularly in the early, eighteenth-century, period (Cai 1987; Liu and Qin 1982; Murray 1993, chs. 1, 4; Qin 1988; Zhuang 1981, 1988). Nonetheless, certain questions remain concerning the depiction of *hui* as mutual aid societies, questions that may help us to gain a fuller understanding of the sociological makeup and historical significance of the *hui*.

The first question has to do with periodization. Were *hui* indeed new in the Qing period? Republican-period scholars misinterpreted the nature of early Qing "secret societies"; maybe they got the dates of emergence wrong as well. Still, reexamination of the sources seems to confirm that few *hui* of the type familiar to us from Qing sources predate the Ming-Qing transition. James Tong's exhaustive work on Ming collective violence, for example, makes almost no mention of *hui*, which are not associated with a distinct type of violence in his analysis (Tong 1991, 58–59). By contrast, there were more than 40 incidents of *hui*-related violence in eighteenth-century Southeast China (Zhuang 1990, 111–20), and C. K. Yang's survey of nationwide violence in nineteenth-century China located 611 secret society "mass action incidents," accounting for 9.2 percent of all nineteenth-century mass actions (Yang 1975, 197). Clearly, *something* was new about the early Qing period, though whether we can attribute this novelty to changes in social practices or peculiarities of our sources remains open to question.

Second, if *hui* were new, how did eighteenth-century Chinese know how to form them? Where did the language and symbols of the *hui* come from, and why were these particular symbols used? Where did eighteenth-century Chinese get their rituals of fictive kinship, and what did they understand by these rituals? In short, what was the cultural—as well as social and political—relationship of these fraternities to mainstream Chinese culture and society?

A third question concerns the issue of violence. If most *hui* were grounded in mutual aid practices, how then do we explain their frequent engagement in violence, and in particular, violence against the state? Of course, mutual aid in a violent environment can easily translate into protective violence, which may account for part of the association of *hui* with conflict. In addition, in many instances the Qing state effectively criminalized mutual aid fraternities, defining what might have been relatively harmless activities as heterodox and dangerous, leaving *hui* little option but to rebel. For the same reason, Qing archival sources on *hui* are heavily biased in the direction of those involved in violence, making it difficult to paint a comprehensive picture of *hui* activities. But at the same time, there is considerable evidence that many *hui* became aggressive and violent without having been provoked by the state; many *hui* appear to have been natural magnets for those interested in entrepreneurial violence. How do brotherly affection and mutual aid lead to violence and rebellion?

Finally, if these "secret societies" are more accurately understood as "mutual aid fraternities," rather than organizations devoted to ethnic opposition to the Qing, how do we explain their proliferation in the early Qing and in Southeast China? More than 90 percent of the *hui* investigated and prosecuted by the state in the eighteenth century were found on the Southeast coast; only after the suppression of the Tiandihui-led Lin Shuangwen uprising of 1787–88 did the *hui* in this form begin to spread out of the Southern Fujian–Northern Guangdong–Taiwan region (Zhuang 1990, 111–20).

By way of providing tentative answers to these questions, this chapter makes the following points:

First, the *hui* that appear so frequently in eighteenth- and nineteenth-century sources were *not* completely new institutions. Instead, they grew out of organizational and cultural practices of traditional Chinese communities that provided either mutual assistance or the administration of community activities. Although many Qing *hui* remained within community structures, others moved out from under the control of traditional communities and community leaders, borrowing the name of this traditional organizational practice for their own purposes.[1] This is what was new and distinctive about eighteenth- and nineteenth-century *hui*, and accounts—at least in part—for their proliferation in Qing sources. During the early Qing period, *hui* became available as informal institutions catering to the needs of marginal, often young, men. Neither the men nor the institutions were always completely alienated from traditional society, nor were all of these associations "secret."[2] Instead, the *hui* often existed alongside or in between traditional institutions, allowing its members to achieve various ends, ranging from mutual aid to criminal entrepreneurship to, on occasion, rebellion.[3]

Second, it follows that eighteenth-century Chinese knew how to form *hui* because most ritual and organizational practices of Qing *hui* derived from traditional institutions and customs. The *hui* as a social form was part of traditional village life, often connected to lineage rites, popular religious practices, or informal structures of mutual aid. The brotherhood oath that accompanied the formation of many *hui* would likewise have been familiar from various contexts, ranging from popular drama and fiction to marriage oaths to declarations of friendship—and to acts of collective violence.

In a new context, however, even the innocent aspects of these familiar forms and practices took on new meanings. Since many *hui* were only partly attached to traditional, orthodox social institutions, *hui* became potentially dangerous on two counts. First, even if the brotherhood "ideology" characterizing many *hui* was not explicitly anti-Confucian, the brotherhood nonetheless remained unigenerational, underscoring the distance of the *hui* from the more typically hierarchical institutions of local society and their built-in age-based authority. The blood oath of fictive kinship and the availability of the *hui* as a social form encouraged late-night drinking and acts of bravado in ways that lineages and village communities, more directly linked to structures of local dominance through local gentry, did not. Second, the blood oath itself, although part of early elite culture, also possessed overtones of danger and heterodoxy, particularly since it was interpreted as such by the powerful Qing state.

Third, the frequent connection between *hui* and violence grew in large measure out of their structural position in Chinese society and out of Qing distrust of non-elite associational activity—the other reason for the proliferation of *hui* in Qing sources. The Qing state was extremely sensitive to *hui* activities, and invested considerable energy in suppressing them. In terms of their structural position, the fact that *hui* were often located between traditional institutions, drawing membership from more than one village, lineage, or ethnic group meant both that *hui* did not always receive the protection afforded more central members of solidary groups and that *hui* were also freer to engage in various types of violence, if violence proved necessary or profitable. Mutual aid in such an environment might easily move from shared crop-watching or common contributions to parental burials, to less innocent forms of "self help." In addition, rebels, malcontents, and messiahs might find themselves naturally drawn to the *hui*, given its tenuous relationship to local society (providing limited protection and yet adequate distance) and its bond of blood brotherhood.

Fourth, although a complete explanation of the proliferation of *hui* in eighteenth-century Southeast China awaits future research, certain speculations suggest themselves. First, Southeast China's position as a distant border area— and in Taiwan's case, as a genuine frontier—surely provides part of the answer. According to one influential theory, the strong lineages of mainland Southeast China were built to compensate for a relative lack of central control and a dangerous social climate (Freedman 1966, 162–64). This danger derived from many sources—difficult topography, inadequate arable land, frequent movement, within and without the macroregion, to and from Taiwan, to and from Southeast Asia—and prevented lineages from achieving complete domination. As a newly settled and undergoverned frontier, Taiwan's social order was even looser throughout the eighteenth century than that of the mainland. Institutions such as *hui* helped to absorb marginal members of the population.

Another part of the explanation invokes the history of the region. The dynastic transition alone, which occupied several decades of the seventeenth century in the Southeast, unsettled the social order and encouraged militarization. Moreover, the rapid population growth of the high Qing, following on the dislocations of geography and history, surely helped to speed the removal of some *hui* from community control.

Without discounting these factors, this chapter—as a heuristic exercise— juxtaposes the emergence and proliferation of *hui* with our understanding of the social forces at work in "early modern" Southeast China. "Early modern" refers to a distinct period, from the late 1500s through the disintegration of the imperial order in the early twentieth century, and a distinctive set of social arrangements. Increased commercialization and a more sophisticated division of labor resulted from foreign trade, New World silver, and population growth. This same population growth encouraged spatial mobility, and commercialization and the spread of literacy facilitated a degree of social mobility as well. A freer social climate emerged, as formal status distinctions were lifted and the lives of the common people of China came to be controlled as much by the marketplace as by the landlord (who moved to the city and hired a manager to administer his properties) or the bureaucrat (who collected his taxes in silver rather than corvée) (Rawski 1985; Rowe 1990; Wakeman 1975).

The emergence of "early modern" China cannot, of course, predict the proliferation of *hui*; if it could, *hui* would have flourished in Jiangnan, where the socioeconomic developments associated with the early modern period were most concentrated and pronounced. But it may be helpful nonetheless to assess the significance of the proliferation of the *hui* in terms of the historical trends associated with early modern China, arguably one of the most important interpretations of Ming-Qing history in the past two decades. Just as commercialization gave rise to guilds in Europe and *huiguan* in China, it may be that the pressure on traditional institutions created by the rise of this early modern order facilitated the formation of *hui* among marginal young men "emancipated" from the protection of lineage and community.

Finally, this chapter suggests many different kinds of *hui* existed throughout the early modern period. There were innocent *hui* fully embedded in law-abiding communities; there were *hui* at the margins of society that divided their time between legal and illegal pursuit of mutual aid; and there were *hui* that harbored con men and rebels. Part of the debate over the nature of the *hui*—were they mutual aid fraternities, secret societies, criminals, or rebels?—stems from an attempt to construct narrow generalizations for a diverse category. Here I concentrate on *hui* located at the margins of settled society but not set up for the specific purpose of rebellion.

The discussion that follows is divided into three parts. The first is a tentative survey of the pre-Qing histories of mutual aid, blood oaths, and fictive kinship. The goal of this section is to examine both the sociological and the cultural-symbolic aspects of *hui* formation in order to illustrate how eighteenth-century Chinese might have understood the establishment of a *hui*. The second is an examination of two particular eighteenth-century *hui*, both based on archival sources, both drawn from the Southeast Coast where I have done the majority of my research. Neither is later than the 1787–88 Lin Shuangwen rebellion, which appears to have been something of a watershed in the history of state-*hui* relations. This section takes a basically sociological tack, illustrating the complicated nature of the relationship between the *hui* and the settled societies of which they remained a part. The final section attempts to link these research findings to our understanding of early modern Chinese society.

Historical Components of Qing Hui

Most Qing *hui* consisted of two components: an organization that brought members together in pursuit of some form of cooperative enterprise and a ritual, frequently including a blood oath of fictive brotherhood, that cemented the organization. Three points are brought out in the exposition that follows:

1. That there was a long history of organization for mutual aid, generally carried out *within* the confines of village society;
2. That the history of the blood oath is longer and more difficult to trace than that of mutual aid, and possesses dangerous symbolic overtones of heterodoxy and rebellion;
3. That the Qing *hui* was a repackaging of earlier social and cultural practices. In other words, even though the *hui* as a social form and the use of the blood oath predated the Qing period by centuries, even though marginal men had certainly banded together in various forms for hundreds of years, there is still little evidence that before the Ming-Qing transition, groups of men at the margins of settled society called themselves *hui* and banded together through a blood oath for the purposes of mutual aid.

Organization for Mutual Aid

There is a long history of local organization for mutual cooperation in Chinese society, spanning a broad spectrum of activities and generally employing terms such as *hui* and *she* as names for the organizations. Most of these organizations were firmly embedded in the institutions of social life, and few engaged in unsupervised violence; hence the "sudden" appearance of large numbers of *hui* in early Qing sources, when their relative "independence" rendered them more suspect .

The research of Japanese scholars suggests that the kind of local organization that eventually grew into the Qing *hui* first emerged in significant numbers in the mid- to late Tang (618–907), and was generally referred to as an *yishe*. The "*yi*" of "*yishe*" refers to an artificial unit of social organization imposed from above, and thus "*yishe*" means "an association of the *yi*,"[4] but for all practical purposes few of the *yishe* seem to have exceeded the boundaries of the village. Another source of cooperation for mutual aid included the vegetarian societies (*zhaihui*), scripture reading groups, and sutra-story telling practices (*sujiang*) originally attached to Buddhist temples. An elite version of these associations, the dharma society (*fashe*), brought together monks and local notables in the homes of the latter for discussions of the sutras, but most *yishe* maintained their concern with the character and morality of *she* members through encouragement of mutual aid in a number of related spheres (Naba 1938, 41ff; Yang 1961, 203–6).

One of the most important of these spheres was that of agricultural production. Early examples of agricultural mutual aid societies include "hoe societies" (*chushe*), small-scale labor-sharing organizations that existed in both northern and southern Song and Yuan China. By the Ming and Qing periods, some of the language describing shared labor seems to have lost its associational tone, but the well-known crop-watching societies (*kanqinghui*) surely drew on this tradition.

In some instances, cooperation was not confined to the busy season of agricultural labor, but extended to the construction of dikes and polders, the collection of stubble, and various other chores in the slack season as well. Some peasants shared draft animals; others made scarce tools available to their neighbors. Still others pooled their funds to purchase animals and tools. Unsurprisingly, most of this cooperation was practiced by neighbors whose fields were located in the same general area. Such cooperation was also sanctioned by the classics and encouraged by the state (Shimizu 1951, 392–98).[5]

Weddings and funerals, as crucial ceremonial junctures in the life cycles of virtually all Chinese families, represented another context in which mutual aid could play an important role. The burial of parents was a crucial obligation in a society that prized filial piety, and many associations were constructed to help either with the organization or with the expense of parental burial. Shimizu Morimitsu again finds the earliest evidence for such societies in the Tang: one of the Tang emperor Gaozong's (r. 650–84) edicts cautions against the proliferation of "private" *she* devoted to weddings and funerals, arguing that such activities placed too much of a burden on the peasantry (who were presumably expected to assist in the ceremonial affairs of the elite) (cited in Shimizu 1951, 456). In another instance, the Tang official Wei Ting complained in a memorial that the practice of forming *yishe* was diverting both noble and peasant from the proper rituals of mourning (cited in Shimizu 1951, 457; more recent examples include Kulp 1925, 196–203; Perry 1980, 53).

Despite such official concerns, the expense of parental burial ensured the popularity of *she* and *hui* devoted to such concerns, and the number of such associations seems to have grown during the Ming. The Wanli period (1573–1620) Ningjin county (Hebei) gazetteer records that

> People establish *yishe* to prepare for mourning. These *she* make no distinction between rich and poor, and select [members] only according to virtue. They meet twice monthly on the first and fifteenth, and everyone contributes a certain amount of money. They choose someone who is honest and generous to be head [of the association]. When there is a death within the *hui*, the leader calls for donations and devotions. (Cited in Shimizu 1951, 460)

Some of these funeral organizations, such as Tang Haoru's Society for the Burial of Relatives (Zangqinshe), appear to have become quite complex during the Qing, keeping elaborate records so as to encourage reverence and penalize financial and moral lapses (described in Shimizu 1951, 463–64). One suspects, however, that most mourning societies were less formal than the Tang Haoru model, as suggested by the following nineteenth-century example from Anhui:

> For the poor to bury their dead requires substantial contributions from relatives and friends, so there have always been Xiaoyihui [Filial Piety and Righteousness Societies]. These meet for a meal once a month and make

common contributions that are held [in trust] by one person. When a grandfather or grandmother, or father or mother, dies, they all help to carry out the mourning and burial, using the [accumulated] funds to help the family in need. If there is extra interest it goes to the surviving members of the families. This is practiced by both elite and commoners. (Cited in Shimizu 1951, 466)

Weddings were another important—and expensive—event in the ritual life cycle of the Chinese family, and similar societies were set up to help to collect adequate funds to carry them out in accordance with the dictates of style and display. Over the whole of the late imperial period scholars have found scattered references to Qinghui ("Sentiments" Societies), Xishe (Happiness Societies), *Hunjiahui* (Marriage Societies), *Hongmaohui* (Red Hat Societies), and *Honglishe* (Red Ceremony Societies), among others. Organizations devoted to preparations for marriage do not, however, appear to have developed as early or to have been as widespread as those concerned with burials and should perhaps be grouped together with more general societies, such as the well-known Hongbaihui (Red and White Societies), as well as the eighteenth-century Henan *hui*, which accumulated funds for newborns as well as for funerals (Shimizu 1951, 469).

Mutual Aid through Finance

Many of these organizations, whatever their stated purpose, shared a common financial mechanism: the pooling of joint funds and their investment in an interest-earning property or enterprise. Again, scholars speculate that this practice may have been imported from India before or during the Tang (Shimizu 1951, 499ff; Wang 1931, 4–6; Yang 1961, 204). The biography of Wei Dan in the *New Tang History* notes that while serving as prefect of Yongzhou, Wei observed that the locals were too poor to afford oxen, so he set up one or more *she* consisting of some 20 families and had each family contribute a certain amount of money to a common fund every month so that, over time, they were able to purchase the oxen they needed (cited in Shimizu 1951, 487). Some of the funeral societies appear to have furnished a mechanism whereby capital was made available to those who contributed the money. In the Qing Daoguang period (1821–50), Lu Yitian describes the establishment of a burial society in Zhejiang that brought together 40 men, each of whom contributed 500 cash at a single annual meeting on the fifteenth day of the fourth month. The men drew lots to determine first use of the money, but the order could be changed for the convenience of all concerned. Lu's description notes that "the money is to remain in the headquarters to prepare for the purchase of bricks and mortar [for the construction of tombs], not for the purchase of bricks and tiles [for the construction of homes] or the purchase of private kilns" (cited in Shimizu 1951, 465). The inclusion of such a prohibition suggests that the fund was likely abused in just such a manner.

However, there was little reason to hide financial exigency behind the facade of ceremonial expense. At least from the Ming period, Chinese set up *hui* or *she* for the sole purpose of providing capital for friends and relatives in need. In the Ming and Qing periods these were referred to generically as *yinhui* (silver associations) or *yaohui* ("shaking" associations), both of which appear to have begun as a form of gambling:

> According to the customs of Jiangsu, whenever someone comes upon hard times, he gets his friends together and they all contribute a sum of money. They enclose dice inside a box and shake it, and the lucky winner takes it all. . . . [This is called a] *yaohui.* (Cited in Shimizu 1951, 500)

Before long, one assumes, this evolved into the *qianhui* or *biaohui*, the revolving credit society familiar to us from late Qing-Republican period China and modern Taiwan, as well as many other societies (for late Qing, Smith 1894, 152–60; for Republican period, Fei 1939, 267–74; Gamble 1944; Kulp 1925, 190–96; Wang 1931; Yang 1935; for Taiwan, Taiwan 1985; Winn forthcoming; for comparative examples, Geertz 1962). A Qing writer notes the advantages and disadvantages of such practices as follows:

> Revolving credit societies [*yinqian yaohui*], in which people surrender their spare change every month and store the combined amount to help friends in need, were originally a good idea. For some reason, though, people today are evil, and I have seen many people, because of problems with *hui*, either disappear completely or go into debt. . . . From this day forward, I will respond to no more requests to enter *hui*, and save myself a great deal of aggravation worrying that I won't have any money when it comes time to contribute. (Cited in Shimizu 1951: 501)

By the latter Qing period, such revolving credit societies were extremely common. They bore various names, some of which revealed the size of the membership or the size of the expected contribution, and others that were simply variations on the theme of revolving credit: the Qixinghui (Seven Star Society), the Qixianhui (Seven Worthies Society), the Baxianhui (Eight Immortals Society), the Junzihui (Gentlemen's Society), the Wuhuhui (Five Tigers Society), the Wuzonghui (Five Leaders Society), the Bashiyuan hui (Eighty Dollar Society), the Erbaiyuan hui (Two Hundred Dollar Society), the Jijinhui (Accumulated Gold Society), the Duijihui (Accumulation Society), and the Shehui (Credit Society). Membership ranged from 7 to 25, in the examples cited by Shimizu Morimitsu from the nineteenth-century and earlier (Shimizu 1951, 489–90, 496–97). Wang Zongpei illustrates that some of these societies grew larger during the Republican period (Wang 1931: 23, 29, 75, 88).

The Hui in Community Ritual Organization

In addition to these examples of *hui* as forums for the organization of mutual aid, we also have numerous historical references to celebratory or ritual occasions and to small groups set up to organize such occasions, both of which were frequently referred to as either *hui* or *she*. The Song dynasty text *Wulin jiushi* (Old Hangzhou), for example, refers to "gatherings" (*hui*) of troupes (*she*) of artisans and performers on certain festive occasions (in Bao 1872, chapter 3, *shehui*) and notes that "every monastery held a Buddha-washing gathering (*yufohui*) at which the monks and nuns competed to collect bronze images [of the Buddha] in little basins" (in Bao 1872, chapter 3, *yufo*). Barend ter Haar has found evidence of similar associational activities, also in the Southern Song, which he characterizes as "assemblies set up by the monasteries themselves; . . . regular Pure Land assemblies held by monasteries; . . . [and] various lay groups . . . who . . . offered tea and hot water on religious festivals" (ter Haar 1992, 30–31). By the late Ming, in North China if not elsewhere, there were urban religious associations, usually called "sacred associations" (*shenghui*), which brought together unrelated individuals to carry out annual pilgrimages and to gather money to repair local temples.

In addition, by the early Ming period, if not before, *hui* and *she* played important roles in community and lineage religious activities, either as subunits of the communities charged with organizing particular activities or as the names for the activities (often feasts or activities culminating in feasts) themselves (for examples, see *Funing zhouzhi* 1593, 2.5a; *Huian xianzhi* 1803, 4.3a; *Xinghua fuzhi* 1503, 15.6b). Anthropologist Myron Cohen found that until recently, lineage members of the North China village of Yangmansa, where Cohen did his field work, formed a Qingminghui every year during the Qingming festival, in order to organize the "only mobilization of the lineage as a group in a ritual context" (Cohen 1990, 521–28).

In his examination of the intersection of religious and community organization in northern Taiwan, historian Wang Shih-ch'ing discusses equally relevant organizations. First, he notes the late eighteenth-century establishment of a *chifuhui* ("Eat Good Fortune Society") by the residents of the village of T'an-ti in the southwestern region of the Tai-pei basin. The association was established "to meet once or twice a year, share a feast, and worship" the local earth god. In addition, according to Wang, the association also provided "the institutional means of organizing work parties to repair irrigation ditches and roads . . . [as well as] a forum for negotiating disputes over boundaries and water rights" (Wang 1974, 80, 85). Wang also discusses the multicommunity spirit association (*shenminghui*), "self-selected communities in which membership is not defined solely on a territorial basis but on the basis of kinship affiliation, ethnic identity, or devotion to a particular god," which played an important role as a substitute for extensive lineage organization in the early development of Taiwanese society. In many such organizations, mutual aid was fused with religious practices to promote community or lineage cohesion (Wang 1974, 71).

In summary, part of the tradition drawn on by eighteenth- and nineteenth-century *hui* was this long-established practice of banding together in various contexts for mutual aid. Most examples of such mutual aid seem to have relied on natural interaction among village or lineage members or among members of subcommunity social units. Indeed, with the exceptions of organization for defense and organization for the construction of irrigation works (Shimizu 1951, 519–60, 610–42), which were often larger, more complex, and less enduring than the associations discussed here, most pre-eighteenth-century *hui* seem to have functioned largely *within* village society, under the fairly watchful eye of the local elite, and with the toleration and even occasional encouragement of the state. Indeed, the incorporation of the *hui* into the workings of community and lineage rituals and the widespread nature of some of the organizational mechanisms associated with the *hui* in twentieth-century Taiwan have prompted anthropologist P. Steven Sangren to characterize the *hui* as a more basic organizational principle in Chinese society than kinship (Sangren 1984). Thus when peasants in 1720s Taiwan set up a *Fumuhui* (Father and Mother Society) to help fellow association members accumulate funds to bury their parents (as Robert Antony describes in his contribution to this volume), they were acting within a long and well-established tradition—even though the leaders were arrested and executed by a zealous Qing state. As I suggested above, many Qing *hui* were to some degree outside community control, which meant that "cooperative" impulses could lead to illegal activities and that "mutual aid fraternities" could recruit unsavory members. But in terms of the basic motivation behind *hui* formation, there seems to have been more continuity than innovation in the proliferation of eighteenth- and nineteenth-century associations.

The Ritual of Association: The Blood Oath of Fictive Brotherhood

A second defining feature of the *hui* during the Qing period was an oath of fictive brotherhood that bound the members to one another. One difference between the *hui* of mutual aid and communal celebration, and the potentially more dangerous *hui* that excited Qing suspicion, must have been the ritual by which the two sorts of association were cemented. The sources collected to explore the history and variety of organization for mutual aid tell us relatively little about the rituals accompanying the formation of such groups. Of the hundreds of sources assembled by Shimizu Morimitsu, one of the few that discusses the ritual aspects of *hui* formation is the Wanli period (1573–1620) Sishui county (Shandong) gazetteer, which records that

> The ordinary people of the cities and villages gather together in *hui*. To the east they make pilgrimages to Taishan, and to the south they make pilgrimages to Wudang [both sacred mountains]. In the idle period at the end of the year they form *she* by the hundreds and call these organizations *xianghui* [incense societies]. (Cited in Shimizu 1951, 462)

This passage clearly refers to the "sacred associations" discussed above, only one of many different kinds of associations, and one of the few extending beyond village or community boundaries. Presumably, the sources are quiet on the nature of the ritual that accompanied the formation of the agricultural, wedding, funeral, and other societies discussed above because these rituals were subsumed in the ceremonial life of the communal group and thus reaffirmed the authority of the leaders of the group. Shimizu produces no sources to identify the ritual of blood-oath brotherhood with the formation of the *hui* and *she* he discusses.

Blood Oaths and the Warring States Transition

Written records of blood-oath brotherhoods predate those of mutual aid associations, and the intersection of these two traditions in the late imperial period is one of the defining features of the early modern *hui*. The most compelling account of the early history of blood oaths is found in Mark Edward Lewis's *Sanctioned Violence in Early China.* Lewis's study reexamines the Warring States transition from an aristocratic, "feudal" regime to a proto-imperial bureaucracy "as revealed by changes in the patterns of sanctioned violence"—warfare, sacrifice, hunting, and other "ritually coded acts of violence" (Lewis 1990, vii, 7). Blood oaths were crucial to this transformation, providing a mechanism of elite political and social cohesion in the wake of the breakdown of the aristocratic religious order of the Shang and early Zhou:

> [The pre-transition] elite [was] defined through sacrifice and warfare, drawn together through kin ties established by the cult of the ancestors and the ritual exchanges of meat, but riven by a segmentary division of authority among men who were devoted to an honor defined by heroism and martial prowess. Inter-state wars, inter-lineage conflicts, and vendettas launched to avenge slighted honor generated incessant conflicts that broke down the old hierarchies of ritual and lineage law and replaced them with an increasingly savage struggle for dominance through armed force. In the conflicts of the Spring and Autumn period, the primary means devised to create new ties among men no longer tightly bound by the old Zhou order was the blood covenant. (Lewis 1990, 43)

In the early Eastern Zhou, these blood oaths became "fundamental to the political and social order," initially facilitating diplomatic pacts under the temporary leadership of an overlord (*ba*), and later permitting alliances between powerful lineages, "alien states, and . . . the various contestants for supremacy as the Zhou disintegrated" (Lewis 1990, 44).

These covenants were binding forms of oaths designed to secure compliance to a common purpose and were "distinguished from ordinary oaths through the killing of a sacrificial animal and the drinking of its blood" (Lewis 1990, 45), a ritual superficially similar to those employed by eighteenth- and nineteenth-century secret societies.

Lewis goes on to argue that these blood oaths, a private response to the disintegration of the old, "feudal" public, gave way in turn to a reimagined public sphere. In this new public sphere, the blood sacrifice was replaced by the written text (now called a "bond" [*yue*]), the sanction of the spirits and ancestors gave way to the moral intentions of the participants, and the relative equality of the parties to the blood oath was transformed into a hierarchical relationship between ruler and servitor, husband and wife, noble and dependent (Lewis 1990, 78). In other words, the transition led to the text-based moral hierarchy of Confucian imperial China.

Blood Oaths and Popular Culture

It is unclear to what extent *popular* rituals adopted the blood sacrifice in this early period; most of our sources focus on elite behavior. Nor is it clear what happened to the practice of blood sacrifice after the Han-period transformation Lewis describes. We do know that bonds and oaths of various sorts functioned in popular contexts from Han times down to the modern age. Barend ter Haar has identified four such practices by Han Chinese, all of which employ the language of bonds and covenants—*jie, ding, yue, meng, shi, jieyi*—while dispensing with the actual blood sacrifice. These practices include: popular bonds promising cooperation between families and couples, generally in the context of marriage; legal bonds in which sworn oaths attest to veracity and personal integrity; community bonds, where oaths serve to cement communal ties, which likely gave rise to official attempts in the neo-Confucian revival from Song times forward to impose "community covenants" (*xiangyue*) from above; and bonds of fictive kinship among unrelated individuals (ter Haar 1991; on *xiangyue*, Cheek 1984; Hsiao 1960, 185–90, 201, 214). This evidence is borne out by literary references. The *Shuihuzhuan* (The Water Margin) and the *Sanguo yanyi* (The Romance of the Three Kingdoms) indicate that the process of brotherhood formation (*jiebai*) is moderately ancient and very popular: The Peach Garden Oath and the assembly at the Zhongyitang were celebrated in late Song story cycles and Yuan drama even before the novels reached more mature form in the Ming (Irwin 1966, 23–60; Plaks 1987, 279–303, 361–76). The first substantive chapter of *Jinpingmei* (The Golden Lotus) includes an account of the formation of a brotherhood (Egerton 1939, 6–31).

Ter Haar also finds evidence that blood-oath rituals strikingly similar to those of the transitional period between the Warring States and the early imperial era were employed by minority ethnic groups throughout Chinese history, including the Mongols and the Manchus in the pre-Qing period (ter Haar 1991). Significantly, blood oaths were also employed, again throughout Chinese history, in various violent, criminal, messianic, and rebellious contexts. The most famous example during the Ming-Qing period in Southeast China is probably that of Deng Maoqi, the fabled "leveling king" (*chanpingwang*) who led a major uprising of disgruntled miners and tenant farmers in western Fujian in the late 1440s; Deng sealed his pact with his followers by killing a white horse, drinking its blood, and sacrificing to heaven (Tanaka 1984, 202–4; Zhu 1986, vol. 2, 113–52 on the rebellion, 134 on the blood oath). But the blood oath was also employed by pirates (for example, the sixteenth-century chaozhou pirate Lin Daoqian) (ter Haar 1991), groups of indentured servants (*nu*) (Fu 1961, 106), and bandits (*Enping xianzhi* 1825, 3.15a), among others. In at least one instance, a Qing official advised local cantons (*xiang*) in Guangdong to form alliances against bandits and to seal these alliances with blood oaths (Qu 1985, vol. 1, 249). Clearly, the blood oath, substituting for ties of genuine kinship, could sanctify undertakings of great danger.

The history of the blood oath is more complex than that of the *hui* or *she*. First, it is clear that the history of it that we have at present is even less complete than that of the *hui*, with important questions unanswered, particularly in the area of popular culture. Second, the act of oath-taking appeared in two different contexts. The blood oath, drawing on the weighty idea of human sacrifice, seems to have been invoked in situations of great political moment—wars and rebellions. The simple oath (without blood), by contrast, seems to have sanctified bonds of a somewhat lesser order—marriage, friendship, community compacts. For reasons that are unclear, many Qing *hui* engaged in fairly innocent pursuit of mutual aid chose to employ a blood sacrifice rather than a simple oath, thereby imbuing their organizations and activities with a powerfully dangerous symbolism that the Qing state could not ignore. One way to understand this choice is to recognize just how dangerous life at the margins of society could be and to note that "mutual aid" among poor young men could often translate into criminal or predatory behavior; the blood oath both bound these young men to one another in the face of potential risk and perhaps made them appear more fearsome to outside groups. In fact, it might not be too fanciful to draw an analogy between the use of the blood oath by early imperial elites and by early modern non-elites: Just as the Warring States nobility employed blood oaths to reconstruct social cohesion in a period when the old sense of "public" was giving way, so the marginalized commoners of the eighteenth century used the blood oath to reconfigure their social order in a period when lineages and villages no longer functioned as an effective "public" for these young men.

The Hui in Eighteenth-Century Southeast China

This section examines mutual assistance, blood oaths, fictive kinship, and *hui* in a specific time and place: eighteenth-century Southeast China. Many of the eighteenth-century *hui* in this region were organizations comprised chiefly of young men[6] and remained marginally attached to existing institutions. In other words, although we can often identify the links between the *hui* and local social groups such as lineages and villages, the leadership, membership, and activities of the *hui* remained in some sense outside these more main-stream institutions.

The treatment of eighteenth-century *hui* in this section is no more comprehensive than that of the history of the components of *hui* above. There are too many known incidents to permit careful treatment in an essay of this length; between 1720 and 1820, in Fujian and Taiwan alone there are 75 examples of *hui*, most of which were probably formed on the basis of a brotherhood oath, and several of which engaged in rebellion (Zhuang 1990, 111–20). Furthermore, even a careful analysis of this group of 75 incidents would bias our understanding of *hui* in the direction of those involved in violence and rebellion and away from those engaged in more innocent pursuits of mutual aid. The incidents I have chosen to examine are two *hui* that came to be involved in rebellion, but which were initially set up for other purposes. I chose these two incidents both because fairly rich archival information reveals more about them than about many other contemporary *hui* and because they illustrate the major theme I am developing—that of the *hui* as an informal institution marginally attached to the more formal institutions of settled society.

The Tiechihui

The case of the Tiechihui (Iron Ruler Society) is a clear example of the ties both between *hui* and local society and between *hui* and rebellion. Qing officials arrested those involved in organizing the near-uprising in the sixth month of QL 18 (1753), in and around the village of Hepingli, in Shaowu county, Shaowu prefecture, western Fujian, but the associations out of which the rebellious activity grew began several years earlier, and for reasons that had little to do with rebellion (unless otherwise noted, all references are to *Shiliao xunkan* 1963, sec. *di*, 409b–450a).

Two originally separate associations eventually came together to form the Tiechihui. The central figure of one was Du Qi, described in the documents as a "bad sort" (*jianmin*) and a martial arts practitioner. Some time during QL 11 (1746), Ma Danjiu, a local bully who lived near Hepingli in the separate settlement of Jiangshixu, attacked Du physically in what was probably a drunken brawl, and Du organized for revenge. He recruited his agnatic younger cousin, Du Guoxiang, a former soldier in the Shaowu military brigade, and 27 others to form an unnamed mutual-assistance brotherhood, but apparently did not immediately avenge Du's injury at the hands of Ma Danjiu.

The other association eventually affiliated with the Tiechihui dated back even further. Luo Jiabi was a Hepingli *jiansheng* of a respectable family, whose father had died in 1736, leaving Luo and his younger brother Luo Jiaqiu in a vulnerable position. To avoid local bullying, Jiabi had formed the Guanshenghui—the name based on that of the popular god of war whose temples were favorite places to swear oaths of brotherhood—consisting of twelve people. When Luo Jiaqiu grew up, he studied martial arts and took over leadership of the Guanshenghui. Over time, Jiaqiu induced 16 more people to enter the *hui*, and every year in the fifth month—which includes the festival of the god of war—they renewed their vows of brotherhood through sacrifices to the spirits and a shared meal. He also became friendly with Du Qi and Du Guoxiang, whose mother had been a member of the Luo clan. To this point, the brotherhood and the *hui* were grafted onto typical village structures, and their ceremonial life borrowed from popular culture.

In 1750, the two associations were brought together by the same bully. One of the members of Du Qi's brotherhood was assaulted by Ma Danjiu—the same man whose violence had prompted the formation of Du Qi's original fraternity. Luo Kangsong, a member of Liu Jiaqiu's *hui*, saw this and was angered, decided to help out, and was injured in the course of his chivalry. At this point the two *hui* decided to join forces. On QL 15.5.13 (1750)—the second day of the festival of Guangong—they met to drink at one of the local temples and agreed to help one another in the event of fights over property, brawls, lawsuits, or personal insults. Their combined number came to 56 and Du Guoxiang recorded their names in a book and penned a fairly orthodox preface, which read in part:

> If we wish to come together to unite our hearts, this will require long study. We must not forget that it is not through wine and meat that one finds true friends (*zhiji*); nor through ignoring others' troubles. [Let us act in such a way that] we feel no shame before the ancients, and distinguish ourselves from the commonplace. (*Shiliao xunkan* 1963, sec. *di*, 443a)

There is some confusion over the name of the association. When Qing officials first learned of the Iron Ruler Society, they assumed that the iron rulers were the symbol of the organization, to be carried on the person as an identifying sign. The documents do in fact record the discovery of two rulers as a consequence of early arrests (*Shiliao xunkan* 1963, sec. *di*, 441a). Other documents also note, however, that the name for the new, enlarged society that came out of this merger came not from the leaders of the society, but from the people of the village who called the enlarged association the Tiechihui because "iron ruler" was local slang for "no-good" (GZZP, NYMJ 793.1). Whatever the truth about the name of the society, it appears that the fact of their organization was widely known and that "secret society" is hardly an appropriate label for the Tiechihui.

The combined associations sought to expand their membership by recruiting underlings from the prefectural and county offices, as well as martial arts adepts and those with ties to the local military. Once such a group achieved a certain size and influence in a locality, it surely made sense for local clerks, runners, policemen, and soldiers to establish ties with the group so as to facilitate their management of "official business." The greater numbers achieved by merging the two organizations eventually facilitated other, more nefarious activities than those of the original *hui*, which had been small, protective, and based largely on ties of surname and marriage. Nonetheless, even the enlarged *hui* remained basically unchanged for almost two years after the merger, until, for unspecified reasons, recruitment efforts accelerated in the spring of QL 17 (1752).

One night in the fourth month, following the recruitment of an itinerant monk and a yamen courier adept in martial arts, 12 of the growing number retired to the monk's cloister to drink and welcome the new members. Late in the night, after several of the party had returned home, those still present began to entertain ambitious notions involving the future of at least part of their association:

> Du Qi and the others began to brag on their abilities and Du Qi suddenly got the idea to become outlaws *[fei]*, *saying that their band was large, and that in years of famine or drought they could gain great influence and have their way without opposition. Everyone agreed. Du Qi said they would have to find more good men [haohan].* . . . [One of the recent recruits] said that without evidence [of their worthiness] they would have a hard time carrying out the recruiting. Du Qi then remembered that his ancestor, Du Shiyuan, had in the early Qing period found a brass seal of a Brigade General in Zheng Chenggong's forces in a fish pond. This was still at Du Guoxiang's house, and could serve as evidence. (*Shiliao xunkan* 1963, sec. *di*, 448b)

Three nights later, having located and polished the seal—a frequently employed symbol of imperial legitimacy—the same men returned to the monk's hut and sealed their intent with prayers, sacrifices, and the blood of a chicken; it is not noted whether previous meetings had also employed blood oaths. In forming their brotherhood, the men ranked themselves by ability in martial arts, rather than by age or experience in the *hui*: Du Guoxiang was named as leader (*huishou*), followed as second leader by *hui* founder Du Qi and as third leader by the newly recruited Du Zhengliang.

Over the next year, the leadership of the pact engaged in a series of somewhat comical efforts to produce convincingly awe-inspiring letters of deputation (*zhafu*), which consisted of rebellious slogans, military ranks (with blank spaces left for the names of recruits), and imperial dragon designs printed on pieces of yellow damask. Part of these efforts involved renting a local temple (*shuguan*) as headquarters, so that Du Guoxiang's wife, who had apparently seen some of the details of the early preparations and had objected strenuously to this threat to her husband and family, would find out no further details.

The peddling of the letters of deputation was an expression of intent to supplant the reigning dynasty and eventually did land the band in trouble, although it took several months before their activities attracted official notice. They claimed that the letters had been authorized by Li Kaihua, an imaginary figure whose name was often used in the planning stage of rebellions (see chapter 6; Kuhn 1990, 63). They presented them either to those who they thought might be helpful to the cause—such as a Jianyang county yamen courier with many contacts in the adjacent county, who was given a "general's letter of deputation" on QL 18.6.25 (1753), or a martial arts adept who was presented with a "brigade general's letter of deputation" on the same day—or peddled them to those who feared being caught out when the rebellion began—such as Wu Zhengzhou, who accepted another "general's letter of deputation" on QL 18.5.9 (1753), promising to contribute 100 piculs of grain when the violence began. The only clear reference to a successful sale was when Du Qi and Du Guoxiang convinced Luo Jiuqiu to pay the outrageous sum of 30 ounces of silver for a letter; Luo had clearly not been part of the plot to rebel and was anxious to buy his way in (although he had only 12 ounces of silver to pay up front, and the two Dus refused to surrender the letter until he had paid in full!).[7] However, the *hui* seems mostly to have had considerable trouble peddling the dangerous letters, as the confessions report numerous fruitless trips through the rural areas.

This incident is an excellent example of the function of the *hui* in the society of Southeastern China, as well as an apt illustration of why the *hui* frightened the Qing state. The leaders of the Tiechihui were well-known (if not respected) members of local society—Luo Jiabi had attained (probably purchased) the status of *jiansheng*, which, even if it had declined in value since the Ming, still "constituted a privileged . . . [status] among the commoners" (Ho 1962, 34)— and if none of those involved appears wealthy, neither do they appear particularly destitute. Granted, many of the members of the *hui* were martial arts adepts, and probably marginally employed and restless, but part of the original rationale for merging the two smaller *hui* in 1750 was to help one another in the event of fights *over property*, which is some indication of their position in the community. In addition, they were able to rent a local temple as a temporary headquarters for their planned rebellion, and Luo Jiaqiu was able to sacrifice the sum of 12 ounces of silver to buy his way into the ranks of the plotters. At the outset, they had banded together in brotherhoods based on surname and lineage ties and devoted to protection against outside violence.

In merging to form the Tiechihui, however, the two original brotherhoods in a sense moved out of the social sphere defined by residential community (although their merger was facilitated by preexisting affinal ties between the two groups) and formed their own *hui* on more neutral ground—at the cloister of the itinerant monk. No community or lineage authority interfered with their late night drinking bouts, which led to plans to expand their organization. Expansion meant recruitment, which brought in more men, more money, larger networks, including further penetration of local civil and military subofficials—in sum, more local power. All this inflated the self-image of the leaders of the *hui*, prompting their hopeless posture of rebellion. The invocation of Zheng Chenggong and the issue of military rank may have been either the acting out of millenarian fantasies or mere devices in an entrepreneurial scheme to bilk locals of their money. In either case, they constituted a direct challenge to the state, in this instance provoked neither by particularly dire economic circumstances nor by official harassment or corruption. Ultimate motivation for rebellion in this case remains obscure, but the re-establishment of the *hui* outside community control seems to be central to the redirection of collective action, even if nothing about the original establishment of the two *hui* suggested rebellious intent.

Lin Shuangwen's Tiandihui

Archival information on eighteenth-century *hui* is most complete in its coverage of the Lin Shuangwen uprising of 1787–88, the second example to be discussed here. The uprising was the first instance of Heaven and Earth Society (Tiandihui, Triad) rebellion,[8] and its success provoked a year-long pacification effort and a subsequent investigation into the origins, practices, and organization of Lin Shuangwen's Tiandihui. Drawing on the materials uncovered during these investigations, we can discuss the nature of this association and its relationship to contemporary Taiwanese society with some precision. Again, we find that Lin Shuangwen and his Tiandihui were only partly alienated from mainstream Taiwanese society: Lin set up a *hui* in order to promote mutual aid among *hui* members and to engage in minor criminal activities. The membership of his original, pre-rebellion *hui* was made up of lower-class young men, but not primarily of drifters or unattached single males. At the same time, and despite his apparent criminality, Lin remained tied to his powerful lineage in important ways. Despite these lineage ties, the cross-ethnic membership of Lin's original *hui*, which included members from both the Zhangzhou and Quanzhou communities in mid-Taiwan,[9] indicates that his association was not completely subsumed in the Lin lineage.

The Tiandihui came to Taiwan through an itinerant cloth merchant named Yan Yan, who migrated to Taiwan and initiated Lin Shuangwen into the association in the mid-1780s. Yan's confession after the suppression of the rebellion outlined both the protective and the corporate security appeals of *hui* membership: "In the beginning, those who entered the *hui* did so to help finance marriages and funerals. Also, if there was a fight, they could help one another" (*Tiandihui* 1980, vol. 1, 110–12). Yan's reference to marriages and funerals draws on the longer tradition discussed above (and illustrated in other contemporary *hui*) of pooling funds to meet the ritual needs of individuals or families too poor to have access to the resources of extended kinship units. His mention of protection against fighting and of banditry resonates with the self-protective aspects we found in the Tiechihui. Part of the initiation ceremony involved a blood oath.

In addition to its traditional corporate functions, Lin Shuangwen's Tiandihui was almost certainly a criminal organization, and another facet of Yan Yan's description of the nature of the Tiandihui was that "if you met up with robbers, the mention of the password [of the Tiandihui] would secure your safety" (*Tiandihui* 1980, vol. 1, 110). At various points in his life, Lin himself seems to have worked as a cart puller and—perhaps, temporarily—as a yamen underling, but at the time of the formation of the *hui* and in the period leading up to the rebellion Lin seems to have been a fence for stolen goods, and his assumption of the leadership of a local Tiandihui may have been in part a complement to various entrepreneurial criminal activities (Ownby 1989, 282–300). Yan Yan also illustrated at least one entrepreneurial strategy associated with the Tiandihui, one very similar to the later developments discussed by Dian Murray in her chapter in this volume:

> The more people you recruited, the more compensation and gratitude you earned, and consequently a great number of people wanted to enter. . . . I got people to enter the *hui* in order to increase the amount of money the *hui* had rather than to make friends. When I first met Lin Shuangwen, I thought that he was generous, not stingy, so I led him into the *hui*, thinking that I could make something off of him. (*Tiandihui* 1980, vol. 1, 116–17)

People in Lin's hometown today speak of him as a local bully—a *tuhao*—which also rings true (personal interviews 1990). He and his Tiandihui may well have been local toughs-for-hire, enforcers, tools of powerful local landlords. In his own confession, Lin said little about the nature of the organization, noting only that "I had often heard that there was something called the Tiandihui in Zhangzhou and Quanzhou, which gathered together many people, who took oaths and formed bands, [pledging to] help one another in time of need" (Liu and Miao 1984, 218–19).

We do not have the same wealth of detail on the individual members of Lin's original Tiandihui that we have for the Tiechihui, nor do we have as complete a narrative of the development of the *hui* over time. The information we do have, nonetheless, at least suggests the type of person attracted to Lin's Tiandihui. Contrary to frequent assumptions about the relationship between demographic mobility, *hui* formation, and violence, Tiandihui members in this instance do not appear to have been dispossessed drifters. Of those for whom we have information, over half had living parents, 60 percent were married, and 36 percent had children. Furthermore, their average age was 37 *sui*, and their average length of residence on Taiwan more than 21 years (Ownby 1989, 375–76).[10] Incomplete information on the economic class and occupations of those who joined Lin Shuangwen both before and after the rebellion reveals a predictable cross-section of generally lower-class society; the occupations of Tiandihui members included one butcher, one farmer, one landlord, three merchants, one painter, two porters, two yamen runners, one "bully," and one tradesman (Ownby 1989, 374). The point that the data from Lin's Tiandihui group makes clear, however, is that one could be poor, but not desperate, and still join the Tiandihui. Many Tiandihui members, like Lin Shuangwen himself, had homes and families, and belonged to communities.

Lin's relationship with his lineage reinforces this image. Lin Shuangwen was part of a large and influential lineage—the Lins of Daliyi and, later, Wufeng, which Johanna Meskill discusses in her study of frontier violence (Meskill 1979). Local officials were wary of this lineage. Naval Admiral Huang Shijian noted in 1783 that "the Lin lineage of the Zhangzhou village of Daliyi is large and has many members. This lineage has always been willful and perverse" (cited in Zhuang 1974–75, 297). The Daliyi Lins had also played an important role in a massive 1782 ethnic feud, some of the Lins (part of yet another *hui*) serving as mercenaries for the larger Zhangzhou community (Ownby 1990, 82ff). Significantly, neither Lin's position as head of the local branch of the Tiandihui nor his involvement in violence and crime seems to have threatened his relationship with his lineage. In fact, on the eve of the rebellion that he eventually led, Lin was ordered by his lineage leadership to take shelter in the mountains and stay out of trouble—and he did (Liu and Miao 1984, 221–22). The Lin lineage may have employed Lin Shuangwen's *hui* for any number of purposes, ranging from collection of rents to prosecution of feud conflicts.

If Lin's relationship with his lineage underscores the closeness of his *hui* to mainstream Taiwanese society, the ethnic composition of Lin's Tiandihui suggests its distance. As noted above, Taiwan during this period was frequently polarized by violent ethnic conflicts, in which the Daliyi Lins had played an important role. Surprisingly, Lin's Tiandihui avoided this ethnic polarization. Evidence from confessions indicates that Lin's original Tiandihui cell contained both Zhangzhou and Quanzhou members; at least three members of Lin's original Tiandihui cell—of the eight for whom we have information on this score—were from Quanzhou (Ownby 1989, 297–98). In addition, even after the rebellion was under way we have evidence that Lin and his leadership cadre recognized the strategic importance of recruiting people from Quanzhou, and deplored the tendancy for the violence of the rebellion to break down along ethnic lines (*Tiandihui* 1980, vol. 1, 153–54). This suggests again that Lin Shuangwen's Tiandihui was not coterminous with the local Zhangzhou community. Instead, the two communities represented separate but interlinking networks of social organization.

Despite extensive Qing investigations into the Tiandihui and its pre-rebellion activities, it remains difficult to chart with precision the evolution of Lin's *hui* from mutual aid/criminal fraternity to challenger to the Qing state. Given the frequent anti-Manchu posture of nineteenth-century Triad groups, scholars have generally assumed that Lin shared this orientation and that this motivation explains his rebellion.[11] The confessions, however, reveal little evidence of restorationist or anti-Manchu intent at any point before, during, or after the Lin Shuangwen uprising. Barend ter Haar has succeeded in locating messianic strains in the confessions of Tiandihui members connected to Yan Yan (see chapter 6), who brought the Tiandihui to Taiwan, but neither the confessions of those who participated in the rebellion nor the documents issued by Lin Shuangwen's "government" resonate with messianic fervor or connect messianic themes with anti-Manchu hostility. In fact, the only action throughout the entire affair that even approaches association with the Ming cause is difficult to interpret: Jin Niang, a female aboriginal shaman recruited by Zhuang Datian, a Tiandihui leader in southern Taiwan who joined forces with Lin Shuangwen after the violence began, would occasionally invoke the spirit of former "king" Zheng Chenggong as Zhuang's men went into battle (*Tiandihui* 1980, vol. 1, 273–73). No one else, not the leaders, not the followers, not even those coerced into joining the rebellion, expressed his understanding of the violence in terms of nationalistic restoration.

This establishes that Lin Shuangwen's rebellion was not anti-Manchu, but leaves open the possibility that his Tiandihui became willfully rebellious in the same way that the Tiechihui did. After the rebellion was under way, Lin did employ the language of Mencian popular revolution. He blamed corrupt local (Han) officials for having incited the wrath of Heaven. He originally chose *tianyun* ("Heaven's revolution") as his reign period, later changing it to *shuntian*, shorthand for *shuntian xingdao*—"following Heaven and carrying out the way" (*Tiandihui* 1980, vol. 1, 153–55). Both of these terms, as Barend ter Haar notes in chapter 6 in this volume, were part of the language of imperial legitimation. Surprisingly, however, there is no evidence from the confessions that the focus of the Tiandihui organization in the pre-rebellion period was on preparations to rise up, and we find no stories in the confessions of late-night drinking and ambitious plotting, as in the case of the Tiechihui. Instead, Lin's Tiandihui seems to have been drawn into the rebellion through the actions of yet another *hui*—the Increase Younger Brothers Society (Tiandihui).

The Increase Younger Brothers Society had been formed in the summer of 1786 in Zhuluo county, to the south of Lin and his Heaven and Earth Society, by a young man angry with his father's division of the family property. The purpose of the *hui* was to bring together enough manpower to challenge the brother who he believed had been unduly favored in the property division. This second brother formed his own hui (the Leigonghui [Thunder God Society[12]]) in anticipation of violence. Before the two *hui* could come to blows, the Qing state discovered their activities and attempted to suppress them, which led to violence between the Increase Younger Brothers Society and officers of the state sent to arrest them. Members of this *hui* sought refuge in Daliyi, though it remains unclear if this was because of previous connections between Lin's organization and the Increase Younger Brothers Society, because Lin Shuangwen was a well-known tough, or because Daliyi was close to Taiwan's dense interior mountains, which provided shelter for many fugitives.[13] In any case, Qing efforts to arrest the Zhuluo fugitives involved coercing the Zhanghua locals to hand over the criminals by burning their homes, an abuse of power that provoked local anger and led to rebellion (Ownby 1989, 300–4).

In sum, the archival documents treating Lin Shuangwen's Tiandihui reveal more about the relationship between *hui* and society than about the relationship between *hui* and rebellion. Lin's Tiandihui was thoroughly embedded in the institutions of local society and yet not subsumed by these institutions. Lin himself, as well as some other members of his *hui*, belonged to the powerful Daliyi Lin lineage, suggesting that the *hui* could extend corporate and protective benefits to those who occupied marginal positions within their own lineages. At the same time, Lin's *hui* was independent enough of lineage control to recruit members of an antagonistic ethnic group, perhaps attracting men who found themselves similarly at the margins of Quanzhou communities. And the information concerning the age, marital status, and length of Taiwan residence of the pre-rebellion members of Lin's Tiandihui clearly suggests that while they may have been down and out, they were probably not homeless and desperate. The *hui* in this instance appears simply as one more institution in the life of the community.

Conclusion: Hui and the Early Modern Order in Southeast China

These two instances of eighteenth-century *hui* suggest the complex relationship of these *hui* to the social order around them. I am not arguing that all early modern *hui*, or even all eighteenth-century *hui* in Southeast China, resembled the Tiechihui or Lin Shuangwen's Tiandihui in every detail. There were no doubt many *hui* that remained firmly under the control of villages and lineages. There were certainly *hui* set up for the specific purpose of launching a rebellion. But there were also many *hui* that do resemble those I have described: a Fumuhui (Father and Mother Society) uncovered in 1728 in Zhuluo county, Taiwan, provided corporate support for the burial of parents (Ownby 1989, 239ff); a Xiaodaohui (Small Knives Society) brought together petty merchants in 1770s and 1780s Zhanghua in order to provide protection against the rapacious local troops (Zhuang 1974–75). I have intentionally chosen *hui* that existed on the margins of orthodox society and have highlighted the links between *hui* and more orthodox institutions in order to make the interpretive point that these particular *hui* members were something other than rebels, bandits, or dispossessed drifters—classic images of the marginal. These *hui* were marginal but still within settled society; the organizations crossed lineage and community lines without breaking all ties with these lineages and communities. Those who joined borrowed the institution of the *hui* to provide a framework for organization and, perhaps, at least partial identity, outside village communities and lineages. The concluding section of this chapter seeks to place the emergence and proliferation of the *hui* in a wider historical context.

It is helpful to juxtapose the emergence and proliferation of *hui* with the formation of an "early modern" social order in China, even if much remains unexplained after this juxtaposition. After we dismiss the assertions of Republican-period historians regarding the origin of secret societies, the field is left with no adequate interpretation of why *hui* emerged when and where they did. The Chinese archival historians who rejected so much of the work of their Republican-period predecessors have attempted partial explanations of the rise and spread of *hui*. Cai Shaoqing and Qin Baoqi argue that overpopulation and commercialization of the economy destroyed natural villages and created marginal porters and peddlers who bound together in *hui* for mutual aid and protection (Cai 1987, 5–10; Liu and Qin 1982, 1029–34). Zhuang Jifa argues that the practice of forming brotherhoods and *hui* grew out of the Fujianese and Cantonese tradition of feuding (*xiedou*), which prompted less powerful lineage and surname groups to band together to protect themselves from other, more powerful groups. One of the ways they joined together was through the creation of fictive kinship relations, similar in principle to the brotherhood ideology of the *hui* (Zhuang 1981, 11–18).

These interpretations, while valuable, are also somewhat limited: the examples of *hui* presented above suggest that not all *hui* members were displaced porters and peddlers, and the historical antecedents to the Qing *hui* presented in the first part of this chapter suggest that fictive kinship in both *hui* formation and in feuds drew on longer traditions than Zhuang Jifa suggests by tracing brotherhoods to seventeenth- and eighteenth-century feuds. Looking at *hui* in the context of a larger interpretive paradigm such as that of "early modern China" might help us to arrive at larger generalizations or to formulate broader questions for future research.

The concept of an "early modern" Chinese social order is a fairly recent attempt to identify certain processes of socioeconomic change, originating in the sixteenth century, which began to move China in the direction of economic growth, involvement in the world economy, and a somewhat freer social order (Eastman 1988; Rawski 1985; Rowe 1985, 1990). Although a full discussion of the early modern social order would range from urbanization (Rowe 1984, 1989) to philanthropy (Fuma 1983) to the emergence of a Chinese version of "civil society" (Rankin 1986)—and much else besides—for the purposes of this discussion I will reduce the idea of the early modern social order to two fundamental developments: economic growth and the emancipation of labor.

Most scholars trace the initial impulse toward economic growth to the sixteenth-century involvement of the Chinese economy in the world economy. New World and Japanese silver reached China through the medium of European traders and significantly monetized China's economy. The expanded money supply facilitated increased domestic trade, which in turn prompted cash-cropping and the further development of handicraft industries. An expanding population and the importation of New World crops provided expanded markets and helped to feed those in the agricultural economy tied increasingly to market forces. In some highly developed parts of China, these processes of development worked near-fundamental changes in economic and social relations, as merchants in newly established *zhen*, or "nonadministrative commercial towns" (Rowe 1990, 245) forged important relationships with the peasants of the hinterland. Although this proto-revolution was restricted to a few flourishing regional cores, it nonetheless seems clear that much of coastal and riverine China was affected to some degree by these profound changes.

The second major transformation involved in the early modern order was the emancipation of labor, which began in earnest—as state policy, at least—after the Qing takeover. One pre-Qing aspect of this emancipation was the merging of the age-old corvée labor tax with the land tax, which eventually reduced the degree of state control over the labor of commoner Chinese. This commutation was facilitated by the monetization of the economy just described and was begun during the late Ming. The Qing rulers, hoping to promote the redevelopment of those parts of China devastated during the course of the dynastic transition, encouraged the free movement of settlers into these depopulated areas through provision of seeds and remission of taxes, and even went so far as to abolish servile status categories in order to foster the image of benevolence and even-handedness.

Another aspect of the emancipation of agricultural labor can be seen in the migration of rural landlords to the flourishing cities, leaving in their stead managerial representatives who often granted rights of permanent tenancy to peasants remaining on the land. In this instance, the "emancipation" was from the "feudal" ties that many scholars believe characterized landlord-tenant relationships in the period before the early modern, and which were largely eclipsed during the bondservant revolts at the end of the Ming (Tanaka 1984; Wiens, 1980; but also McDermott 1981). In some parts of China, including the Southeast Coast, the development during the Ming-Qing period of the "one field–two [or three] owners" system of land tenure helped farmers secure access to needed land, as well as facilitating the sale of this land (or the right to its use) should liquidity become necessary (Fujii 1984). These various "emancipations" came together with the population explosion beginning in the eighteenth-century to produce what may have been the most geographically mobile peacetime population in Chinese history.

Economic growth and relative emancipation from the controls of the imperial state and the "feudal lord" marked the early modern period. These developments, along with migration to new areas and reclamation of new land, surely suggest hopeful signs of energy and renewal. How, then, do we relate these developments to the poor and marginal members of the *hui* of eighteenth-century Southeast China? Part of the answer to this question must lie in Philip Kuhn's depiction of the attitude of commoner Chinese to the "Prosperous Age"—the period of economic growth just described. In the context of the soul-stealing panic of 1768, Kuhn notes:

> [It is hard] to estimate . . . what the Prosperous Age really meant to ordinary people. Attitudes about where life was leading, whether toward better conditions or worse, whether toward greater security or less, may have been rather

different from what we would expect in a growing economy. From the stand-point of an eighteenth-century Chinese commoner, commercial growth may have meant, not the prospect of riches or security, but a scant margin of survival in a competitive and crowded society. . . . A free-wheeling labor market, the decline of personal dependency and servile status . . . [were] [n]o doubt . . . appreciated by families struggling to survive on small parcels of land, who urgently needed to sell their excess labor power to fend off starvation. . . . [But s]urely the underlying fact about "free labor" in the eighteenth-century economy is that it was sold in a buyer's market. (Kuhn 1990, 35–36)

Kuhn is suggesting, in other words, that the underside of economic expansion and the emancipation of labor may well have been an unprotected confrontation with an increasingly competitive economy. The fragmentation of community and the proliferation of the *hui* in eighteenth-century Southeast China may well have grown out of just such a confrontation.

Furthermore, when we turn from a general picture of the early modern order to an examination of the Southeast Coast, it is clear that economic development and the emancipation of the commoner existed alongside other counter currents. First, the wars and disruptions that accompanied the Ming-Qing dynastic transition in the Southeast Coast endured for decades. The Ming government began to lose control of the region by the 1620s, and the Southeast Coast subsequently fell into the hands of trader-militarists such as the Zheng family, whose battles with the Manchu forces have been well chronicled elsewhere. The extended transition lasted until the 1680s, when the Qing finally subdued the remnant Zheng forces and established control over Taiwan. Second, it is unclear to what extent Fujian and the Southeast Coast profited from the general eighteenth-century prosperity—even after the recovery from the dynastic transition. Of course, the economy of the Southeast Coast had been connected to overseas trade for centuries, as the research of Hugh Clark and Evelyn Rawski makes clear (Clark 1991; Rawski 1972): the geographical position and the commer-cially oriented economy of the Southeast Coast meant that it was one of the first regions in China to experience the transformations associated more generally with the "early modern" order. Scholars offer competing depictions of the eighteenth-century economy, however, and it may be safe to conclude that the Southeast Coast, despite its historically commercial focus, did not experience the eighteenth-century growth and prosperity in any general or sustained fashion (Ng 1983, 162; Skinner 1985, 278–79; Vermeer 1990; Zhu 1986, vol. 2, 431–73, 495–521).

If the Southeast Coast did not enjoy the same economic boom as other regions of China, it does nonetheless appear to have experienced similar population growth and mobility. Unreconstructed population figures for Fujian province from the late seventeenth through the mid-nineteenth century suggest rapid growth (Li 1982, 34; Wang 1986, 85). It is difficult to know at what point such population growth "saturated" a region, or even at what point increased numbers imposed a burden on local economies. But if, as some scholars argue, "shortage of land had already become serious after the mid-Ming" (Ng 1983, 15), then surely eighteenth-century growth posed even more acute problems. Additional signs of overpopulation include land fragmentation,[14] increasing urbanization (Naquin and Rawski 1987, 172; Skinner 1977, 229), increasing grain prices (Ho 1959, 267–68; Wang 1958; Wang 1986, 94, 100), and out-migration to Southeast Asia, Taiwan, and other frontier areas within China proper.[15]

Taiwan functioned as a safety valve for the burgeoning population of the Southeast Coast during much of the eighteenth century, the Han population growing from 130,000 in the immediate post-transition period (1684) to more than 800,000 by 1777 and almost 1.8 million by 1824 (Shepherd, 1993, 161). Vast fortunes were made in real estate and modest fortunes in commerce, as Taiwan's land was reclaimed and its economy incorporated into that of the Southeast Coast. And at least until the final decades of the eighteenth century, enough fertile land was available to improve substantially the life chances of those who simply wanted to farm (Ch'en 1987). Even during peacetime, however, Taiwan's society remained fluid and mobile—an exaggerated version of the early modern order as a whole. Given Qing restrictions on immigration, even extended families found it difficult to immigrate together, and the reconstruction of social life on Taiwan evidenced considerable flexibility. Temples and common-surname and common-origin groups provided associational functions that lineages had traditionally filled on the mainland.

Taiwan also suffered from frequent violence, which made association for protection all the more urgent. Some of the reasons for this violence were unique to Taiwan. The distance of the island from Beijing meant a certain difficulty of control, and the Qing decision to quarantine the island for much of the eighteenth century meant that many of the migrants were young, single, and occasionally desperate men. Other factors, however, again reflected the more general characteristics of the early modern order. These young, single men were part of the more general population growth, and their migration to Taiwan reflected their mobility and their "emancipation." The raw opportunism of life on the Taiwanese frontier reflected the more general commercialization and atomization of life in the eighteenth century. At least some of this mobility, insecurity, and violence characterized the society of the mainland Southeast Coast as well as Taiwan, as frequent feuds and *hui*-organized violence suggest (Lamley 1990; Ownby 1989, 1990). Philip Kuhn suggests in his study of eighteenth-century Jiangnan that the potentially frightening aspect of a new kind of economic growth may have been an impersonal job market, which provided "a scant margin of survival in a competitive and crowded society" (Kuhn 1990, 36). On the Southeast coast, the danger of the early modern order may have been physical as well as economic.

It is in this context that the proliferation of the *hui* in eighteenth-century Southeast China becomes clear. The Southeast coast in the eighteenth century was a mobile, competitive, fragmented, violent society. Some members of society were fortunate enough to benefit from the protection of powerful lineages or well-organized communities, but others were not. For those who found themselves at the margins of community life, the *hui* offered a framework within which to organize for the pursuit of mutual benefit, be it protective or predatory, economic or defensive. From this perspective, the *hui* appears an informal, supplemental social institution, roughly comparable to the Friendly Societies of eighteenth-century England (Godsden 1967), the Sociétés de secours mutuel in France (Sewell 1980), or the Freemasons of the nineteenth-century United States (Clawson 1989). Two important distinctions separate this depiction of the *hui* of Southeast China from these working-class institutions of the early West: first, neither the reconstruction of Chinese society on Taiwan nor the development of the early modern order as a whole seems to have involved the same fundamental transformations as the similar processes in the West; and Western states took a far more benign attitude toward non-elite associations than did the jealous Qing government.

Ultimately, there can be no definitive "proof" that the eighteenth-century emergence and proliferation of the *hui* was a "product" of the early modern order, and I hope that readers will find my argument suggestive rather than teleological. Perhaps a more systematic comparison of frontiers, dynastic transitions (or other periods of protracted instability), and regional levels of socioeconomic development across several centuries of Chinese history would yield more profound insights than the approach adopted here. Nonetheless, if the idea of "early modern" China is to stand as more than a provocative juxtaposition of Chinese and European history, historians should attempt to integrate popular experience into the broader themes of the paradigm. Evelyn Rawski, making a similar point, has noted that

> [E]conomic growth during the Ming-Qing could not have been significant if it did not produce a discernible impact on the lives of ordinary people. . . . Was there . . . [significant] change in peasant *mentalité* after the late Ming–early Qing trade expansion? What were the psychological costs (as well as benefits) of participation in a market system? Can we delineate the alterations in *mentalité* through shifts in childrearing, new family strategies, kinship or community organization? (Rawski 1991, 100–01)

The evidence presented here suggests that the history of the *hui* in eighteenth-century Southeast China represents one such shift.

Notes

The author would like to thank Timothy Brook, Timothy Cheek, Harry J. Lamley, and Susan Naquin for their generous and helpful comments on this chapter.

1. I leave *hui* untranslated because of the large variety of related organizations referred to by the term. Neither "secret society" nor "mutual aid association" accurately describes all varieties of early modern *hui*, and neither "association" nor "society" adds

precision to the admittedly vague term "*hui*." For the purposes of this chapter, I adopt a very broad definition of *hui*, including chiefly groups calling themselves *hui* (or the rough equivalent, *she*) but also some groups that did not name themselves while still occupying similar social positions or fulfilling similar social functions.

2. One might note a rough parallel between the establishment of semi-independent *hui* in the early modern period, and the Song-period pseudo-monastic movement of the People of the Way, who were outside monastic Buddhism and state control, but remained a "socially well-accepted group." See ter Haar (1992, 28–43).

3. Tanaka Issei mentions the role of secret society leaders in sponsoring dramatic performances in Ming-Qing China, a particularly apt example of the range of *hui* activities, and of their embeddedness in local society. See Tanaka 1985, 143.

4. "In the past, eight families [*jia*] made up a *lin*, three *lin* made up a *peng*, three *peng* a *li*, and five *li* an *yi*." See entry #40136, *Zhongwen dacidian* 1973, vol. 9, 263.

5. An example of state encouragement is the passage in the 1660 *Da Qing huidian shili*, which urges "the establishment of village *she*, so that the people will concentrate in groups of 20 or 30, 40 or 50 families, who will provide agricultural assistance during the busy season in the event of death or illness." Cited in Shimizu (1951, 419).

6. Although the evidence presented in this chapter cannot prove that *hui* membership appealed chiefly to younger men, this was one of the more general conclusions of my dissertation. See Ownby (1989, 339–53).

7. Twelve taels of silver would have bought roughly 8.5 *shi* of rice, more than three times the average annual per capita consumption in the late imperial period. This estimate is based on figures in Wang (1986, 88).

8. Investigations after the Lin Shuangwen rebellion into the origins of the Tiandihui uncovered some evidence that the Lu Mao rebellion of 1768 and the Li Amin uprising of 1770, both in southern Fujian, had been led by Tiandihui members, which had not been reported by local officials at the time (Murray 1993; ch. 1; Qin and Li 1988). I discuss the credibility of this evidence in Ownby (1989, 303ff). In any case, the Lin Shuangwen rebellion marked the first time that the Qing court was aware of the Tiandihui as the recognized force behind an uprising in progress.

9. During the late eighteenth century, one of the most important sources of conflict in Taiwanese society was the division of the population according to mainland provenance. The most important of these divisions was among those from Zhangzhou prefecture, those from Quanzhou prefecture (both in southern mainland Fujian), and Hakkas (from the inland regions of both southern mainland Fujian and northern Guangdong). These divisions were reflected in settlement patterns as well as in "ethnic" feuds and rebellions (Lamley 1981; Ownby 1990).

10. These figures include all those arrested who claimed Tiandihui membership and thus do not refer to Lin's original, smaller group. Twenty-five of the 89 Tiandihui members provided information about marital status, their parents, and their children. Thirty-eight gave their ages, and 16 provided information on their length of stay on Taiwan. Liu Niling analyzes the same data in a slightly different way (1983, 282–83).

11. Even Zhuang Jifa, who has been instrumental in the reinterpretation of the "secret society," begins his 1981 treatment of the Lin Shuangwen rebellion with the statement that it was a "revolutionary anti-Manchu movement" (Zhuang 1981, 34).

12. The confession of the brother who founded this *hui* noted that his brother's "evil nature assured that he would be struck by thunder" (*Tiandihui* 1980, vol. 1, 170–75). One suspects, however, that the choice of the *hui* name comes from popular religion and mythology. See Lagerwey (1987, 81, 97), for the role of the God (or Duke) of Thunder in Daoist ritual practices in contemporary Taiwan. The God of Thunder also appears in the Taiping Rebellion (Wagner 1982, 18).

13. Zhang Tan argues that the two societies were in fact branches of the larger Heaven and Earth Society and that the "Increase Younger Brothers Society," which in Chinese is a homonym for the Heaven and Earth Society, was invented by local officials trying to cover up their failure to preserve social order. I discuss Zhang's position in Ownby (1989, 306–9), and argue that while evidence concerning the name of the second *hui* is inconclusive, the two do not appear to have been linked before the quarrel between the two brothers. The Increase Younger Brothers Society reappears in the nineteenth century as a frequent variant for "Heaven and Earth Society," suggesting that the name was not solely an official invention. See Zhuang (1981, 83–91).

14. As early as the 1740s, Fujian Governor Wang Shu (served 1740–42) noted that "Fujian is mostly mountainous, and the fields are scattered. . . . Even if the people can reclaim a *mou* or two, it is always at the corners of [already cultivated] land, or on the tops of the mountains." See Wang's biography in Zhao (1928, j. 314/95, p. 1190).

15. There was, for instance, considerable migration from Fujian to Sichuan, which had been depopulated by the peasant wars at the end of the Ming. In fact, some versions of the Tiandihui origin myth connect Fujian with Sichuan. See Sasaki (1970, 167–73). Han Yulin, governor-general of Fujian-Zhejiang, reported in 1733 that 100,000–200,000 people from the Zhang-Quan region had already settled in the Philippines. Cited in Wang (1986, 92).

References

Bao Tingbo, comp. 1872. *Zhi buzu zhai congshu* [Collectanea from the "awareness of inadequacy" studio]. Shanghai.

Cai Shaoqing. 1987. *Zhongguo jindai huidangshi yanjiu* [Studies of the history of secret societies in modern China]. Beijing: Zhonghua shuju.

Ch'en, Ch'iu-k'un. 1987. "Landlord and Tenant: Varieties of Land Tenure in Frontier Taiwan, 1680–1900," Ph.D. diss., Stanford University.

Cheek, Timothy. 1984. "Contracts and Ideological Control in Village Administration: Tensions in the 'Village Covenant' (*xiangyue*) System in Late Imperial China." Unpublished paper presented at the 36th annual meeting of the Association for Asian Studies, Washington, D.C.

Chesneaux, Jean, ed. 1972. *Popular Movements and Secret Societies in China 1840–1950*. Stanford: Stanford University Press.

Clark, Hugh R. 1991. *Community, Trade, and Networks: Southern Fujian Province from the Third to the Thirteenth Century*. Cambridge: Cambridge University Press.

Clawson, Mary Ann. 1989. *Constructing Brotherhood: Class, Gender, and Fraternalism*. Princeton: Princeton University Press.

Cohen, Myron L. 1990. "Lineage Organization in North China." *Journal of Asian Studies* 49, no. 3: 509–34.

Davis, Fei-ling. 1977. *Primitive Revolutionaries: A Study of Secret Societies in the Late Nineteenth Century*. Honolulu: University of Hawaii Press.

Eastman, Lloyd E. 1988. *Family, Field, and Ancestors: Constancy and Change in China's Social and Economic History, 1550–1949*. New York: Oxford University Press.

Egerton, Clement, trans. 1939. *The Golden Lotus*. London: Routledge and Kegan Paul, 1939.

Enping xianzhi [Gazetteer of Enping county, Guangdong].1825.

Fei, Hsiao-t'ung. 1939. *Peasant Life in China*. New York: E. P. Dutton.

Freedman, Maurice. 1966. *Chinese Lineage and Society: Fukien and Kwangtung*. London: Athlone Press.

Fu Yiling. 1961. *Ming-Qing nongcun shehui jingji* [The social economy of the Ming-Qing rural village]. Beijing: Sanlian Press.

Fuma Susumu. 1983. "Zenkai to zentō no shuppatsu" [The origins of *shanhui* and *shantang*]. In *Min-Shin jidai no seiji to shakai*, ed. Ono Kazuko. Kyoto: Kyōto daigaku jinbun kagaku kenkyūjo.

Funing zhouzhi [Gazetteer of Funing department]. 1593.

Fujii Hiroshi. 1984. "Ichiden-ryōshushi no kihon kōzō" [The basic structure of the one-field two-owners system]. *Kindai Chūgoku* 15: 46–107.

Gamble, Sidney D. 1944. " A Chinese Mutual Savings Society." *Far Eastern Quarterly* 4: 41–52.

Geertz, Clifford. 1962. "The Rotating Credit Association: A 'Middle Rung' in Economic Development." *Economic Development and Cultural Change* 10: 241–74.

Godsden, P. H. J. H. . 1967. *The Friendly Societies in England, 1815–1875*. New York: Augustus M. Kelley.

GZZP, NYMJ. *Gongzhong zhupi, nongmin yundong, mimijieshe* [Imperially rescripted documents from the palace fond, peasant movements, secret societies]. Unpublished documents from the Number One Historical Archives, Beijing, People's Republic of China. (Dates range from the eighteenth to the twentieth century.)

Ho, Ping-ti. 1959. *Studies on the Population of China, 1368–1953* . Cambridge: Harvard University Press.

———. 1962. *The Ladder of Success in Imperial China*. New York: Columbia University Press.

Hsiao, Kung-chuan. 1960. *Rural China: Imperial Control in the Nineteenth Century*. Seattle: University of Washington Press.

Huian xianzhi [Gazetteer of Huian county, Fujian]. 1803.

Irwin, Richard G. 1966. *The Evolution of a Chinese Novel*. Cambridge: Harvard University Press.

Jones, Susan Mann, and Philip A. Kuhn. 1978. "Dynastic Decline and the Roots of Rebellion." In *The Cambridge History of China*, vol. 10, part 1, ed. John K. Fairbank, 134–36. Cambridge: Cambridge University Press.

Kuhn, Philip A. 1970. *Rebellion and Its Enemies in Late Imperial China: Militarization and Social Structure, 1796–1864*. Cambridge: Harvard University Press.

———. 1990. *Soulstealers: The Chinese Sorcery Scare of 1768*. Cambridge: Harvard University Press.

Kulp, Daniel H. 1925. *Country Life in South China: The Sociology of Familism, Volume I, Phenix Village, Kwantung, China*. New York: Columbia University.

Lagerwey, John. 1987. *Taoist Ritual in Chinese Society and History*. New York: Macmillan Publishing Company.

Lamley, Harry J. 1981. "Subethnic Rivalry in the Ch'ing Period." In *The Anthropology of Taiwanese Society*, ed. Emily M. Ahern and Hill Gates, 282–313. Stanford: Stanford University Press.

———. 1990. "Lineage Feuding in Southern Fujian and Eastern Guangdong under Qing Rule." In *Violence in China: Essays in Culture and Counterculture*, ed. Jonathan N. Lipman and Stevan Harrell, 27–64. Albany: State University of New York Press.

Lewis, Mark Edward. 1990. *Sanctioned Violence in Early China*. Albany: State University of New York Press.

Li Guoqi. 1982. *Zhongguo xiandaihua de diyu: Min-Zhe-Tai diqu, 1860–1916* [Studies of the modernized regions of China: The Fujian-Zhejiang-Taiwan area]. Taipei: Modern History Research Institute, Academia Sinica.

Liu Meizhen and Qin Baoqi. 1982. "Guanyu Tiandihui lishishang de ruogan wenti" [Some questions concerning the history of the Heaven and Earth Society]. In *Ming-*

Qing shi guoji xueshu taolunhui lunwenji, 1023–39. Tianjin: Tianjin renmin chubanshe.

Liu Niling. 1983. *Qingdai Taiwan minbian yanjiu* [Studies of popular uprisings in Qing Taiwan]. Taipei: Historical Research Institute of Taiwan Normal University.

Liu Ruzhong and Miao Xuemeng, eds. 1984. *Taiwan Lin Shuangwen qiyi ziliao xuanbian* [Selected materials on the Lin Shuangwen uprising on Taiwan]. Fuzhou: Fujian People's Press.

Luo Ergang. 1943. *Tiandihui wenxianlu* [Heaven and Earth Society documents]. Shanghai: Zhengzhong shuju.

McDermott, Joseph P. 1981. "Bondservants in the T'ai-hu Basin during the Late Ming: A Case of Mistaken Identities." *Journal of Asian Studies* 40, no. 4: 675–701.

Meskill, Johanna Menzel. 1979. *A Chinese Pioneer Family: The Lins of Wu-feng, Taiwan, 1729–1895*. Princeton: Princeton University Press.

Murray, Dian H. 1993. *The Origin of the Tiandihui (Heaven and Earth Society)*. Stanford: Stanford University Press.

Naba Toshisada. 1938. "Tōdai no shayo ni tsuite" [On Tang dynasty *sheyi* (*yishe*)]. *Shirin* 23, no. 2: 223–65; 23, no. 3: 495–534; 23, no. 4: 729–93.

Naquin, Susan, and Evelyn S. Rawski. 1987. *Chinese Society in the Eighteenth Century*. New Haven: Yale University Press.

Ng Chin-keong. 1983. *Trade and Society: The Amoy Network on the China Coast 1683–1735*. Singapore: Singapore University Press.

Ownby, David. 1989. "Communal Violence in Eighteenth Century Southeast China: The Background to the Lin Shuangwen Uprising of 1787." Ph.D. diss., Harvard University.

———. 1990. "The Ethnic Feud in Qing Taiwan: What Is This Violence Business, Anyway?" *Late Imperial China* 11, no. 1: 75–98.

Perry, Elizabeth J. 1980. *Rebels and Revolutionaries in North China, 1845–1945*. Stanford: Stanford University Press.

Plaks, Andrew H. 1987. *The Four Masterworks of the Ming Novel*. Princeton: Princeton University Press.

Qin Baoqi. 1988. *Qing qianqi Tiandihui yanjiu* [A study of the early Qing Heaven and Earth Society]. Beijing: People's University Press.

Qin Baoqi and Li Shoujun, eds. 1988. "Youguan Tiandihui qiyuan shiliao" [Historical materials on the origin of the Heaven and Earth Society]. *Lishi dang'an* 1: 30–39.

Qin Baoqi and Liu Meizhen. 1980. "Shilun Tiandihui" [A tentative study of the Heaven and Earth Society]. *Qingshi yanjiuji* 1: 154–82.

Qu Dajun. 1985 (reprint of original 1700 edition). *Guangdong xinyu* [New commentary on Guangdong]. Beijing: Zhonghua shuju.

Rankin, Mary Backus. 1986. *Elite Activism and Political Transformation in China: Zhejiang Province, 1865–1911*. Stanford: Stanford University Press.

Rawski, Evelyn S. 1972. *Agricultural Change and the Peasant Economy of South China*. Cambridge: Harvard University Press.

———. 1985. "Economic and Social Foundations of Late Imperial Culture." In *Popular Culture in Late Imperial China*, ed. David Johnson, Andrew J. Nathan, and Evelyn S. Rawski, 3–33. Berkeley: University of California Press.

———. 1991. "Research Themes in Ming-Qing Socioeconomic History: The State of the Field." *Journal of Asian Studies* 50, no. 1: 84–111.

Rowe, William T. 1984. *Hankow: Commerce and Society in a Chinese City, 1796–1889*. Stanford: Stanford University Press.

———. 1985. "Approaches to Modern Chinese Social History." In *Reliving the Past: The Worlds of Social History*, ed. Olivier Zunz, 236–96. Chapel Hill: University of North Carolina Press.

————. 1989. *Hankow: Conflict and Community in a Chinese City, 1796–1898*. Stanford: Stanford University Press.

————. 1990. "Modern Chinese Social History." In *Heritage of China*, ed. Paul S. Ropp, 242–62. Berkeley: University of California.

Sangren, P. Steven. 1984. "Traditional Chinese Corporations: Beyond Kinship." *Journal of Asian Studies* 18, no. 3: 391–415.

Sasaki Masaya. 1970. *Shinmatsu no himitsu kessha: zempen, Tenchikai no seiritsu* [Secret societies in the late Qing period: The founding of the Heaven and Earth Society]. Tokyo: Gannanto shoten.

Sewell, William H. Jr. 1980. *Work and Revolution in France: The Language of Labor from the Old Regime to 1848*. Cambridge: Cambridge University Press.

Shepherd, John R. 1993. *Statecraft and Political Economy on the Taiwan Frontier, 1600–1800*. Stanford: Stanford University Press.

Shiliao xunkan [Historical Documents].1963 (reprint of 1930 original). Taipei: Guofeng Press.

Shimizu Morimitsu. 1951. *Chūgoku kyōson shakairon* [On Chinese village society]. Tokyo: Ganba shoten.

Skinner, G. William. 1977. "Regional Urbanization in Nineteenth Century China." In *The City in Late Imperial China*, ed. G. William Skinner, 211–49. Stanford: Stanford University Press.

————. 1985. "Presidential Address: The Structure of Chinese History." *Journal of Asian Studies* 44, no. 2: 271–92.

Smith, Arthur H. 1894. *Village Life in China*. New York: Fleming and Revell.

Taiwan. 1985. *Taiwan diqu minjian hehui xianzhuang zhi yanjiu* [Studies on the current situation regarding popular rotating credit societies in the Taiwan region]. Taipei: Legal Affairs Bulletin Press.

Tanaka, Masatoshi. 1984. "Popular Uprisings, Rent Resistance, and Bondservant Rebellions in the Late Ming." In *State and Society in China*, ed. Linda Grove and Christian Daniels, 165–214. Tokyo: University of Tokyo Press.

Tanaka Issei. 1985. "The Social and Historical Context of Ming-Ch'ing Local Drama." In *Popular Culture in Late Imperial China*, ed. David Johnson et al., 143–60. Berkeley: University of California Press.

Tao Chengzhang. 1943. "Jiaohui yuanliu kao" [Examination of the origin and development of sects and secret societies]. In *Tiandihui wenxianlu*, comp. Luo Ergang, 61–76. Shanghai: Zhengzhong shuju.

Ter Haar, Barend J. 1991. "Sources of the Heaven and Earth Gathering Tradition." Unpublished paper presented at the 43rd annual meeting of the Association for Asian Studies. New Orleans, LA.

————. 1992. *The White Lotus Teachings in Chinese Religious History*. Leiden: E.J. Brill.

Tiandihui [The Heaven and Earth Society]. 1980–88. Qing History Research Institute of People's University, and Number One Historical Archives of China eds. Beijing: China People's University Press. Vols. 1–7.

Tong, James W. 1991. *Disorder under Heaven: Collective Violence in the Ming Dynasty*. Stanford: Stanford University Press.

Vermeer, Eduard B. 1990. "The Decline of Hsing-hua Prefecture in the Early Ch'ing." In *Development and Decline of Fukien Province in the 17th and 18th Centuries*, ed. Eduard B. Vermeer, 101–61. Leiden: E. J. Brill.

Wagner, Rudolf G. 1982. *Re-enacting the Heavenly Vision: The Role of Religion in the Taiping Rebellion*. Berkeley: Institute of East Asian Studies.

Wakeman, Frederic, Jr. 1975. "Introduction: The Evolution of Local Control in Late

Imperial China." In *Conflict and Control in Imperial China*, ed. Frederic Wakeman, Jr., and Carolyn Grant, 1–25. Berkeley: University of California Press.

Wang Shiqing. 1958. "Qingdai Taiwan de mijia" [Rice prices in Qing Taiwan]. *Taiwan wenxian* 9, no. 4: 11–20.

———. [Wang, Shih-ch'ing]. 1974. "Religious Organization in the History of a Taiwanese Town." In *Religion and Ritual in Chinese Society*, ed. Arthur P. Wolf, 71–92. Stanford: Stanford University Press.

Wang, Yeh-chien. 1986. "Food Supply in Eighteenth Century Fukien." *Late Imperial China* 7, no. 2: 80–117.

Wang Zongpei. 1931. *Zhongguo zhi hehui* [Chinese mutual benefit associations]. Nanjing: Chinese Cooperative Study Society.

Wiens, Mi Chu. 1980. "Lord and Peasant: The Sixteenth to the Eighteenth Century." *Modern China* 1: 3–39.

Winn, Jane Kaufman. Forthcoming. "Not By Rule of Law: Mediating State-Society Relations in Taiwan through the Underground Economy." In *The Other Taiwan, 1945–1992*, ed. Murray A. Rubinstein. Armonk, NY: M. E. Sharpe.

Xiao Yishan. 1935. *Jindai mimi shehui shiliao* [Historical materials on modern secret societies]. Beiping: Beiping yanjiuyuan. Reprint Taipei: Wenhai chubanshe, 1965; and Taipei: Yonghezhen wenhai chubanshe, 1972.

Xinghua fuzhi [Gazetteer of Xinghua prefecture, Fujian]. 1503.

Yang, C. K. 1975. "Some Preliminary Patterns of Mass Actions in Nineteenth-Century China." In *Conflict and Control in Late Imperial China*, ed. Frederic Wakeman, Jr., and Carolyn Grant, 174–210. Berkeley: University of California Press.

Yang, Lien-sheng. 1961. "Buddhist Monasteries and Four Money-Raising Institutions in Chinese History." In *Studies in Chinese Institutional History*, ed. Lien-sheng Yang, 198–215. Cambridge: Harvard University Press.

Yang Ximeng. 1935. *Zhongguo hehui zhi yanjiu* [Studies in Chinese mutual benefit societies]. Shanghai: Commercial Press.

Zhang Tan. 1983. "Tiandihui he Tiandihui" [The Heaven and Earth Society and the Increase Younger Brothers Society]. *Taiwan fengwu* 33, no. 3: 11–20.

Zhao Yi. 1928. *Qingshigao* [Draft history of the Qing]. Beijing: Qingshiguan.

Zhongwen dacidian [Comprehensive Chinese dictionary]. 1973. Taipei: Zhonghua xueshuyuan.

Zhu Weigan. 1986. *Fujian shigao* [Draft history of Fujian]. Fu'an, Fujian: Fujian Educational Publishing Press.

Zhuang Jifa. 1974–75. "Taiwan Xiaodaohui yuanliukao" [A study of the origins of the Taiwan Small Knives Society]. *Shihuo yuekan fukan* 4, no. 7: 293–303.

———. 1981. *Qingdai Tiandihui yuanliukao* [Studies of the origins of the Heaven and Earth Society of the Qing dynasty]. Taipei: Gugong congkan bianji weiyuanhui.

———. 1990. "*Cong Qingdai lüli de xiuding kan mimi huidang de qiyuan jiqi fazhan*" [The origin and development of secret societies as seen through the amendments to Qing laws]. *Guoli Taiwan Shifan Daxue lishi xuebao* 18: 107–68.

3

Chinese Organizations in West Borneo and Bangka: Kongsis and *Hui*

Mary Somers Heidhues

During the eighteenth century, Chinese emigration to Southeast Asia increased rapidly. The increase was partly because Qing prohibitions on coastal settlement and trade had been relaxed, partly because of growing economic and social tensions, but also because opportunities in the Nanyang, as the Chinese called the region, were increasing. The Chinese population in and around Batavia more than doubled between 1680 and 1740 (Blussé 1986: 84), but immigrants also settled in rural areas of the Malay Peninsula and the Indonesian Archipelago, as Carl Trocki's work on Riau shows (Trocki 1979), and engaged in mining in Bangka and Borneo.[1] Native rulers encouraged the Chinese to settle in frontier areas not yet touched by colonial influence or even native government. These rulers taxed export products made by the Chinese. By controlling the harbors, they could sell these wares to Chinese, Dutch, British, and other traders who visited the region.

Having left the Celestial Kingdom behind, the immigrants, nearly all of them single young males, adapted their organizations to the new situations they faced. The mining settlements of West Borneo and Bangka, in particular, demonstrate how Chinese organizations based on mutual support, especially *hui* and kongsi, helped them organize profit-making ventures on an alien frontier.

Kongsi, from *gongsi,* meaning "public company," is widely used in Southeast Asia to describe a common undertaking, and has been for centuries. Although the names kongsi and *hui* are sometimes used as synonyms (as shown in chapter 9), *hui* will be used here to mean "secret society," kongsi to refer to a common undertaking based on shares. In much of Dutch colonial literature, *hui* appear as conspiracies, while kongsis are economic organizations, various kinds of associations to pool capital or labor, especially in mining, as in Bangka and Borneo. *Hui* were seen as hierarchical, kongsis as egalitarian; *hui* rebellious, kongsis

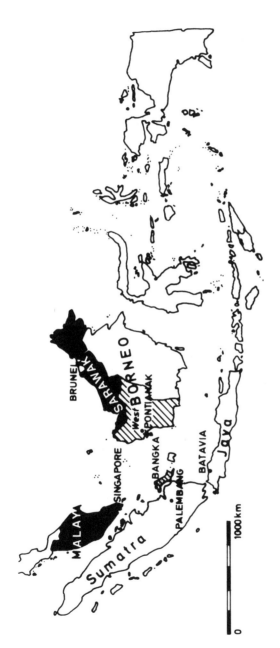

The Netherlands Indies and adjacent territories in the nineteenth century. Bangka and West Borneo are indicated by diagonal shading.

profit-oriented. Similarities between *hui* and kongsis have always been evident, and, in fact, both took on different functions in Southeast Asia after colonial influence made itself felt in rural areas in the late nineteenth century. This chapter acknowledges that common features of the two stem from a common, more basic tradition of ritual brotherhood, even where organizational links are not evident.

After 1816, the Dutch expanded and consolidated their rule, co-opting local rulers into the colonial administration, extending control over territories and peoples, and, especially after 1850, opening the economy to state and private enterprises. This forward movement brought them into contact and conflict with immigrant Chinese societies, mining kongsis, and secret societies or *hui*.

A close look at the evidence concerning kongsis in Borneo and Bangka will show that, partly because of the influence of colonialism, nineteenth-century kongsis were becoming more like authoritarian units and less like egalitarian mutual benefit societies. In fact, even before the nineteenth century, as kongsis became larger, they became less egalitarian.

Historical Background: Borneo

Until recently, Borneo was a sparsely populated island, covered almost totally by jungle. Inhabitants of the interior were the so-called Dayak peoples, who lived from hunting, gathering forest products, shifting cultivation, and, in the west, a bit of gold- or diamond-mining. Along the coast, Malay settlements grew up under sultans (the oldest, that of Brunei, gave its name to the island and is the only ruling line to survive to the present day). These sultans, by controlling the mouths of the rivers, were in a position to manage and profit from the exchange of forest products from upriver areas for imported rice, salt and other goods, most of which came from outside the island. By doing so, they extended a claim to control over interior territories and authority over the peoples of the interior as well.

Local sultans probably first encouraged Chinese miners to come to Borneo to mine gold during the first half of the eighteenth century. These rulers discovered that Chinese mining technology and organization greatly increased production and therefore profit, compared with earlier, native efforts. The sultans initially provided capital for these ventures in the form of rice, oil, tools, opium, and other materials. Costs were billed to the mining groups, the kongsis, which in turn delivered part of their gold to the court in payment (Schaank 1893, 561), in theory a lucrative arrangement for the sultan—so long as he remained in control of exports.

No "typical" mining kongsi worked the sites; organization varied with the number of workers and the amount of capital involved, as illustrated by an early nineteenth-century description, based on information from a Chinese who had lived in the area (Crawfurd 1820, vol. 3, 474–75). A handful of laborers, often from the same village or with the same family name, worked the smaller mines with hoes and other simple tools. Larger operations, where waterworks, reservoirs, sluices, and chain pumps enabled continuous, large-scale operations, might employ several dozen men (Veth 1854, vol. 1, 331–35; Schaank 1893, 518n).

For reasons of defense, politics or economic efficiency, these mines gradually coalesced into larger units and expanded in numbers and power at the expense of the sultans. While the sultans controlled the mouths of the rivers, where there were Malay settlements, and the Dayaks populated the interior, the kongsis came to control much of the upland river valleys north of Borneo's great Kapuas River, between Pontianak and Sambas, by the end of the eighteenth century. In the process, they formed alliances or federations of kongsis, increasing their power. By the early nineteenth century, the larger kongsi federations were virtually independent of the sultans.

In 1791, the Dutch East India Company, which had maintained a trading station on the coast, withdrew its presence in West Borneo. The Dutch returned to the area in 1818 and found that much of the territory they had claimed through agreements with the sultans was effectively under kongsi authority. Prepared to let kongsis run the mines as institutions of economics and industry, the colonialists would not tolerate them as a "state within a state." The ensuing struggle for power, which pitted Dutch, local rulers, and some individual kongsis against the more powerful federations, lasted until 1854; the great kongsi federations were the losers. Several authors have already described this conflict and its aftermath (for example, Jackson 1970; Langelaan 1984; Rees 1858, 1859; Veth 1854).

In war, a kongsi could be a formidable opponent. Van Rees, a military historian, describes how the Dutch went to battle in August 1850 with the largest kongsi federation of West Borneo, led by the Thaikong[2] ("great harbor" or "great river," probably a translation of the Malay "Sungai Raya," the river where the kongsi was situated) Kongsi of Montrado. Colonial forces faced up to 7,000 fighting men who were well armed, trained, and paid a regular salary, as well as a large number of auxiliaries who performed coolie services and were not necessarily armed. Regular soldiers were organized in *khie* (flags or pennants) of about 80 men. Military commanders took over administrative duties in time of war and oversaw the provision of food and ammunition (Rees 1859, 108–9).

Kongsi federations had been able to break free of the sultans' control because they smuggled goods through rivers not controlled by the sultans, organized their own food production in addition to mining, and developed fighting capacity. They fought Dayaks, Malays, the Dutch, and, above all, each other. There were fewer and fewer, but larger, kongsi federations, because the winners absorbed the territory of the losers or weaker kongsis joined with stronger ones.

The process of consolidating existing mines and federations into larger kongsi federations in the Montrado area is striking. In 1776, 14 existing kongsis or groups of kongsis, Thaikong being the leader, formed the Fo-Sjoen federation. In 1808, only seven member kongsis remained; in 1822 four, in 1830 three. Finally, Thaikong alone controlled Fo-Sjoen between 1837 and 1850, when two new

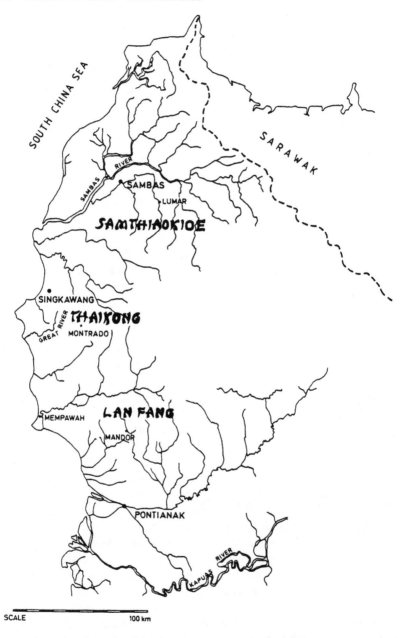

Northern West Borneo in the early nineteenth century, indicating approximate areas of influence of the three great kongsi federations.

allies joined. Fo-Sjoen was finally defeated and dissolved by the Dutch in 1851 (Jackson 1970, 56, 58n; Schaank 1893, Bijlage appendix A).

After about 1820, depletion of the best gold sites and competition for control of water added to conflict among mines and kongsis. In Mandor, to the south of Montrado, the Lanfang federation, a former rival of Thaikong, held sway; both expanded their territory at the expense of others after this time. Farther north, Thaikong drove its other major rival, Samthiaokioe, out of its most profitable territory, and many of Samthiaokioe's members fled to Sarawak. (On the fate of Samthiaokioe in Sarawak and its conflict with the Brooke regime there, see Lockard 1978.) However, this federation continued to exercise authority in the area near the Sambas River. There was little scope for others. At a few sites, small kongsis may have continued to work under the aegis of the powerful federations, or, if they were isolated enough, remained independent (Jackson 1970, 24–25, 58–59).

In any case, the sultans were no longer in control of the kongsis and were unable to collect revenue from them. They, as well as some kongsis defeated in battles for territory, turned to the Dutch for help, but only in 1850 was the colonial power, which had Lanfang and Samthiaokioe on its side, strong enough to face Thaikong/Fo-Sjoen.

History of Tin Kongsis on Bangka

Tin was found on the island of Bangka in about 1710 and subsequently (probably about 1740) the sultans of Palembang, who were rulers of the island, turned mining over to Chinese kongsis working under the supervision of regional head-men (also called kongsi) on the island. Muslims of Chinese descent at the Palembang court, who were called "*Tikos*," managed the operation from a distance. The sultan obtained capital from the Dutch East India Company, which enabled him, working through the *Tikos*, to provide advances for opening the mines, supply rice, and buy the tin; he then sold it to the company at a substantial profit (Heidhues 1992, 15–18).

By the end of the eighteenth century, piracy, disorder, and smuggling had reduced tin deliveries to Palembang to a trickle, and most mines fell into disuse. In 1812 the British and in 1816 the Dutch took over the island and ruled it directly, ending the influence of the sultan and the *Tikos*. For the next century, the mines continued to be worked by kongsis, but the Dutch colonial government financed all operations and took the tin at a fixed price, leaving no room for kongsis to be politically or financially independent (Heidhues 1992, 30–53). The kongsis were thus very different from what they had been in the sultans' times— or in West Borneo.[3]

In the 1840s, elections of headmen in the mines of Bangka were boisterous and apparently "democratic" affairs. Kongsi headmen often rotated in office, returning to mine labor after a year or so. Miners paid no more respect to a mine head than to any other miner. As far as the Chinese were concerned, a mine boss existed "more because there must be a head, than to exercise real authority" (Fraenkel 1843, 57–59).

Thus in the early days of colonial control, kongsi organization on Bangka appears to have been characterized on the one hand by rotating leadership and on the other by the sanctions of mutual trust and of indebtedness, especially in the case of new laborers or *sinkeh* (Fontaine 1823, n.p.). New laborers worked for a year or more to pay off the cost of their passage from China; once free from debt, they might become shareholders. The financial and disciplinary aspects of the kongsi, however, were more important in larger mines, because of the larger number of workers, the greater investment—the same kind of technology that was used to mine gold—and higher risk involved. With time, this changed the character of the kongsis themselves.

Kongsi Organization

Describing what kongsis did is easier than determining how they were organized. The word, also used in Malay and Indonesian, can have a variety of meanings:

1. A kongsi, especially in mining areas, might be a group who agreed to divide capital and labor responsibilities, each member having a share (*hun*), and to divide profits among themselves. These kongsis had from a few to several dozen members. Such a group usually worked a single site (for the purposes of this chapter, this is the meaning of kongsi).
2. In the gold-mining territory of West Borneo—and this seems unique in Chinese experience—there were associations or federations of mining kongsis. These were also called kongsi, and they controlled hundreds or even thousands of persons. These are called here "kongsi federations," because they were governed by a board of representatives of major constituent kongsis. As noted above, the three major federations in West Borneo were Fo-Sjoen (including Thaikong), Lanfang, and Samthiaokioe.
3. In the twentieth century, kongsi can mean "any kind of association, from a club to a limited company" (Ward 1954, 359n). In modern times, kongsis might form the basis of business partnerships, analogous to limited liability companies (Vleming 1926, 57–70).
4. *Hui*, perhaps as a cover for their activities, often took the name kongsi. The influential secret society Ngee Heng (Ghee Hin, Ngee Hin) of Singapore and Malaya, which Carl Trocki discusses in chapter 4, officially called itself Ngee Heng Kongsi.

As noted, colonial officials and others who observed Chinese mining kongsis in Southeast Asia, particularly as they existed in the gold mines of West Borneo, or in Bangka's tin mines, had different opinions on what kongsi organization meant. Undoubtedly, the institution was imported from China, and David Ownby in chapter 2 points out that mutual aid groups were multiplying in South China at this time because of the stresses evident in society. Wang Tai Peng (1977) shows that similar shareholding organizations engaged in mining and trade in China. However, even if kongsis had egalitarian membership and rotating leadership in their early years, reports from areas like Borneo and Bangka begin only in the late eighteenth or early nineteenth century, after kongsis had been established for some time, so assertions about their earliest organization are speculative.

Literature on the internal organization of kongsis and on the kongsi associations often goes to extremes. The assertions of various commentators include:

1. That they are no different from secret societies or *hui*, an attitude colonial officials, who were often suspicious of Chinese, readily adopted;
2. That they are egalitarian institutions or at least oligarchic republics led by far-sighted leaders. Early European visitors, who only penetrated to mining areas in the nineteenth century, favored this interpretation:

   > They live in a kind of Republic, which is presided over by the head of the mine. (Resident of Bangka A. de la Fontaine 1823, n.p.)

3. That they are a transplanted version of Chinese village society, which again is either "republican" or paternalistic, a view promoted by the Dutch sinologist J. J. M. de Groot (Blussé 1989, 133; Groot 1885), which will be taken up below.

Labor and Finance

The names of many of the original kongsis in West Borneo show that they began as partnerships: "Eight Shares," "Fourteen Shares," and so forth. But once kongsis combined into larger associations, not every laborer was or could be a shareholder.

Most vital to all mining operations was the guarantee of a constant flow of new laborers. Small mines might operate over a short time with a number of relatives, men from the same village or former mining comrades; large mines needed to sustain this effort over decades. During the best years of gold production, up to 2,000 new workers (called *sinkeh* or *sinhak*) arrived annually, while from 200 to 300 left on junks, returning to China with their savings (Langelaan 1984; Veth 1854, vol. 1, 313–14).

Only the larger kongsi federations, which had the resources to maintain contact with China, could organize immigration on such a large scale. Similarly, only those organizations that had their own temple, or *toapekong*,[4] could initiate *sinkeh* in a ceremony emphasizing ritual brotherhood (described below). In this way the federations provided workers, once initiated, for the smaller mines (Schaank 1893, 526–28). Capital requirements—immigration had to be financed—also increased the power of the larger kongsis and the federations, and limited the egalitarianism implicit in the ideal of equal shareholding.

Crawfurd, citing an informant who had lived in Borneo, noted in 1828, before Dutch influence could have had time to change the character of the kongsis there:

> The great mines are wrought by companies [a translation of kongsi?] of persons of property and capital, *who employ monthly labourers*. The smaller mines, on the other hand, are worked by the mere laborers who at once conduct the operative parts, and share the proceeds, on terms of perfect equality. [Emphasis added.] (Crawfurd 1820, vol. 3, 474–75)

Limits to Shareholding

The historical development of the kongsi federations shows how important it was to be able to band together to support a standing army. Although they were also vital to the kongsi federations, farmers, many of them local-born Chinese and children of Dayak mothers,[5] were not shareholding members of the mining kongsis or the federations. They might, however, form their own kongsis, as did a group of farmers of Chinese origin who took the name Tiandihui(!) in the eighteenth century. They attempted to monopolize rice and sugar deliveries to the mining operations, but were defeated and destroyed by a coalition of 14 mining kongsi federations in 1775. Unfortunately, little more is known about the affair, which illustrates the conflict between immigrant miners and settled farmers (Schaank 1893, 520).

In addition to local-born Chinese, who could not vote or hold shares in the kongsi federations, other groups were not eligible to be shareholders. *Sinkeh* were not shareholders—and could not be, for they had no capital and were in debt for their passage. Admission to shareholding, if ever, came only after they had worked off their debts and either purchased a share or struck out in a newly formed kongsi.

However, kongsis had non-working shareholders, as is clear from Crawfurd's description above. Veth confirms this, and even suggests that financing of mining was more important than providing labor:

> The necessary funds were put together in the form of shares . . . and according to the number of his shares, everyone took part in profit or loss. Whoever had more than one share had to take part in the work by means of a laborer, whose wage he himself paid, for each of his shares. (Veth 1854, vol. 1, 303)

Similar arrangements were common on Bangka. There, the opening of the kongsis to investment by outsiders arose very early. Furthermore, some workers —those who had not yet paid off their debt for passage—were not shareholders (*kuli*, that is, coolie, *kongsi*) and some shareholders in the kongsis were not workers but instead hired other men (*kuli hun*) to work their share for them.

> The shares . . . in a mine are usually divided equally among the miners; however there are some private Chinese, whether traders or other *kampung-* [town] dwellers, who take or purchase a couple of shares in a mine and have it worked by coolies who are paid a wage. (Fraenkel 1843, 397)

By mid-century, a non-working shareholder in a prosperous mine on Bangka could earn 100 or more silver dollars per year, paying a coolie a small monthly wage to do his share of the work (Croockewit 1852, 15). While this is a modest sum compared with the profits in the peak years of gold mining on Borneo, the cost of importing a coolie, who might work for up to three years before being free to join a kongsi himself, was less than 30 silver dollars at this time, and the wage was low, so the return on the investment of the Chinese, who probably lived in the district capital or market town (Malay, *pangkal*) was considerable.

On Bangka, the discrepancy between rewards to labor and to non-laboring shareholders increased from year to year as Dutch control of the mines intensified. Shareholding became concentrated in the hands of a few persons, many of whom were not miners at all. Government-supervised kongsis counted 1 shareholder to 1.6 laborers in 1877, 1 to 8.7 in 1897, and in 1900, 1 to 10.6. Some kongsis had dozens of shareholders at the end of the century, many had only one. Shareholders were only 7 percent of the work force in 1906 (Heidhues 1992, 73).

Kongsi Leadership

Even in early times in Borneo, leadership in kongsis was restricted. Kongsi members were from a small area in China; in small mines they often came from a single village. Jiayingzhou Hakkas dominated the Lanfang Kongsi (federation) in Mandor, together with Dabu men, while Huizhou Hakkas ruled the Fo-Sjoen federation of Montrado. One or a few family names controlled most federations; in Thaikong, ruling families were the Ng (Wu), Wong (Huang) and Tjang (Zheng) (Schaank 1893, 524–26). Outsiders not from the same homeland in China might be admitted to the kongsi, but their rights were often restricted. Non-Jiayingzhou Hakkas could, for example, be members, but not headmen, of the Lanfang Kongsi. Leadership of the Lanfang Kongsi did not rotate, headmen remained in office for years, and the job sometimes passed from father to son or son-in-law (Groot 1885, 16).

This overview suggests that, while small, new kongsis might be egalitarian, the older and larger the operation, the less likely it was to be an association of equals. In West Borneo, leadership and followers also pursued different interests. After 1851, part of the top leadership of Fo-Sjoen-Thaikong cooperated with the Dutch, becoming Chinese kapitans or other officers (Rees 1858, 177).

Lower-level leaders[6] went into opposition, even though the colonial government tried to reassure them that it would not disturb the basic mining organizations. The miners' discontent was explainable: many mines may have been unproductive by this time—and where would the miners obtain capital or new laborers without the federations?

On Bangka, the transition was rapid after the mid-nineteenth century. Mine bosses by this time had ceased to rotate in office. Colonial officials preferred to deal with more permanent mine chiefs, and a mine boss was the contractor and with the government and responsible for mine operations. He exercised police power over miners and could call on the government for help in enforcing discipline, chasing runaways, and selling supplies to the miners at inflated prices. In the twentieth century, the mine boss was simply an employee of the mining enterprise. Usually these men were local-born, while about 90 percent of coolies were immigrants.

Because Bangka suffered from periodic labor shortages in the late nineteenth century, coolies began to be recruited from the far south of Guangdong and Guangxi (Leizhou, Gaozhou, Hainan) instead of Jiayingzhou and nearby core Hakka areas, where the first miners originated. Rather than being controlled by bonds of shareholding, common origin, or even ritual brotherhood, they could be controlled only by the threat of force. Although the name kongsi continued to be used in Bangka, its meaning was lost.

The status of most laborers in Bangka was no longer like that in Borneo during the supposed golden age of the kongsi or in Bangka in some distant past. In fact, they differed little from the coolies in East Sumatra's plantations—contract laborers, without any share in profits. Not surprisingly, kongsis in Bangka were replaced in the twentieth century by a system of work-teams that, although designed to retain the egalitarian and sharing aspects of the kongsi, resembled that of the tobacco plantations of Sumatra, with its heavy emphasis on control of coolie labor (Heidhues 1992, 57–60, 75–77).

Colonial Experience with *Hui* in Borneo and Bangka

In 1853, reports reached Dutch authorities in the Residency of West Borneo that Chinese living in remote areas were forming a *hui*, and probably planning a revolt (Rees 1858, 218; 221). When an attack on Tjang Pin, the kapitan of China, took place in the market town of Singkawang, no one doubted that the "Sam Tiam Foei" or "Three Finger Band"[7] was behind the unrest. This society, whose name was spoken "only in a whisper" (Rees 1858, 222), soon put a price on the heads of all Chinese cooperating with the Dutch; in April, a suspected spy for the Dutch, who could have identified Tjang's attacker, was knifed during a theater performance *(wayang)* at the town market of Singkawang: "no doubt, the murder . . . was the work of the Three Finger Band and an act of revenge" (Rees 1858, 225).

The rebels' names were legion: not only were they called Sam Tiam Foei, but Thien-Thi-Foei (Tiandihui, Heaven and Earth Society), Kioe-Liong-Kongsi (Nine Dragons), and, finally, Ngee-Hin-Kongsi (Kielstra 1890, 458–74; Schaank 1893, 595).

> Ngihin [Ngee Hin, Ngee Heng] is the name of one of the most powerful democratic societies in China, which causes empires to shake on their foundations, creates new dynasties and has branches wherever Chinese settle. (Rees 1858, 260)

Ngee Hin was indeed one of Singapore's most influential Triad societies, as chapter 4 demonstrates. From its headquarters, apparently in Singapore, ties extended to businessmen in other parts of the Indonesian Archipelago, such as Riau—why not to West Borneo as well? Yet, just as the Ngee Heng in Penang was independent of that in Singapore, there is no apparent organizational connection with West Borneo. What was shared were symbols, tracts, and lore.

The 1853 conspiracy in Singkawang, actively recruiting members, appeared to have penetrated even the Dutch-appointed Chinese officials. Recruitment methods were known to the authorities: a man would find a message that he should go to a hidden crossroads in the forest at a certain time or face reprisals. From the rendezvous, a member led him, along with other recruits, to a secret meeting. There, a cock was killed, its blood mixed with *arak* (wine), a needle dipped in the brew. Each initiate pricked his lip as a promise of silence, then drank. New members received a red-stamped certificate of membership, which, like everything else connected with the initiation, was to remain secret (Rees 1858, 232–33).

With a mixture of military action, bribery, threats, and forced resettlement, the colonial authorities finally scotched the rebellion. They located the jungle headquarters of the rebels, killing or wounding the inhabitants, and capturing their books, membership lists, and seals. This would effectively deal the "Sam Tiam Foei" a death-blow in the Singkawang-Montrado area, or so they thought. Although a reward of 50 silver dollars was offered for his arrest, the ringleader of the conspiracy, Liau Njie Liong (Liau's name means "second dragon" and is probably a pseudonym), made a dramatic escape to Sarawak in October 1855, hidden in a coffin (Kielstra 1890, 2208; Rees 1858, 258–61, 266). Not long afterward, however, in 1856, the society was again implicated in uprisings in Lumar and Mandor. More trouble followed in 1874 in Mempawah (Kielstra 1890, 1922–40; 1892, 956).

The story seemed to repeat itself in October 1884, when Chinese in Mandor fomented an uprising against the colonial authorities. A Dutch official (*controleur*) and some of his policemen were murdered, the river blocked to Dutch traffic. Official opinion was that the Sam Tiam Foei, active in the area during the previous months, was taking advantage of a change of administration in Mandor, where the Lanfang Kongsi, the last remaining kongsi federation, had recently been dissolved. In early November, the uprising expanded to nearby areas, gaining more recruits (Kielstra 1893, 973–76).

In many of these instances, the governance of the Chinese had recently passed into Dutch hands. The Dutch had replaced an independent or at least autonomous kongsi federation with Chinese officers appointed by the colonial power. With the end of the federation, new taxes, duties, and regulations also came into effect.

Similarly, in Bangka in 1899, a conspiracy utilizing *hui* practices broke out among tin miners in the Koba area on the northern coast. Colonial reports identify the "ringleader," a new immigrant who was a fortune-teller, medium, and apparently a *hui* initiate before he left China. He presided over the nightly initiation ceremonies for which coolies, who were forbidden to leave the mines, secretly assembled in the forest. Initiates passed through a symbolic gate of swords and swore brotherhood, secrecy, and death to the mine bosses (Heidhues 1992, 140ff).

In 1912, two Chinese officers were murdered in West Borneo and there were rumors of an impending uprising that threatened to affect widespread areas. The rebels formed a sworn brotherhood in July 1914, initiating several hundred members, including not only Chinese but Dayaks and Malays. A chicken was killed; participants swore a blood oath (The 1981, 138–39).

Although the rise of *hui* activity seemed to be linked to the decline of the kongsis, *hui* were not a new phenomenon in the colony. The Dutch had already had ample experience with *hui* as they understood them, even in the mid-nineteenth century, when the first of these episodes broke in West Borneo. Such activities had occurred in various parts of their territory, and they had seized society trappings—books, membership certificates ("diplomas"), and banners—in the Riau Archipelago, in Borneo, and in parts of Java. Having dealt with Chinese since the seventeenth century, the Dutch seem to have had an almost equally long contact with *hui*. Blythe claims that experience with Koxinga (Zheng Chenggong) in Formosa tipped them off to the dangers of such organizations (1969, 49). Although that is unproved, a search of colonial relations with the Chinese in Java during the seventeenth and eighteenth centuries may well turn up other examples. In 1693, something very much like a secret society (the report speaks of *vloekverwanten,* sworn kin or sworn brothers) caused trouble near Semarang, Central Java (Nagtegaal 1988, 115). The fact that this happened a century before the presumed founding of the Tiandihui appears to confirm ter Haar's assertion in chapter 6 in this volume, and the conviction of the authors of the other chapters, that such brotherhoods pre-dated the Tiandihui and had deep roots in Chinese tradition. In the case of West Borneo, it may be better to look for common roots of kongsi and *hui,* rather than seeing conspiratorial identities between them.

Kongsi and *Hui*—Two Sides of a Coin

Were the *hui* activities in West Borneo and perhaps even those in Bangka, which seem to have appeared only after the kongsis in these areas were abolished or emasculated, the continuation of the kongsis under another name? Certainly, common elements existed:

For one thing, the use of the name "tiko" in Palembang or "thaiko" on Borneo, both meaning "elder brother," for the headman of a kongsi, resembles the practice of secret societies. The head of a *hui* was also a *dage.* If the common term does not prove identity, it at least shows the importance of ritual brotherhood in both kinds of institutions.

Mak Lau Fong has characterized the *dage* of twentieth-century *hui*; their position resembles that of the *thaiko*:

> According to informants, a general headman or *ta ko* does not interact closely in daily life with any member within the organization. . . . [He] is actually a headman of a distinct major secret society which has its own organizational structure. . . . In other words, a general headman is himself the headman of a single secret society, while simultaneously overseeing a group of secret societies each with its own headmen. (Mak 1981, 67)

Mak's description could apply to kongsi practices, too.

Second, the most striking element of *hui* rituals was the initiation ceremony, with the killing of a cock, the drinking of its blood, or alternatively, the blood from the forefingers of the initiates, mixed with wine, the gate of swords, and the oath of allegiance. Kongsis in Borneo also held an initiation for new members that contained elements of the blood oath in abbreviated form. No cock was killed, but a mixture of blood and *arak* was passed among initiates and members. Kongsi initiation was also not held in secret, as *hui* initiations usually were. A sample text of a ceremony is:

> Q. Do you know that the kongsi food is not tasty?
> A. Since all the brothers eat it, why should I not be able to eat it?
> Q. If the kongsi is in danger, what must you do?
> A. I must help it.
> Q. And if you do not help?
> A. Then may 10,000 knives cut me to pieces. (Schaank 1893, 585–86)

Third, many trappings of *hui* and kongsi were similar: Guandi, the god of merchants, war, and brotherhoods, was present in the main houses or temples (*thang*) of the kongsis, just as he was present in society temples. Claudine Salmon has raised the question of links between five Guandi temples in Bangka and local *hui* (Salmon 1991, 5). *Hui* membership certificates spoke of membership in a kongsi; as seen above, the terms might be interchangeable. Both associations used symbols such as flags and seals. However, the kongsi federations apparently did not use secret passwords or certificates of membership (Langelaan 1984, 13, based on Schaank 1893).

Last, both organizations had other religious functions. Societies, like kongsi, maintained temples and organized the celebration of major feasts (New Year, Qingming, and the so-called Festival of the Hungry Ghosts). For bachelor immigrants, the kongsi or *hui* took the place of his family or clan and provided him with burial and offerings after his death.

This catalogue of similarities is not new. Even Veth (1854, 300) pointed out that the two organizations were in many ways similar—one secret, one open. If the two had common or even identical origins and the difference between kongsi and *hui* lay in the Dutch attitude to them, that might explain why little is heard of *hui*, and only of kongsis, in West Borneo before the Dutch extended their rule. Even among colonial officials, opinions varied as they began to learn more about the Chinese and their institutions in the late nineteenth century.

Kongsi as "Village Republics"

One of the best-known of these officials was J. J. M. de Groot, sinologist, author of a monumental work on the religious system of China, and Chinese language interpreter in Pontianak from 1880 to 1883. He undertook to analyze the nature of kongsis and to distinguish them from secret societies. His 1885 work on the kongsis of Borneo includes the Chinese text and (Dutch) translation of the history of the Lanfang Kongsi, probably the only Chinese-language source preserved on the early history of Chinese settlement there, apart from temple and tomb inscriptions.[8] This text was apparently compiled in the 1880s by Yep Siong-yoen (Ye Xiangyun), the son-in-law of the last head of the kongsi federation. De Groot's interpretation helped redefine colonial policy toward the Chinese (Blussé 1989, 133).

De Groot's defense of the kongsi federations is comprehensive. They are not secret societies. Their link with *hui* stems from their common origin in Chinese village society. Like Chinese villages, kongsis are little republics, "well-organized free states" (Groot 1885, 63, 172–74). *Thaiko*, he insists, simply means "*primus inter pares.*"

> This spirit of brotherly cooperation, helpfulness and mutual support [is] a child of the clan system and of village autonomy. (Groot 1885, 113)

De Groot's intention is not just to de-criminalize the kongsis, but to plead for the retention of the kongsi federation as a form of indirect rule for the Chinese, just as the Malays and Dayaks of Borneo were under indirect rule through the sultans. Recognition of the kongsis as autonomous under Dutch rule would eliminate the reason for conflict and for the outbreaks of violence that had followed the abolition of Fo-Sjoen and, later, Lanfang. The Dutch could control the kongsi through a kapthai (captain, the new title given the *thaiko*) of their own choosing, as they had Mandor's Lanfang Kongsi from 1823 to 1884 (Groot 1885, 5, 127). Dissolving Lanfang had been a mistake. Another China specialist of his day, Schlegel (1885), agreed with him: Abolishing the kongsis had been deleterious for peace and order, and for the economy of the area.

Hui were not necessarily criminal, but rather, in de Groot's eyes, an expression of the Chinese "love of joining" (Groot 1885, 114). The Chinese system of mutual aid thus extended to the colonies, and secret signs and passwords enabled newcomers to find their way about in a strange land. Both these arguments were cited subsequently by colonial officers for Chinese affairs in other parts of the colony, who would have read de Groot's works.

De Groot certainly exaggerated the "republican" character of Chinese villages, but other additional factors weaken his argument. By 1851, *hui* were outlawed in Dutch territory (Sandick 1909, 418–24). The writer of the history of the Lanfang Kongsi may well have known that anything resembling a secret society was illegal and would have refrained from describing oaths and other suspicious activities, so the document is not informative about kongsi practices. Writing a few years after de Groot, Schaank, also familiar with the Chinese language, showed that kongsis did use similar trappings to those of *hui* (Schaank 1893, see above).

Furthermore, although the kongsi federations may have had much in common with Chinese villages, for example, such as common origin or dominance of one or a few surnames, there were important differences. Kongsis were primarily economic enterprises and in the federations, farmers—the backbone of China's villages—were second-class members, as were all local-born. In kongsis, single adult males were the bulk of the population, and they dominated the most important economic sector, mining.

Colonial Policy as Provocation

Something more than the abolition of the kongsis gave rise to *hui*. All the above uprisings were responses to what many Chinese perceived as serious provocations. De Groot, for example, does not report that Lanfang had been almost bankrupt at the time of its dissolution, partly because the Dutch had so reduced its territory that it could no longer support itself. Its gold was practically exhausted and many Chinese had left for other districts (Groot 1885, 55; report of military commander Andresen of February 1856 cited in Kielstra 1890, 1714; Kielstra 1892, 1266).

The extension of Dutch rule to the former Fo-Sjoen area of Montrado in 1851 was another such provocation. After the kongsis were dissolved, the Dutch introduced a poll tax, required all adult males to carry identity papers, and used compulsory labor, corvée, to build a road linking Montrado to the coast. A reluctant populace underwent smallpox vaccination; arrest threatened those who failed to show signs of a reaction to the inoculation (Rees 1858, 230). Illicit (in Dutch eyes) exchange with Singapore stopped, and government revenue farms monopolized the delivery of opium and salt. In dissolving the Lanfang Kongsi 30 years later, the Dutch also had planned to destroy the kongsi headquarters without providing a suitable substitute temple to house the tablets of its two patrons, Guandi and the founder of the Lanfang Kongsi, Lo Fong Pak. Although they were willing to name Lanfang officials to administrative posts, less malleable elements from the dissolved kongsi federation raised a rebellion (Kielstra 1893, 971–85).

In the case of Bangka in 1899, the mine bosses themselves seem to have provoked trouble. Finding the mines in the Koba area unprofitable, they bilked the coolies of their pay and resorted to vicious reprisals against runaways. Even newly arrived *sinkeh* knew of Koba's bad reputation and mutinied rather than be sent to work there (Heidhues 1992, 140).

A generation after the dissolution of Lanfang, trouble recurred. Colonial reports put the blame for the incident of 1912 in West Borneo on Chinese nationalism, which had introduced movements such as the *shubaoshe* (lit., book and newspaper society). (These were political reading clubs that became popular at the time of the 1911 Revolution in China.) Yet it appears on closer examination that tax increases, corvée demands, and the strict enforcement of the requirement that Chinese carry passes also contributed to Chinese rebelliousness (The 1981, 150–51). In addition, after 1905, the Chinese population was growing through an influx of new immigrants, who might have been less easy to control (Cator 1936, 158–59).

In the introduction to his examination of secret society practices, Schlegel remarked that "what distinguishes the genuine Hung League [Triad, *hui*] is its indestructibility" (Schlegel 1866, 6). The incidents related here show that *hui* were also ephemeral, displaying little continuity of action, activity, or even membership. The colonial authorities quickly deported or imprisoned supposed ringleaders, yet when problems arose, the *hui* reappeared. It was not the organization that persisted, however, but its forms.

Seen in this light, *hui*—and to some extent kongsi as well—are not so much conspiratorial or political organizations as kinds of ritual brotherhood. The *hui* appear to have emerged together with changes in the administration of the Chinese or arose to meet serious oppression. *Hui* thus were singled out as uniquely culpable in the violence that accompanied expansion of colonial control.

Formation of so-called secret societies was, in the instances cited here, a response to a provocation and served to organize and strengthen that response, one of several uses of ritual brotherhood. When the provocation was extreme, these rites and traditions bound the conspirators together. Violence seemed to crop up so easily among Chinese, less because of the presence of an organization than because of the presence of a widely available tradition with which they could organize. By the same token, kongsis could be expanded and changed to meet economic and even administrative purposes beyond their original goals.

Traditions of ritual brotherhood were widely known in Southeast Asia; for one thing, they traveled with the immigrants. Ritual specialists (called *xiansheng*, master) moved to Southeast Asia, sometimes to escape the law in China. Both in Bangka in 1899 and in West Borneo in 1854 (Kielstra 1890, 463–64), leaders of the uprisings were men who had been initiated into *hui* before leaving China. *Hui* may have actually organized migration before the second half of the nineteenth century (Yen 1985, 40–41). Men from overseas communities who visited their homelands in Southern China may have become initiates during their visits.

More important, as Barend ter Haar shows in this volume, traditions of sworn brotherhood were widely known in Chinese society. Even the literary sources of *hui* lore must have been widely known in Southeast Asia, expecially the *Romance of the Three Kingdoms*. Claudine Salmon points to the frequent use of the word *yi* (righteousness) in nineteenth-century temple inscriptions in Bangka as an indication that the donors, which were themselves kongsis, were familiar with the concerns of the *Three Kingdoms* (Salmon 1991, 5). This same character is also the first ideograph in the name of the Ngee Hin (Ngee Heng) society.

Written sources would have been available to the literate. The leaders of Chinese society, Chinese officers, mine heads and clerks were literate; schools were apparently common in the market towns (Veth 1854, 312; sources on Bangka confirm this). The *Three Kingdoms* in particular was also told, retold, read aloud, and even translated for those who read languages other than Chinese.

For the illiterate, as Sharon Carstens relates, popular Chinese theater was another source of the tradition of ritual brotherhood. Theater, or *wayang*, performances by wandering troupes were an integral part of New Year and other festivities, for example in Bangka (Epp 1841, 181). Finally, contacts with Singapore facilitated transmission of paraphernalia such as texts, diplomas, and so forth, as the many items of Ngee Hin documentation found in various parts of the archipelago demonstrate.

Conclusions

In the face of brutality, exploitation, and competition from colonial regimes, native rulers, and from other Chinese, Chinese in Southeast Asia, like their counterparts in China, could activate sworn brotherhoods and other rituals and organization to form *hui*. They could also use these traditions with great flexibility to build a pseudo-family, beyond clan or village solidarity, as sanction for loyalty in business, mining, or other enterprises. When expansion demanded organization of larger amounts of capital or control of large numbers of laborers, the supposed egalitarianism of the kongsi gave way to more autocratic forms. Mining kongsis, having lost their initial purpose and becoming more an organization to exploit labor than to share its rewards, finally disappeared from their last bastion in Bangka in 1919, not only because they were disbanded by the Dutch but because they no longer met the needs of either miners or bosses.

Among Chinese immigrants in eighteenth- and nineteenth-century Southeast Asia, as Maurice Freedman (1960) pointed out, ritual brotherhood was the only kind of institution available—not family, not clan, and not voluntary association. Colonial policy finally forced (or better, facilitated) a differentiation of these brotherhoods, leaving the fields of extortion, petty rackets, and other criminal activities to the *hui* in the twentieth century. Political movements, labor unions, burial, place of origin, and other associations supplanted the societies in the settled communities (compare Mak 1981). Having served an immigrant, frontier society, the "legitimate" functions of kongsis and *hui* were transferred to new organizational forms, ones more acceptable to colonial powers.

Notes

1. The Indonesian part of the island of Borneo is now called Kalimantan. West Borneo is the present-day province of West Kalimantan, but because this chapter deals with the nineteenth century, I have retained the older name.

2. Spellings of Chinese names are retained as used in Southeast Asia, although they are often inconsistent. The Glossary provides character equivalents, where known.

3. Wang Tai Peng (1977) has compared kongsis in the two locations, but has, in my opinion, misunderstood the relationship of the *tiko* and the headmen to the Palembang Court.

4. Pinyin, *dabogong*; in Indonesia the term oftens means an idol or simply a Chinese temple. De Groot sees the Toapekong or Thai-pak-kwong as the great "*Pak*" or uncle of the "*kong*" or kongsi, that is, the patron-founder. When the founder of the Lanfang Kongsi, Lo Fong Pak, died, his tablets were placed in the *thang* or great hall of the kongsi federation and he became the Toapekong. The Hakka honored a god *bogong* or *dabogong* and may not only have "transported" him to Southeast Asia but identified him with the settlement's founder. Franke sees the Toapekong as similar to the *tudi*, the spirit of a locality or Earth God (1989, 381).

5. Traders and those few miners who managed to save enough money to acquire a bride married Dayak women. Sources are unanimous in claiming that the immigrants seldom brought women (except for prostitutes or a handful of wives of the very rich) abroad before the end of the nineteenth century. Marriage to a Dayak meant forming bonds with her family. Dayaks, in turn, learned to speak Chinese. For example, Veth cites a report of 1844 that Dayaks of West Borneo lived among Chinese, married their daughters to them, attended their feasts and spoke their language (Veth 1854, vol. 1, 100, 104).

6. Contemporary Western sources spoke of "ultra-democratic" elements, meaning, presumably, the miners themselves. The epithet "democratic" carried overtones of being radical, populist, or anarchic. Colonial authors also refer to both kongsis and *hui* as "communist," "republican," or "socialist," all of which carried pejorative connotations.

7. Actually *sandianhui*, three drops society, a synonym for the Tiandihui or Triads, from the practice of writing "three drops of water" in front of certain characters as a secret sign. Van Rees, a military man who has written rather chauvinistic histories of expeditions in Bangka and Borneo, explains that the name comes from the practice of grasping objects with three fingers as a secret sign of membership in the brotherhood.

8. Wolfgang Franke has collected many such inscriptions in the West Borneo area, and is preparing a publication.

References

Blussé, Leonard. 1986. "Batavia 1619–1740: The Rise and Fall of a Chinese Colonial Town." In *Strange Company: Chinese Settlers, Mestizo Women and the Dutch in VOC Batavia*, 73–96. Dordrecht: Foris.

———. 1989. *Tribuut aan China: vier eeuwen Nederlands-Chinese betrekkingen* [Tribute to China: four centuries of Netherlands-Chinese relations]. Amsterdam: Cramwinckel.

Blythe, Wilfred. 1969. *The Impact of Chinese Secret Societies in Malaya: A Historical Study*. London: Oxford University Press for the Royal Institute of International Affairs.

Cator, W. L. 1936. *The Economic Position of the Chinese in the Netherlands Indies*. Oxford: Blackwell.

Crawfurd, John. 1820. *History of the Indian Archipelago*. Edinburgh: Constable.

Croockewit, J. H. 1852. *Banka, Malakka, Billiton*. The Hague: Fuhri.

Epp, Franz. 1841. *Schilderungen aus ostindiens Archipel* [Descriptions of the East Indian Archipelago]. Heidelberg: J. C. B. Mohr.

Fontaine, A. de la (Resident of Bangka). 1823. Report on Bangka, manuscript. Algemeen Rijksarchief, The Hague, Elout Collection No. 57–121.

Fraenkel, S. 1843. "Beschrijving van de bewerking der tin-mijnen op het Eiland Banka en van de gebruiken der mijnwerker [Description of the operation of the tin mines on the island of Bangka and of the customs of the mineworkers]." *Tijdschrift voor Nederlandsch-Indië*, no. 10: 392–419.

————. 1844. "Bijdrage tot de Kennis der tinmijnen van het eiland Banka [Contribution to understanding of the tin mines of the island of Bangka]," *Tijdschrift voor Nederlandsch-Indië*: 49–85.

Freedman, Maurice. 1960. "Immigrants and Associations: Chinese in Nineteenth-Century Singapore." *Comparative Studies in Society and History* 3, no. 1 (October 1960): 25–48. Reprinted in *The Study of Chinese Society: Essays by Maurice Freedman*, ed. G. William Skinner, 61–83. Stanford: Stanford University Press, 1979.

Franke, Wolfgang: 1989. *Sino-Malaysiana: Selected Papers on Ming and Qing History and on the Overseas Chinese in Southeast Asia, 1942–1988*. Singapore: South Seas Society.

Groot, J. J. M. de. 1885. *Het kongsiwezen van Borneo: eene verhandeling over den grondslag en den aard der chineesche politieke vereenigingen in de koloniën* [The organization of the kongsis of Borneo: a treatise on the basis and the character of Chinese political associations in the colonies]. The Hague: M. Nijhoff.

Heidhues, Mary F. Somers. 1992. *Bangka Tin and Mentok Pepper: Chinese Settlement on an Indonesian Island*. Singapore: Institute of Southeast Asian Studies.

Jackson, James C. 1970. *Chinese in the West Borneo Goldfields: A Study in Cultural Geography*. Hull: University of Hull Publications, Occational Papers in Geography No. 15.

Kielstra, E. B. 1889–1893. "Bijdragen tot de geschiedenis van Borneo's Westerafdeeling [Contributions to the history of Borneo's Western District]." *Indische Gids*, 11(1889): 321–60, 505–44, 705–42, 941–91, 1141–51, 1352–83, 1721–31, 1918–31, 2119–48; 12 (1890): 450–74, 682–91, 857–78, 1085–1112; 1482–1501, 1694–1723, 1922–41, 2185–2226; 14 (1893): 1264–81, 1441–64, 1679–96, 2072–88, 2300–2316; 14 (1893) 952–86, 2091–2104.

Langelaan, Quirijn S. 1984. *De Chinezen van Sambas, 1850* [The Chinese of Sambas, 1850]. M.A. thesis. University of Amsterdam. Mimeo.

Lockard, Craig. 1978. "The 1857 Chinese Rebellion in Sarawak." *Journal of Southeast Asian Studies* 9, no. 1: 85–98.

Mak Lau Fong. 1981. *The Sociology of Secret Societies: A Study of Chinese Secret Societies in Singapore and Peninsular Malaysia*. Kuala Lumpur: Oxford University Press.

Nagtegaal, Lucas Wilhelmus. 1988. *Rijden op een Hollandse tijger: De noordkust van Java en de V.O.C.* [Riding on a Dutch tiger: the north coast of Java and the Dutch East Indies Company]. Ph.D. diss., University of Utrecht.

Rees, W. A. van. 1858. *Montrado: Geschied- en krijgskundige bijdrage betreffende de onderwerping der Chinezen op Borneo, naar het dagboek van een Indisch officier over 1854–1856* [Montrado: historical and military contribution concerning the conquest of the Chinese on Borneo, after the diary of an Indian officer from 1854–1856]. 's-Hertogenbosch: Gebr. Müller.

————. 1859. *Wachia, Taykong en Amir, of het Nederlandsch-Indisch Leger in 1850* [Wachia, Taykong and Amir, or the Netherlands Indies Army in 1850]. Rotterdam: H. Nijgh.

Salmon, Claudine. 1991. "The Three Kingdoms in Insular Southeast Asia—Religion and Literature." Paper presented to Symposium on the Culture of the Three Kingdoms, Chengdu, Sichuan, November 1–8.

Sandick, L. H. W. van. 1909. *Chineezen buiten China: Hunne beteekenis voor de ontwikkeling van Zuid-Oost-Azië, speciaal van Nederlandsch-Indië* [Chinese outside China: their importance for the development of Southeast Asia, especially of the Netherlands Indies]. The Hague: M. van der Beek's Hofboekhandel.

Schaank, S. H. 1893. "De Kongsis van Montrado: Bijdrage tot de geschiedenis en de kennis van het wezen der Chineesche vereenigingen op de Westkust van Borneo [The kongsis of Montrado: contribution to the history and understanding of the Chinese associations on the West Coast of Borneo]." *Tijdschrift voor Indische Taal-, Land en Volkenkunde* 35, no. 5–6, 498–612.

Schlegel, G. 1866. "Thian Ti Hwui: The Hung-league or Heaven-Earth-league: A Secret Society with the Chinese in China and India." *Verhandelingen van het Bataviaasch Genootschap van Kunsten en Wetenschappen* 32: *passim*.

———. 1885. "L'Organisation des kongsi à Borneo [The organization of kongsis in Borneo]," *Revue coloniale Internationale* 1: 448–465.

The Siauw Giap. 1981. "Rural Unrest in West Kalimantan: The Chinese Uprising in 1914." In *Leyden Studies in Sinology*, ed. W. L. Idema (Sinica Leidensia XV). Leiden: E. J. Brill.

Trocki, Carl A. 1979. *Prince of Pirates: The Temenggongs and the Development of Johor and Singapore, 1784–1885.* Singapore: Singapore University Press for the Institute of Southeast Asian Studies.

Veth, P. J. 1854. *Borneo's Wester-Afdeeling: geographisch, statistisch, historisch, vorafgegaan door eene algemeene schets des ganschen eilands* [Borneo's Western Division: geography, statistics, history, preceded by a general sketch of the entire island]. Zaltbommel: Joh. Nomanen Zoon.

Vleming, J. L. 1926. *Het chineesche Zakenleven in Nederlandsch-Indië* [Chinese business life in the Netherlands Indies]. Weltevreden: Landsdrukkerij.

Wang Tai Peng. 1977. *The Origins of Chinese Kongsi with Special Reference to West Borneo.* M.A. thesis, Australian National University.

Ward, Barbara E. 1954. "A Hakka Kongsi in Borneo." *Journal of Oriental Studies* 1, no. 2 (July): 358–70.

Yen Ching-hwang. 1985. *Coolies and Mandarins: China's Protection of Overseas Chinese during the Late Ching Period (1851–1911).* Singapore: Singapore University Press.

4

The Rise and Fall of the Ngee Heng Kongsi in Singapore

Carl A. Trocki

This chapter offers a Marxian analysis of the rise and fall of the Ngee Heng[1] secret society in Singapore during the nineteenth century. The analysis stresses four fundamental points. First, the Ngee Heng, like most Chinese secret societies in Southeast Asia at that time, was an important economic institution. Second, as an economic institution, it came into contact with the forces of British imperialism and global capitalism, and to some extent actually facilitated their expansion. Third, the so-called secret society riots of this period should be considered aspects of class struggle characteristic of the expansion of bourgeois capitalism. Fourth, the colonial state pushed the Ngee Heng and other secret societies beyond the pale of legitimate economic activity and stigmatized them as criminal organizations.

Singapore Island became a British colony in 1819 when Thomas Stamford Raffles established a free port there on behalf of the English East India Company. Thousands of Chinese rapidly migrated to the new center. Among these migrants were many merchants and traders, but far more were laborers who found employment in the expanding pepper and gambier plantations in Singapore's interior. By 1825, Europeans realized that these plantations housed a large and active secret society, known variously as the Tiandihui, the Ngee Heng Hui (or the Ngee Heng Kongsi), or the Ghee Hin Hui. Given the size and the economic importance of the Ngee Heng, it was impossible and actually undesirable for the colonial authorities to remove the Chinese or to outlaw the society. In fact, the British actually governed the Chinese in cooperation with the society. Likewise, economic contacts between the European merchants and the laborers were dominated by the society—which thus became known among some Europeans as the "Grand Triad Hoey [hui]."

In subsequent years, new secret societies appeared, and the colonial government regarded conflicts between various secret societies, between secret societies and the government, and among other organized groups of Chinese as a major challenge to their system of control. Ultimately, secret societies, along with many other forms of Chinese voluntary organizations, including political parties, were subjected to police regulation and suppression. A considerable literature relating to these organizations has focused on their role as agencies of criminal and antigovernmental activity. The economic analysis offered here counters these earlier views of the Tiandihui, or Ngee Heng, and of nineteenth-century Singapore Chinese society in general.

The history of the Ngee Heng was more complex than the simple story of criminal expansion and suppression by the state found in the European accounts. The society went through a metamorphosis of several stages in its encounter with British imperialism. At first, it seems to have been an autonomous socioeconomic system coexisting alongside the British colonial system. Later, it became the unofficial partner of the *laissez-faire* state in governing the Chinese populace of Singapore. As this happened, the character of the society's leadership changed. Charismatic military and political leaders were replaced by successful merchants who began to identify more with the European merchant class than with the Chinese. Wealth and economic dependency replaced loyalty and solidarity as the foundations of Chinese life. The ties of brotherhood and mutual support that had originally reinforced economic relations within the society became the foundation for a complex debt structure, and the secret society itself became a coercive agency in the service of moneylenders and tax farmers, the wealthiest of the Chinese *taukeh* or bosses. As this happened, the Ngee Heng began to fragment along ethnic and surname lines, while direct control of the most lucrative elements of the local economy gravitated into the hands of the *taukeh* and their families. By the 1870s, the Ngee Heng and its new competitors had been criminalized and made objects of British suppression.

Several corollaries follow from this argument. The first is a challenge to the traditional view of secret societies as mere criminal gangs. Whatever their nature within China, the character of secret societies changed significantly after Chinese laborers brought them to the Nanyang. Chapters 2 and 7 in this volume suggest that Chinese brotherhoods and secret societies were characterized by marginality. Members were migrants or young single men with attenuated connections to lineage associations and to mainstream society. As they migrated overseas, these individuals carried secret society traditions with them. However, when they subsequently established prosperous and autonomous communities in the jungles of Southeast Asia, the secret society was transformed into a legitimate social entity. This tradition was grafted onto common Chinese patterns of economic organization to form a widespread grouping known as the kongsi. The end result was that the secret society became the actual "government" of the local Chinese social order. This mutation shows the latent potential of "renegade" elements of popular Chinese culture that became apparent only after individuals were freed from the political and social environment of imperial Confucian rule and the limited resource base of their homeland.

Second, egalitarianism, perhaps even a kind of incipient democracy, appeared in the kongsis of Southeast Asia. The social order of the kongsi represented an alternative vision, a challenge, to both the hierarchical traditions of China and the bourgeois impulses of European imperialism. At some level, this social vision may have challenged the British colonial social order more than the alleged criminality that led to the Kongsis' suppression. The British, however, did not immediately move to eliminate the societies in the early nineteenth century. The ubiquity of this socioeconomic form in Southeast Asia together with its success in pioneering large-scale commercial agriculture and mining operations made the kongsi necessary to colonial rule. The kongsi remained a powerful institution among the Chinese migrants of this era, providing both an agency of social control and an avenue of economic progress.

These findings challenge the accepted view of economic development in colonial Southeast Asia, which emphasizes British initiative and Chinese industry. By contrast, I would stress the significance of organizational aspects of Chinese economic enterprises in the region before and in conjunction with the activities of European companies and colonial establishments. When they established a base at Singapore, the British brought new infusions of capital and through free trade facilitated the region's connections to world markets. These alone, however, would have been ineffectual without the social and economic contributions of the Ngee Heng and other Chinese kongsis.

**The Kongsi and Chinese Migration
to Southeast Asia**

No account of secret societies in the Nanyang would be complete without economic analysis. It is well known that Chinese laborers and merchants came to Southeast Asia neither to overthrow the Chinese or any other government, nor to engage in prohibited ritual practices, but, rather, to make money. The Southeast Asian version of the Tiandihui, or Heaven and Earth Society, in the eighteenth and nineteenth centuries had an economic and social function that could achieve only rudimentary development in China. Secret societies should therefore be studied in association with the kongsi, and economic factors should be seen as helping drive social and political change.

At the beginning of the nineteenth century, the economies of Southeast Asia were, in general, fragmented and characterized by self-sufficiency and the absence of cash. So far as the ultimate producers of wealth were concerned, the cash economy did not exist, and their products were most frequently absorbed into the commercial economy by confiscation. Most political structures in Southeast Asia were built around the control of manpower, and there was no "free labor." The cash economies of the commercial centers, the entrepôts of the region, prospered or languished within restricted spheres of influence and were connected to the economies of the outer world through myriad complex links. Domestically, they too survived by confiscation and conquest, most particularly through piracy and slave trading. In every case, these centers were governed by royal or company monopolies.

The arrival of the Chinese laborers in the jungles of Southeast Asia began to change this picture radically. The Chinese seem to have been the first representatives of wage labor in the region. They were organized around a uniquely Chinese form of capitalism (or perhaps proto-capitalism), in which the partnership of the kongsi and the brotherhood ideology of the secret societies cemented the economic relations between plantation and mine laborers and their financial backers.

Because these settlements produced commodities for export, their entire economy was commercialized. Individuals worked for either shares or a cash wage. Imported consumable provisions and exported products all had cash values. These exchanges were often conducted at entrepôts that were under colonial or indigenous royal or aristocratic control; however, these rulers did not actually control the Chinese laborers' settlements. The miners and planters were often located far in the interior or in otherwise uninhabited areas, and thus developed their own forms of local government based on the secret society and the kongsi. In other words, Chinese began to create autonomous communities in these rural settings. Their economies were likewise independent of European commerce, because they focused on a Chinese market and initially did not participate in the European-dominated commercial networks.

This conclusion is based partly on the analysis put forward by Wang Tai Peng (Wang 1977), who studied the Hakka gold mining kongsis of western Borneo that flourished from the mid-eighteenth to the mid-nineteenth centuries. While his approach may be flawed, he offers insights that compel a reconsideration of the history of the Chinese migration to Southeast Asia.

Wang has drawn attention to the kongsi as a distinctive socioeconomic formation—unique to the colonies of Chinese miners and planters—which first appeared in Southeast Asia at the beginning of the eighteenth century. He points to the combination of two important factors: the shareholding principle and the ideology of brotherhood. The division of an economic venture into shares within a kongsi underpinned by oaths of sworn brotherhood are the two factors distinguishing these kongsis from purely commercial ventures as well as from the economically marginal secret societies of China.

Wang maintains that the heart of the Hakka mining kongsis in western Borneo was the brotherhood of the laborers. Groups of miners, both laborers and capitalists, pooled their resources in a particular venture to form a kongsi. They agreed to distribute the produce on a share basis: to each according to his contribution. The principle was further democratized in order to allow even the lowest coolies to obtain shares through labor. Community organization was achieved through the federation of individual kongsis. Thus one share holding kongsi would operate a particular mine or group of mines. In areas where many kongsis operated separate mining concessions, the members formed broader coalitions, which undertook the functions of community government, including public works, regulation of property rights, defense, taxation, and the management of relations with other political entities such as local Malay rulers, other indigenous peoples, and European trading companies. These broader coalitions, likewise called kongsis, were governed through representative institutions. In Borneo, these "community" kongsis were, in fact, self-governing and autonomous proto-states, which some observers called "republics" (see discussion in chapter 3). The members were bound together by oaths of brotherhood, based on secret society rituals, and operated in what Wang has termed a democratic and egalitarian fashion.

The interest of *kongsi* coolies lay entirely in the *kongsi*-house. Through distinction in war, coolies were rewarded with shares in the *kongsi* mines. A new member or *Hsin-k'o* could also become share-holder after a year working in the *kongsi*-mine. The old coolies who had retired from work were given a share each for their long service to the *kongsi*. The profits of the *kongsi*-miners after setting aside part of it for the *kongsi* fund, were divided by the share-holders or mine workers. When the profit was huge, everyone of them could expect a bonus to be added to their dividend. The *kongsi*-house provided them a roof under the sky, meals, democratic life and brotherhood and a share in gain and loss. (Wang 1977, 94)

Some observers, such as Mak Lau Fong (Mak 1981, 23), maintain that there were no secret societies in Borneo, only mining partnerships. Wang suggests that the Tiandihui was not present at first, but was later organized by coolies in opposition to wealthy pro-Dutch merchants who tried to take over the kongsi. It may be that there was no "secret" society in the Lanfang, Thaikong, or the other Borneo kongsis, secrecy being unnecessary in a community made up entirely of Chinese members, and dominated by the Tiandihui. Whether or not there was a secret ritual, there was certainly ritual sanctifying the oaths of brotherhood that bound the entire kongsi together. Secrecy became necessary only when the Chinese lived near or under the control of an actual state authority.

I agree with the points made by Barend ter Haar and Mary Somers Heidhues in this collection, that *hui* and kongsi both stem from a common Chinese tradition of ritual brotherhood. Heidhues's reconstruction of the historical development and decline of the Borneo kongsis is also probably closer to historical reality than Wang's more idealistic scenario. By the beginning of the nineteenth century, the egalitarian promises of justice and common welfare were more rhetoric than reality. Nevertheless, the fact that the ideals of brotherhood and the promise of social and economic justice continued to characterize the rituals and ideology of groups like the Ngee Heng throughout the nineteenth century is testimony to the power of these beliefs and to the aspirations of the Chinese laborers who joined them. The economic accomplishments of the kongsis must be understood within the context of the ideological promise offered by the secret society oath of brotherhood.

These rituals presented the migrant Chinese with a familiar and persuasive body of symbols and a mythology that grew out of the traditions of their own villages. As migrants living in a dangerous world, they could readily identify with the militant traditions of banditry, daring, and adventure championed in the traditional Chinese epics such as *The Water Margin*, or the stories of loyalty, brotherhood, military strategy, and personal courage found in *The Romance of the Three Kingdoms*. The initiation rituals and the traditions of the societies reinforced and commemorated the promise of brotherhood that is a basic theme in these epics (Mak 1981, 31–33). Sharon Carstens shows in her chapter in this volume that the secret society ideology and the charismatic authority of local leaders were buttressed by the theatrical performances of traveling players and itinerant storytellers who made their living by performing these epics in the kongsi villages of Southeast Asia.

By the nineteenth century, variations on the type of kongsi described by Wang Tai Peng seem to have permeated the Chinese settlements in Southeast Asia, and many types of joint undertakings bore the name. In addition to Borneo and Bangka, mining or planting kongsis were found in Riau, Selangor, Perak, Phuket, Linggi and many other locations in the Malay world and Siam. Newbold's remarks about these settlements are instructive:

> It is not unreasonable to infer that the Chinese colonists at Melaka, in Java, Borneo and other parts of the Indian Archipelago at an early period after emigration would find the advantages of binding themselves together as a means of self-protection in a foreign land. Many of them had probably been members . . . in their native land. Henceforth the numerous "Kongsees" or public clubs with which we find them invariably linked particularly at the mines and plantations of the interior. (Newbold 1841, 130)

Many of these kongsi settlements predated the period of British expansion and operated independently of the English or other European powers. Later, in the nineteenth century, when individual Chinese immigrants arrived in the Nanyang, they were confronted with Chinese social forms that had been constructed by their predecessors. They had to fit into these forms if they were to survive as aliens in a "barbarian land." The kongsi was one of those social and economic institutions that can be considered a "carrier" of Chinese culture and history. The kongsis made it possible for the Chinese to leave their homes; to occupy territory in foreign lands; to set up functioning communities; to establish viable economic systems; and to maintain an organized social structure.

The Kongsis and the Pepper and Gambier Society in Singapore

Each secret society or complex of secret societies in nineteenth-century Southeast Asia belonged to an economic system. In the case of nineteenth century Singapore and the Ngee Heng, that meant pepper and gambier. The kongsi economy of the area around Singapore (Riau and Johor) differed from the Borneo kongsis described by Wang, and from that of the Malayan states (ca. 1860), where the economies were based on mining. The pepper and gambier economy of Riau-Singapore-Johor was centered at Singapore while the mining economies of the west coast states were based in Pinang. The secret societies and economic kongsis of both regions were similiarly divided.[2]

The pepper and gambier economy of Singapore employed the largest single work force and literally dominated much of the adjacent countryside. While this was clearly not the only or even the most lucrative element of the Singapore economy, the sheer numbers it employed gave its controllers an enormous degree of leverage in local affairs (Trocki 1990, 63–81). The Ngee Heng was intimately tied to pepper and gambier agriculture, even if the exact nature of that relationship was sometimes unclear. Most European observers indicate that the Ngee Heng exercised the power of life and death over the Chinese inhabitants of the Singapore countryside. John Cameron speaks of "courts" and punishments, even executions.

> At the time, these societies possessed great power among the Chinese; and though there was no direct evidence of the fact, it was strongly suspected that at the courts they were known to hold, they frequently awarded and carried out the sentence of death. Many murdered bodies were found about the country, each mutilated in a peculiar manner: generally with either the right or left hand chopped up into a certain number of parts, left hanging together by the skin; and in these cases Chinamen never were the informants, nor could they ever be induced to give evidence. (Cameron 1865, 265)

J. D. Vaughan suggests that the secret societies maintained order among the "unlettered Chinese" of the colony (Trocki 1990, 35–37; Vaughan 1879, 99). The institutional links between the society and the pepper and gambier kongsis are indisputable and well documented. Evidence indicates that important *kangchu* (the local term for the chiefs of the pepper and gambier settlements) were also Ngee Heng headmen (Trocki 1979, 101–8).

The Ngee Heng was the original Chinese institution in Singapore. Despite British perceptions in 1819, Singapore was not really a tabula rasa. Rather, Singapore and the area around it had already long since been part of a specific Sino-Malay economic system that was closely linked to the dominant secret society. The progressive absorption of this Chinese economic system by the free trade economy of British capitalism became a dynamic element in Singapore's history. The struggle was carried out between what Lee Poh-ping has called the

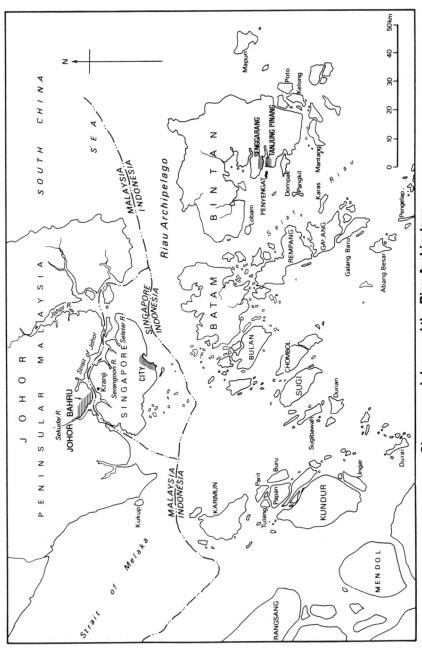

Singapore, Johor, and the Riau Archipelago

"pepper and gambier society," represented by the Ngee Heng, and the "free trade society" of the British imperial establishment (Lee 1978).

Underlying the secret society riots of nineteenth-century Singapore was also a conflict of ideology. The ideology of Chinese brotherhood contrasted with the European principles of market capitalism and economic individualism. The "secret society riots" of the nineteenth century were more than simple squabbles for economic predominance among groups of Chinese distinguished only by ethnicity.[3] They were, rather, surface manifestations of the struggle between distinctive economic systems and different economic classes.

It seems likely that, in the early years of the century, the Ngee Heng stood as the agency through which the Chinese involved in plantation agriculture interacted with each other, legitimizing their mutual economic obligations. As such, it may have considered itself representative of all Chinese engaged in agriculture to the Malay rulers and European colonial structures in the areas where it was established. Its role was to represent the organized voice of the "planting community" (e.g., planters, coolies, traders, and boatmen).

Pepper and gambier agriculture and the institutional superstructure that controlled it in Singapore derived from the forms developed in eighteenth-century Riau (Trocki 1979), with an overall framework provided by the *kangchu* system. Groups of Chinese planters organized by a leader (the *kangchu*) took over a small river valley and established a group of plantations or *bangsal*, around a central village on the river. The village, called a *kangkar*, or "river foot," served as a kind of market center. The first of these settlements was probably established on Bintan Island in the early eighteenth century and, before 1784, operated with the permission of the local ruler of the island (Trocki 1976, 132–55).

In terms of economic organization, each *kangkar* settlement was formed by a kongsi. In nineteenth-century Johor, each kongsi included some or all of the planters (many of whom shared the same surname), the *kangchu*, and sometimes a merchant who had advanced provisions and tools in return for produce. Coolies or laborers were probably not members, unlike in Borneo, where kongsis did not accept coolies as members. Each member of the pepper and gambier kongsi held at least one share; *kangchu* or merchants might hold two or more. Generally, each kongsi constituted about 10 shares. While the system may have changed between its first appearance in eighteenth-century Riau and the mid-nineteenth century, when the Johor documents were produced, the fundamental structures (that is, a shareholding kongsi occupying a river valley under a *kangchu*) seem to have existed in Riau before 1784.

On this basis, Lee Poh-ping's characterization of the "original" society of Singapore as having been a "pepper and gambier society" seems reasonable. It had come to Singapore from neighboring Riau, which had been a thriving port-polity in the eighteenth century. There were, according to Dutch reports, two *kampongs*, or settlements, of Chinese in eighteenth-century Riau, a division that has continued. On the southern shore of the harbor in the mouth of the Riau

River is the main settlement of Tanjung Pinang. Today, as in the eighteenth century, this was dominated primarily by Chinese from Fujian province. The people are locally known as Hokkiens. The Dutch called this the "Amoy Kampong," and established their own headquarters there. On the northern side of the harbor, across the river mouth and reachable only by boat, is the settlement of Senggarang. Here, the Chinese population is made up largely of settlers who originally came from Chaozhou prefecture in Guangdong province via the port of Shantou (Swatow). These people are identified as Teochew. In the eighteenth and nineteenth centuries, the Dutch called this the "Canton Kampong" because of the provincial origin of the settlers. Senggarang is rather unique among Chinese settlements in Southeast Asia in that it is built on stilts at the edge of a swamp and is atypical of other Chinese market towns, with their rows of brick and stucco shops. In the eighteenth century, these Teochews dominated the pepper and gambier industry, and the commercial center was in Senggarang. The settlement had its own kapitan, its own temple, and apparently its own kongsi, the Ngee Heng. Dutch reports tell of conflict between the "Canton" and "Amoy" Chinese in the late eighteenth century, and it seems clear that the colonial power felt more closely allied to the Hokkien mercantile community than to the Teochew traders and planters (Trocki 1979, 32–33). Despite occasional conflict, there seems to have been an active economic connection between the two communities, with the Hokkiens probably dominating the flow of capital goods to the Teochews, while the Teochews dominated the labor force. Ng Chin-keong's discussion of these settlements suggests that while the Teochew settlement was older, the Hokkien community was initially more prosperous (Ng 1976, 15–33).

These relationships may have changed with the founding of Singapore. Many Teochew traders and Hokkien merchants moved their headquarters to Singapore, which rapidly became the market center for the pepper and gambier industry. New plantations were opened in Singapore, and older ones in Riau simply began shipping their produce across the strait to the British free port in order to avoid Dutch taxes. In Singapore, the Teochew pepper and gambier traders established themselves in one of the prime locations of the port, along the south bank of the Singapore River on Boat Quay Road. Economic and social relationships surely changed when the Teochew merchants found themselves cheek-by-jowl with Hokkiens, Cantonese, Hakkas, and British in the same urban space, although precise details of the social atmosphere are lacking.

What then was the status of the Ngee Heng in early Singapore? First, the Teochews, because of their numerical superiority in the years between 1819 and 1850, initially dominated the colony's Chinese society on the mass level.[4] Second, the Ngee Heng Kongsi, the Teochew-dominated "branch" of the larger secret society complex, became the only society in Singapore. Until 1846, there is no evidence of any other secret society in Singapore, despite a Chinese population marked by a diversity of speech groups. Third, as a result of ignorance, impotence, and a *laissez-faire* attitude on the part of the British, the Ngee Heng was able to exercise nearly supreme power in the countryside. While the Ngee Heng must have exercised influence among the Chinese townspeople, it had to share power there with the British colonial government. Moreover, the linguistic diversity among the Chinese in the town and the existence of other forms of social organization, not all of them secret, must have counterbalanced the Ngee Heng power. Finally, the Ngee Heng did not dominate the elite of Singapore Chinese society, especially that of the Melaka Chinese.

Following Wang Tai Peng's hypothesis about the brotherhood ideology of the kongsi, we can conclude that the majority of Chinese laborers looked to the Ngee Heng as the upholder of the communal and collectivist ideals that promised them justice and fair shares within a community of shared labor. It is doubtful, however, that either the pepper and gambier kongsis or the Ngee Heng itself actually promoted working-class interests in Singapore. After Singapore was founded, a group of merchants, shopkeepers, *kangchu*, and larger planters probably dominated the society. They appeared to have a commonality of interests that worked to the disadvantage of the average coolie. Nevertheless, the average Chinese periodically, especially in times of economic stress, undertook violent mass action in response to the promise of justice (in accord with the meaning of the name "Ngee Heng"). These actions were evident in the large-scale outbreaks of violence in 1846–47 and again in 1852 and 1854.

While not so autonomous and isolated as the Lanfang Kongsi in Borneo, the Ngee Heng represented a kind of kongsi government in Singapore. This group was the successor to one that had earlier existed on Riau; Singapore was its colony and at some point it established a headquarters there. The first reports of its existence came with the famous description given by Munshi Abdullah bin Abdul Kadir (Abdullah 1970, 204–17). In about 1825, Abdullah witnessed an initiation ceremony in the interior of the island. A close reading of his report showed that the Singapore Tiandihui (or "Thian Tai Huey," as he called it) was in fact a pepper and gambier kongsi. The ceremony he witnessed took place within a well-established gambier planting community that existed beyond the reach and apparently beyond the knowledge of Singapore's colonial government. In 1827, the cultivated area was nearly ten miles long, stretching across the center of the island's interior (Buckley 1903, 198). All this had happened since 1819. Together, the Hokkien and Teochew pepper and gambier shopkeepers in Boat Quay, the plantations, their population, and the Ngee Heng can be taken for what Lee Poh-ping has styled the pepper and gambier society (Lee 1978).

By 1850, the Chinese pepper and gambier agriculture extended from Dutch-controlled Riau to British-controlled Singapore to Malay-controlled Johor. The "political" boundaries, so important to colonial authorities, were almost insignificant in the face of the socioeconomic contiguity of the Chinese pepper and gambier society. Money, goods, opium, people, the chain of debt, and the authority of the Ngee Heng itself flowed back and forth across these administrative constructs with little regard to their existence.

The British Free Trade Society

If the British mercantile community of nineteenth-century Singapore can be said to have had a religion, it was the ideology of free trade. The first British merchants were former "country traders" or free European merchants who had come to Singapore from India or Pinang. Most were "agency" merchants who set up trading houses that functioned as agents for firms in India, Britain, and Europe. They sold goods consigned to them by their clients and procured local goods and produce on their behalf. The Singapore merchants, together with their allies in Britain and India, successfully lobbied the British government and colonial authorities to guarantee that no taxes were ever levied on Singapore trade (Turnbull 1975, 194–95).

While they benefited from the influx of Chinese, Malay, and other Southeast Asian traders, Europeans dealt at a disadvantage in that their transactions were largely tertiary. It was difficult for them to invest directly in primary production or even in retail undertakings: they simply lacked the infrastructure. They were thus dependent on Chinese merchants to act as intermediaries with the local economies, both Chinese and Southeast Asian. Most important, they had no access to the labor force. A system developed in which European merchants made advances of their own goods (cloth, provisions, iron tools, opium) as capital to Chinese merchants in return for promises of local goods such as jungle produce,[5] tin, pepper, and gold. These merchants, in turn, advanced the goods to smaller merchants, who lent them to people such as the *kangchu* and mine bosses of the kongsis scattered around the Malay world. There was thus a chain of debt linking the European merchants and large Chinese merchants of Singapore with the hinterland.

Singapore's economic culture was dominated by the European merchants who were the source of most of the operating capital in the area. This nexus is what Lee Poh-ping has called the "free trade society."[6] Even if only the few hundred European merchants and their employees actually subscribed to something resembling the classic ideology of free trade, their economic influence remained extensive. However, this free trade influence was exercised through Chinese institutions such as the kongsi and the Ngee Heng.

At the beginning of the nineteenth century, the pepper and gambier society was, in many respects, self-contained. It was not a free market economy, but rather one that depended on the chain of indebtedness and mutual obligation upheld by the kongsis and the Ngee Heng. These obligations included monopolistic agreements regarding the purchase of provisions and the disposal of produce, often at predetermined prices. There were also conditions that theoretically guaranteed a minimum living standard for coolies despite periods of unemployment and low prices. Market forces did not fully penetrate the industry. This changed very slowly before 1830.

In these early years, most of the produce went to China, where the use of gambier as a tanning agent had been pioneered as early as the eighteenth century. There was no market for gambier in Europe. Perhaps some of the pepper was purchased by Europeans, but it is difficult to tell. The expansion of the cultivation in Singapore between 1810 and 1830, however, must have demanded a certain amount of capital and it is probable that European traders in Singapore were the ultimate source of this capital. The connection between the pepper and gambier society of the interior and the free trade society of the European merchants was shaky. Europeans had little control over their investments, which were often quite risky. The Chinese planters, for their part, seem to have been little concerned over the vagaries of the market.

One last point about the free trade society concerns the role of its Chinese allies. Chief among these were the so-called Baba merchants or Straits Chinese, most of whom had come to Singapore from Melaka. They represented a culture and a community of indigenized urban Chinese whose relationship with the Ngee Heng and the more "ethnic" elements of the Chinese population was always ambivalent. Many of them spoke some English, which gave them a certain credibility with the European community; they often spoke Malay at home and did business in a patois of Hokkien. They were thus one of the key intermediary classes in the multi-ethnic community of Singapore.

The Opium Farming System

Opium, or more precisely, the opium revenue farm, was the means by which the colonial state first gained control over the political life of the Chinese during the middle of the nineteenth century. This was the source of profit for the merchants and frequently the major source of revenue for the colonial government.[7] The "farm" was a monopoly concession that the government sold to independent contractors who paid an annual rental for the right to manufacture and retail smokable opium, or *chandu,* to the local population. In the 1840s, the pepper and gambier kongsis became intertwined with the revenue farms. In the end, opium came to reinforce the system of debt and, at the same time, permanently distorted the social fabric of the kongsis.

Revenue farming was not completely new to the kongsis; pepper and gambier kongsis had always performed some sort of tax collection function in situations where it was necessary to maintain relations with local political structures. In Johor, between 1846 and the 1920s, the *kangchu* of the various pepper and gambier settlements not only regulated economic relations between merchants in the town and planters in the country, but also held tax farming privileges from the Malay government and exercised powers of law and order over the residents of their settlements. The *kangkar,* or headquarters of the *kangchu,* were characterized by opium shops, liquor shops, gambling dens, pawnshops, pig farms, and local provision shops, all of which were sources of profit for the kongsi that ran the settlement and which were thus jealously guarded monopolies. The indebtedness of the coolies was maintained through these monopolies, particularly the opium farm (Trocki 1979, 160–86).

The *kangkar* functioned as a company store. More precisely, it was a kongsi store, which allowed the shareholders to profit from both the production and the consumption of the coolies. Gambier planters or shopkeepers could not possibly gain an appreciable profit unless they retrieved from the coolies most of their wage ($3 to $4 per month).[8] This apparently was quite easy: virtually all nineteenth-century reports indicate that Chinese coolies (both in the mines and on the plantations) were inveterate users of opium. In nineteenth-century Southeast Asia, wherever there were Chinese, there were opium farms. Opium sales facilitated the "recycling" of wages. The markup on *chandu* sales was so high (about 300 percent) that the cost of purchasing raw opium was almost negligible. Since there was only a marginal profit to be made from pepper and gambier alone, pepper and gambier merchants had to hold shares in an opium farm or an opium shop in order to secure a level of profit justifying their investment.

The British government of Singapore, however, did not deal with individual *kangchu*. They did not even recognize the existence of *kangchu* in Singapore, even though they clearly existed. Rather, the government selected one individual to act as head of the entire opium farming operation for the entire colony and then left these subsidiary matters to him. His most pressing need was to organize a syndicate, or a kongsi, of his own to finance and to manage the opium farm. Each year, the government put up the revenue farms for auction and hoped that several potential farmers would compete for the privilege and thus offer bids guaranteeing the government a "reasonable" portion of the profit from the sale of taxable items.[9] Since the pepper and gambier planters and coolies, by virtue of their overwhelming numbers, represented the major group of consumers for items such as opium, alcohol, and pork, the health of the farms (and therefore the state's finances) was intimately tied to the prosperity of the pepper and gambier cultivation.

The pepper and gambier dealers took a personal interest in the formation of revenue farming syndicates. These were large corporate organizations with hundreds of shareholders, almost all of them Chinese. In the 1840s, Teochow merchant Seah Eu Chin claimed that there were 300 pepper and gambier dealers involved in advancing goods and capital to planters in return for the right to purchase their products at fixed (usually below-market) prices. To supplement their income, they relied on some connection with the farms. The Johor Archives records show that shopkeepers in both Johor Bahru and Singapore commonly held shares in the various *kangchu* concessions in Johor (Trocki 1979, chs. 5 and 6).

Although there is little information on the identity of revenue farmers during the early decades of Singapore's history, the farms were probably organized and dominated by groups of Melaka Chinese who had some credibility with the European authorities. The Melaka Chinese possessed the ability to raise capital to finance the farms, and could probably marshal an effective organization to

control distribution of their products in Singapore. However, their urban networks did not extend to the planters' settlements in the countryside. If they
wished to collect a tax on the vast amounts of opium consumed by the planters
and their coolies, it would be necessary to have some sort of arrangement with
the *kangchu* and kongsis and, thus, with the Ngee Heng.

The nature of this connection is not entirely clear, and changed over time. The
opium farmers profited most directly from their control of the opium shops in
town that were frequented by coolies who occasionally came in from the jungles.[10] Before 1840, opium distribution to the countryside was most likely managed through the pepper and gambier shopkeepers who had shares in the kongsis.
One can easily imagine some sort of segmented distribution system for opium, in
which the farmers simply sold large lots of *chandu* to the shopkeepers at farm
prices. The shopkeepers then advanced the opium, at a markup, to their *kangchu*
who managed sales within the *kangkar*. The opium dealers would have insisted
on arrangements that would prevent people in the countryside from preparing
their own *chandu* or from buying smuggled *chandu*. Whatever system was practiced, it was never very satisfactory for the farmers. Throughout the early nineteenth century, smuggling frequently occurred. Singapore was a free port;
anyone could buy raw opium. Turning it into *chandu* required nothing more than
a cooking fire and a couple of pans. Smuggling and the manufacture of illegal
chandu were regular sources of conflict in nineteenth-century Singapore.

Transformation and Conflict

So long as the economies of the town and the rural areas operated in relatively
separate universes, the debtor relationships and the opium distribution arrangements described above may have endured without too much difficulty. However,
demographic growth and improved communications brought the two worlds into
more frequent and less regulated contact. Extensive Chinese unemployment in
the late 1820s and early 1830s reportedly was caused by low gambier prices.
These conditions led to an outbreak of gang robberies conducted by out-of-work
coolies. An abrupt rise in gambier prices (from $1.30 to $3.25 per pikul[11]) after
1836 brought a boom in planting activity. This led to a scarcity of land at the
very time additional Chinese migrants began to arrive in the settlement. The abun-
dance of pepper and gambier produced by these new planters quickly glutted the
market and drove gambier prices down to only 85 cents per pikul by 1838.

After 1836, European involvement with and investment in pepper and gambier increased markedly. This investment came at a time when the Chinese
economy of Southeast Asia was collapsing. Both Jennifer Cushman and Wong
Lin Ken indicate that the junk trade was falling off, partly because of the growing popularity of square-rigged vessels among Chinese as well as European
shipowners and partly because of the opening of the treaty ports in China after
1842 (Cushman 1975, 90–93; Wong 1960, 82). A final circumstance was that

Chinese purchasing patterns were changing, and the ability of the Chinese market to absorb Southeast Asian produce was declining, largely as a result of increasing opium purchases. Thus it was only a matter of time before the ethos of free trade and European economic thinking, together with European capital, invaded the Chinese economy of Southeast Asia.

Despite the strategic, technological, and financial advantages of the British, the colonial takeover of the Chinese economy of Singapore was slow and tentative. Because British forces were so few and the Chinese were so numerous, the British first had to cooperate with the Ngee Heng. The British sought domination only gradually, until finally the economic center of gravity shifted in their favor, and the balance of military and policy power followed suit.

Several circumstances aided the British takeover of the economy, including demographic and economic changes. As the Chinese population increased, cultural and linguistic differences in the population became more important. One source of tension in the 1850s was the status of the newly arriving Hokkien migrants, many fleeing the disturbances then sweeping southern China. Colonial government records indicate that between 10,000 and 20,000 Chinese arrived in Singapore annually during these years. It was during the 1850s that the subethnic balance of Singapore's Chinese population decisively shifted. Until 1848, the Teochews had made up the largest speech group in Singapore (Siah 1848, 290). By 1860, however, the Hokkiens comprised the largest speech group and were beginning to crowd the Teochews in the pepper and gambier plantations. The eruptions of violence in Singapore after 1846 were not simply the result of different speech groups. Rather, the violence indicated that the balance of numbers and economic power was shifting toward the Hokkiens during the 1840s and 1850s.

At the same time, Roman Catholic Chinese planters appeared in Singapore and were themselves grouped together by French priests from the *Société des Missions Etrangères* in communities called *hongkah*. The Catholics thus appeared as communities separate from the Ngee Heng's kongsis and clearly represented a challenge to their authority. These may have been the 400 Cantonese planters mentioned by Seah Eu Chin (see note 3).

These demographic shifts complicated the ethnic structure of the agricultural population. To these changes were added the declining Chinese market in gambier and the stresses of the depression of 1830–35. In 1834, the British Parliament decided to remove the duty on the import of gambier to Britain. In 1836, gambier exports to Britain totaled 9,921 pikuls, or over 25 percent of all gambier exported from Singapore. This was a new development. Taken together, these conditions presented Europeans and their Chinese allies with an opportunity to invest in cultivation of gambier on new terms that brought about a major restructuring of the gambier economy.

Chinese allies of the British, such as Seah Eu Chin, began to invest heavily in gambier planting (Trocki 1979, 94–95). It appears that Seah was not associated with the Ngee Heng Kongsi and the Teochews who had initially established pepper and gambier planting in Singapore. An indication of his independence from groups like the Ngee Heng was the establishment of his own kongsi, the Ngee Ann, at about this time in order to mobilize his own support base within the Teochew community. This was not a secret society and appears to have existed outside the Ngee Heng's orbit.[12] At the same time, other wealthy Chinese began to organize their own planting efforts, but it is uncertain whether these were undertaken with the cooperation of the Ngee Heng. Later evidence suggests that at least some may have operated outside its umbrella.

With increased amounts of capital now flowing into the plantations, British merchants became more concerned about the conduct of the gambier business. There were several attempts at control aimed in part at protecting investments. These included policies to bring the gambier plantations under European law as well as attempts to manipulate and divide the Ngee Heng and Chinese mercantile factions in Singapore. In 1841, John Turnbull Thomson arrived to take up his duties as government surveyor, and the government began to consider issuing land titles and collecting quit rents and other land taxes from the planters who had hitherto been ignored by the state (Buckley 1903, 363). This eventually led to the introduction of European economic principles into the Chinese economy. In 1856, Seah Eu Chin took out titles on an entire block of plantations.[13] This acknowledged the principle of bourgeois private property where it had never existed and thus removed the land from the Ngee Heng's control.[14] The expansion and prosperity of this period caused the first fracture lines in the originally unchallenged dominance of the Ngee Heng.

The First Secret Society Riots

Tensions began building among the gambier planters in the early 1840s. Many newspaper articles commented on disputes between Chinese planters over land and timber rights. At about this time a new secret society emerged, and by 1845 or 1846, polarization among the factions led to a clash between two large and well-organized Chinese groups in Singapore. This situation must be seen in the context of similar and related developments in Riau and Johor. Secret society fighting erupted in Riau and spread to Singapore. The plantation economy was extended to the neighboring territory of Johor to relieve overcrowding. This expansion was initiated by the Ngee Heng itself and marked the migration of a significant part of the society's organization to Johor in March and April 1846, just when street fighting was breaking out in Singapore (Trocki 1979, 104–109).

The Singapore newspapers reported that the secret society had split as a result of the death of an old leader. This event led to the so-called Chinese funeral riots. The new secret society was known as the Kwan Teck Hui (Comber 1959, 42–45, 60–63; Wynne 1941, 101–2). Newbold indicates that this new society had been formed after 1840 and that it was a Hokkien society. Describing the reaction of the Tiandihui, or Ngee Heng, to the establishment of the Kwan Teck Hui, he remarked,

> They are strongly suspected of concerting and executing most daring robberies and murders, particularly at Singapore where a large body resides among the jungles and fastness in the interior of the island. This body consists chiefly of the emigrants from Canton, and there does not exist much good-will between it and the Fokien society, lately established in the town of Singapore. (Newbold 1841, 134)

The riot in Singapore seems to have been the result of either inept police work or possible collusion between the superintendent of police and the Kwan Teck headman. The head of the Tiandihui in Singapore, a man known as Ho Yam Ko or Ho Ah Yam ("*Ko*" simply means "elder brother," a common title for a secret society leader), had died. The members of the society had applied to the police for a permit for the procession, but there had been a disagreement over the route. The leaders wanted the procession to go from the temple on Rochore Road through the middle of Kampong Glam and then on to the Chinese burial ground near the military cantonment on the western side of the town. The police denied such permission because it led through the territory of the other secret society.[15] They designated another route, which would follow Rochore Road and then skirt the most populous part of Kampong Glam. The police also limited the number of people allowed to march in the procession.

The regulations no doubt frustrated the Ngee Heng members, and they were certainly suspicious of the government's sincerity and sympathies when, on the day of the procession, they saw one Ho Cheo Teck (or Chew Tock) walking beside the police superintendent as his "interpreter." Ho Cheo Teck was the head of the Kwan Teck Hui. Some 2,000 to 3,000 members of the Kwan Teck Hui were gathered at the intersection leading to Kampong Glam. The funeral procession was led by the head of the Ngee Heng, Chew Swee, who had with him 6,000 members. When the procession attempted to turn into Kampong Glam the police formed a line to stop them. A police officer called Chew Swee to ask why he had broken the rule. Suddenly there was a great deal of noise and confusion, and then the police moved to arrest some coolies, and the riot began (Comber 1959, 65–73; *SSR* BB 63, no. 218). The governor later reported that both headmen of the societies had been beaten up and that the chief culprits were "a party of coolies from the Jungle who appeared to be unknown to both parties"(*SSR* R 13, no. 66, 446). Actually, it was not much of a riot. After a few people were beaten, the two crowds were separated and the Ngee Heng marchers continued their procession according to the police plan. This clash marked the beginning of a period of conflict between the two societies in and around Singapore that continued for several months.

Many observers have simply accepted the explanation given by Wilfred

Blythe in his *The Impact of Chinese Secret Societies in Malaya*, which points to "ideological" differences. He noted that a funeral was an important event for the Chinese, one where they could display the wealth, power, and prestige of the deceased. He pointed out that funeral processions were frequent occasions for secret society fights.

> A procession provided a setting for the display of power and arrogance by the society, and the opportunity was frequently sought when members were thus massed together, bearing the emblems and insignia of their brotherhood, to insult members or officials of rival societies as a result of which a quarrel would flare up. (Blythe 1969, 67–68)

Certainly there was an element of ethnic and group rivalry involved in the riot, but Blythe's explanation takes no note of prevailing economic and social conditions that contributed to the conflict.

Events in Riau link these disturbances to the pepper and gambier and opium economy. Observers in Singapore noticed the prominence of individuals from Riau. On March 14, 1846, Tan Tock Seng, an important Straits Chinese merchant, wrote a letter to the resident councillor, Thomas Church, complaining of another disturbance that he had witnessed. He asked for action from the government, pointing out that some of the participants had come from Riau (*SSR* BB 63, No. 227; *SSR* R 13, p. 447). In his report, Church asked for additional military support as he felt the disturbances would continue.

> It appears a bitter and hostile feeling exists between the members of the two Secret Societies, Tan Tay Huey [Tiandihui or Ngee Heng] and Quan Yah Huey [Kwan Teck Hui] and both parties are prepared to proceed to open violence; I have been confidentially informed by the Resident of Rhio that at Bintang there had been most sanguine contests between the members of the rival Hueys, accompanied by the burning of Villages and considerable loss of life, a goodly number of the adverse party have crossed over to Singapore and are industriously engaged in exciting and fomenting disturbances with a view to revenge. (*SSR* CC 16, no. 315)

The disputes at both Singapore and Riau were fought between members of the two rival societies that had branches in both places. The refugees from Riau no doubt added to the ferocity of the battle against the Kwan Teck Hui in Singapore.

After the March 3 riot, other disturbances took place. A disturbance reported by Tan Tock Seng on March 14 was followed by a gunfight on March 19 between the members of the two societies in Kampong Glam. On March 30, a gang of Ngee Heng members attacked and robbed the house of Thomas Hewetson, a magistrate's clerk. Although a truce was announced between the two societies toward the end of March, later events indicate that ill-feeling still ran very deep (Buckley 1903, 445–446; Comber 1959, 71–73; *SFP* 19 March 1846).

The following year a party of Ngee Heng members launched a devastating attack on their rivals, led by Neo Liang Guan, a refugee from Riau who had settled in Singapore and had become fairly wealthy. Neo owned several plantations around Seletar. In 1847, he organized a daring raid against the pepper and gambier plantations, or *bangsals*, which had been opened, presumably by Kwan Teck affiliates, on Galang Island.

> Their plans were laid with the greatest skill, and the effect was most complete. They took the inhabitants of the different *bangsals* or *kampongs* most completely by surprise, affording time neither for defense nor escape. The inhabitants were given to the sword, while everything in the different *kampongs* was destroyed, the houses and their furniture being burnt, and all trees, pepper vines and gambier plants cut up and laid waste. Twenty-eight . . . plantations were thus treated in the course of one night, upwards of one hundred persons having been killed; their bodies having been found, in nearly every case, deprived of the heads, and shockingly mangled and disfigured. (Buckley 1903, 463–64)[16]

The two secret societies represented two factions fighting for control of the pepper and gambier agriculture, in both Singapore and Riau. In both places the Kwan Teck appears to have gained some measure of official support. In Riau, the Kwan Teck Hui's leader was appointed kapitan by the local chief, the Yang di-Pertuan Muda.[17] Even in Singapore, the leader of the Kwan Teck Hui, Ho Chew Teck, had gotten closer to the government than the Ngee Heng leaders. It is difficult, however, to see the face of deep-seated, rival forces in these two societies alone.

Opium Farming Syndicates and the Secret Societies

There is no direct evidence of a connection between the Kwan Teck Hui in Riau and the local revenue farms, but generally the office of kapitan carried with it control of the farms. The Yang di-Pertuan Muda would benefit from the establishment of a rival organization because it would provoke competition for the farms and thus increase his profits. Similar concerns generally motivated the Singapore government. That is to say, the Singapore government could be implicated in the cultivation of both the rival secret society as well as the rival revenue farming syndicate that appeared in Singapore at this time.

In Singapore, a Melaka Chinese named Kong Kiong Tuan, a newcomer, took control of the Singapore farms in 1846 by offering the government a considerable increase in rent. The details of Kong's background are unknown, but his wealth and position might have been connected to the upsurge in tin mining in Melaka during the 1840s. He may also have been related to a Melaka secret society.[18] While Kong's takeover of the Singapore farms was a boon to the government, there was also a losing syndicate, although the records do not indicate the identity of those involved in this syndicate. Subsequently, Kong suffered considerable losses because of smuggling by those whom he had ousted. He was also faced with a threat from Johor, where Temenggong Ibrahim, the local Malay ruler, had opened his own revenue farm to service the plantations newly established in his territories. The Temenggong is said to have entered into an arrangement with a Singapore Chinese merchant known as "Ang Ah."[19] Johor presented less a direct economic threat than a nuisance in that the Johor farmer could easily supplement his income by smuggling *chandu* across the narrow strait to Singapore.

The Johor settlement on the Tebrau River was under the control of a Ngee Heng headman, Tan Kye Soon. It follows that Ang Ah was also connected to the Ngee Heng. In fact, strong evidence suggests that the Temenggong's family had always maintained a close relationship with the society. If secret society and revenue farm alliances crossed borders—and it is almost certain that they did—then it is reasonable to assume that Kong's opponent in Singapore was likewise backed by the Ngee Heng and that Kong himself was probably aligned with the Ngee Heng's opponents, the Kwan Tek. Similar alignments probably extended to Riau as well, and two coalitions of revenue farmers, pepper and gambier merchants and secret societies likely competed for control of the entire area (Trocki 1979, 102–10).

The simultaneity of these events indicates the linkages between two levels of the Chinese economy: between the pepper and gambier kongsis and the opium farm syndicates. The sudden appearance of the Kwan Teck has all the earmarks of an attempted coup by a well-financed clique that also had good relations with the European and Malay power structures in Singapore and Riau. Newbold's comment that the Kwan Teck was formed in the *town*, and not the countryside, adds further support to the assumption that Kong Kiong Tuan and the Kwan Teck were both part of the same operation. Another factor in the equation was the question of ethnicity. Kong Kiong Tuan was a Hokkien Baba, a Melaka-born Chinese. The circumstances suggest that the Kwan Teck may have been composed of newly arrived Hokkien coolies in alliance with well-established Baba merchants who had the backing of the colonial power structure in both Singapore and Riau.

The progress of the conflict and the ultimate outcome are somewhat difficult to trace. The Kwan Teck Hui disappeared after these riots and was never heard from again. Kong and his Hokkien affiliates appear to have won the first round in the struggle in 1846, by virtue of getting the Singapore farms and probably the Riau farms as well. Their victory, however, was short lived. R. Little, who apparently got most of his information from Kong, reported that the fight with his rival was disastrous for Kong and that he was ultimately forced out of the opium farming syndicate altogether. Kong's rival for the Singapore farms appears to have been an alliance of two groups of merchants, Hokkiens and Teochews. The leading Hokkien was Cheang Sam Teo and the Teochew was Lau Joon Tek (Trocki 1990, 94–119).

Both were relative outsiders so far as the farms were concerned. Each seems to have represented a separate constellation of interests and alliances within Singapore's Chinese society. Cheang Sam Teo, according to Yen Ching-hwang, had recently emerged as the head of a major subgroup of the Hokkiens, the Changtai.[20] Their rivals were the Haichang group led by Tan Tock Seng and later by his son, Tan Kim Ching, representing an old Melaka family. From this time until the 1880s, no member of the Tan Tock Seng family, or any Melaka Chinese, held a position in a Singapore revenue farming syndicate. All Hokkiens connected to the opium and spirit farms were in one way or another associated with the Cheang family.

The Cheang family allied with what seems to have been two groups of Teochews. One Teochew clique was dominated by Seah Eu Chin and the Ngee Ann Kongsi. The other group was the remainder of the Teochew planters, *kangchu*, and shopkeepers who were associated with the Ngee Heng and remained separate from the Ngee Ann. The status of their relationship was at best tenuous. Over the course of time, Seah and his family eroded the Ngee Heng's position. The coalition of interests represented by the new revenue farming kongsi entailed a fatal compromise for the Ngee Heng.

The 1847 alliance took this direction because of Ngee Heng's needs at that time. If the Teochew partner, Lau Joon Tek, was also a Ngee Heng headman, as seems likely, he needed both to mobilize the capital to control the farms and to gain the respect of the British government. While the colonial government might have relied on secret society headmen for certain functions, it would not have allowed the revenue farms to fall entirely under the control of a secret society leader. A partnership of sorts appears to have formed between Seah Eu Chin and Lau Joon Tek. This combined Seah's wealth and reputation with the military and political strength of the Teochews in the Ngee Heng. Seah's name lent Lau a certain legitimacy and Seah's wealth behind the farms was apparently enough of a guarantee for the British. Despite his earlier obscurity, Lau dominated the revenue farms for a generation after 1847 and was apparently quite well-known and respected at the time of his death in 1860. Lau and Cheang Sam Teo went on to control the farms for the next thirteen years, while Seah appears to have made his fortune by controlling plantations and acting as a silent partner in the farms. They formed a syndicate that held both the opium and the spirit farms of Singapore and Johor from 1847 until 1860.

How did this resolution of the conflicts of 1846 affect the status of the Ngee Heng? Even though the society reasserted its power both by establishing a base in Johor and by destroying its rivals in Galang, it was seriously weakened in Singapore. Although it may not have been entirely apparent at the time, the center of power had clearly shifted to the town and to groups of very wealthy merchants who were not dependent on the Ngee Heng for their power. The Cheangs and the Seahs were each backed by their own organizations: the Changtai of the Cheangs and the Ngee Ann Kongsi of the Seahs.

The Ngee Heng did not just disappear. It still represented thousands of planters and *kangchu* in the jungles and remained a power among the Chinese of Johor for a long time. The shift in leadership, however, brought a reorientation of the internal organization. The death of the old leader (whose funeral caused the riot) and the subsequent conflict suggests that a new leadership group was emerging in 1846. The departure of Tan Kye Soon to Johor indicates that the rural-based pioneer leaders, the *kangchu*, were losing influence in Singapore to the town-based shopkeepers. The coherence of the rural kongsis, which had been the basis of *kangchu* power, must have also been compromised by the appearance of Hokkien planters and coolies in areas that had previously been dominated by Teochews. Hereafter, divisions appeared in the Ngee Heng that were based either on membership in a *pang*, or speech group, or in a *seh*, a surname group. Within these *pang* and *seh* were powerful family cliques that dominated important businesses and a wide range of economic resources through marriage connections, political influence, patronage, and debt. In late nineteenth-century Singapore, families such as those of Seah Eu Chin, Cheang Hong Lim and Tan Kim Ching were at the apex of Chinese society. Later evidence speaks of the Ngee Heng (now more generally known as the Ghee Hin, following the Hokkien pronunciation) as comprising a Hokkien branch, a Teochew branch, a Hakka branch, and so on. Whether the rise of *taukeh* influence within the kongsis actually caused this ethnic fragmentation within the larger secret society complex is difficult to say, but the two trends seemed to occur together. Wang Tai Peng noted that a similar trend was responsible for the weakening of the Lanfang Kongsi in Borneo.

At the same time, strong tendencies toward exploitation of coolies and the growing predominance of the profit motive over the "share-the-wealth" principle became more evident. Ideals of brotherhood and egalitarianism were probably always more rhetoric than reality, but by the 1860s, even the rhetoric was disappearing. Perhaps the most influential element in this reorientation of the Ngee Heng was the association that the society had formed with the revenue farmers. The strongmen of the societies became the enforcers of the monopolies, and the farmers became the paymasters and the most abundant sources of largesse. By 1860, the society needed the farmers more than the farmers needed it. The appearance of overt ethnic conflict in the 1850s shows the weakness of the Ngee Heng's former unity; and the rise of the surname groups after 1860 is evidence that the opium farmers now drove events.

After 1860, when another split arose in the revenue farming kongsi, the relative weakness of the Ngee Heng was quite apparent. For a decade after Lau Joon Tek's death in 1860, conflict raged for control of the farms. Lines were drawn between the Hokkien kongsi dominated first by Cheang Sam Teo and later by his son, Cheang Hong Lim. Their opponents was a Teochew kongsi dominated by the brother-in-law of Seah Eu Chin, Tan Seng Poh, who at that time controlled the Seah family's substantial economic holdings.[20] Yet another fissure appeared in the revenue farming kongsis in 1864, when the new ruler of Johor, Maharajah Abu Bakar, appointed a different Teochew merchant, Tan Hiok Nee, as the Major China of Johor and he became the holder of the state's opium farm. The Johor group probably represented what remained of the Teochew Ngee Heng organization after it lost much of its control inside Singapore. There was also a split in the Riau farms, which from this time on were even more closely bound to the Singapore farms.

These years of conflict were marked by open clashes between the farmers and their affiliated secret societies. In the end, the two opposing Singapore farmers joined with the Johor *taukeh*, Tan Hiok Nee, and formed what I have described as the "Great Opium Syndicate" of the 1870s (Trocki 1987). This syndicate had the distinction of being the first that succeeded in separating itself from the formal organization of the secret societies. Tan Seng Poh is reported to have formed an enforcement organization made up of the "Seh Tan."[22] This group made its appearance in 1860 as a breakaway component of the Ngee Heng. At that time, the Seh Tan and other surname groups were said to have split from the Ngee Heng. Henceforth, the Seh Tan was Tan Seng Poh's private army. He employed them as his revenue police, and alternatively as smugglers in his attempts to break his competitors. The final settlement of the Great Syndicate seems to have institutionalized the Seh Tan as the revenue farm army and resulted in a considerable loss of power and prestige by the old kongsi brotherhood. Tan Seng Poh's victory was not simply his control of the opium farm, however; the real prize was control of the entire pepper and gambier industry in Singapore and its surrounding area.

The only successful secret society of the 1860s and 1870s was the Ghee Hock Hui, which also emerged in 1860 as a breakaway from the Ngee Heng. Most scholars have identified it as having been largely Teochew and dominated by Chua Moh Choon.[23] Chua was known as a pepper and gambier dealer and most prominently as a coolie broker. The Ghee Hock was largely a crimping organization that dealt in the trade in human labor centered in Singapore.

The loss of the Ngee Heng's claims to a legitimate source of income, whether from opium or from pepper and gambier, constituted a serious erosion of the links between the "respectable" Chinese elites and viable "popular" organizations. This marked the beginning of the end for secret societies in Singapore. They began the slide into illegitimacy, and became subject to regulation and eventual suppression. After a series of riots in the 1870s (the "Veranda Riots" of 1872 and the so-called Chinese Post Office riots of 1876 in Singapore), the Ngee Heng went into a serious decline. While it continued to exist and to show significant membership, its social power declined along with its economic power. At the same time, the colonial government had set up the Chinese protectorate under William Pickering and had begun the process of registering the societies and gradually restricting them.

Conclusions

The 1846–47 events marked the beginning of the Ngee Heng's transformation. Before this time it seems to have been a worker- or at least producer-dominated organization. Henceforth, it came under the domination of the same clique of *taukeh* who controlled the revenue farms. This was not such a great change, since wealthy men had always had great influence within the Ngee Heng. That influence was based to some extent on patronage links which connected them to the planters. These links were consecrated in the brotherhood oaths of the Ngee Heng.

A crucial change took place as the loyalty of the revenue farmers began to shift away from the men on the plantations and toward the colonial state. In the 1850s and 1860s, the society was transformed into an agency of labor control, concerned with domination of the coolie trade with China and with protecting the privileges of the pepper and gambier *taukeh* and of the revenue farmers. The ostensible purpose of securing basic welfare, justice, and fair shares for the coolies and planters was lost as the Ngee Heng joined the establishment and helped itself to a share of the legitimate economy. Outbreaks of violence among the Chinese during the 1850s and 1860s were of two kinds: "ethnic" protests, such as the 1854 Hokkien-Teochew riot, triggered by the inroads of mercantile domination; and attempts to defend or attack the interests of one or another mercantile clique, as in the early 1860s. In fact, elements of both were often present in most conflicts.

Most of the violence in Singapore between 1830 and 1870, whatever its immediate cause, was connected in some way with the pepper and gambier agriculture and its associated financial superstructure. It was linked to deep-seated economic divisions usually rooted in tensions between the opposing ideologies of economic brotherhood and *laissez-faire* capitalism. While the "class struggle" was not always obvious, the conflicts should be viewed in the total context, bearing in mind the economic difficulties, the immediate stakes, and the long-term winners and losers.

Singapore should be analyzed from a Marxist viewpoint because the settlement was founded on the first principle of capitalist economics—free trade. It is the classic model for Gallagher and Robinson's "free trade imperialism" (Gallagher and Robinson 1953). Through Singapore, economies such as those of the Chinese kongsis in the Southeast Asian "periphery" were linked to the global market as dependent commodity producers. Internally, the process was not so simple. Rather, it meant an uncomfortable compromise for the British. The British, both merchants and colonial officials, needed Chinese allies in their attempts to dominate the productive economies of Asia. These allies included members of the Chinese merchant classes and the secret societies themselves.

There are problems with this explanation. Although economic and class factors were the most important causes, ethnicity certainly played a role. Second, much of the evidence is only circumstantial. There are no real internal Chinese sources for this period, and British sources offer few authoritative insights about the aims and motives of the Chinese. Some elements of the story are thus speculative. It is difficult to apply any sort of textbook Marxist analysis to this situation. While there was certainly conflict, it cannot always be identified as class-based, or even economically motivated. This is especially true of the treatment of the Ngee Heng and the extent to which it was an agency of Chinese working-class interests. Typically, these conflicts have been explained as manifestations of ethnic animosity, and with good reason. However, the evidence offered here shows that ethnicity and other such "cultural" factors must be understood within the fundamental economic struggle.

The ultimate collapse of the Ngee Heng's legitimacy constituted an absolute loss of power for the Chinese of Singapore. In the nineteenth century, the secret society constituted the only vehicle capable of mobilizing the Chinese masses for what might be termed "political" action. Its actions may appear traditionalist, reactionary, and inchoate to outsiders, but during this period, it was the only social entity with which many migrant Chinese could identify and in which they could find a source of community. To the colonial powers, this community represented real political competition, and thus it had to be destroyed. With the destruction of this community, secret societies turned to criminal activities: extortion, kidnapping, prostitution, illegal drugs, and gambling. Singapore Chinese culture was thus stripped of its political dimension, and the community was fragmented. Until the appearance of "modern" political entities such as the Kuomintang (Nationalist Party) and the Communist Party in the 1920s, there was no political community that sought to stand for the average Chinese. Both parties suffered the same fate as the Ngee Heng and were prosecuted and oppressed with the same legal measures that had been erected to destroy the secret societies. Neither Singapore nor Malayan Chinese were allowed to organize politically.

In one sense, this history describes a kind of trajectory in which a marginal and sometimes criminal organization left China, gained social legitimacy through its control of productive enterprises, and then lapsed back into marginality. As it lost a role in the legitimate economy, it was ultimately recriminalized. This criminalization was partly the work of the colonial state and the European merchants acting as agents of free trade imperialism. The Ngee Heng was exactly what the British accused it of being: an *imperium in imperio*. It had to be destroyed because it gave voice to the people and the society that colonialism sought to control.

This destruction also required the cooperation of locally based Chinese merchants. Initially, they had accepted the Ngee Heng as an integral element of their economy. By defecting to the colonial economic powers, they undercut the economic foundations of the secret societies. They further crippled the social prestige of the Ngee Heng by developing the same institutions that had marginalized it in China: clan groups, surname groups, family businesses, and other organizations stressing "exclusivist" regional and ethnic identities over the all-inclusive "brotherhood" ethic of the Ngee Heng.

It is ironic that the merchants' power also declined over time. Their predominance depended on two factors: control of agriculture production and control of the revenue farms. With the decline of plantation agriculture, they lost their usefulness to the colonial government. In 1880, a group of *taukeh* from Pinang who had grown wealthy from the tin mines of the western Malay states were able to buy the Singapore revenue farms out from under the successors of Cheang Hong Lim and Tan Seng Poh. The lesson of these events was that wealthy Chinese would be treated as the legitimate leaders of the "community," but only on the basis of wealth and their acceptance by the colonial state. They could own property, but not wield political power. At any given time, they could be replaced by someone else with a little more money.

The Chinese mercantile elite had been fashioned into an instrument of colonial control. They could exploit the masses, as it were, but they could neither seek to win their support nor exercise control on the basis of popular approval. Thus Chinese society in Singapore was divided, with the colonial police in the form of the "Chinese Protectorate" standing between the elite and the masses. The process that occurred in nineteenth-century Singapore was not unique in the way it affected the Chinese. In fact, it was the very core of European colonialism. Indigenous institutions that could give voice to what J. S. Furnivall has termed the "social will" could not be permitted to stand in any society (Furnivall 1956: 304–5). It was this delegitimation of popular institutions that facilitated the takeover of the economic resources of the region by global capitalism, and allowed the incorporation of Southeast Asia into its periphery.

Notes

Parts of this chapter are based on my book, *Opium and Empire: Chinese Society in Colonial Singapore, 1800–1910* (Ithaca: Cornell University Press, 1990). Earlier versions were read by Benedict Anderson, Jean DiBernardi, Heng Pek Koon, Audrey Kahin, Donald Nonini, and G. William Skinner. Their comments and criticisms helped me avoid many errors.

1. "Ngee Heng" (Mandarin pinyin *yixing*) has been translated as "righteousness rising," or "justice aroused." Kongsi (Mandarin pinyin *gongsi*) means "company," "association," or "partnership." I will use the colloquial "kongsi" rather than the Mandarin version, since the local pronunciation and spelling of this term has passed into common usage.

2. Parkinson 1960; Wynne 1941; and most other colonial writers have assumed that the Ngee Heng of Singapore and the "Ghee Hin" of Pinang were branches of the same institution. They give no evidence that there was a connection between the Singapore and Pinang secret societies, and there is no circumstantial evidence to link the secret societies of the two areas in any practical way. The names were written with the same Chinese

characters, and their relationships to the local economy may have been comparable, but they were components of different solar systems and revolved around different suns: one based on planting and centered in Singapore and one based on mining and centered in Pinang. This autonomy may have broken down after 1870, when communications improved and local economies began to interact more regularly.

3. Blythe 1969; Comber 1959; and Wynne 1941 all give extensive accounts of these disturbances as well as their own explanations of secret society violence. The major outbreaks occurred in 1846, 1852, 1854, 1861, and 1870–71, with other less significant events throughout the late nineteenth century.

4. Siah (1848, 290) gives the breakdown of Singapore's Chinese population by speech group and by occupation ca. 1848. He shows that Teochew pepper and gambier planters numbered 10,000 out of a total of 39,700 Chinese. There were 19,000 Teochews altogether, including 200 listed as pepper and gambier dealers. There were 9,000 Hokkiens of whom there were 100 pepper and gambier dealers and no pepper and gambier planters. There were 6,000 Cantonese (listed as "Macao") of whom 400 were pepper and gambier planters. There were also 1,000 Melaka Chinese, 4,000 Hakkas, and 700 Hainanese.

5. This was a general category of commerce at the time that included many natural products of the rain forest, including camphor, damar, gutta percha, and other types of resin and tree sap, different types of wood, aromatics, peacock and bird of paradise feathers, animal skins, horns, antlers, and so on.

6. While I do not fully accept the content that Lee has given this social construct, I do believe that it existed among the European merchants of the port. Certainly, there were, both in Singapore and in England, allied forces who actively promoted the establishment and practice of laissez-faire economic principles. It is unlikely that Chinese merchants ever fully understood or fully shared the philosophy of Adam Smith; nonetheless, there was clearly a group that saw personal advantage in allying themselves with Europeans and who, as time went by, found less and less advantage in making common cause with the secret societies and the social order they represented.

7. The opium farm regularly contributed between 40 percent and 60 percent of the locally collected revenue of Singapore for every year between 1820 and 1920 (Trocki 1990, 96–97, 188).

8. Throughout this chapter, "$" refers to Spanish silver dollars, originally minted in Mexico and later in other parts of North and South America. These were brought to Asia first by the Spanish galleon trade and after the American Revolution by Yankee shippers. By the eighteenth century, they became the general circulating currency of Southeast and much of East Asia. They had the same value as all American silver dollars of the period and were valued at 4 shillings on $2.60 to Pound Sterling. Two Indian rupees (Rs) were worth about $1.

9. I have discussed the revenue farms of Singapore in some detail in Trocki 1987 and 1990. In addition to opium, there was a spirit farm, a pig farm, a pawnbroking farm, a *sirih* (betel nut) farm, a *baang* (ganja) farm, and, for a few years, a gambling farm in Singapore. Similar systems operated in all the colonies of Southeast Asia in the nineteenth century. See, for instance, Rush 1990.

10. Little (1848, 20–21) remarks on the large number of opium dens located on the streets frequented by coolies and planters from the jungles.

11. A pikul is equivalent to 133.3 pounds and is comprised of 100 catties (1.33 lb.), which are divided into 16 tahils (taels) of 1.33 oz. each.

12. Yen (1986, 185–91). Yen's analysis of the divisions within the Teochew community focuses on the emergence of Seah Eu Chin's group, which was initially called the Ngee Ann Kun in 1830. In 1848, it was renamed the Ngee Ann Kongsi. It was essentially

an alliance of Teochews around a temple and a burial society. From the 1830s to the 1880s, Seah and his sons dominated both the Ngee Ann Kongsi and the Teochew community in Singapore. However, in the 1880s other Teochew groups, dissatisfied with Seah's leadership, came to positions of authority and ultimately organized a powerful financial clique around the Sze Hai Tong or Four Seas Bank, which still exists.

13. In 1856, he claimed the ownership of several plantations when the government finally decided to issue titles to those who could afford to pay a rate of Rs5 to Rs10 per acre ($2.50 to $5) depending on the locality. He offered a flat rate of $40 per plantation and gave the government $4,760 for 119 plantations on February 18, 1856, and a week later deposited an additional $2,400 for 60 more plantations (cf. *SSR* AA 35, 68, Resident Councillor to Governor, 14 March 1856).

14. Before this time, Chinese planters had simply occupied empty land and then moved on when the soil was exhausted. Gambier planting was characterized as a form of "shifting cultivation." In any case, the concept of land values, the issuance of title deeds and the collection of quit rents in the region was entirely a British innovation, and only became enforceable as the population increase made land a relatively scarce commodity and improvements in communications made the lands accessible to the state.

15. The city of Singapore was divided into areas dominated by different ethnic groups and by certain secret societies. Mak Lau Fong (Mak 1981, 79, and 136–37) has a detailed treatment of the ethnic mapping of Singapore.

16. While there is no indication of what subsequently became of Neo Liang Guan, his *bangsal* on the Seletar River represented the pioneering settlement, which later became Chan Chukang and Nam To Kang; later the area was renamed Nee Soon Village (Pitt 1987, 195–96; and *SSR* U 13, 56–57). As an aside here, it is worth noting the impunity with which Neo and Ngee Heng operated in the Singapore countryside. This village was not even on British maps until the 1860s. In the mid-nineteenth century, the entire northern two-thirds of the island were dotted with these *kang* settlements, many of which still exist today. All were founded by Ngee Heng pepper and gambier planters and represent continuing reminders of the "pepper and gambier society."

17. This chief, also known as the Yamtuan Muda, or as the "viceroy" of Riau by the Dutch, was the descendent of the Bugis warriors who had established themselves under the sultan in the early eighteenth century.

18. I am grateful to Sharon Carstens for suggesting this connection. While there was a link between Singapore farms and the Riau and Johor farms in the 1840s, it is not clear that the Melaka farms were related to the Singapore farms at that time. Later on, in the late 1860s and 1870s, the Melaka farms were regularly held by the same syndicates that held the Singapore farms. Comber's contention (Comber 1959, 40–42) linking the Melaka Chinese to the Kwan Teck Hui may point to Kong's alliance with a Melaka secret society.

19. This was probably the merchant Sim Ah Nga who was later involved in a partnership with Tan Seng Poh. It is likely that he was one of the major participants in the kongsi formed by Cheang Sam Teo and Lau Joon Tek.

20. Yen Ching-hwang (Yen 1986, 177–91) shows a division between the two Hokkien place-of-origin subgroups: the Haichang (H'ai Ch'ang) founded by Tan Tock Seng and the Changtai (Ch'ang T'ai) of Cheang Sam Teo. Each was backed by the foundation and support of various temples, cemeteries and other "charitable" organizations. Both were subgroups of the Zhangzhou Hokkiens otherwise known as "Hokkiens."

H'ai Ch'ang	*Ch'ang T'ai*
Tan Tock Seng (1839–60)	Cheang Sam Teo (1846–60)
Tan Kim Ching (1860–92)	Cheang Hong Lim (1863-ca.1900)
T'ien Fu Kung Temple	Ch'ing-yuan chen chun Temple

Even though Yen maintains that these groups were rooted in places of origin in China, both were also intimately connected with the leadership of certain wealthy patrons. It was not enough just to be from that county; membership in the group also signified acceptance of the patronage of the leading families.

21. Song Ong Siang (Song 1967, 19–20 and 131) reports that Seah Eu Chin had married the daughter of the "wealthy Kapitan China of Perak." After she died, he married her younger sister. The girls' younger brother, Tan Seng Poh, came to Singapore to live with the Seah household, and he took over the management of the businesses in 1864 when Seah Eu Chin retired.

22. *Straits Times*, 27 April 1861, carried an interview with the secret society leader Chua Moh Choon, who stated that the Tiandihui or the "Grand Triad Hoey," or the "Hoey of the Heaven and Earth and Man connection" had broken up into its component *seh* or clan groups, because the former "grand master" had recently died. See my discussions of these events in Trocki 1987 (70–71), and 1990 (128–29).

23. The idea that the Ghee Hock was a breakaway from the Ngee Heng is suggested by the fact the Chinese characters for Ngee Heng are carved on Chua's headstone, which was discovered in Singapore in 1989 (Trocki 1990, 157, n. 21).

References

Abdullah bin Abdul Kadir, Munshi. 1970. *The Hikayat Abdullah*, trans. A. H. Hill. Kuala Lumpur: Oxford University Press.

Blythe, Wilfred L. 1969. *The Impact of Chinese Secret Societies in Malaya: A Historical Study*. London: Oxford University Press

Buckley, Charles Burton. 1903. *An Anecdotal History of Old Times in Singapore*. Repr. Kuala Lumpur: University of Malaya Press, 1965.

C. K. 1893. "Yap Ah Loi." *Selangor Journal* 12, no. 1: 184–85.

Cameron, John. 1865. *Our Tropical Possessions in Malayan India: Singapore, Penang, Province Wellesley, Malacca*. Repr. Kuala Lumpur: Oxford University Press, 1965.

Comber, Leon. 1959. *Chinese Secret Societies in Malaya, A Survey of the Triad Society from 1800 to 1900*. New York: Association of Asian Studies.

Cushman, Jennifer W. 1975. "Fields from the Sea: Chinese Junk Trade with Siam during the Late Eighteenth Century and Early Nineteenth Centuries." Ph.D. diss., Cornell University.

_____. 1991. *Family and State: The Formation of a Sino-Thai Tin Mining Dynasty 1797–1932*. Singapore: Oxford University Press.

Furnivall, J.S. 1956. *Colonial Policy and Practice: A Comparative Study of Burma and Netherlands India*. New York: New York University Press.

Gallagher, J., and R. Robinson. 1953. "The Imperialism of Free Trade." *Economic History Review* 6: 1–15.

Lee Poh-ping. 1978. *Chinese Society in Nineteenth and Early Twentieth Century Singapore: A Socioeconomic Analysis*. Kuala Lumpur: Oxford University Press.

Little, R. 1848. "On the Habitual Use of Opium in Singapore." *Journal of the Indian Archipelago and Eastern Asia* 2, no. 1 (January): 1–79.

Mak Lau Fong. 1981. *The Sociology of Secret Societies: A Study of Chinese Secret Societies in Singapore and Peninsular Malaysia*. Kuala Lumpur: Oxford University Press.

National Archives of Singapore. 1987. *A Pictorial History of Nee Soon Community*. Singapore: Grassroots Organisations of Nee Soon Community, National Archives, Oral History Department.

Newbold, T. J. 1841. "The Chinese Secret Society of the Tien-Ti-Huih." *Journal of the Royal Asiatic Society (JRAS)* 5, no. 6: 120–58.

Ng Chin-keong. 1976. *The Chinese in Riau: A Community on an Unstable and Restrictive Frontier.* Singapore: Research Project Series, no. 2, Institute of Humanities and Social Sciences, College of Graduate Studies, Nanyang University, December.

Parkinson, C. Northcote. 1960. *British Intervention in Malaya, 1867–1877.* Singapore: University of Malaya Press.

Pitt Kuan Wah. 1987. "From Plantations to New Town: The Story of Nee Soon." In National Archives, *The Development of Nee Soon Community.* Singapore: Grassroots Organisations of Nee Soon Constituency, Oral History Department, National Archives, 195–96.

Rush, James R. 1990. *Opium to Java: Revenue Farming and Chinese Enterprise in Colonial Indonesia, 1860–1910.* Ithaca, NY: Cornell University Press.

SFP. Singapore Free Press, various dates, Singapore National Library.

Siah U Chin (Seah Eu Chin). 1848. "The Chinese of Singapore." *Journal of the Indian Archipelago and Eastern Asia* 2: 283–90.

Song Ong Siang. 1967. *One Hundred Years History of the Chinese in Singapore.* Singapore: University of Malaya Press.

SSR. Straits Settlements Records, 1819–67. Singapore National Archives (Vols. A-Z, AA, etc.).

Trocki, Carl A. 1976. "The Origin of the Kangchu System, 1740–1860." *Journal of the Malaysian Branch, Royal Asian Society* 49, pt. 2: 132–55.

_____. 1979. *Prince of Pirates: The Temenggongs and the Development of Johor and Singapore 1784–1885.* Singapore: Singapore University Press.

_____. 1987. "The Rise of Singapore's Great Opium Syndicate, 1840–1886." *Journal of Southeast Asian Studies* 18, no. 1 (March): 58–86.

_____. 1990. *Opium and Empire: Chinese Society in Colonial Singapore, 1800–1910.* Ithaca, NY: Cornell University Press.

Turnbull, C. M. 1975. *The Straits Settlements: From Indian Presidency to Crown Colony 1824–1867.* Singapore: Oxford University Press.

Vaughan, J. D. 1879. *Manners and Customs of the Chinese in the Straits Settlements.* Singapore: Mission Press.

Wang Tai Peng. 1977. "The Origins of Chinese *Kongsi* with Special Reference to West Borneo." M.A. thesis, Australian National University.

Wong Lin Ken. 1960. "The Trade of Singapore, 1819–1869." *Journal of the Malaysian Branch, Royal Asian Society* 35 (December).

Wynne, Mervyn Llwellyn. 1941. *Triad and Tabut: A Survey of the Origins and Diffusion of Chinese and Mohammedan Secret Societies in the Malay Peninsula 1800–1835.* Singapore: Government Printing Office. (Released in 1957 with an introduction by W. L. Blythe).

Yen Ching-hwang. 1986. *A Social History of the Chinese in Singapore and Malaya, 1800–1911.* Kuala Lumpur: Oxford University Press.

5

Chinese Culture and Polity in Nineteenth-Century Malaya: The Case of Yap Ah Loy

Sharon A. Carstens

On a side wall in the ancestral hall of the Yap Clan Association, located in the heart of Kuala Lumpur's Chinatown, hang pictures of the last three Chinese kapitans of nineteenth-century Kuala Lumpur: Yap Ah Loy, Yap Ah Shak, and Yap Kwan Seng. The latter two kapitans are shown clothed in the embroidered gowns and conical hats of Mandarin officials; Yap Ah Loy wears a plain black tunic top, wide white trousers, and a small dark circular cap. These two styles of dress caught my attention on my first visit to the Yap Clan Association, their iconography suggesting tantalizing variations in Chinese leadership styles during this period of Malayan history. A closer look at the lives of these men, particularly that of Yap Ah Loy, shows that these variations reflect competing and overlapping views about social status and political legitimacy in nineteenth-century Malayan Chinese society.[1]

The style of leadership most widely written about and clearly dominant in the Straits Settlements by the later decades of the nineteenth century was that of a wealthy, philanthropically oriented Chinese merchant elite (Turnbull 1972; Wang 1981; Yong 1967). At the same time, Chinese leaders in the interior parts of the Malay peninsula between 1830 and 1880 appear to have been men of a different type. In the highly risky and often tumultuous world of the gambier estates of Johor in the 1840s and 1850s, or in tin mining camps in areas of Melaka, Negri Sembilan, Selangor, and Perak from the 1830s to 1880, the leaders were often men known more for their fighting skills and their ability to organize others than for their comparative wealth. Appointed to official positions as kapitan or *kangchu*[2] by local Malay royalty, these Chinese strongmen served simultaneously as military leaders, mediators between the local Chinese and Malays, and private entrepreneurs who eventually amassed considerable wealth for themselves and their families. This wealth, however, did not usually translate into leadership positions for their sons or other kin, as often happened among Chinese kapitans and wealthy merchant leaders in Melaka and Singapore; it was more likely to be passed on to another strongman, often a close associate who had served as bodyguard and partner in various endeavors.

One common interpretation of the relationship between these interior kapitans and the wider political and economic order suggests that dialect-based secret societies served as the connecting link between Straits merchant leaders and leaders of the interior communities.[3] In a classic statement of this model, Gullick (1955, 12) describes how wealthy financiers in the Straits Settlements controlled secret societies, arranging for newly arrived immigrants to be inducted into the appropriate secret society (corresponding with their dialect group) and sent to the interior tin mines funded by the financier. These mines were in turn operated by secret society leaders, including among them the local kapitan, who relied on the Straits merchants for capital and for manpower and who organized the coolies in defense of the mines against challenges from other secret societies in the same area.[4]

Although the neatness of this model has an intuitive appeal, a closer examination of the evidence shows that it fails in both factual and conceptual terms. To begin with, secret societies could and did include members from different dialect groups (Freedman 1960, 36–37; Khoo 1972, 201–25). Second, although there were clear links between certain wealthy Pinang merchants, secret societies, and the tin mining camps in Perak during the 1860s and 1870s, these may have been special cases, for no such relationship can be proved for Singapore or Melaka merchants and other interior areas (Khoo 1972, 201–25). Secret society leaders in Singapore during the mid- to late nineteenth century were not usually wealthy merchants (Lee 1978, 52–53). On occasion, certain Chinese merchants petitioned the British government for protection *against* these very societies (Turnbull 1972, 121).[5]

The conceptual difficulty with Gullick's model lies in its seeming conflation of cultural categories with social groups, a common failure of structural functionalists of his time and later.[6] Chinese society in Singapore and Malaya *did* segment along the lines of dialect, subdialect, territorial, and surname identities. In a world of strangers, these identities were continually used to form dyadic ties with men from similar backgrounds. Such identities could also be used as the basis for organizing more formal groups such as clan or dialect associations, agricultural and mining kongsis, or even secret societies.[7] Yet one did not automatically lead to the other, and even where such groups existed, they could include a heterogeneous membership and involve only a portion of the population.[8]

Other authors who have attempted to untangle the complicated relationships between dialect groups, secret societies, wealthy merchants, and kapitans include Lee Poh-ping (1978), writing on the structure of economic relations in nineteenth-century Singapore, and Mak Lau Fong (1981), examining Chinese secret societies in Singapore and Peninsular Malaya. Both Lee and Mak argue for the primacy of economic motivations, opposing what they identify as "culturalist"

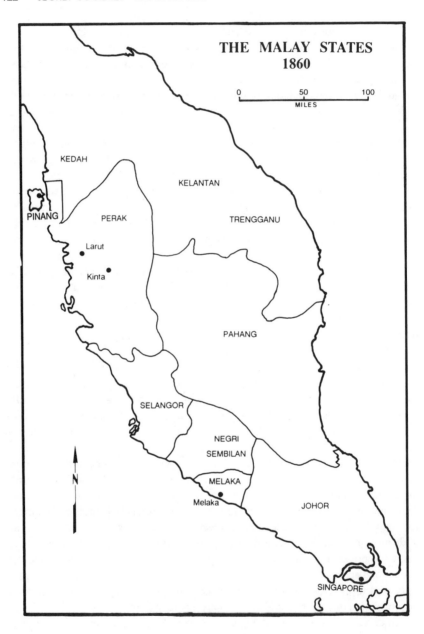

THE MALAY STATES
1860

views that are overly concerned with dialect divisions and secret society ideology derived from mainland China. And both authors also view culture as something distinct from economic and political spheres, and secondary to them. However, while Lee and Mak locate their explanations within the changing political economies of the Straits Settlements and Malaya, they fail to understand the cultural underpinnings and transformations occurring within the very practices they describe. By confining their concept of culture to phenomena such as temples, secret society rituals, and formal ideologies, they overlook the manner in which cultural beliefs and practices, embedded in the daily lives of Chinese immigrants from all social classes, interacted with the wider political economy of the time.[9]

The following analysis attempts to construct a more complicated model of nineteenth-century Malayan Chinese cultural formations in order to better interpret the variations in leadership styles within Chinese society of that period. The view of culture explicitly espoused by this model assumes the interpenetration of economic, sociopolitical, and ideological domains, and suggests that people both consciously and unconsciously draw on a range of cultural values as they seek to understand their worlds and choose between various courses of action (Benjamin 1985, 220–21). Such worlds are always historically situated, shaped by events both internal and external to the people who inhabit them; thus, cultural values must always be understood within their particular historical context.[10] Through examining events in the life of a single individual such as Yap Ah Loy, some of the choices and strategies available to Chinese in nineteenth-century Malaya are thrown into sharp relief. As socioeconomic contexts changed, so too would successful cultural strategies. Yap Ah Loy's life includes both models of leadership already cited. As a young man, his rise to power was associated as much with military prowess and other personal skills as with success in business; yet during the last part of his life, as the local economic and political environment changed, his political style conformed more closely to that of the wealthy merchant elite.[11]

Unlike most other Chinese leaders of this period, especially those operating outside the British-controlled spheres of the Straits Settlements, Yap Ah Loy's life is fairly well documented. This is largely the result of the efforts of S. M. Middlebrook, a British civil servant who, in the 1930s, gathered together personal family documents and information from other sources to construct one of the most detailed biographies of any Chinese Malayan leader of this time. The following account of Yap Ah Loy's life, while heavily indebted to Middlebrook's work, includes additional information from other, sometimes contradictory sources, which are noted in the text. It also pays particularly close attention to the two most important primary sources used by Middlebrook: a record of Yap Ah Loy's life, said to have been produced by Yap Ah Loy himself, hereafter referred to as the "Record" (Anon. 1957), and a short history dictated by his close associate Hui Fatt some time after Yap Ah Loy's death, hereafter referred to as the "Short History" (Hui 18??). These documents offer accounts of Yap Ah Loy's activities from the viewpoints of the participants themselves, and both narratives end in an interesting fashion in 1873 with the close of the Selangor wars before the final rebuilding of Kuala Lumpur, giving special prominence to Yap Ah Loy's rise to power through means other than business success.[12]

Yap Ah Loy: Early Years in Malaya

Yap Ah Loy was only seventeen years old when he traveled in 1854 from his Hakka home in Huizhou prefecture, Guangdong province, to the Malayan port of Melaka.[13] Details of his family background are not known, but his parents were probably poor tenant farmers, unable to provide their son with more than a year or two of lessons in the village school, and no significant economic opportunity if he remained at home.[14] In Melaka, young Yap's first contacts were with kinsmen, men who carried the same surname and who arranged for him to work first in a nearby tin mine and then, upon its closing, as an assistant in a small shop. After a little more than a year, the proprietor of the shop, Yap Ng, advised Yap Ah Loy to return to China, giving him sufficient money for his ticket home. But "fate" appeared to have other things in store for him; while waiting for his ship to sail from Singapore, Yap Ah Loy lost his ticket in a gambling game, leaving him no choice but to stay on.

Yap Ah Loy's next destination was Lukut, at this time a flourishing tin mining settlement in southern Selangor. A certain Yap Fook (identified in the "Record" as a cousin of Yap Ng) helped him find employment here in a tin mining kongsi headed by a Huizhou Hakka named Chong Chong. After working for three years as mining coolie and cook, Yap Ah Loy had saved enough money to begin a pig trading business, which soon expanded from Lukut to include the nearby tin mining area of Sungei Ujong in Negri Sembilan as well. Here he met two other Huizhou Hakkas who were to play important roles in his rise to power: the Chinese kapitan of Sungei Ujong, known as Kapitan Shin (Sheng Ming Li) and his bodyguard Liu Ngim Kong, who invited him to serve as another bodyguard for the kapitan. Yap Ah Loy must also have joined the Hai San secret society, if he did not already belong, for both Kapitan Shin and Liu Ngim Kong are identified by other sources as probable Hai San leaders (Khoo 1972, 117).

In 1860, serious fighting erupted in Sungei Ujong when the Chinese miners rebelled against what they considered excessive taxation by the local Malay chiefs (Khoo 1972, 122). Yap Ah Loy fought with Kapitan Shin's group, which was severely defeated. The kapitan was himself slain, but was rumored to have died a miraculous death when white blood flowed from his severed head, and his body was returned to Melaka for burial. An injured Liu Ngim Kong was treated for his wounds at Yap Fook's kongsi in Lukut and soon after departed for Melaka.

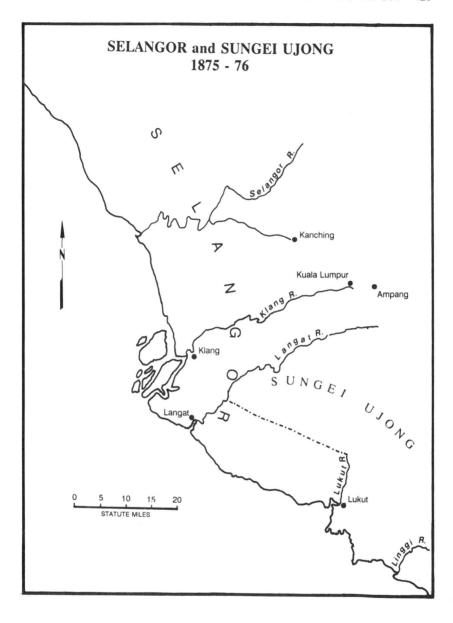

SELANGOR and SUNGEI UJONG
1875 - 76

Although Yap Ah Loy was also wounded in the fighting, he remained in the area, and it was the power vacuum left by Kapitan Shin's death that gave the young Yap Ah Loy, now aged twenty-four, his first opportunity for leadership. It is not entirely clear what his new position entailed or why he was chosen to fill the post he did.[15] Kapitan Shin left behind both a son, known as Ah Sam, and a son-in-law, Lam Ma, a Huizhou Hakka who was later identified as a headman of the Hai San secret society (Gullick 1955, 134; Khoo 1972, 78). Nevertheless, another Hai San headman, a prosperous Cantonese miner named Wong Ying (Khoo 1972, 219) and several others selected Yap Ah Shak, a wealthy Huizhou Hakka merchant with Hai San connections (Gullick 1955, 134), to take over the late kapitan's position. Yap Ah Shak then passed this title to Yap Ah Loy, who proceeded to serve as Sungei Ujong's kapitan for the next year. Middlebrook (1951, 16) comments that Yap Ah Shak must have chosen Yap Ah Loy because of the courage he had displayed as a fighter and his apparent ability to control the miners and maintain order.

No details concerning the nature of Yap Ah Loy's rule as Sungei Ujong's kapitan survive, other than the "Short History's" comment that "peace now reigned in the area." Given the heterogeneous composition of Sungei Ujong in terms of both dialect groups and secret society affiliations, keeping the peace probably presented a considerable challenge,[16] and it may have been the rather precarious nature of this position that convinced Yap Ah Loy to put it aside and journey further north to Selangor in 1862 at the invitation of his old friend Liu Ngim Kong, who was now serving as kapitan for the fledgling but growing settlement of Kuala Lumpur.

The Move to Kuala Lumpur and the Selangor Wars

Yap Ah Loy traveled to Kuala Lumpur in the company of three friends, two of whom remained Yap Ah Loy's close comrades in arms and served as military leaders in the later battles of the Selangor wars. Employed as Liu Ngim Kong's personal assistant and the overseer of his mines, Yap Ah Loy soon began to profit considerably on his own account: within two years he owned two tin mines and had opened a "druggist shop" in town.[17] Shortly after this, Liu Ngim Kong assisted him with arrangements for his marriage to a Melaka Chinese woman, Kok Kang Keown.

Yap Ah Loy also played a leading role in the construction of Kuala Lumpur's first temple, dedicated to the deceased Kapitan Shin of Sungei Ujong, who was believed to have become a powerful god. Reports from Melaka said that a worshipper at the former kapitan's grave had been possessed by his spirit, directing that he henceforth be called Si Sen Ta, a title derived from another Chinese deity already worshipped in temples in Melaka as Thai Sen Ta, and identified as the spirit of a former Chinese government official (Letessier 1893, 320–21). After a series of miracles, a special temple had been erected for Si Sen Ta in

Melaka, with the main body of worshippers being Huizhou Hakkas. However, other Chinese also attended the annual birthday celebrations where religious plays were performed and, through spirit mediums, sought the advice of the deified kapitan in matters of health and business. Reports of these activities must have encouraged Yap Ah Loy and other Huizhou Hakkas in Kuala Lumpur to establish their own branch of this temple at a spot indicated by a Chinese possessed by Si Sen Ta's spirit.

Yap Ah Loy's increasing success in Kuala Lumpur paralleled the flourishing growth of the entire area. Yet it was this very growth that set the scene for the fierce competition over commercial and mining profits soon to follow among Malays and Chinese alike, culminating in the Selangor wars. Within the general vicinity of Kuala Lumpur, two different groups of Hakkas were involved in tin mining development. To the north, in the Selangor River district, Jiayingzhou Hakkas had mined tin around Kanching since the 1840s, while in Ampang and Kuala Lumpur most of the miners were Huizhou Hakkas. As their operations expanded, growing competition over the same resources led to quarrels and fighting.

Although the subdialect division between the two communities was fairly clear, secret society connections were more complex. Shortly after Yap Ah Loy's arrival in Kuala Lumpur, word came that a group of about a thousand Huizhou miners belonging to the Ghee Hin society had been pushed from their mines in intense fighting in Larut (Perak) by members of the Hai San society there. A decision was made to invite these men to come to work in the Kuala Lumpur mines, even though Liu Ngim Kong, Yap Ah Loy, and probably many others were members of the Hai San secret society.[18] Meanwhile, in Kanching, although the strongest society was the Song Pak Kun, a branch of the Ghee Hin, the Hai San society was also said to be present (Gullick 1955, 135).

Divisions among the Selangor Malay royalty were potentially even more serious. The expansion of tin mining activities in Selangor presented lucrative opportunities to Malay chiefs as well as Chinese, particularly in the collection of revenues on tin and other commodities entering and leaving the state. Unfortunately, the death of Sultan Muhammed of Selangor in 1859 led to three years of succession disputes and the appointment of a weak successor, Raja 'Abdu'l-Samad, who was unable or unwilling to equalize and rationalize the revenues being collected by local chiefs in the five districts of Selangor. Further divisions existed in Selangor between the Malays of Bugis descent who controlled the coastal areas, and thus benefited most from increasing trade revenues, and the Sumatran Malays of the interior. All these conditions contributed to the attack and ultimate seizure of the port of Klang in 1866 by Raja Mahdie, an act that set into motion ten years of civil warfare, first between Malays but eventually including warring factions of Chinese as well.

Liu Ngim Kong, acting kapitan of Kuala Lumpur, traveled to Klang in 1866 in an attempt to mediate between Mahdie and his rival Raja 'Abdu'llah, obviously fearing the possible chaos such disagreement could bring, but he was not successful. Within a year or two, he had become a sick man and began to make arrangements for someone to take over as kapitan after his death. His own succession to the kapitan's post had followed from his close relationship to Kuala Lumpur's first kapitan, Hiu Siew, another Huizhou Hakka reputed to have been a member of the Ghee Hin society (Khoo 1972, 117). There is some indication that Liu Ngim Kong had also seized the personal property of the former kapitan at his death, even though Liu had a son who could have inherited it.

One possible successor to Liu was Yap Si, a Huizhou Hakka and former partner of Hiu Siew. Recent purchases had made Yap Si the largest and wealthiest miner in Kanching, and his acceptance of the position would have united the two areas. But Yap Si was a retiring man and not interested in becoming kapitan, so the choice now settled on Yap Ah Loy. After consulting with the local Sumatran Malay chiefs, Liu Ngim Kong obtained the final agreement of Sultan 'Abdu'l-Samad. Just before his death, he summoned the thirty-two-year-old Ah Loy back from Klang, where he had been looking after Liu Ngim Kong's business interests, and told him of his decision, asking that the young Yap arrange for his body to be buried in Melaka and his personal property protected and passed to his family, who would also return to Melaka.

Yap Ah Loy's ascension to the kapitancy of Kuala Lumpur in 1868 was immediately challenged by "relatives" of the former kapitan, identified as men with the surnames Liu, Kon, and Chong, who claimed rights both in the kapitancy and to Liu Ngim Kong's personal property.[19] The dispute was settled only with assistance from the local Malay chief, Sutan Puasa, who informed the "relatives" that the sultan and local chiefs had already approved Yap Ah Loy's appointment. In keeping with the former kapitan's wishes, Yap arranged his burial, transferred his personal effects to his family, and probably appropriated Liu's business interests for himself. Realizing that he had clearly made enemies in his ascension to power, his first act as kapitan was to recruit more fighters for his personal bodyguard. He also promulgated a list of criminal offenses and their punishments, instituting a public policy of strict law and order reputed to have been very successful (Anon. 1927, 5).

About six months after Liu's death, a new and more serious challenge to Yap Ah Loy's authority was presented by Chong Chong, the Huizhou Hakka who had first employed him in Lukut. Arriving in Kuala Lumpur with about twenty followers during the New Year's celebrations of 1869, Chong Chong visited Yap at his house, but declined to stay with him. Rumors quickly spread of the trouble that he and his men intended to cause during the New Year's festivities, a time when the town was crowded with miners invited by their employers and the kapitan to feast, gamble, and watch theatrical performances. However, close surveillance of the potential troublemakers effectively blocked whatever disorder they might have planned.

According to Middlebrook, Chong Chong had probably assumed leadership of the disenfranchised relatives of Liu Ngim Kong. Failing to dislodge Yap Ah Loy's authority on his home ground, he proceeded to organize opposition among the Jiayingzhou Hakkas in Kanching, the growing rivals of the Huizhou Hakkas of Ampang and Kuala Lumpur. Within a month, and probably at Chong Chong's instigation, the acting headman of Kanching, Yap Ah Loy's friend Yap Si, was murdered while trying to flee to Kuala Lumpur. Chong Chong himself escaped from the area when Yap Ah Loy and his men went to investigate the matter in Kanching, but this incident further poisoned relations between the two camps of Hakkas.

A combination of Malay and Chinese political insecurities appear to have contributed to Yap Ah Loy's first formal installation as kapitan. Raja Mahdie, who had forcibly taken Klang in 1866, was interested in legitimating his own position and in restraining possible disturbances among Chinese in the interior, which would slow the flow of tin and other taxable goods through Klang. His first action was to have two Huizhou Hakkas who were Kuala Lumpur residents but allies of Chong Chong (and thus enemies of Yap Ah Loy) arrested and punished as troublemakers. Next, acting as if he were the sultan's representative, he organized a ceremony to formally invest Yap Ah Loy in the office of kapitan. The festivities of June 1869 included a mixture of Chinese and Malay entertainments, with both Chinese and Malay actors performing *wayangs*.[20] For the formal ceremony, Yap Ah Loy wore the Malay dress of a raja and was flanked by his head fighting men in military uniform. After the proclamation was read and approved by the audience (as the "Short History" says, "things were already destined by heaven and all expressed their approval"),[21] Yap Ah Loy was carried in a sedan chair in a procession through the town in the manner of a Chinese official. Less than a year later, Raja Mahdie was attacked and pushed out of Klang by the sultan's new son-in-law, Tunku Kudin of Kedah.

Yap Ah Loy also took more practical measures to prepare for what appeared to be an inevitable conflict. He had around him a select group of capable men who would prove their talents and their loyalty on numerous occasions in the years ahead. Among them were Voon Siew, Yap Ah Loy's counsel and diplomat; Hui Fatt, his close friend and personal protector; and Chong Piang, his able general in battle.[22] Yap Ah Loy's younger brother was sent to Singapore and then back to China to recruit fighting men. Others were recruited locally, with promises of generous provisions of payment and aid to the families of men killed or wounded in battle.[23] Yap Ah Loy also traveled with eighty men to visit the sultan in Langat to inform him of the unsettled conditions and seek his support. Here he unexpectedly found Tunku Kudin visiting his father-in-law and was now compelled to formally recognize and side with Kudin's position at Klang, thus making a guaranteed enemy of Raja Mahdie.

After the autumn of 1870 followed two years of campaigns and battles between shifting alliances of Chinese and Malays. In the first series of battles, Chong Chong was the main Chinese protagonist, drawing his followers largely from dissatisfied Jiayingzhou Hakkas to the north and south of Kuala Lumpur. Malay forces were led mostly by Sayid Mashor, an avowed enemy of Tunku Kudin, while Sutan Puasa and other local Malay chiefs supported Yap Ah Loy. After a second unsuccessful attack on Kuala Lumpur in June 1871, Chong Chong disappeared from the scene and it is unclear who, if anyone, led Chinese troops against Yap Ah Loy in the final battles resulting in the fall of Kuala Lumpur in 1872. By this point, however, the local Malay chiefs had switched sides, a situation that no doubt contributed significantly to Yap Ah Loy's (temporary) defeat.

The earlier campaigns were directed by Yap Ah Loy from the relative safety of Kuala Lumpur, but when Kuala Lumpur was surrounded by the enemy in 1872, Yap personally assumed command of his troops in the field and appears to have served in this capacity throughout both the retreat from Kuala Lumpur in August 1872, and the successful retaking of the town in March 1873. He was aided in this by Malay soldiers sent from Pahang and, according to one source, the advice of the deity Si Sen Ta as well (C. K. 1893, 185).[24] With the Selangor wars now ended, Tunku Kudin organized a new installation of Yap Ah Loy as kapitan under his authority, with the kapitan wearing Chinese ceremonial robes rather than Malay ones and the ritual following Chinese practices.

Kuala Lumpur Kapitan in a New Era

The British intervention in the Malay States in 1874 brought further important changes to the area. Moving quickly to establish control over revenue collection and the use of force, the British installed police posts at several places in the interior. Even Yap Ah Loy was forced to accept a contingent of six police who lived in his compound and were paid by him.

However, from 1873 to 1879 Yap Ah Loy's problems were more economic than political. Large amounts of capital were needed to restore the mines and buildings devastated by three years of civil war, and laborers had to be recruited or called back to work in these mines. Meanwhile, tin prices remained low, making it increasingly difficult to keep the mines going and to keep his creditors, who included Chinese and British merchants in Melaka and Singapore and the Selangor government, at bay. On the verge of bankruptcy in 1879, Yap Ah Loy was saved by a stroke of luck: a sudden dramatic increase in tin prices. By 1880 he was free of debt and energetically involved in a growing number of new businesses.

The sudden rise in tin prices brought a rush of miners to Kuala Lumpur, swelling the town's population by 30 percent in a single year and convincing the British that their presence in Kuala Lumpur made more sense than it did in Klang. The stationing of the British resident in Kuala Lumpur in March 1880 meant a further diminishing of Yap Ah Loy's power as an administrator, but he continued to serve as magistrate for the settlement of Chinese disputes along with his old friend Yap Ah Shak, who had moved from Sungei Ujong to Kuala Lumpur at the end of the Selangor disturbances.

Yap Ah Loy's most important roles during this period were economic and philanthropic. The kapitan personally held title to approximately two-thirds of the urban property in Kuala Lumpur east of the Klang River, including the main market, the gambling sheds, and the brothels. In addition to controlling the market in tin, he was an enthusiastic supporter of new economic enterprises, installing Kuala Lumpur's first steam pump in his Ampang mine, experimenting less successfully with plantation crops, and operating a brickfield and kiln near town. As a philanthropist, he built a refuge that offered food and shelter for the sick, and he played a leading role in building Kuala Lumpur's first Chinese school.

Yap Ah Loy's dealings with British administrators were considerably more complex than they had ever been with the Malay royalty. Documents in the Selangor Secretariat Files show him borrowing money; seeking reimbursement for roads built at his own expense; acting as spokesman and apologist for Chinese miners accused of disturbing the peace in Ulu Selangor; and requesting naturalization as a British subject.[25] The motivation for this last move, which created some confusion about questions of political sovereignty for the British, was unclear. The colonial documents suggest that he wanted the right to fly the British flag as protection for his ships, but Gullick (1955, 29) mentions possible challenges to Yap Ah Loy's authority from Chinese miners coming from the Straits Settlements who claimed to be British subjects and thus not under the domain of the kapitan China.

Yap Ah Loy was routinely praised by British administrators for his perseverance in developing the Kuala Lumpur area despite great adversity. Nevertheless, as British control expanded, these same administrators could find the kapitan's attitudes about the extent of his power quite exasperating, as noted in the following excerpt from a letter by then Resident Frank Swettenham to the colonial secretary in 1882,

> I asked then to widen and extend some street through his property offering other land in return for what I took. He agreed but he always says what I offer him is his already. I think a letter from the Governor or yourself to him in Chinese setting him right on these points would do much good.[26]

The two main areas where British administrators and Yap Ah Loy clashed were in municipal planning and control of the revenue farms.[27] Although Yap Ah Loy considered control of the farms one of his perquisites as kapitan, the British were determined to use the farms for their own purposes. Thus in 1882 they refused to consider petitions from Yap Ah Loy and other Selangor Chinese requesting that the farms automatically be given to Kapitan Yap, and by opening competition for them to the highest bidder, managed to raise the price paid by

Yap Ah Loy by 330 percent (Chew 1967–68, 71–72). Two years later, in 1884, the British simply decided to give the farms to a group of Hokkien financiers from Pinang, in an attempt to attract new capital into Selangor, much to the displeasure of Yap Ah Loy and his supporters (Gullick 1955, 75).

During this same year Yap Ah Loy made plans for a long-awaited visit to China, asking his friends Yap Ah Shak and Chow Yoke, leader of the Cantonese in Kuala Lumpur and a reputed Ghee Hin headman (Sadka 1968, 181), to take care of his business while he was gone. But his trip was postponed, and toward the end of the year he fell ill. In the middle of April 1885, he died at the relatively young age of forty-eight. According to the family genealogy, in addition to his Melaka wife and her three sons and daughter, he left behind him three other secondary wives, four sons, and three daughters.[28]

Yap Ah Loy's sons were too young to succeed their father as kapitan. After consultation with representatives of the different dialect groups in Kuala Lumpur, the merchant Yap Ah Shak, the same man who had given over the kapitan's position to the young Yap Ah Loy in Sungei Ujong in 1859, was chosen by the British as Selangor's new kapitan. He was succeeded at his death in 1889 by Yap Kwan Seng, another wealthy Huizhou Hakka merchant, who served until his death in 1902, when the position was abolished.

Strategies, Culture, and Context

The constantly shifting events and relationships in Yap Ah Loy's life illustrate well the dynamic interplay between the economic, political, and ideological contexts of particular periods and the possibilities of individual choice, influenced and shaped by cultural values. Affected by factors such as fluctuations in world tin prices, quarrels between Malay royalty, or the changing demography of the tin mining community, Yap Ah Loy and other leaders responded by drawing on culturally constructed ideas about risk and fate and the proper manipulation of social relations to shape their actions. Moreover, the behavior of individuals such as Yap Ah Loy served to change both culture and context, dramatically affecting the choices available to individuals who followed.

The relationship between context and cultural values will be explored in the following sections through a more detailed analysis of the three interpenetrating domains referred to earlier: the economic, the sociopolitical, and the ideological. Of course, culture and context are arbitrary divisions, for contextual elements can always be understood at another level as culturally shaped. In a similar manner, the organization of particular data into these separate domains is, as the arguments about their interpenetration infer, highly artificial, and is used here only as a means to focus our attention on particular issues. Finally, the order of presentation in the following sections, beginning with economic questions, reflects no belief in the priority of this or any other domain.

The extent to which cultural values change with one's position in a society, and the level of hegemonic dominance they may impose, has been a topic of recent interest in studies of Chinese society, most notably in David Johnson's (1985) pioneering article "Communication, Class, and Consciousness in Late Imperial China" and the 1987 collection of articles edited by Hill Gates and Robert Weller on hegemony and Chinese folk ideologies. According to Gates and Weller (1987, 6),

> The concept of hegemony also directs attention toward how the daily experiences of economic systems and class membership help shape ideas, and particularly asks how such ideas may support some groups more than others. This is a more subtle process than attempts at ideological domination; such a cultural hegemony grows naturally out of daily life, and thus carries an inherently convincing quality that may be missing from more clearly manipulative attempts to promote a particular ideology.

The fluidity of social mobility in Chinese Malayan society during this period makes analysis in terms of formal class divisions problematic. Nevertheless, Chinese workers, at whatever level they were actively engaged, were greatly influenced by their participation in particular economic and political spheres, whether serving as mining coolies, petty traders, mining advancers, or large-scale mine owners. How this participation shaped and reinforced cultural values of a hegemonic nature is a question worth asking. Yet a closer look at the constantly changing circumstances suggests that the extent of hegemonic dominance must be treated as an empirical question, tied to factors in the larger socioeconomic context. For example, we will see that changes in systems of labor recruitment and labor availability affected both the working conditions and the forms of payment for the common laborer. Hence, cultural values of risk-taking and beliefs in fate that in one situation might reinforce the dominance of mine owners and advancers, worked in other contexts to benefit common laborers.

Context and Strategy in the Economic Domain

The general economic strategy practiced by Yap Ah Loy throughout his life was fairly typical for Malayan Chinese of this period. The basic pattern for someone who began as a penniless immigrant was to save money earned through one's own labor and then invest these savings in enterprises that would grow and eventually be diversified with further accumulations of wealth. The ultimate success of this strategy was highly variable, depending on both shifting contextual factors and the clever manipulation of a combination of cultural strategies at crucial moments.

The dominant economic enterprise for Yap Ah Loy and for other Chinese working in the Malayan interior after the mid-nineteenth century was tin mining, an industry dependent on world markets, and one whose history in Malaya has been well documented (Wong 1965). A short review of the socioeconomic organization of tin mining at this time illustrates some of the key variables in economic practices and strategies available to miners engaged at various levels. Tin was mined by groups of Chinese organized by financiers who arranged for the necessary supplies to be shipped into the interior to support the miners; made arrangements for sale of the final product (at fluctuating world prices); and paid taxes on supplies and tin (as required first by Malay rulers, then by the British). The capital necessary for opening a tin mine was relatively modest, and the financing of such enterprises was further facilitated by an extensive system of credit operating among merchants, traders, and smaller mine owners. Wages paid to laborers were the major expense for mine owners, making the recruitment of workers a crucial component in any tin mining venture.

The harsh, disease-ridden conditions in the interior posed great risks for would-be miners and steadily depleted the labor pool. The most common source of labor supply before the mid-1870s consisted of new immigrants who traveled to Malaya under the credit-ticket system, working for a set period of time as indentured laborers to mine owners who paid for their passage. One method for extending the period of indenture was to entice the worker into debt through gambling or opium, supplied and controlled by the financiers.[29] Even with such techniques, by 1876 the number of new (indentured) immigrants arriving was insufficient, and labor scarcity had become a problem (Wong 1965, 66–69).

Tin mining was always a risky business, with final profits dependent not only on the quality of ore deposits and world tin prices, but on proper relations with both workers and local authorities. The actual organization of tin mining kongsis and the systems of payment used were combined products of the contextual realm of tin mining and labor availability, and the wider cultural values of Chinese workers. Positions within the kongsi were clearly demarcated in terms of required tasks and forms of payment, from overseers, to clerks, cooks, and common laborers.[30] Yet the exact distribution of the profits from mining depended on several situational factors.

Mine owners and financiers preferred to pay wages to workers according to time worked, providing food and discretionary supplies on credit, while paying actual wages only on an annual or biannual basis. Often the profits made through artificially high prices on provisions were sufficient to keep mine owners in business even when tin prices were low. But labor scarcity enhanced the bargaining power of Chinese workers, leading, among other things, to a steady decline in the markup of provision prices from the mid-1870s on (Wong 1965, 75).

Alternative systems of payment for labor also became more common during this period. Chinese workers, whenever possible, showed a marked proclivity to work for themselves.[31] Chinese coolies often preferred what was known as the *fun-si-ka*, or share system, where laborers worked for a set share in the final profit of the mine, relying on advancers to support the enterprise by supplying money and provisions on credit (Wong 1965, 60–63).[32] If the mine did not pan out, the laborers risked working for free, but if the ore deposits were extremely rich, then share workers had a chance for sizable profits.[33] Another form of payment that emphasized individual initiative but did not bring a similar possibility of great profit for the mining worker was the piece-work system used by mining financiers such as Loke Yew in the later decades of the nineteenth century (Pasqual 1895, 44).

Relations between workers and financiers were, in many respects, always adversarial, with each seeking his own personal advantage at every turn. While financiers are often depicted as having the upper hand through their control of provisions, the sale of opium, and the long terms between wage settlements, workers had their own sets of strategies. These ranged from simple tactics such as faking illness to the more serious absconding of indentured coolies. Workers were also known to strike over a range of issues, from bad food, to reductions in wages, increases in the price of provisions, or attempts to break workers' contracts (Pasqual 1895). Nevertheless, such measures taken by the coolies were mainly defensive (and not revolutionary), for most of them retained the hope of eventually turning the tables and one day becoming employers themselves.

The general economic strategy for getting ahead, practiced by workers and mine owners alike, was, as previously mentioned, founded on hard work, savings, and investment: what Harrell (1985) has labeled "the Chinese entrepreneurial ethic." This ethic assumed, of course, that the poorest man could indeed work his way up the ladder, an assumption mirrored by European observers such as Pasqual, who remarked that he "always looked upon a Sinkheh (newcomer) as a Towkay Labur (financier), Towkay Bantu (advancer), or a Capitan China in embryo, and respected him accordingly" (1895, 102). Yap Ah Loy provided yet another example of this possibility.

A related component in this strategy was the diversification of investments as one's capital increased. Thus we see Yap Ah Loy investing in both a medicine shop and tin mines during an earlier period, and expanding to a great many other enterprises in his later years, including not only plantations and brickyards, but also prostitution houses, gambling booths, and opium farms. The higher up the socioeconomic ladder one climbed, the more likely that "investments" would include enterprises of a somewhat different nature, such as the feasting and entertainment of employees and others; support of bodyguards and other defensive measures; or the building of temples, hospitals, and schools. Of course, the order in which one supported such enterprises reflected somewhat different images of social status and political leadership.

Another set of activities and practices associated with tin mining, while having clear ties to both the sociopolitical and ideological domains, was nevertheless important in shaping and reflecting cultural values linked to economic behaviors. These practices included ceremonial and "ritualistic" activities such as the hiring of Malay *pawangs* (shamans) for divining the location of tin deposits (Hale 1885, 304–5); feasting, burning joss sticks, and shooting firecrackers on a "lucky day" chosen to open a new mine (Pasqual 1895, 27) or to begin smelting the ore (Croockewit 1854, 119); the use of special mining vocabularies that tabooed words whose sounds conveyed unfortunate meanings (Pasqual 1895, 138–39); and lists of behaviors either prescribed or proscribed for their effects on the spirits of the ore (Braddell 1853, 80; Croockewit 1854, 118–19; Hale 1885, 307–9; Pasqual 1895, 139). These practices, many of them embedded in the daily activities of the miners, reflected Chinese folk beliefs in the importance of staying in harmony with the natural and cosmic orders. However, the high level of specifically symbolic activities associated with the mundane world of tin mining must also have derived in part from a general recognition of the intense risks mining posed to both personal and financial health.

We have noted repeatedly that risk and luck were major components in all mining endeavors in the interior. The events of Yap Ah Loy's life clearly demonstrated this central premise, and it is significant that his style of mining was specifically linked to the "superstitious practices" cited above, in contrast to the Kuala Lumpur mining leaders who followed after him (Pasqual 1895, 43–44). These ritualistic activities served as constant reminders of surrounding dangers, offering the miners both instrumental means to seek to control these dangers, and partial explanations for why some men succeeded while others failed. Such explanations related to more generalized Chinese ideas about luck and fate. As Harrell (1987) notes, while Chinese beliefs in fate served as important rationales for differential success among individuals, these "fatalistic" attitudes did not in themselves encourage passivity, for one's current luck or fortune could still be manipulated by knowing when to take risks and when to "play it safe." Thus cultural values emphasizing beliefs in fate may have served hegemonic functions during periods when mining workers had little control over their conditions of employment, but as the situation changed, these same values could provide powerful spurs to enterprising coolies working under the share system or even as entry-level entrepreneurs.

The Sociopolitical Domain

Social relations, and the cultural values that shape them, are in some sense always political, if we understand politics as having generally to do with power and control, and see social relations as a means to influence others or rally people to one's cause (Benjamin 1985, 220–21). This section examines the mix of sociopolitical strategies used by Yap Ah Loy and others of his time, shaped, once again, by the interaction of cultural values and wider contextual features.

Any description of the sociopolitical context of the Malayan interior during the last half of the nineteenth century must include major changes in both population demographics and the identity of the central political authorities. The growth of mining activities in the interior attracted large numbers of single Chinese males from different regions of Southeastern China, who left family and village in search of new economic opportunities. Although no population census figures exist for the period preceding British intervention, reports on individual mining settlements in the present-day states of Melaka, Negri Sembilan, Selangor, and Perak document Chinese mining populations in the thousands, which increased and decreased with the availability of tin deposits and conditions of local political stability.

Competing interests in taxing mining activities among the Malay royalty and the necessity of cooperation with local Malay rulers were important ingredients in the larger sociopolitical situation to which the Chinese had to respond. Both the Malay rulers and the British, during the earlier stages of their intervention in the 1870s, chose to govern Chinese communities by principles of indirect rule, either through kapitans or local headmen who were in turn responsible for the behavior of their compatriots. Some Malay royalty also turned to Chinese kapitans for political and military support in local struggles with competing Malay factions, as happened with Yap Ah Loy. During the last decades of the century, however, the British began increasingly to take over both central administrative and policing functions, leaving the Chinese kapitans with largely advisory and ceremonial roles to play.

The various types of social ties formed by Yap Ah Loy with others during the different stages of his life illustrate well the mix of possible social relations and the appropriate strategies for their use. In general, kinship, surname, home district, and dialect similarities formed a foundation for dyadic ties and more corporate groups among Chinese of this period. Actual blood relatives had the strongest obligation to aid an individual, as the young Yap Ah Loy was assisted on first arrival in Malaya by his relatives, Yap Ng and Yap Fook. Yet kinsmen, for most new immigrants, were in short supply and not necessarily well placed enough to be useful to an ambitious individual. Wider categories of association, based on subdialect or dialect, cast the net much further, allowing for ties like those between Yap Ah Loy and the powerful Kapitan Shin and Liu Ngim Kong.

However, social similarities in and of themselves were not necessarily sufficient for the creation of such social relations, nor did they guarantee cooperation between individuals. Such was clearly the case with Chong Chong, the former Huizhou Hakka employer of Yap Ah Loy, who became his most bitter enemy and eventually served as leader of the Jiayingzhou Hakkas of Kanching. Alternatively, men who shared none of the above-mentioned criteria in common could still develop into friends and allies, as with the Cantonese Ghee Hin headman Chow Yoke, who served as one of Yap Ah Loy's military leaders during the civil war and later became one of his most trusted friends (Gullick 1955, 34). Nevertheless, these "secondary" sorts of ties were inherently more unstable, always subject to challenge by those who possessed the more "primary" bonds of kinship.

Given the variability and individual choice noted in the above sets of social relations, it is useful to review some other basic patterns found in the structuring of Chinese social relations, patterns based on the dynamic interplay between ideas about hierarchy and egalitarianism, and ascribed and achieved status. Although Confucian Chinese society was clearly hierarchical in orientation, this social hierarchy (like the economic hierarchy) was neither strictly inherited nor fixed, partly as a result of the system of competitive examinations for government office. Even while successful candidates were drawn disproportionately from the most privileged social and economic backgrounds, the examination system reinforced beliefs that held that individuals could, with effort and good fortune, improve their social status and that of their families.

The more egalitarian traditions of blood brotherhood, patterned after celebrated relations between heros in Chinese history and folk literature, also found expression in numerous relations in Chinese society. These ideals of blood brotherhood were at the heart of nineteenth-century secret society organizations, which often recruited members from a diversity of kinship and social backgrounds.[34] Although there were graded statuses and leadership positions within these societies, such statuses were won through individual achievement. Moreover, the basic rule of helping any "brother" in trouble reinforced more general ideas about social equality.

Finally, note should be taken of the overall self-governing nature of smaller communities in China, whose main links with officials of the central government were in the payment of taxes and infrequent legal cases. Local-level leaders, drawn from a variety of social backgrounds, served in both official and non-official capacities. Acting as middlemen in relations with higher officials, men from prominent gentry families often served as powers behind the scene (Fei 1953, 79–84), usually avoiding more formal positions like that of village headman, which would place them in a subordinate position vis-à-vis state officials.[35] The qualifications for village headman and the exact nature and duties of this office varied with time and place (See Duara 1988; Fei 1980/1939, 106–9; Smith 1899, 170–76; Yang 1945, 173–89), yet such positions were usually elective, suggesting that leaders of this type needed to rely on personal abilities to attract the support of those they served. Once in office, these men were known to use this position to further enhance their power and economic standing in the local community.

Thus within Chinese society there existed a range of alternative social and political relations including both inherited and achieved statuses, which fluctuated between rather rigid hierarchies and more fluid egalitarian relations of blood brotherhood. While the state decreed that power of appointment and dismissal came from above, local-level leaders relied on personal skills and the support of their followers to advance their causes. These various modes of social organization, while distinctively different in style, generally contained within them elements of the opposing mode (rather like the germs within yin and yang symbols), which seem to have encouraged fairly smooth transitions from one style to another as situations changed.

Nineteenth-century Chinese residents of Southeast Asia drew on these varied ideas of power and social status in structuring relations with each other, both in dyadic ties and through more organized groups such as kongsis, clan associations, and secret societies. There was, however, one crucial difference: in place of Confucian education and landed estates, wealth and social philanthropy now became the primary measures of social success and social status. Nevertheless, the tension between a relatively fixed or stable social hierarchy and more egalitarian competition for social recognition continued. Whenever possible, successful families passed both wealth and position to their male descendants, as with several of the Chinese kapitans in Melaka under the Dutch or the late nineteenth-century Chinese leaders in Singapore (Wong 1963, 3–4; Yong 1967, 16–17). The establishment of the powerful Keng Tek Hoey by Melaka-born Singapore merchants in the mid-nineteenth century demonstrates a similar pattern, with membership limited to the original thirty-six members and their male descendants (Khoo 1972, 63, 117).[36] Similarly, those who challenged Yap Ah Loy's first appointment as kapitan of Kuala Lumpur justified their claims by identifying themselves as "kinsmen" of the late Liu Ngim Kong.

Presumably, the inheritance of wealth and position was most successful under stable political conditions and most likely to be put aside under conditions of turmoil and change, especially with the presence of alternative forms of social organization such as those found in secret societies. Thus while the more settled Melaka-born Chinese community in the early nineteenth century organized itself in ancestral worship societies, conditions changed with the discovery in the 1840s of tin in nearby Kesang, which brought a great inundation of single male immigrants from other dialect groups to the area. During the 1850s, secret societies, such as the Hai San, were able to attract members from all strata of Melaka Chinese society, including the established merchant groups (Khoo 1972, 114).

Leadership positions in the Straits Settlements and the Malayan interior before the 1880s similarly displayed two contrasting models of leadership. Most Chinese leaders in the Straits Settlements were wealthy merchants from dominant dialect groups who were recognized for their philanthropic contributions both within their own groups and to the community at large, and who acted as liaisons between the Chinese and the British. For example, of the fifteen Chinese leaders identified by Yong (1967, 4–5) as the most prominent in nineteenth-century Singapore, ten belonged to the dominant Hokkien community and none was of minority Hakka or Hainanese background. In a similar manner, Mak (1987) found that Hokkien elites in nineteenth-century Pinang were also the most dominant figures in donating money to associations both within and outside their own dialect group. Such men did not necessarily hold official political office,[37] or if they did, these official positions served largely as symbolic legitimation of a power they already possessed, rather than as avenues to power itself. This was certainly true of positions awarded by the British, such as Asian justice of the peace or honorary magistrate, and by the late nineteenth century the office of kapitan in Kuala Lumpur or Perak had taken on a similar character. The style of leadership in such situations was almost mandarin in tone: often indirect, paternalistic, and honorary.[38]

The second type of leadership position stood in direct contrast to this: power here was based on more direct support by a group of followers and a political title or office was as much a means to increase one's economic or political power, as a reward for having it. Furthermore, while these positions did bestow honor, they were also potentially dangerous, as the incumbents were vulnerable to challenges from opponents who used the same sort of strong-arm tactics that they themselves had employed in rising to office. The acting heads of many secret societies and certain interior kapitans, such as Yap Ah Loy, were clearly leaders of this type.

During his early years in Sungei Ujong and Kuala Lumpur, Yap Ah Loy's leadership was based neither on his comparative wealth nor on philanthropy, but relied on other qualities, chief among them his fighting prowess. Although neither the "Record" nor the "Short History" comments directly on Yap Ah Loy's personal fighting skills, their concentration on battle strategies directed by Yap Ah Loy during the Selangor disturbances reinforces his image as a military leader and a fighting man. Interpreted by some authors as simply the acquisition of power through naked force (Wan 1967, 136), such views ignore the cultural significance of fighting skills and expertise in late imperial China, where the use of military force was not only considered legitimate in certain situations but was, at least among some social groups, actively celebrated. Chinese sojourners in Singapore and Malaya came from an area of China known for its tradition of interlineage feuding (Freedman 1958, 105–13; 1966, 104–7; Lamley 1990), which by the nineteenth century had become part of a pattern of increasing militarization of the entire society (Kuhn 1970, 9, 78). The unrest created by lineage feuding, secret society activities, and other localized rebellions drew even Confucian-educated officials into service as military leaders of local armed militia groups, or *tuanlian* (Kuhn 1970). In a similar manner, in nineteenth-century Taiwan, members of the local elite were known to choose careers of private armed power. According to Johanna Meskill (1979, 88–91), these local strongmen represented a social type, attracting followers by appealing to cultural traditions of fighting heroes common in Chinese folk literature and theater.

The two contrasting styles of leadership found in Chinese communities of this period were thus associated with cultural values of a diverse and at times seemingly contradictory nature. These values, rooted in beliefs about hierarchy and equality, in the importance of status passed from father to son as opposed to status earned through personal achievement were, like other cultural values, continually expressed in the nature of the very relations they shaped, as men sought out kinsmen for assistance, swore brotherhood to one another in secret societies, or chose to support one potential leader over another. Such values were also symbolically communicated in more formal ideological constructs, the domain that constitutes the final section of our analysis.

Ideology and Power

Our discussion of ideology begins by clarifying what we mean by this term, for the concept has been used in many analytically discrete ways, both within and outside Marxist analysis. As Raymond Williams observed, even within Marxist writings the ideological domain has signified phenomena ranging from systems of false consciousness, which may or may not be tied to particular classes, to "the general process of the production of meanings and ideas" (1977, 55). While acknowledging that certain ideas have been used to support particular class interests and that mystification often comprises an important element in this process, the more general definition of ideology as the production of meanings and ideas will be used in the following discussion. This approach has the advantage of recognizing the positive creation of meanings by conscious individuals, while treating more hegemonic features of ideological systems as an empirical question worthy of exploration rather than as their assumed function.

The ideological domain refers not only to the production of meanings, but focuses in particular on the communication of these ideas in symbolic forms that are both visible and public. Thus while ideology is closely related to (and intertwined with) cultural values in the economic and sociopolitical spheres (Williams 1977, 61), the public expressions of these ideas in specific religious and creative endeavors are what make ideological formations worthy of separate analysis. Like their economic and sociopolitical counterparts, ideological systems are historic products of the interaction between specific local contexts and sets of wider cultural values. Hence in a manner similar to what we have noted elsewhere, shifting contexts may present enterprising individuals with opportunities to draw on various cultural values to create or support different ideological formations that further enhance their own goals, effecting in the process of their manipulation possible shifts in ideological meanings as well.

Among the most central arenas for ideological production and communication in China were educational and literary institutions, religious rituals, and forms of popular entertainment such as story telling and theatrical productions. Each of these arenas promulgated and supported distinct and overlapping sets of cultural values: values such as the importance of literacy, Confucian learning, and filial piety; the desirability of remaining in harmony with natural and supernatural forces; or loyalty to kin and pseudo-kin in a variety of sociopolitical settings.

The adaptation of these and other ideological formations to the Malayan situation depended largely on contextual factors that varied in terms of location (rural or urban) and time period. For example, the low educational levels of most Chinese immigrants certainly affected the manner in which certain types of information and ideas could be shared. Popular entertainments and religious institutions were far more common in the urbanized world of the Straits Settlements than in the hinterlands, where temple celebrations and theatrical shows were limited mainly to holidays and special occasions. This may have offered leaders who sponsored such activities in more isolated areas possibilities for firmer control over the types of messages portrayed. Local demography was another important factor, for messages that appealed to a mostly single male population might not carry the same appeal for men who had married and taken on family responsibilities. Thus with slow shifts in gender ratios and an increasing number of local marriages among more successful immigrants, institutions such as clan associations or Chinese schools that promulgated messages of Confucian filial piety also grew.

From his early days in Kuala Lumpur, Yap Ah Loy appears to have been an active manipulator of ideological symbols. His sponsorship of Kuala Lumpur's first temple, the Xian Si Shi Ye Miao, dedicated to the deified Kapitan Shin, carried messages on different levels. Not only was the founding and generous endowment of Chinese temples a common practice for Chinese Malayan leaders, but religious leadership of key temples in some instances, such as the Cheng Hoon Temple in Melaka, paralleled secular leadership in the community itself (Wong 1963). It is significant that the central god in the Xian Si Shi Ye Temple was not a major Chinese deity such as Guanyin, Mazu, Guangung, or even Dabogong, but a former Chinese kapitan, whom Yap Ah Loy had personally served and fought for. In his reincarnation as Si Sen Ta, linked to a former mandarin, Kapitan Shin joined together two of the most powerful images of leadership in Chinese society—that of military hero and martyr and that of educated official. Because of their previous relationship, Si Sen Ta may have been seen as particularly responsive to Yap Ah Loy's prayers, for he was said to have brought military advice to Yap Ah Loy in his dreams (C. K. 1893). In a more abstract sense, this god might also have been perceived as representing a continuum of power and legitimacy between strongman kapitans in this world and their counterparts in the next.

On a sociological level, the Xian Si Shi Ye Temple appears to have served as a focal community temple, rather than one catering exclusively to Huizhou Hakkas. Descriptions of temple processions in the 1890s note the inclusion of not only the headmen of the different Chinese subethnic groups in the population, but even a "band of Klings, playing tomtoms and dancing" and "a company of Japanese."[39] As founder and principal leader of this temple in its formative period, Yap Ah Loy thus portrayed himself as someone who represented not just the narrow interests of his own clan or dialect group, but the wider community as well. One final feature of this temple, its close association with spirit mediumship, carried further implications relating to another of Yap Ah Loy's activities in early Kuala Lumpur. Chinese supplicants sought the god's advice on issues including ill health, for which the spirit medium routinely provided medical prescriptions (Letessier 1893, 321). It is tempting to see a relationship between this temple function and the one retail business founded by Yap Ah Loy: the Chinese drugstore. The ability to cure illness must have been highly regarded in the unhealthy climate of early Kuala Lumpur, and ownership of a Chinese medicine shop could have provided one more link in a chain of powerful and empowering symbolic messages that Yap Ah Loy sought to convey.[40]

Other arenas of ideological support for military-type leaders found in Chinese Malayan society of this time included secret society rituals and the tradition of popular theater. As ter Haar's chapter in this volume indicates, martial traditions like those celebrated in the novel *The Water Margin*, were important contributors to many of the symbols used in Triad initiation rituals. Theatrical performances, whether by human actors or hand-held puppets, were virtually a requirement of temple festivals, New Year's celebrations, and other special festivities in Chinese Malayan towns and mining camps.[41] While we do not know precisely what the topics of these plays were, martial arts themes were evidently not unusual.[42] J. D. Vaughan, an acute observer of nineteenth-century Chinese society in the Straits Settlements wrote,

> The Chinese are ardent admirers of the drama and will night after night sit to see what appears to us unmeaning spectacles. Theatrical performances consist of endless processions of soldiers, relieved occasionally by single combats of the most ludicrous nature. (1971/1879, 85)

The extent to which cultural messages communicated through plays were either consciously manipulated or encouraged specific actions is always difficult to judge.[43] As kapitan of Kuala Lumpur, Yap Ah Loy sponsored theatrical shows to entertain miners at the New Year and on other festive occasions. Although there is no information about the types of stories performed, he exhibited a direct appreciation for the usefulness of theater as communication on at least one occasion. When the governor of Selangor, Sir Frederick Weld, visited Kuala Lumpur in 1880, Yap Ah Loy entertained his group with a Chinese theatrical performance, which Weld described as "representing a Sultan and great Rajas quarreling, but laying aside their quarrels on appearance of a 'Governor' who pacifies the country" (Gullick 1955, 28).

While the sponsorship of temples and theatrical performances continued throughout Yap Ah Loy's tenure as kapitan, his style of leadership as Selangor kapitan in the 1880s, and the messages this seemed to convey, resembled much more closely the honorary and paternalistic styles of the wealthy merchant leaders of the Straits Settlements. Denying any connection with secret societies (like merchant leaders elsewhere),[44] he devoted his attention to building up his own economic enterprises. Like the Straits leaders, he also engaged in philanthropic works, sponsoring a shelter for the sick and the first Chinese school in Kuala Lumpur. His successors as kapitan, the wealthy merchants Yap Ah Shak and Yap Kwan Seng, carried on in a similar fashion, acting as honorary officials, deserving of the recognition conveyed in their mandarin attire.[45]

Concluding Remarks

This chapter has explored the way in which Yap Ah Loy and other Malayan Chinese leaders of his time drew on different and somewhat contrasting ideas about leadership prevalent in Chinese society of this period. Recent studies by other historians of Chinese society have suggested that one approach to understanding regional variations in Chinese sociopolitical organization might be to focus on cultural adaptations to the different conditions found in core versus peripheral areas (Cole 1986; Schoppa 1982). The situation of the Chinese in the Straits Settlements and the Malayan interior provides a comparable case. As interior areas like Kuala Lumpur increasingly took on political and economic characteristics analogous to those of the Straits Settlements, the expected patterns for elite status and leadership adjusted to fit these new circumstances. Hence, by looking at the actual economic, sociopolitical, and ideological contexts of these areas at particular points in time, the varying appropriateness of different cultural strategies becomes clear.[46]

The story of Yap Ah Loy and his times illustrates well the manner in which specific cultural strategies could be adjusted to changing contexts. It also thoroughly negates a view of nineteenth-century Chinese Malayan society as ruled simply by strong-arm kapitans backed by the power of their dialect-based secret societies. Yap Ah Loy drew on a complex mix of social relations, political strategies, and ideological images in his ascent to power, based on cultural values that were themselves both complementary and contradictory. While Yap Ah Loy may have first made the acquaintance of important contacts like Kapitan Shin and Liu Ngim Kong through the Hai San secret society, the values inherent in this type of organization, rather than the organizational structure itself, were the most crucial in supporting his rise to power. Thus while Yap Ah Loy was almost certainly a Hai San leader in his early days as kapitan of Kuala Lumpur, this did not prevent him from welcoming to Kuala Lumpur other defeated Huizhou "brothers" from Perak who had fought as members of a different, antagonistic secret society. His public promulgation of laws and punishments as well as his use of economic incentives to attract the support of fighters and mining workers suggest that he could not simply rely on his secret society position for either economic or political support. In a similar manner, his sponsorship of the Si Sen Ta temple and theatrical entertainments for the miners communicated a complex mix of messages about power and political legitimacy.

One final point concerns some of the more specific interrelationships between context and cultural values in the economic, sociopolitical, and ideological domains. It would be tempting to suggest that as the British assumed growing responsibility for policing and central administrative functions, they created a situation favoring leadership and control by a wealthy and increasingly entrenched Chinese merchant class. Yet even while the late nineteenth century did see a growth in inherited wealth and power among Chinese leaders, contextual factors relating to labor availability and world commodity prices continued to work in favor of the economic advancement of poor immigrants, who were given better choices in forms of labor payment and less exploitative pricing on their supplies. At the same time, the "superstitious" practices and rituals associated with tin mining in Yap Ah Loy's time—practices that reinforced beliefs in possible supernatural avenues to success for even the poorest coolie—were said to be gradually disappearing. The message encouraged by mine owners and financiers now apparently linked success strictly to hard work, suggesting that those who succeeded had done so through their own efforts and cleverness, thus downplaying cultural support for the possibility of sudden advancement through lucky breaks and cultural excuses for failure.

Changes like this in ideological messages underline the importance of an interpretive approach that takes into account interactions between all spheres of human activity. At first sight, someone like Yap Ah Loy is interesting primarily for what he can teach us about variations in Chinese patterns of leadership and power. Yet the more one examines his life, the clearer it becomes that sociopolitical relations, and the cultural values that support them, can be understood only in relation to the wider economic and ideological contexts in which they occur. Furthermore, the availability within Chinese culture of a variety of patterns for sociopolitical relations once again reminds us that, in some respects, Chinese adaptations to overseas life were not so different from adaptations to varying conditions in China and that scholars can continue to benefit from mutual attention to one another's sources.

Notes

1. Research on Yap Ah Loy and nineteenth century Chinese Malayan leaders was supported by a Cullister Grant from Beloit College (Summer 1982) and a Fulbright Faculty Research Abroad Grant (1983–84), which are gratefully acknowledged. Numerous individuals in Malaysia and Singapore generously assisted me with this research; I would like to particularly thank the grandson of Yap Ah Loy, Yap Swee Hin, for sharing his memories and family genealogy. Don Nonini, Stevan Harrall, Ben Anderson, and Julie Nemer provided helpful critiques and comments on various versions of this chapter. The final interpretations and errors, as always, are strictly my own.

Chinese names and terms commonly cited in the secondary literature on Malaysia conform to these romanizations; other Chinese words are romanized in pinyin. Please refer to character references in the glossary.

2. A *kangchu* was a Chinese river headman in nineteenth-century Johor, Singapore, or Riau, with authority from the local Malay ruler to open plantations, collect taxes, and exercise the functions of government (Trocki 1979, 90–91, 114). According to C. S. Wong (1963, 1), a kapitan was "the recognised captain, chief or headman of a community on foreign soil . . . officially vested with certain executive, administrative and, in some cases, judicial powers over his own people, and invariably acting as the channel between the Government and the community."

3. While undoubtedly not always "secret," sworn brotherhood organizations such as the Tiandihui or Ghee Hin Kongsi have been consistently referred to as secret societies in literature on Malayan Chinese. For simplicity's sake, this chapter uses the term "secret society" in its broadest sense to include legal and illegal sworn brotherhoods of all types.

4. Similar interpretations are advanced by Wong (1965, 41–42) and by Godley (1981, 27) who cites the writings on Malayan Chinese secret societies of Comber (1959) and Blythe (1969). See also Sadka (1968, 25). Freedman (1960) comments on the close

connection in the Straits Settlements between political and economic power, but refrains from models that posit direct relationships between merchants, kapitans, secret societies, and mining coolies.

5. Turnbull (1972, 125–26) mentions the possibility that wealthy merchants covertly controlled these secret societies, but no data exists to substantiate this.

6. See, for example, Crissman's much cited work on the segmentary structure of overseas Chinese social organization, where after distinguishing between different levels of ethnic organization, the author simply asserts that corporate ethnic groups constitute the major components in the structure of overseas Chinese society (1967, 188). For a critique of this approach, see Sangren (1984).

7. Kongsis were cooperative labor groups with profits distributed on a modified share system. See chapters 3 and 4 by Heidhues and Trocki in this volume for further discussion of the structures of kongsis and *hui*.

8. Singapore society supplies a good example of this latter principle. After arguing for the importance of secret societies in the integration of new immigrants into the local community, Freedman provides figures showing that less than half of the male Chinese population of the city were registered members of secret societies in 1881 (1960, 32).

9. Trocki's recent (1990) study of kongsis, secret societies, and opium farms in nineteenth-century Singapore, while also arguing for the primacy of economic factors, does not entirely rule out cultural practices as important elements for consideration.

10. Harrell's (1982) model of culture and context, developed in his ethnography of a Taiwanese community, has been very influential in shaping this definition of cultural formations. While Harrell focuses on the explication of social behavior, his general model has been extended, in the analysis that follows, to include more abstractly formulated notions of cultural values and the production and communication of meanings and ideas in the ideological realm.

11. These two leadership styles are actually represented in two different photos that have survived of Yap Ah Loy as kapitan: the first, of the "common man" displayed in the Yap Clan Association and the Xian Si Shi Ye Temple, and the second showing him in mandarin attire, found in the Malayan archives and in many published accounts of his life.

12. See Middlebrook (1951, 120–24) for a complete description of these documents. The "Record" was used by Yap's heirs after his death as part of a petition to the British government requesting reimbursement for funds spent by Yap Ah Loy on public services, even though, as Middlebrook notes, the activities chronicled concentrated on military activities between 1869 and 1873, and did not include his sustained efforts to rebuild Kuala Lumpur during the subsequent twelve years.

13. Yap Ah Loy was clearly of Hakka parentage and identified himself as a Huizhou Hakka in his associations throughout his life. According to the Yap family genealogy (shared with me by his grandson, Yap Swee Hin), his ancestors moved from Fujian province to Meixian (Jiayingzhou) in Guangdong province during the Yuan Dynasty and then to nearby Xingning twelve generations later. The move to Huizhou, an area much closer to Canton, took place eight generations before Yap Ah Loy's birth. Subdialect group identification, tied to local areas of origin in China, often constituted a divisive factor among Hakkas and other southern Chinese working in Southeast Asia. The distinction between Jiayingzhou Hakkas and Huizhou Hakkas was an important one in the geopolitical events of Yap Ah Loy's life.

14. The family genealogy lists Yap Ah Loy as the eldest in a family with four sons and one daughter. Numerous apocryphal stories of Yap Ah Loy's childhood appear in renditions of his life from Chinese sources, reflecting Chinese ideas about childhood revelations of predestined character traits. For comments on these stories see Carstens (1988).

15. As Khoo notes (1972, 218–20), our knowledge of the structure of the Sungei Ujong Chinese community is limited by the type of reports available. The relationship between the Sungei Ujong kapitan and the local Malay royalty, as well as the precise duties of this office, are never described, making it difficult to speculate on why the wealthier miners and merchants who ultimately selected Yap Ah Loy as kapitan did not aspire to this post themselves.

16. With Yap Ah Loy's departure, the area reverted to the control of three men identified as Wong Ying, a Cantonese; Hui Sam, a Huizhou Hakka; and Ng Kim, a Jiayingzhou Hakka. Khoo (1972, 116–17, 218–20) notes the presence of at least two antagonistic secret societies in Sungei Ujong in the 1860s: the Hai San and the Sung Pak Kun, an affiliate of the Ghee Hin. A list of secret society leaders in Sungei Ujong from an 1884 government report includes Hokkien, Hakka, and Cantonese representatives. According to Khoo (1972, 218–20), Hakkas were further divided into Jiayingzhou and Huizhou factions supporting rival secret societies, and even where the Cantonese and the Huizhou Hakkas belonged to the same secret society, "clashes between them neverthe-less occurred."

17. No further description of this "druggist shop" is given beyond mention of its establishment in the "Short History."

18. Middlebrook (1951, 20–21, 103) mistakenly identifies the defeated Huizhou Hakkas from Larut as members of the Hai San society, even though reports clearly stated that it was the Ghee Hin who were defeated and pushed from the area. But Middlebrook insists that the Huizhous who arrived in Kuala Lumpur *must have been* Hai San members or they would not have been welcome. Khoo (1972, 118, 138, 158) cites a government report on the Larut disturbances identifying the defeated Huizhou Hakkas as members of the Ghee Hin society and suggests further that it may have been later disturbances in 1865 that produced the Huizhou refugees who were invited to Kuala Lumpur.

19. These three surnames, in Mandarin Liu, Guan, and Zhang, are among four histori-cally linked to the shared brotherhood of the leading figures in *The Romance of the Three Kingdoms*. Their bearers recognized fictive kin ties, which were used by Cantonese speak-ers to found a multiple surname association in Singapore in 1866 (Yen 1981, 66).

20. Although *wayang* now refers generally to the Malay shadow puppet play, the word is frequently used in historical sources to mean any sort of Chinese or Malay theatrical entertainment, using either puppets or live actors.

21. For further discussion of Chinese beliefs in the predestination of leaders see Car-stens (1988). Ideas about fate and destiny were important elements in the culture of Chinese miners, as mentioned below.

22. Middlebrook (1951, 52) notes that we do not know whether Yap Ah Loy could either read or write Chinese or speak Malay, but that he seems to have relied on Voon Siew to act as interpreter-secretary on many important occasions.

23. Similar provisions are mentioned by Kuhn (1970, 78) for the recruitment of fight-ers by local lineages in southeastern China, suggesting that even particularistic loyalties such as lineage, dialect, or secret society sometimes needed to be strengthened by specific terms of payment to attract sufficient numbers of fighting men.

24. This source is a short biography of Yap Ah Loy published in the *Selangor Journal* in 1893 and said to be an English translation of a Chinese version current in Kuala Lumpur at this time. Although highly inaccurate in many ways, its reference to Si Sen Ta offers insight into beliefs not expressed in either the "Short History" or the "Record."

25. See *Selangor Secretariat Files* 1876, no. 4; 1879, no. 11; 1880, no. 272; 1882, no. 542.

26. *Selangor Secretariat Files* 1882, no. 669. See Chew (1967–68; 1984) for a more detailed account of the changing relationship between Yap Ah Loy and Frank Swettenham.

27. The revenue farms were government monopolies on the sale or control of opium, alcohol, gambling, or other goods auctioned off to wealthy Chinese individuals or syndicates for set periods. These "farms" were both the major source of income for the British colonizers and lucrative and contested enterprises for Chinese businessmen.

28. The family genealogy lists a woman surnamed Liao as first wife. According to Wang (1958, 48), she was a *tong yang xi*, an adopted daughter-in-law, who died of illness. The Melaka wife is designated as successor to a deceased wife (*ji shi*), and the other women are labeled as *qie*, concubines.

29. The revenue farm system in the Malayan interior differed from that of the Straits Settlements, where revenue farmers had monopolistic rights on both the manufacture and retail of the opium product, *chandu*. In the interior tin districts, the revenue farmer collected duty on all raw opium imported into the area, but did not control the manufacture and sale of *chandu*, which was often sold on credit to mining workers by the financiers (Wong 1965, 78–79). For an insightful analysis of the political coalitions and cleavages produced by the Straits system, see Trocki (1987).

30. Pasqual's (1895) detailed account of Chinese mining practices, including the organization and financing of tin mining kongsis, provides information of ethnographic quality that has proved very useful to my own understanding of the interface between "economic" and "cultural" practices. The careful demarcation of statuses among tin mining workers corresponds with Chinese notions of social differentiation mentioned below.

31. Croockewit (1854, 122), discussing the best methods for organizing mining workers, remarked that "anyone who knows the Chinese and has seen them work must be convinced that more than any other nation, it is necessary they should have a personal interest in their work."

32. Balazs (1964, 48–49) mentions a similar share system among Chinese laborers in the Yunnan copper mines of the eighteenth century.

33. Pasqual (1895, 45–46) reported that even if the mine were not profitable, workers under the share system still owed the cost of their provisions to the financier; later he contradicted this, saying that share coolies risked only their time and labor "for which they may be said to be more than compensated by their having obtained free board and lodging, clothing, opium, cash and generally having enjoyed what they would admit to be a jolly good time during their connection with the mine."

34. See Ownby's and ter Haar's chapters in this volume for more detailed historical analyses of the blood oath and blood brotherhood traditions in China.

35. According to Martin Yang (1945, 185), "No villager of social rank or much self esteem wanted to be a (local) official, for he would lose face in dealing with those who outranked him in authority but not in social status. Besides, no one wanted to be at the beck and call of the government or to have to take orders." Duara's study (1988) of villages in North China shows that the rewards of village leadership changed with increasing penetration of the state during the early twentieth century.

36. The Keng Tek Hoey displayed an intriguing amalgam of organizational principles, which to some extent mirrored the evolution of Chinese social forms in the Malayan environment described below. While Khoo (1972, 63, 117) identifies this group as a secret society, a more recent study by Chng (1986, 107–23) clarifies the function of this group as providing a type of insurance to family members of a group of merchants who feared for their support in the event of death or bankruptcy.

37. After the British discontinued the kapitan system in the Straits Settlements in 1826, certain Chinese leaders in Melaka, Singapore, and Pinang continued to be recognized as "unofficial" kapitans. See Turnbull (1972, 106); Wong (1963, 31–37).

38. The honor involved in leadership positions among overseas Chinese is clearly demonstrated in the elaboration of offices in voluntary associations. As Freedman noted,

"the triad of benefaction, conferred honor, and office-holding emerge in the general estimations of a man's social worth" (1957, 94–95). By the late nineteenth century, wealthy Malayan and Straits Chinese were given another opportunity to purchase more traditional symbols of high social status, through the sale of official degrees by the Qing government (Yen 1970).

39. This description appears in the *Selangor Journal* 2, no. 3 (October 20, 1893). Klings referred to Indian members of the community.

40. This part of my argument must unfortunately remain speculative, in part because there has been little research on the interrelationship between Chinese herbal medicine and spiritual healing. I do know that in the Malaysian Chinese community of Pulai, there was an overlap between these types of practitioners and that both herbal doctors and spirit mediums used their knowledge as a source of power that they controlled in part through secrecy (Carstens 1980). We do not know whether Yap Ah Loy was ever consulted for cures or whether his main interest in the medicine shop lay with his own personal belief in Chinese medicine. There was, in fact, some speculation by the British that his death was caused by his stubborn refusal to use Western medicine. See his obituary in the *Straits Times*, April 20, 1985.

41. Permanent *wayang* stages were found not only in larger cities and towns, but, according to reports by British travelers, in much more isolated mining camps as well. (This information comes from copies of British colonial documents collected by Paul Kratoska and shared with me in Pinang in 1984.)

42. Tanaka Issei, a noted Japanese scholar on Chinese popular theater, has recently argued that plays about martial prowess were especially popular in small market towns dominated by secret societies (1985, 149).

43. One account of the Zhu Yigui rebellion in Taiwan in 1721 provides a possible example. After being arrested by the magistrate for singing opera and swearing brotherhood, Zhu Yigui's followers reportedly used temple altar cloths to fashion clothing and hats for themselves similar to those worn by their heros on stage before rebelling and occupying Taiwan's provincial capital (Chiu 1983, 137).

44. Although secret societies were illegal in the interior Malay states, Turnbull (1972, 125–26) notes that even before secret societies had been banned by the British in the Straits Settlements, no respectable Chinese merchant would admit to membership, even though many were rumored to belong. If one sees secret societies as offering an alternative and opposing image to a more "mandarin" style of leadership, then the public disavowals of connections by wealthy merchants who sought recognition through a different avenue of power makes sense.

45. The activities of the last kapitan of Kuala Lumpur and other Chinese leaders of this period, as documented in the pages of the *Selangor Journal*, parallel almost exactly those of Chinese leaders in the Straits Settlements described in the well-known works of Song Ong Siang (1975/1923) and C. B. Buckley (1965/1902). Mention is made, for example, of dinners given by Kapitan Yap Kwan Seng, Loke Yew, and Yap Ah Loy's sons for British officials; the sponsorship of schools (both Chinese and English) and hospitals; and other more "British-style" activities such as participation in sports clubs and horse racing.

46. For a similar argument about the adaptation of lineage structures in seventeenth- and eighteenth-century Amoy, see Ng (1983).

References

Anon. 1927. "The Biography of Yap Ah Loy." English translation of Chinese biography published in unidentified Chinese periodical. Middlebrook papers, Singapore National Archives.

Anon. 1957. "Translation of Extracts from a Record Made in Chinese by Yap Ah Loy

Relating to the War in Selangor Before the Year 1874." *Journal of the South Seas Society* 13, no. 1: 1–26.

Balazs, Etienne. 1964. *Chinese Civilization and Bureaucracy, trans., H. M. Wright.* New Haven: Yale University Press.

Benjamin, Geoffrey. 1985. "In the Long Term: Three Themes in Malayan Cultural Ecology." In *Cultural Values and Human Values in Southeast Asia,* ed. Karl L. Huttere, A. Terry Rambo, and George Lovelace, 219–78. Michigan Papers on South and Southeast Asia No. 27. Ann Arbor: University of Michigan Center for South and Southeast Asian Studies.

Blythe, Wilfred Lawson. 1969. *The Impact of Chinese Secret Societies in Malaya: A Historical Study.* Kuala Lumpur: Oxford University Press.

Braddell, T. 1853. "Notes on a Trip to the Interior from Malacca." *Journal of the Indian Archipelago and Eastern Asia* 7: 73–104.

Buckley, C. B. 1965/1902. *An Anecdotal History of Old Times in Singapore 1819–1867.* Singapore: University of Malaya Press.

C. K. 1893. "Yap Ah Loi." *Selangor Journal* 12, no. 1: 184–85.

Carstens, Sharon A. 1980. "Images of Community in a Chinese Malaysian Settlement." Ph.D. diss., Cornell University.

_____. 1988. "From Myth to History: Yap Ah Loy and the Heroic Past of Chinese Malaysians." *Journal of Southeast Asian Studies* 19, no. 2: 185–208.

Chew, Ernest. 1967–68. "Frank Swettenham and Yap Ah Loy: The Advance of British 'Influence' in Kuala Lumpur, 1871–1885." *Journal of the Historical Society, University of Singapore*: 65–76.

_____. 1984. "Frank Swettenham and Yap Ah Loy: The Increase of British Influence in Kuala Lumpur, 1871–1885. *Journal of the Malaysian Branch Royal Asiatic Society* 57, no. 1: 70–87.

Chiu Kun Liang. 1983. *Xiandai shehui de minsu quyi* (Folk Arts in Modern Society). Taipei: Yuan Liu Publications.

Chng, D. K. Y. 1986. *Xinjiapo Huarenshi luncong* (Collected Essays on Chinese in Nineteenth-Century Singapore). Singapore: South Seas Society.

Cole, James. 1986. *Shaohsing: Competition and Cooperation in Nineteenth Century China.* Tucson: University of Arizona Press.

Comber, Leon F. 1959. *Chinese Secret Societies in Malaya: A Survey of the Triad Society from 1800–1900.* New York: J. J. Augustin.

Crissman, Lawrence. 1967. "The Segmentary Structure of Urban Overseas Chinese Communities." *Man* (new series) 2, no. 2: 185–203.

Croockewit, H. 1854. "The Tin Mines of Malacca." *Journal of the Indian Archipelago and Eastern Asia* 8: 112–33.

Duara, Prasenjit. 1988. *Culture, Power, and the State: Rural North China, 1900–1942.* Stanford: Stanford University Press.

Fei Hsiao-tung. 1980/1939. *Peasant Life in China.* London: Routledge and Kegan Paul.

_____. 1953. *China's Gentry.* Chicago: University of Chicago Press.

Freedman, Maurice. 1970/1957. *Chinese Family and Marriage in Singapore.* New York, London: Johnson Reprint.

_____. 1958. *Lineage Organization in Southeastern China.* London: Athlone Press.

_____. 1960. "Immigrants and Associations: Chinese in Nineteenth Century Singapore." *Comparative Studies in Society and History* 3: 25–48.

_____. 1966. *Chinese Lineage and Society: Fukien and Kwangtung.* London: Athlone Press.

Gates, Hill, and Robert Weller. 1987. "Hegemony and Chinese Folk Ideologies." *Modern China* 13, no. 1: 3–16.

Godley, Michael. 1981. *The Mandarin-capitalists from Nanyang.* Cambridge: Cambridge University Press.

Gullick, J. M. 1955. "Kuala Lumpur: 1880–1895." *Journal of the Malayan Branch Royal Asiatic Society* 28, no. 4: 1–171.

Hale, A. 1885. "On Mines and Miners in Kinta, Perak." *Journal of the Royal Asiatic Society Straits Branch* 16: 303–10.

Harrell, Stevan. 1982. *Ploughshare Village: Culture and Context in Taiwan.* Seattle: University of Washington Press.

_____. 1985. "Why Do the Chinese Work So Hard?" *Modern China* 11, no. 2: 203–26.

_____. 1987. "The Concept of Fate in Chinese Folk Ideology." *Modern China* 13, no. 1: 90–109.

Hui Fatt. 18??. "A Short History of Yap Tet Loy." English translation of Chinese text. Middlebrook papers, Singapore National Archives.

Johnson, David. 1985. "Communication, Class and Consciousness in Late Imperial China." In *Popular Culture in Late Imperial China*, ed. David Johnson, Andrew J. Nathan, and Evelyn S. Rawski, 34–72. Berkeley: University of California Press.

Khoo Kay Kim. 1972. *The Western Malay States 1850–1873.* Kuala Lumpur: Oxford University Press.

Kuhn, Philip A. 1970. *Rebellion and Its Enemies in Late Imperial China: Militarization and Social Structure, 1796–1864.* Cambridge: Harvard University Press.

Lamley, Harry J. 1990. "Lineage and Surname Feuds in Southern Fukien and Eastern Kwangtung under the Ch'ing. In *Orthodoxy in Late Imperial China*, ed. Kwang-Ching Liu, 255–78. Berkeley: University of California Press.

Lee Poh-ping. 1978. *Chinese Society in Nineteenth Century Singapore.* Singapore: Oxford University Press.

Letessier, Charles. 1893. "Si Sen Ta: A Chinese Apotheosis." *Selangor Journal* 1, no. 20: 320–22.

Mak Lau Fong. 1981. *The Sociology of Secret Societies: A Study of Chinese Secret Societies in Singapore and Peninsular Malaysia.* Kuala Lumpur: Oxford University Press.

_____. 1987. "Chinese Subcommunal Elites in 19th Century Penang." *Tonan Ajia Kenkyu* (Southeast Asian Studies) 25, no. 2: 254–64.

Meskill, Johanna. 1979. *A Chinese Pioneer Family: The Lins of Wu-feng Taiwan 1729–1895.* Princeton: Princeton University Press.

Middlebrook, S. M. 1951. "Yap Ah Loy." *Journal of the Malayan Branch Royal Asiatic Society* 24, no. 2: 1–127.

Ng Chin-Keong. 1983. *Trade and Society: The Amoy Network on the China Coast 1683–1735.* Singapore: Singapore University Press.

Pasqual, J. C. 1895. "Chinese Tin Mining in Selangor." *Selangor Journal* 4, no. 2: 25–29; 4, no. 3: 43–46; 4, no. 6: 99–103; 4, no. 8: 137–40; 4, no. 10: 168–73.

Sadka, Emily. 1968. *The Protected Malay States: 1874–1895.* Kuala Lumpur: University of Malaya Press.

Sangren, P. Steven. 1984. "Traditional Chinese Corporations: Beyond Kinship." *Journal of Asian Studies* 43, no. 3: 391–415.

Schoppa, R. Keith. 1982. *Chinese Elites and Political Change.* Cambridge: Harvard University Press.

Selangor Journal, 1893–1897.

Selangor Secretariat Files, 1875–1885.

Smith, Arthur H. 1970/1899. *Village Life in China.* Boston: Little, Brown, and Company.

Song Ong Siang. 1975/1923. *One Hundred Years History of the Chinese in Singapore.* San Francisco: Chinese Materials Center.

Straits Times (Singapore), 1885.

Tanaka Issei. 1985. "The Social and Historical Context of Ming-Ch'ing Local Drama." In *Popular Culture in Late Imperial China*, ed. David Johnson, Andrew J. Nathan, and Evelyn S. Rawski, 143–60. Berkeley: University of California Press.

Trocki, Carl A. 1979. *Prince of Pirates*. Singapore: Singapore University Press.

_____. 1987. "The Rise of Singapore's Great Opium Syndicate, 1840–86." *Journal of Southeast Asian Studies* 8, no. 1: 58–80.

_____. 1990. *Opium and Empire: Chinese Society in Colonial Singapore, 1800–1910*. Ithaca: Cornell University Press.

Turnbull, C. M. 1972. *The Straits Settlements 1826–1867*. Singapore: Oxford University Press.

Vaughan, J. D. 1971/1879. *The Manners and Customs of the the Chinese of the Straits Settlements*. Kuala Lumpur: Oxford University Press.

Wan Ming Seng. 1967. "The History of the Organization of the Chinese Community in Selangor with Particular Reference to Problems of Leadership, 1857–1962." M.A. thesis, Universiti Malaya.

Wang Gungwu. 1981. "Traditional Leadership in a New Nation: The Chinese in Malaya and Singapore." In *Community and Nation: Essays on Southeast Asia and the Chinese*, ed. Wang Gungwu, 159–72. Singapore: Heinemann Educational Books.

Wang Zhiyuan. 1958. *Ye Delai juan* (The Biography of Ye Delai). Kuala Lumpur: Yihua Publishers.

Williams, Raymond. 1977. *Marxism and Literature*. Oxford: Oxford University Press.

Wong, C. S. 1963. *A Gallery of Chinese Kapitans*. Singapore: Ministry of Culture, Government Printing Office.

Wong Lin Ken. 1965. *The Malayan Tin Industry to 1914*. Tucson: University of Arizona Press.

Yang, Martin. 1945. *A Chinese Village*. New York: Columbia University Press.

Yen Ching-hwang. 1970. "Ch'ing's Sale of Honours and the Chinese Leadership in Singapore and Malaya (1877–1912)." *Journal of Southeast Asian Studies* 1, no. 2: 20–32.

_____. 1981. "Early Chinese Clan Organizations in Singapore and Malaya, 1819–1911." *Journal of Southeast Asian Studies* 12, no. 1: 62–92.

Yong Ching Fatt. 1967. "Chinese Leadership in Nineteenth Century Singapore." *Journal of the Island Society* 1, no. 1: 184–85.

6

Messianism and the Heaven and Earth Society: Approaches to Heaven and Earth Society Texts

Barend J. ter Haar

During the last decade or so, social historians in China and the United States seem to have reached a new consensus on the origins of the Heaven and Earth Society (Tiandihui; "society" is the usual translation for *hui*, which, strictly speaking, means "gathering"; for the sake of brevity, the phenomenon is referred to below with the common alternative name "Triad," a translation of *sanhe hui*). They view the Triads as voluntary brotherhoods organized for mutual support, which later developed into a successful predatory tradition. Supporters of this interpretation react against an older view, based on a literal reading of the Triad foundation myth, according to which the Triads evolved from pro-Ming groups during the early Qing dynasty. The new interpretation relies on an intimate knowledge of the official documents that were produced in the course of persecuting these brotherhoods on the mainland and on Taiwan since the late eighteenth century. The focus of this recent research has been on specific events, resulting in a more detailed factual knowledge of the phenomenon than before (Cai 1987; Qin 1988: 1–86; Zhuang 1981 provides an excellent historiographical survey).

Understandably, contemporary social historians have hesitated to tackle the large number of texts produced by the Triads because previous historians have misinterpreted them and because they are full of obscure religious information and mythological references. Nevertheless, the very fact that these texts were produced (or copied) continuously from the first years of the nineteenth century —or earlier—until the late 1950s, and served as the basis for Triad initiation rituals throughout this period, leaves little doubt that they were important to the members of these groups. Historians, therefore, need to make a serious effort to understand them.

The principal mistake of previous historians in reading the texts has been to take them as sources of historical facts and dates. While the texts may reflect actual events, other readings of them might be more fruitful. Alternative approaches could include:

1. A historical or diachronic approach, relating early evidence on Triad ritual and mythology to similar pre-existing traditions;
2. A textual approach, reading the texts within themselves as a closed system, explaining elements and structures only by referring to other parts of the same system;
3. A normative approach, collecting all extant interpretations by adherents from confessions, changes in the transmission of the tradition, field reports, and so forth;
4. A contextual approach, comparing elements and structures from the tradition with elements and structures from other contemporary traditions, in an effort to obtain the cultural framework with which adherents themselves approached Triad ritual and mythology.

Ideally, each reading should result in fairly similar interpretations. In fact this is by no means the case. On the contrary, as I shall argue below, the first and second approaches indicate that Triad ritual and mythology derived from a messianic tradition. However, the available normative interpretations relate the texts to an initiation ritual, in which elements from funerary and birth rituals are reenacted. This last interpretation also best reflects the kind of rituals and beliefs with which the average member would have approached Triad lore.

This chapter adopts the first approach, a historical reading of elements from Triad ritual and mythology. These elements have not been chosen haphazardly; together, they constitute an essential part of the plot of the Triad foundation myth and ritual including the form, transmission, and content of the political and religious message, some principal figures in the myth, and the most basic elements of the initiation ritual. Almost all these elements can be traced from the earliest appearance of the Triads in historical sources in 1787 down to the second half of the twentieth century.

Like messianic traditions elsewhere, Chinese messianism builds on the concrete expectation that one or more saviors will descend to earth to rescue a select group of human beings from imminent or currently raging apocalyptic disasters. These saviors often appear as human rulers, who will subsequently reign over a radically changed world. The disasters include fierce attacks by all kinds of gruesome demons, such as those of plagues and other diseases. The group of elect would be protected from such demons by an army of spirit soldiers. Thus, Chinese messianism has both strong political and exorcist dimensions. These two aspects of messianic and millenarian prophecies are elaborated on below. Here it should be pointed out that preachers of these prophecies often played the role of healers in the present world as well.

In any analysis of Triad beliefs and mythology, the foundation myth occupies an important place. This story of support of the Qing court by the monks of the Shaolin monastery and their subsequent betrayal upon the advice of jealous ministers is probably the part of Triad lore that is best known to many readers, not only from Triad texts but from typical Hong Kong martial arts movies. It can be shown not only that this myth contains well-known literary themes, but even that several late Ming and Qing religious groups possessed a surprisingly similar foundation myth. Crucial elements from this myth can be ascertained as early as the first confessions by Triad adherents, in 1787.

In addition to the foundation myth, the initiation ritual of the Triads merits close analysis. This chapter summarizes the results of this analysis with respect to the messianic background of this ritual, but much evidence has had to be left out for reasons of space. Crucial parts of the ritual are the blood oath, that is, an oath, accompanied by drinking blood mixed with wine and by passing through a gate of knives, and a set of ritual implements (contained in a wooden rice bucket). The blood oath in this particular form seems to stem from rituals practiced only—by the late Ming and Qing periods—among ethnic minorities. The ritual implements are extremely common in Chinese rituals, usually involving exorcism of evil demons.

Because the Triads continued and further developed existing beliefs and practices, this raises the question of whether we can identify particular earlier groups that already contained essential characteristics of the later Triads. Traditionally, scholars have pointed to the widespread—and therefore also rather general—phenomenon of the sworn brotherhood, but I propose two more specific traditions. One is a predatory tradition that operated since the late Ming in northeastern Guangdong and southern Fujian provinces, which like the Triads possessed a mix of self-defense or predatory practices, substantial religious rituals, and a distinctive jargon. Some nineteenth-century Triad jargon ("secret language") was already used in this older tradition. The other possible precursor is a messianic group led by a certain Ma Chaozhu, whose teachings show many similarities to Triad mythology.

This chapter is part of a larger study and, as a result, detailed discussion of specific cases, as well as full evaluation of the source materials, have had to be omitted. In order to enable the reader to put the present discussion into its proper perspective, it seems advisable to give some general idea of the larger study on which it is based. Instead of focusing on specific events, the dating of the precise origins of the Triads, or actual uprisings, this larger study attempts a reconstruction of the extremely well-documented beliefs and mythology of the Triads.[1] Consequently, events are of interest insofar as they provide information about the interpretation or function of these beliefs by adherents or opponents of the Triads. Since the temporal perspective is not restricted to a specific period, this allows the use of a much broader set of source materials than is available to most historians of the Triads. These range from forced (and therefore distorted) confessions and descriptive pieces by contemporary Chinese as well as Western officials, journalists, or historians, to texts and pictures produced by Triad adherents, and even include a short film reenacting the initiation ritual, produced by the Hong Kong police force in the late 1950s with the assistance of former high-ranking members of the Triads.

A further concern in my larger study is the question of how much adherents really knew about the Triad beliefs and stories, or even how seriously they took them. The answer to this question largely determines the historian's evaluation of the relevance of Triad ritual and mythology to an understanding of the nature of the Triad groups themselves. The available confessions by Triad adherents in the Qing archives actually have little to say about the content and meaning of the Triad texts. This problem of relevance is also tied to more general questions about the nature of Chinese ritual practice and religious beliefs. On the one hand, captured adherents probably concealed as much as possible of their knowledge of Triad traditions; on the other hand, anthropologists of Chinese religion have observed that in the Chinese religious context, worship and participation *(orthopraxis)* are much more important than beliefs and actual comprehension. During recent fieldwork in Taiwan, Hong Kong, and Xiamen, I had the opportunity to confirm this observation. In my view, this last point is basic to our understanding of the relationship of Triad adherents to their ritual and mythology. While my larger, ongoing study should permit a more detailed investigation of these matters, my approach in the present chapter is purely historical. Leaving aside the other three approaches—especially the normative one—is, however, a practical expedient because of space limitations.

Form and Transmission of the Messianic Message

Messages from the world of the gods were always encoded in special allusive and arcane language, including the use of split characters, as if these were the real meaning-carrying elements. This testified to the heavenly origin of the message and facilitated flexibility of interpretation. Some of the symbolism involved is discussed below, in relation to the names of messianic saviors. Split characters were (and still are) familiar to most Chinese from fortune-telling (Smith 1991: 201–4 and *passim*). They were particularly common in messianic prophecies. Already in the oldest Triad confessions, such characters appear frequently as a means of expressing special names.

A frequent example of splitting a character is the character *ming*, which can stand for the name of the former dynasty or a messianic figure (see below). *Ming* is often split into *ri* (sun) and *yue* (moon). The common surname of Triad adherents, Hong, is frequently split into *wu dian er shi yi* (lit. five dots and twenty-one), or later into *san ba nian yi* (lit. three-eight-twenty-one).[2]

The most important case of split characters in Triad lore undoubtedly is the phrase *muli doushi zhi tianxia*. In confessions extracted by Qing authorities, Triad members did not (or at least professed not to) know what the phrase *muli doushi* meant. In one confession from 1787, the four characters are interpreted as a reference to specific years, but three of the four years are actually the first years of the first three Qing reign periods.[3] This seems rather trivial. Neither contemporary confessions nor later confessions, nor other independent sources, confirm this interpretation. It makes more sense to take *mu* and *dou* together, since the *mudou*, or wooden rice-measure, is a crucial object in Triad ritual, even in simplified versions. The characters *mudou* were already used during the late ninth century as a reference in split characters to the family name Zhu (Sun 1981, vol. 16: 117 [in 874–79]). I would propose this reading here as well. The complete phrase might be translated literally as "when 'wood *(mu)*' stands and it is the age of 'the bushel *(dou)*', [somebody] will rule all under Heaven." This can then be interpreted as "the Zhus will rule all under Heaven."

At least as important as its form and content was the carrier of the supernatural message. This could be a real person, an object, or a written text. The primary revealed text in the mythology of the Triads was transmitted by an incense burner. A religious cult in Chinese culture minimally consists of presenting incense to the gods, and therefore the incense burner has always been central to religious practice (Lagerwey 1987; Schipper 1982). An oath from 1787 specifically mentions the burning of incense, which is confirmed in slightly later sources from 1808 and 1811 (Qin 1988: 153, 154, 161). Furthermore, Heaven might send precious objects such as an incense burner, a seal, or even a rare book as physical evidence of its support for a ruler (or a claimant to the throne) or for a religious cult.

In the founding myth of the Triads, the incense burner occurs at a pivotal point early in the plot and brings the will of Heaven to the fleeing monks of the Shaolin monastery. The burner already features as such in the earliest full-fledged version (from 1811).

> An incense burner of white stone (weighing fifty-two ounces) floated upward to the surface of the sea. On the bottom of the incense burner were the four characters [meaning] "Restore the Ming and Extirpate the Qing." The men then took the incense burner [made of] Baiding [porcelain], and swore an oath before heaven. . . . [They choose Wan Tiqi as their leader and gathered 108 persons, who] (bound together) their righteousness before heaven, and (indicated) Hong as their surname, smeared blood and worshipped the covenant, becoming one Hong family. (*Tiandihui* 1980, vol. 1, 4; on Baiding, see Schlegel 1866, 14 n. 4).

This myth makes explicit the significance of the incense burner as a ritual object and as a provider of legitimacy. It was sent by Heaven and carried a sacred text that summarized the aims of the tradition. For centuries, both actual rulers and aspirants to the throne had made use of dynastic treasures such as incense burners to substantiate their claim of having received the Heavenly Mandate. During the Qing, dynastic treasures had lost their formerly central position in elite perceptions of legitimacy; instead, they now emphasized the moral virtues of the ruler as shown in ritual and political practice. Rebels, however, still made use of them. They were long ago incorporated into Daoist rituals and ordinary temple cults, where they are still very much alive today (Seidel 1983; ter Haar 1992). This story is, therefore, a very strong politico-religious statement about the central mythological aims of the Triads, one that most people would have comprehended easily. Not only does the burner bring an important message, but its weight *(wu shi er)* hides the common surname *(hong)* of the Triad adherents!

One of the first paragraphs of the 1811 initiation manual states that in 1643 an "Inscription by Liu Bowen" was spit out by the (Yellow) River in Kaifeng. A text with this name had been circulating since at least the early eighteenth century (and can still be found today in many temples on Taiwan). It predicted the return of the Ming under the Zhu family, bringing peace to the nation.[4] The historical Liu Ji had been one of the most important advisers to the founder of the Ming, Zhu Yuanzhang. In later mythology, he is always referred to by his courtesy name *(zi)*, as Liu Bowen. A tradition well established since the Ming made him a prophet who forecast the future of the Ming and all later rulers. The widely known *Baked Cake Ballad* (Shaobingge), a famous prophetic text dating back in one form or another to the late Ming, was eventually also ascribed to him. The ballad in its present form is full of anti-Manchu and pro-Ming sentiment. The text stresses the barbarian threat (Chan 1970, 1973). Barbarian invasions had been a typical apocalyptic disaster in eschatological texts since at least the third century. By placing the "Inscription by Liu Bowen" so prominently in the text, the author(s) of the 1811 manual suggest that the Triads would guarantee the fulfillment of the widespread prophecies about the return of the Ming.

The Nature of Triad Ming Loyalism

The Political Dimension of Messianism

The past views that the Triads arose from the purely political Ming loyalism of early Qing literati or from the resistance led by the merchant-pirate Zheng Chenggong are surely incorrect (Cai 1987; Qin 1988; Zhuang 1981). But does this mean that the many political statements about restoring the Ming dynasty in one form or another, which we find in Triad sources, are a later and unimportant development, and not representative of the earliest Triads? A detailed analysis of the earliest confessions from 1787 and later written texts shows that this is not the case.

Apart from insufficient understanding of some specific terminology (to be discussed below), in my opinion, this confusion results from a fundamental misunderstanding about the nature of the references to the Zhu imperial family and the term or name "*Ming*." Rather than purely political references, these are both messianic and political in nature. "*Ming*" can mean "luminous" or specifically refer to the former Ming dynasty. As we shall see, this convergence of meanings is probably not a coincidence.

In Chinese messianism the savior was often perceived as an ideal king who would not only dispel all diseases and disasters but would also become a secular ruler. The saviors in messianic prophecies frequently bore the family names Li, Liu, Zhao, and Zhang. These names were often written in split characters. Imperial houses or aspirants to the throne would use such beliefs to support their claims of legitimacy. In the case of the Song, the ruling Zhao family even actively created such beliefs, which remained popular after the fall of the dynasty in 1279 (Mollier 1990, 22–25 and 56–58; Noguchi 1986, 141–212; Seidel 1969–1970, 216–47; ter Haar 1992, 115–16).

The Tradition of the Luminous King

A relevant case is the messianic tradition of the assistant of the Buddhist savior Maitreya, the *mingwang,* or Luminous King. This tradition antedates the Ming dynasty by many centuries. In 1351, Han Shantong (succeeded by his son Lin'er) and his general, Liu Futong, started an uprising against the Mongol Yuan dynasty, which eventually brought the Ming dynasty to power. He gathered support among people in the Huai region who were working on repairs of the Grand Canal by claiming to have found a statue carrying a prophecy of the advent of apocalyptic disasters. He announced the coming of the savior Maitreya and his assistant, the Luminous King. Significantly, the uprising began in a *mao* (1351) year; since the late Tang, this date has figured, together with the preceding *yin* year, in millenarian prophecies, and often appeared together with elements from the Luminous King tradition. Han claimed to be a descendant of the Northern Song emperor Huizong, despite his different surname. In those same years and in the same region, prophecies also circulated about the advent of Great Equity *(taiping)* (ter Haar 1992, 115–23 and the primary sources referred to there; on the significance of the *yin* year, see Ke 1983, 188–89; 1987, 364–71).

The founder of the Ming dynasty, a former traveling monk called Zhu Yuanzhang, started his career as a rebel in one of the bands that followed Han's son Lin'er, who was also called the Small Luminous King *(xiao mingwang).* Although after 1355 his own military power far exceeded that of Han Lin'er and Liu Futong, Zhu Yuanzhang continued to accept the religious authority of Han Lin'er until the latter drowned in 1366. The name of Zhu's dynasty, Ming, and the first year title, Hongwu (Vast Martiality, using the same character *hong* that is so prominent in messianic prophecies about apocalyptic disasters), were likely an effort to incorporate some of the messianic charisma for Zhu's own benefit. After the dynasty had been established, however, different choices about the legitimation of power were made that excluded the use of messianism. As a result, few documents exist about whether and how ordinary subjects connected messianism to the Ming dynasty. After the dynasty had fallen, however, the much older tradition of the Luminous King was soon combined with beliefs in the restoration of the Ming imperial family. Something similar had happened after the Han, Tang, and Song dynasties fell, when rebels also often claimed to be descendants of the imperial families of these dynasties: Liu, Li, and Zhao, as well as messianic saviors.

Political Claims of the Triads

Both the political and messianic dimensions of the belief in the restoration of a descendant of the imperial Zhu family of the Ming, or a Luminous King/Ruler, go back to the earliest documented stage of the Triads, around 1787. This section discusses the political aspect first, in a more concise manner, and reserves a more detailed treatment of messianic aspects for the following sections. In reality, however, they are closely intertwined and thus some repetition of the evidence is unavoidable. The political dimension of the belief in restoration takes various forms. Here, three aspects will be presented: legitimation of religious and political charisma by physical descent, the restoration of the Ming as a political unit (a nation); and the receipt of the Heavenly Mandate.

Many examples exist of the belief that religious and political legitimacy (and therefore charisma) are transmitted by descent. It is the basis not only of rulership by a dynasty but also of the recurrent claims by messianic saviors and nonreligious rebels that they descend from past imperial houses. We already encountered the example of Han Shantong, who claimed descent from the Song house. The following section discusses several examples of non-Triad claims about saviors descending from the imperial family of the Ming.

The foundation myth of the Triads (first related as a complete story in the 1811 manual, although many constituent elements are already present in much earlier material) claims a physical line of descent of its founders from the Ming imperial family. An Imperial Concubine Li (which means "peach") is said to have fled the palace after Li Zicheng had rebelled. She bore a son, the Young Lord *(xiaozhu)* in the Gaoxi Temple, who went on to found the Triads. The five cofounders of the Triads are described as his physical sons, even though they have different surnames. These are referred to by a standard kinship term as the Five Houses *(wufang)*, *fang* being a common way of referring to a sublineage (Freedman 1958, 36).[5]

From the beginning, the elements of physical descent from the Zhu family, motherhood in connection with a peach, and a Gaoxi temple or cloister occur together. A written oath found in 1787 speaks of a Luminous Ruler *(mingzhu)* who transmits the lineage in this cloister. In confessions from that same year, a Young Ruler called Zhu is mentioned, who had been begotten from eating a peach (which can be *li*, the name of the concubine, *tao*, or *taoli*) of the immortals (lit. *xiantao*). Evidently, the Young Ruler Zhu was the same as the Luminous Ruler, who transmitted the lineage of the Zhu imperial family (see above, "The

Luminous King and Other Saviors"). The messianic element of the Luminous Ruler is discussed in more detail below.

The mention of the phrase "subjugating oneself to/supporting the Ming (or: the Luminous One)" in two documents uncovered in 1791 proves that this political ideal existed very early, if not from the very first appearance of the Triads in our sources in 1787. The two texts had been composed in that same year by Triad adherents who had been arrested and banished to Xinjiang in 1787 and had lost touch with local developments in the south (*Tiandihui* 1986, vol. 5, 413). In written oaths uncovered in 1800 and 1808, as well as in the story of the incense burner in the 1811 manual, the full ideal of restoring the Ming and overthrowing the Qing is always explicitly mentioned.[6] Furthermore, the name of the Ming dynasty is often concealed in the form of the split characters *ri* and *yue (ming)*. The earliest example of this might be a poetry line from 1787, and clearer references can be found from the rudimentary manual of 1806 onward (see note 1).

Of course, the claim of having received the Heavenly Mandate always had to be underpinned with physical evidence: miracles, natural occurrences, or actual objects, such as the incense burner mentioned above. There were also old fixed phrases for expressing this claim. Triad texts make abundant use of such phraseology, which they could have borrowed from different sources: government publications, Daoist texts, millenarian and messianic texts, previous uprisings, and so on.[7] Particularly important are the phrase "following Heaven and carrying out the Way" (*shuntian xingdao,* often abbreviated to *shuntian*) and the term "Heaven's Revolution" *(tianyun)* Qin 1988, 153–61 [1787, 1806, 1808, 1812 documents]; (*Tiandihui* 1982, vol. 1, 70, 71, 87 [1787 confessions]; 1986, vol. 5, 413 [1791 documents]). The phrase "following Heaven and carrying out the Way" must be understood as "following the will of Heaven" or "following the Heavenly Mandate *(tianming)* and bringing into practice the Royal Way *(wangdao)* of governance." Historically, the phrase goes back to writings about the Heavenly Mandate in Han and pre-Han political thinking.[8] The term "Heaven's Revolution" in this context refers to the period of rule allotted to a dynasty by Heaven. It can be traced to at least the Period of Disunion, but I have been unable as yet to find its precise source (Mollier 1990, 164; Zürcher 1982, 38 n. 70 and 41 n. 77). The participants in the 1787 uprising of Lin Shuangwen on Taiwan already used this terminology, but it was also common among contemporary adherents of the Triads on the mainland. All literate as well as many illiterate Chinese would have known this terminology and its meaning.

Even if we look only at the political dimension of Triad beliefs, the elements of physical descent of the founder of the Triad tradition from the Ming imperial house, the restoration of the Ming as a political entity and conventional concepts of legitimation are present in the earliest sources from 1787. In no way does this substantiate the traditional claim of a link to the pro-Ming loyalist feelings among literati of the early Qing. There are two much more likely sources for the Ming loyalist message in Triad lore. One is the existence of the messianic tradition of the Luminous King, which is discussed below, and the other is the likely continuance of pro-Ming feelings among local bandit and pirate groups, which I discuss in detail in a forthcoming study.

The above section ignores one knotty problem: the relationship among messianism, political ideals, and actual practice. In a way this problem resembles the question referred to in the introductory remarks, whether and how people actually believed in the messianic contents of Triad ritual and mythology. Chinese messianism was and is inherently political in theory and implications, and there can be no doubt about the political nature of the common legitimation terminology used in Triad texts from the earliest evidence onwards. Nevertheless, the preceding discussion concerns only the historical origins and the internal context of the written material (in other words, the first two approaches outlined initially). The normative reading by actual adherents themselves may well have diverged considerably.

Messianic Saviors

The Luminous King and Other Saviors

In Triad ritual and mythology, three saviors are frequently mentioned, a figure alternatively called Luminous King or Prince or Ruler *(mingwang, mingjun, mingzhu)*, and two figures with the surnames Zhu and Li. The previous sections introduced the Luminous Ruler and a savior with the surname Zhu. They function against the background of ideals about the restoration of the Ming.

The belief in the Luminous King dates back to a tradition from the sixth century, which featured three figures who act as saviors: Maitreya, the young Prince Moonlight *(yueguang tongzi)*, and the Luminous King as their assistant (Zürcher 1982, 1–59). The belief in the Luminous King was transmitted, for instance, in the still extant *Classic of the Five Lords* (Wugongjing). This text inspired many uprisings from the late Tang until this century, including the most important messianic tradition of nineteenth- and twentieth-century Vietnam, the Buu Son Ky Huong tradition that evolved into the Hoa Hao religious group (or "sect"; on my objections to this term, see ter Haar 1992) founded in 1939. Sometimes, the Luminous King appeared together with Maitreya, but more often he appeared alone or with the figure of Luo Ping (Ke 1983, 1987; on Vietnam, see Tai 1983). These beliefs played an important role in late Yuan uprisings, especially the one inspired by Han Shantong. The Luminous King, the importance of *yin* and *mao* days, and the era of Great Equity are all prominent in this *Classic of the Five Lords*. Other works also mention the Luminous King (see Ma 1989, 48, for additional references).

During the Qing, incidents involving prophecies of impending doom and the advent of saviors were at least as frequent as during preceding dynasties. Especially prominent were saviors from the Li and Zhu families, starting with the figures of Third Prince Zhu and Li Kaihua. Four cases, all close in time to 1787, the year that the Triads first appear in historical sources as a distinct phenomenon, illustrate the links of Triad mythology with Qing messianism. Without going into detail about them, it is possible to select elements that are directly relevant to our topic.

In the first example, the 1729–30 case of Li Mei in Enping (Guangdong), the saviors are called Third Prince Zhu and Li Jiukui (Nine Sunflowers Li)(Sasaki 1970, 188; Suzuki 1982, 239). Their followers believed that Third Prince Zhu and Li Jiukui lived in the "Little Western Heaven," situated in Vietnam, and would come with a large army. Li Mei himself claimed that "[the] Heaven[ly Mandate] has been given and the Way will be carried out *(tianyu daoxing)*." He also sold certificates *(zha)*, which would provide protection against the disasters of plagues and demons *(Kangyongqian* 1976, 613–16; *Shiliao xunkan tian*, 1930 especially 21a–b, 24a, 53a–b).

A case that caused the central government real headaches was that of Ma Chaozhu (Suzuki 1982, 267–80). He had been active from 1747 onward in the Hubei region, preparing a messianic uprising. Most of his followers were rounded up in 1752, but he himself was never caught. His teachings concerned a young descendant of the Ming imperial house, called Zhu Hongjin, whose assistants included, among others, one Li Kaihua. Zhu Hongjin was called a Young Ruler *(youzhu)* and a Luminous Ruler *(mingzhu)*. From his kingdom in the Western Ocean—believed to be situated in Sichuan—he would come leading a large army of spirit soldiers to conquer China and restore the Ming. Followers had to pay a fee in silver and conclude a blood oath covenant. Ma Chaozhu presented himself as one of Zhu Hongjin's generals. The profusion of historical documents on this case preserved in the Qing archives on Taiwan and in Beijing shows in considerable detail that the beliefs spread by Ma reflect an earlier stage of the same tradition from which the Triads originated *(Kangyongqian* 1979, 657–60).

In 1752, at about the same time as the Ma Chaozhu case, authorities arrested a group of people in Shangrao, Jiangxi. They had been inspired by the claims of their leader, Li Dexian, that he possessed the magical technique of summoning spirit soldiers. They carried flags bearing, among others, the names Li Kaihua, Zhu Hongzong, and Zhu Hongzhu. Unfortunately, historical sources on this group are rather scarce *(Kangyongqian* 1979, 664–65).

The three cases of Li Mei, Ma Chaozhu, and Li Dexian antedate the first appearance of the Triads in our sources, but equally interesting are the almost contemporary prophecies that circulated before the great uprising of 1796–1804 in the Sichuan-Hunan-Hubei border region, which is traditionally called a White Lotus uprising (see Satō 1983, 109–29; on the White Lotus teachings, see ter Haar 1992, 250–61). One of its preachers, Zhang Zhengmo, confessed in 1796 that he had been told in 1794 of the birth of a True Ruler *(zhenzhu)*, called Li Quanr or Canine Li, who had the characters for sun *(ri)* and moon *(yue)* on his hands. He was to be assisted by Zhu Jiutao, "Nine Peaches" Zhu, who is never identified as a specific historical person. Apocalyptic disasters, including floods, fires, and plagues, were approaching and would kill countless people.[9] Li Quanr himself had already been arrested in 1794 and had testified that he was only 18 *sui* and was actually called Liu Xi Gour (or Canine Liu Xi). His stepfather had told him that his deceased natural father had been called Li and was a Maitreya, or an Immortal *(shenxian)*. This made him, the son, an Immortal Lad *(xiantong)*, that is a Maitreya as well *(Qingzhongqi* 1981, vol. 1, 14–15 [1794], same text as *Shiliao congbian* 1983, vol. 9, 191–92).

Prophecies also circulated at the same time in roughly the same region about the advent of another Maitreya who would help a certain Niu Ba (the split character form of Zhu) to "start an undertaking" *(qishi)* to save people from apocalyptic disasters.[10] His present reincarnation was as a youth. By paying money to join the group and by worshipping Maitreya and Niu Ba, people could avoid the coming disasters. Fierce rows developed between this group and the group supporting the Li Quanr/Liu Xi Gour figure, both claiming to have the real Maitreya *(Qingzhongqi* 1981, vol. 1 3ff [confession 1794]; *Shiliao congbian* 1983, vol. 9, 203–4). Other people who were arrested at the time also spoke of a Zhu Hongtao "red peaches Zhu," who is not further identified *(Qingzhongqi* 1981, vol. 1, 4, 14ff [1794 confessions]). These saviors were not regarded primarily as political leaders. Worship of them was supposed to offer an escape from human misery and apocalyptic disasters. The original prophecies were hardly rebellious, because everything was preordained and there was no need for action. Only increased Qing pressure on the personal networks of the various messianic preachers eventually made violence inevitable.[11]

Several symbols, above all the surname Zhu of the saviors and the characters for "sun" and "moon" on the hands of Li Quanr/Liu Xi Gour, suggest that in addition to messianic expectations, political pro-Ming sentiments were involved in these movements. Explicit confirmation of this can be found in a proclamation pasted to a wall in Xing'an (modern Shaanxi) in 1797. It stated unequivocally that the authors' aim was "to resurrect the Han and destroy the Man[chus]" *(xinghan mieman),* and declared that the "Son of Heaven of the True Ming" *(zhenming tianzi)* had already appeared. The document addressed the local inhabitants as "subjects" of the former Great Ming. Furthermore, it claimed the receipt of the Heavenly Mandate, using standard terminology: "to accept the affairs of the Revolution on behalf of Heaven" *(weitian cheng yunshi)* (Zhang 1980). Several confessions by members of the rebel army that posted this proclamation confirm that this use of the phrase *"zhenming tianzi"* was political, and they refer to their leader Wang Fasheng as a descendant of the Ming imperial house *(Qingdai nongmin* 1990, vol. 6, 73, 205, 208–9). Admittedly, no extant confessions mention the claim of restoring the Ming and overthrowing the Qing, but this simply suggests that the information in the confessions is incomplete. Either the rebels never confessed to the claim, or unknown officials who edited the material deleted the reference. The evidence of the publicly posted proclamation is unequivocally Ming restorationist. Such discrepancies between the evidence in forced confessions and in documents produced voluntarily by the rebels themselves show that the absence of references to the Luminous King does not prove that the belief was not involved.

Collective Characteristics of Messianic Saviors

Despite the apparent disparity of the evidence summarized in the preceding overview, numerous themes recur. In order to understand the connections between Triad mythology and Qing messianism, I shall first recapitulate the evidence from the preceding section in a more systematic fashion. First of all, several features indicate the mythical nature of the saviors and their safe havens. For instance, the curious personal names: beginning with the figure of Li Kaihua, there is a consistent use of flower (especially peach) symbolism, a wealth of puns on the sound "*hong*" and the recurrent use of the number nine *(jiu)*. The descendant of the Zhu family is first called Third Prince Zhu, but later the characteristics of the Li figure, *viz.* the flower, peach and other symbolism, are transferred to the Zhu figure as well.

The flower symbolism combined several associations that must have been familiar to most Chinese. Peaches (*tao* or *taoli*) have always been linked with the messianic surname Li and the ideal of long life.[12] The blossoming of flowers in political, messianic, or millenarian prophecies always announced an important event, such as the restoration of the Ming or the advent of the savior.[13] In Chinese folklore, at least in southern China, there was (and still is) a widespread belief that women were represented in Heaven (called, for instance, the Heavenly Flower Garden) by plants. The birth of a child was thought of as the opening of a new bud on the parent plant.[14] Thus, even the straightforward name of Li Kaihua could be taken to mean literally "the Li that will be born."

The puns on the sound *hong* may reflect the old tradition of the savior Li Hong, but also the term *hong* "floods, vast." Floods are a standard eschatological disaster (Mollier 1990, 22–23, 159–62, 173; Seidel 1969–1970, 236–46; Zürcher 1982, 38, 41–42, 53). The same Hong occurs in the year title of the founding emperor of the Ming, Hongwu, "Vast Martiality." It was suggested above that the emperor or his advisers might have chosen this year title because of its millenarian connotations. *Hong*[a] (red) is the dominant Chinese auspicious color. The importance of the number nine in Chinese religion and mythology hardly needs to be pointed out.

Although the modern observer easily recognizes these saviors and their safe havens, such as the Little Western Heaven or the Western Ocean, as mythical, Qing officials (for example in the case of Ma Chaozhu) spent months looking for them. Beijing exerted immense political pressure to come up with real physical places and persons.

A second point to be noticed is the youth of the incarnations of the Li and Zhu saviors (whether real or fictional). This is a peculiar feature of the tradition of the Luminous King. It further confirms that the saviors themselves were not political figures, but functioned most of all as symbols on whom people could project their hopes during the imminent apocalypse. Because of their youth, they were still close to an ideal unspoiled state of human nature.

The final point concerns the transmission of messianic and millenarian prophecies. There was no standardized transmission of these prophecies through specific organizations ("sects," "secret societies"), even though some written texts circulated and had considerable impact. The changing names of the Li and Zhu saviors, as well as the varying combinations of constituent beliefs, all show that they were transmitted orally. Elements from various traditions could be combined differently by an individual preacher and serve as the basis for forming ad hoc religious groups.

Saviors in Triad Mythology

The preceding analysis demonstrates that the figures of the Luminous King/ Ruler and the two saviors from the Li and Zhu families were well-established personae in Qing messianism. What was their place in early Triad lore? The oath from 1787 already mentions a Luminous Ruler: "Today, because the Luminous Ruler (*mingzhu*) from the Phoenix Flower Pavilion (*fenghua ting*), in the Gaoxi Cloister, in the Maqi Temple, in Guangdong, transmits the lineage, this night we smear blood and conclude a covenant" (Qin 1988, 153). This last phrase was a standard formula to describe all types of blood oath covenants and reveals nothing about its form; drinking (human or chicken) blood mixed with wine was the common method.

Other confessions from 1787 as well as later material confirm the existence of a savior with the surname Zhu, who is also associated with the Luminous King. Thus, one confession from 1787 mentions a mysterious figure: "there was a certain Zhu Hongde, who was begotten from eating a peach of the immortals." He was about 15 or 16 *sui*.[15] Some depict him as a monk. Other adherents confirm the belief in this young person, whom they call Zhu or Zhu Dingyuan (Qin 1988, 311–13; *Tiandihui* 1980, vol. 1, 90, 97, 111–12; confessions by three different persons). Most likely, this person was actually the same Luminous Ruler who "transmits the lineage" (in the 1787 oath) and the (very young) son of the concubine Li (in the 1811 manual). In the 1811 manual, the Luminous King is mentioned frequently (and independently of references to the Ming as a political unit). The shorter term, "Ruler" *(zhu)* is used in both the 1808 oath and the 1811 manual; it refers to either the son of the concubine Li or to the Hongwu Emperor. In the 1811 manual, the son of the concubine is also depicted as a monk (Qin 1988, 154 [1808 oath]; for the 1811 manual, see *Tiandihui* 1980, vol. 1, 4–6, 11, 12, 17, 18, 22).

From the beginning, the evidence shows a belief in a principal savior, who is a young descendant of the Ming imperial family and a monk. He is identified as the Luminous King/Ruler. His status as a monk probably reflects the fact that Zhu Yuanzhang (Hongwu) also started his career as such.

Another mysterious figure in the 1787 confessions is Li Taohong ("peaches are red Li") or Hong Litao ("Vast Li peaches").[16] The surname Li is, of course, the old messianic surname. Here it is combined with the terms "peaches" (tao) and "vast" or "red" (hong and hong [a]). The names of the Li Taohong/Hong Litao figure can be interpreted as a hidden reference to Zhu Hongde's mysterious birth, similar to the name Li Kaihua.

The 1787 confessions also mention an even more mysterious figure, called Monk Hong Erfang, who either remains obscure or is identified with a figure called Monk Wan Tuxi (a mythical founder of the Triads and the same as Wan Tiqi).[17] The name Hong Erfang simply means Hong of the Second House and in later mythology he is alternatively called Fang Dahong or Hong Dasui. This figure is almost always presented as being in charge of the Second House.[18]

Apart from its occurrence in the names of important figures in Triad mythology, the messianic pun on the sound "hong" is continued in one very unexpected way by the Triads. All those who took the blood oath became members of one family with the common surname Hong (hong, "vast" or "flood"). As noted before, the name was often transcribed in split characters.

Thus significant resemblances exist between the contemporary messianic traditions and the Triads with respect to the leading figures in the two traditions. These are the recurrent puns on the sound "hong," the use in the names of persons of the same flower symbolism, the appearance of the Luminous King/Ruler and the saviors from the Li and Zhu families, and finally the crucial place of the youthful founding father. The messianic traditions and the Triad versions constantly restate the same mythological and religious themes.

Messianic Apocalypse and the Triad Foundation Myth

Cities as Places of Refuge

The similarities between Triad mythology and the messianic tradition of the Luminous King go much further than merely having several saviors in common. A summary of the most relevant aspects in the messianic tradition concerning the advent of the apocalypse and the rescue of a limited number of chosen people will form the basis for a general discussion of similar elements in Triad mythology.

In the sixth-century messianic tradition of Maitreya and Prince Moonlight, accompanied by the Luminous King, the world is plagued by apocalyptic disasters: epidemics, floods, and barbarian invasions. Maitreya, Prince Moonlight, the Luminous King, and other saviors appear in the human world to lead the elect away from this world, across a bridge into the Magic City. Before this happens, the chosen few are to be gathered in numerous safe havens, which are also conceived of as cities or fortresses (actually the cumbersome translation "walled enclosures" for "*cheng*" would be more correct). Two of these are Yangzhou (note the special Chinese character) and Liucheng, both meaning "willow." The text also describes the use of secret finger signs (Zürcher 1982, 36, 41–42, 50).

Although Yangzhou and Liucheng are only two in a much longer list of cities that serve as safe havens in this tradition, we also find these two cities—especially Yangzhou—appearing as safe havens from apocalyptic disasters in other early eschatological scriptures.[19] This belief in a city as a refuge for the elect in the case of apocalyptic disaster continued to inspire believers of messianic prophecies from the Tang through the Ming and into the nineteenth century. Qing adherents of the Eternal Venerable Mother tradition commonly believed in a Cloud City or Golden City as the location of paradise. Through buying certificates from the leaders of their religious groups, they would be assured the right of passage into this city after their death, instead of being left to continue the vicious cycle of birth and rebirth. In this way, the millenarian belief became routinized and lost its original urgency. In the Eternal Venerable Mother tradition, strictly speaking, the Cloud City/Golden City had taken over the role of Amitabha's Western Paradise.[20] However, the messianic dimension of the belief lived on in other contexts, such as the *Classic of the Five Lords*. According to this work, the Luminous King would rule the world in Jinling (that is, Nanjing).

During the eighteenth and nineteenth centuries, at least three important (near-) rebellions were fueled by the belief in a city as a safe haven. Ma Chaozhu ultimately planned to attack Nanjing in 1752. Lin Qing actually penetrated the Forbidden City of Beijing in 1813 in the hope of founding a messianic kingdom from there (Naquin 1976, 13–14 and 291 n. 27). The Taipings conquered Nanjing, where they indeed started to put their messianic ideals into practice (Wagner 1982, 67–81). These cities were not merely imperial capitals to be captured for political or military purposes, but also possessed a religious dimension as a safe haven.

The Triad initiation ritual also makes this identification of city and safe haven, calling this place by the name City of Willows *(muyang cheng)*. In the ritual, candidate members are led over a bridge into the City of Willows, where they are then initiated. The structure of this ritual (as well as the foundation myth on which the ritual is partially based) must ultimately go back to the sixth-century tradition of the Luminous King, because it uses the same name for the city and possesses the same structural element of the bridge, as well as the common savior figure of the Luminous King. The city is clearly presented in textual material as a safe haven for the adherents. The name City of Willows is used as early as the 1806 rudimentary manual (*Tiandihui* 1980, vol. 1, 12). *Yang* is synonymous with *liu,* and the two characters are frequently used together to denote willows. *Muyang* is the split and recombined version of *yang*. Interestingly, an alternative name for the City of Willows in the 1811 Triad manual is Forbidden City (Qin 1988, 159 [1806 rudimentary manual]; *Tiandihui* 1980, vol. 1, 12 [1811 manual]).

Barbarian Invasions as an Apocalyptic Threat

The above three elements, the Luminous King, the City of Willows, and the bridge, are all typical of and more or less unique to the sixth-century tradition of Prince Moonlight and the Luminous King. Other elements of Triad ritual and mythology can be documented in other messianic and millenarian traditions as well. Some elements can definitely not be traced to the sixth-century tradition of the Luminous King, but only to other messianic traditions.

Of the several standard apocalyptic disasters, plagues do not seem to play a prominent role in Triad lore. Floods, however, appear more frequently, and the word *hong*, as already discussed, appears extremely often in Triad texts.[21] Nevertheless, floods are not crucial to the mythology of the Triads. Quite the reverse is true of barbarian invasions. In Chinese messianism, barbarian invasions are one of the archetypal apocalyptic disasters (Bauer 1973, stations 10, 13, 15, 30, 32; Ma 1989, 45–48, 157, 165–74; Mollier 1990, 22–25, 68–71; Zürcher 1982, 32–33, 48, 50–51). In the Triad foundation myth, their role is absolutely essential. First of all, they appear as the *xilufan* ("Western Lu barbarians"), whom the Shaolin monks defeat on behalf of the Qing (Manchu) emperors. Because of plotting by jealous ministers at the court, these same rulers turn against the monks. This betrayal eventually leads to the founding of the Triads by a young Ming prince in order to take revenge on the Manchus.

Given that barbarian invasions are a typical eschatological disaster, I would even go so far as to suggest that the anti-Qing and anti-Manchu posture of messianic groups in general and of the Triads in particular is not primarily a reaction to a declining or oppressive Qing government or to socioeconomic tensions. Rather, it represents the traditional place of barbarians in Chinese religious beliefs.

The Role of Signs, Numbers, and Contracts

Secret finger signs constituted a core part of Triad lore since its beginnings. Such signs enabled adherents to recognize each other and thereby served as a means of mutual protection. One had to stretch out three fingers, hold a teacup or a pipe of tobacco with three fingers, or press three fingers to one's breast (*Tiandihui* 1980, vol. 1, 69–72, 87, 104, 111, 121). The thumb symbolized Heaven, the small finger earth (*Tiandihui* 1980, vol. 1, 69, 70, 71, 121). A comparison of these signs with the relevant (though very cryptic) passage in one of the texts from the tradition of the Luminous King does not indicate any similarities in content (Zürcher 1982, 41 n. 77, 44–45, 58, and 74, lines 289–90). Of course, such signs may well have changed considerably over time, or, alternatively, the source of inspiration for the Triad's finger signs may have been elsewhere. Finger signs are, for instance, found in Daoism. The various parts of the fingers and the hand (especially the left hand) represent the Eight Trigrams and the Twelve Earthly

Branches. In addition, the little finger, index finger, and the thumb represent the stars above the Big Dipper (Lagerwey 1987, 17, 70, 113). Clearly, the finger signs of the Triads use exactly the same type of symbolism. Before we identify with certitude the origins of the Triad finger signs, we need to know more about the use of finger signs by (semi-)messianic groups, such as perhaps the modern *Yiguan dao*, an extremely popular Daoist religious group on Taiwan, which is still prohibited on the mainland.

As is common in Chinese millenarianism and messianism, Triad lore shows a fascination with numbers (for example, the split forms of the common family name Hong) and dates. Especially important is the use of the same cyclical date for crucial events. The advent of a savior or of eschatological disasters is often predicted for years with the cyclical characters *jiazi* (which is the first combination of the cycle of sixty) (for instance, Zürcher 1982, 3, 20–22). In the *Classic of the Five Lords*, the Luminous King is said to appear in a year with a cyclical combination that has as its second character *yin* or *mao* (which actually occur consecutively in the cycle). Many uprisings involving beliefs from this book actually took place in such years (Ke 1983, 199–200, and 1987, 367).

Significantly, the 1811 manual uses the cyclical characters *jiayin* (the fiftieth combination of the sixty-year cycle) four times for crucial events, namely the day of the blood oath by the 108 founding monks, the "appearance in the world of the tree from the pit of a peach" *(taozishu chushi)* to signify the appearance of the savior, the burning of the Shaolin monastery, and the advent of the brothers in the world *(Tiandihui* 1980, vol. 1, 4, 15, 17, 19). The obviously mythical nature of *jiayin* years also casts doubt on many of the theories that ascribe a specific year to the founding of the Triads on the basis of its founding myth.

Finally, an element that is not present in the sixth-century tradition but is quite common in messianic and millenarian beliefs during the Qing is the belief in purchasing certificates (*zha* or *hetong*, "contracts") as a guaranteed means of avoiding the apocalypse. This has been mentioned above in connection with the Eternal Venerable Mother tradition and was quite widespread.[22] The Triads also used certificates (called *zha*) for their adherents, which functioned primarily as membership certificates. However, another important function of these certificates was protection. They were, I believe, conceptually modeled on certificates such as those sold by Li Mei in 1729–30 to guarantee protection against the imminent apocalypse. The earliest examples of such certificates among adherents of the Triads are probably two small sheets carrying crucial mythical information, given in 1791 by adherents (who had been banished in 1787) to Liu Zhaokui, a follower of the Eight Trigrams tradition (*Tiandihui* 1986, vol. 5, 404–24).

Considering the present state of the evidence, as analyzed above, I would therefore suggest that the Triads culled both from a specific, probably written (but as yet unidentified), messianic tradition of the Luminous King and the City of Willows, and from more widespread oral traditions, evolving continuously during the Qing, about saviors from the Li and Zhu families. The associations of the name of the savior Luminous King/Ruler had been further enriched during the Ming by its use as a dynastic title. During the Qing, anti-Manchu feelings, too, were reinforced—if not produced outright—by the adoption of these messianic beliefs, which saw barbarian invasion as one of the traditional apocalyptic disasters.

Concluding Remarks

This preliminary analysis of the historical origins of crucial and mutually coherent elements from Triad lore raises several new questions—questions that could never have been asked on the basis of a purely social-historical approach in which one looks only at the activities and social backgrounds of adherents. In this chapter I have taken the reverse track, stressing the meaning(s) of the texts rather than the scarcely documented interpretations and activities of the adherents. Even if we assume that the messianic contents of the rituals and myths did not matter to the majority of the adherents, this leaves the important problem of why those who eventually transmitted the tradition to later generations did care and what the messianism meant to them. Did the Triads remain messianic in orientation (that is, was the messianic focus regenerated from time to time), or—as is my impression—did the messianic aspect become routinized? In the latter case, we can find parallels with the Eternal Heavenly Mother groups described by Susan Naquin; these groups often restructured the messianic ideal of a post-apocalyptic paradise into a long-term expectation, which could be guaranteed by buying certificates. Moreover, did the religious element in general become more and more subjugated to the social activities of various individual groups? These are questions for further research, but it is quite clear that there are significant parallels to the evolution of the messianic Eight Trigrams tradition (which influenced many predatory groups in northern China, although the tradition itself retained its original messianic nature) and the change of the devotionalist Non-Action movement, founded by Luo Qing, into a mutual-aid organization of laborers on the Grand Canal, and eventually into a scarcely disguised criminal organization.

A major issue in scholarly work on the Triads has always been their attitude toward the Qing and the Manchus. Past scholars have seen the Triads as a proto-nationalist political movement, whereas recent scholars have attempted to underplay this political dimension. This investigation points to an altogether different interpretation, founded on a more detailed understanding of legitimation terminology and of the nature of politico-messianic traditions. In my opinion, the anti-Qing posture of the Triads, and—lest this be forgotten—other roughly contemporary messianic traditions, reflects the traditional role of barbarians as an apocalyptic threat. Thus it did not originate in Ming loyalism among literati (with whom the Triads had little connection historically) or the socioeconomic or political decline of the dynasty, both of which have been adduced to explain the appearance of this element. Pro-Ming and anti-Qing notions were already present in the teachings of Ma Chaozhu (1747–52), in the 1797 proclamation by a rebel army during the so-called White Lotus uprising of 1796–1804, and in the earliest material on the Triads itself. Rather, the anti-Qing and pro-Ming posture of the Triads originated in a messianic tradition that antedated the Qing and the Ming by many centuries.

The fact that this originally messianic expectation does not seem to have been prominent in the minds of most Triad adherents need not mean that it was unimportant in their overall beliefs. One might, perhaps, compare it to the general Christian expectation of the kingdom of Christ that will come one day, and for which each good believer should prepare. Although this conviction is actualized only in some smaller religious groups within Christianity, it is quite basic to the beliefs of all Christians.

Notes

1. This research is being carried out with a Research Fellowship of the Royal Dutch Academy of Arts and Sciences.

2. On *ming*: Qin 1988, 160 (1806 manual); *Tiandihui* 1980, vol. 2, 71 (1787 confession); and 8 and 9 (1811 manual). On *wu dian er shi yi*: *Tiandihui* 1980, vol. 1, 97 (same as Qin 1988, 310); on *san ba nian yi*: *Tiandihui* 1980, vol.1, 7.

3. *Tiandihui* 1980, vol. 1, 69–71. The phrase is repeated in many confessions and ritual texts, such as the earliest full-fledged manual (from 1811, hereafter referred to as the 1811 manual), see *Tiandihui* 1980, vol. 1, 8. The interpretation has been copied by all later scholars, starting from Schlegel 1866, 24–25. See Qin 1988, 97–98, for the most recent statement.

4. *Tiandihui* 1980, vol. 1, 4. Earliest mention of this title is 1729, see Sasaki 1970, 167–73; Suzuki 1982, 241. Earliest preserved version, see Ma 1989, 166–67; the text was found in 1813.

5. *Tiandihui* 1980, vol. 1, 4–5, 12 (1811 manual). On the Gaoxi Cloister, see also: Qin 1988, 153 (1787 oath), and *Tiandihui* 1986, vol. 5, 413 (1791 documents by people banished in 1787).

6. *Tiandihui* 1987, vol. 6, 420 (1800); Qin 1988, 154 (1808); *Tiandihui* 1980, vol. 1, 4–6, 8, 11, 13, 15–18, 21, 22 (1811 manual). The ideal of restoring the Ming is often phrased as the need to recover "the rivers and mountains," which is a *pars pro toto* for "the nation," see Qin 1988, 154 (1808 oath) and 159 (1806 rudimentary manual).

7. For their use in Daoist texts, see Lagerwey 1987, 28–29, 66. For their use by the government, see for instance the posthumous titles of the first Ming emperors and the phraseology of imperial edicts, as they are quoted in the Veritable Records of the Ming and Qing dynasties. Many rebels also used this terminology, as early as the late Tang. I present the evidence in full in my forthcoming study.

8. The concepts are, for instance, fundamental to Dong Zhongshu's thought on legitimation and rulership, see *Hanshu* 1962, 56, 2495–2528.

9. *Qingzhongqi* 1981, vol. 5, 37 (confession 1796). Riddle poems and apocalyptic prophecies circulated from 1768 onward within the same network of preachers: *Shiliao congbian* 1983, vol. 9, 159, 160–61 (1768), 166, 169 (1775), 173 (1785); *Qingzhongqi* 1981, vol. 1, 6, 7 (1794 confessions), and so forth.

10. Naquin 1976, 21 and 90, translates *shi* as "rebellion." I prefer the more literal "undertaking": followers of the prophecies did not perceive of their activities only (or primarily) as a rebellion, but as something that was fated to happen by Heaven.

11. See for instance the confession by Liu Song, a major teacher, in *Shiliao congbian* 1983, vol. 9, 202–4. The confessions abound with such remarks. See also ter Haar 1992, 250–61.

12. In *Shuyiji, xia*: 3a, people eating *taoli* (peaches) become immortals. This shows that the term was used as a synonym for *tao* (peaches) in its function of providing immortality. At the end of the Sui, prophecies on *taolizi* (the son of the peaches/the son of peaches-Li) about the advent of a savior called Li circulated widely, discussed by Bingham 1941, 51–54, 68. On peaches in millenarian/messianic prophecies, see also Mollier 1990, 96. In descriptions of the countries of immortals behind grottoes and in mountains, special trees, including peach trees, are always a prominent element; see, for instance, Bokenkamp 1986, 77.

13. In political apocryphal prophecies: *Zhongguo erqiannian zhi yuyan*, in different sets of prophecies: 1970, 42, 46, 86, 91. In messianic and millenarian prophecies: *Qingzhongqi* 1981, vol. 1, 40, on the advent of the Buddhas, when the flowers blossom on the 15th day of the second month, and Naquin 1976, 112, 321 n. 137, on the projected start of the 1813 Eight Trigrams uprising, namely when the yellow flowers blossom on the 15th day of the eighth month (as well as an example of red [*hong*[a]] flowers blossoming). The 1811 manual *(Tiandihui* 1980, vol. 1, 15, 16, 21) contains very explicit references to this effect.

14. The precise ethnographic history of this custom is as yet unclear, but there can be no doubt that in the nineteenth and twentieth centuries this mythology existed throughout southern China. A complete survey of the secondary literature would take us too far. See, for instance, Berthier 1988, 123–36, 210–21, 259–71.

15. *Tiandihui* 1980, vol. 1, 87. There are many references in the 1811 manual to the flowering of peaches as a sign of the advent of a savior *(Tiandihui* 1980, vol. 1, 15, 16 and 21) and the "appearance on earth" (*chushi*, the common term for the incarnation on earth of a savior) of a tree from the pit of a peach *(Tiandihui* 1980, vol. 1, 15).

16. Qin 1988, 311; *Tiandihui* 1980, vol. 1, 87, 111–12; also compare the surnames of three of the founders in *Tiandihui* 1980, vol. 1, 6 –7 (1811 manual). Most confessions mention only the surnames Li and Zhu, without the personal names.

17. *Tiandihui* 1980, vol. 1, 90 (two confessions), 97, and 111–12 (Yan Yan's confession), 139, and Qin 1988, 310 (by the supposed son of Monk Wan, who claims his father also was Monk Hong).

18. Qin 1988, 154 (1808 oath: Fang Dahong of the Second House), and 157 (1797 summary: Fang Dahong of the Second House), 158 (1806 rudimentary manual: Fang Dahong of the Third House); the 1811 manual is inconsistent, *Tiandihui* 1980, vol. 1, 5–7 (Hong Dasui of the Second House) and 11 (Fang Dahong).

19. Apart from the texts mentioned by Zürcher, also see various texts pointed out to me by Ad Dudink, such as *Daozang* 1195 (Schipper enumeration) lines 147–152 and *Daozang* 322, 5a8. Seidel 1984, 312 and 344, mentions the *sanyang di* (Three Willow land) as a place where people will be elected to be saved from the apocalypse.

20. Schafer 1965, 549; Seidel 1984, 310 and 348 (in a late sixth-century messianic text, although not as a central element). Luo (1509) contains a complaint about preachers of Maitreyan prophecies who claim that the elect can take refuge from disasters in the city. The commentary specifies that this is the Silver City. On the belief in the Cloud City or Golden City during the Qing, see Naquin 1976, 13–14, and 1985, 268.

21. On *hong* meaning "flood" in Triad lore, see *Tiandihui* 1980, vol. 1, 87 (1787 confession) and 8 (1811 manual); compare other references to disasters and the fall of the dynasty in the 1811 manual, *Tiandihui* 1980, vol. 1, 7.

22. Suzuki 1982, 163–64, uses this as a criterion for distinguishing religious groups (he differentiates this type from that of the Triads, which he defines primarily by the use of the blood oath) and illustrates this type with numerous cases in the rest of his article. Also see Naquin 1985, 267–268.

References

Bauer, Wolfgang. 1973. *Tuibeitu. Das Bild in der Weissage-Literatur Chinas*. Munich: Heinz Moos Verlag.

Berthier, Brigitte. 1988. *La Dame-du-bord-de-l'eau*. Nanterre: Société à l'Ethnologie.

Bingham, Woodbridge. 1941. *The Founding of the T'ang Dynasty*. Baltimore: Waverly Press.

Bokenkamp, Stephen R. 1986. "The Peach Flower Font and the Grotto Passage." *Journal of the American Oriental Society* 106: 65–77.

Cai Shaoqing. 1987. *Zhongguo jindai huidang shi yanjiu* [Research into the History of Gatherings and Bands in Late Imperial China]. Beijing: Zhonghua shuju.

Chan, Hok-lam. 1970. "Du Liu Bowen Shaobingge" [On the *Baked Cake Ballad* by Liu Ji]. In *Shou Luo Xianglin jiaoshou lunwenji* [Collection of Essays on the Occasion of Professor Luo Xianglin's Venerable Age]. Hong Kong: Wanyou tushu gongsi.

———. 1973. "Chang Chung and His Prophecy: The Transmission of the Legend of an Early Ming Taoist." *Oriens Extremus* 20: 65–102.

Daozang: Laojun bianhua wuji jing. 1924–26. [The Daoist Canon: Non-extreme Classic on Lord Lao's Transformations]. Shanghai: Commercial Press.

Freedman, Maurice. 1958. *Lineage Organization in Southeastern China*. London: Athlone Press, 1980 reprint.

Hanshu [Dynastic History of the Former Han]. 1962. Beijing: Zhonghua shuju, 1975 reprint.

Kangyongqian shiqi chengxiang renmin fankang douzheng ziliao [Sources on the Resistance Struggles of City People during the Kangxi, Yongzheng and Qianlong Periods]. 1979. Beijing: Zhonghua shuju.

Ke Shuxian. 1983. " 'Zhuantian tujing' kao" [An Investigation of the 'Classic of the Map of the Turning of Aeons']. *Shihuo* 13, nos. 5, 6: 197–203.

———. 1987. " 'Zhuantian tujing' xukao [A Sequel Investigation of the 'Classic of the Map of the Turning of Aeons']. *Shihuo* 16, nos. 9, 10: 364–71.

Lagerwey, John. 1987. *Taoist Ritual in Chinese Society and History*. New York: MacMillan.

Luo Qing. *Wubu liuce* [Six Books in Five Volumes]. Original edition 1509, commentary 1596. Reprinted, Taizhong, Mindetang 1980.

Ma Xisha. 1989. *Qingdai bagua jiao* [The Eight Trigrams Teachings of the Qing]. Beijing: Zhongguo renmin daxue chubanshe.

Mollier, Christine. 1990. *Une Apocalypse taoiste du Ve siècle: le livre des incantations divines des grottes abyssales*. Paris: Collège de France, Institut des Hautes Etudes Chinoises.

Naquin, Susan. 1976. *Millenarian Rebellion in China: The Eight Trigrams Uprising of 1813*. New Haven: Yale University Press.

———. 1985. "The Transmission of White Lotus Sectarianism in Late Imperial China." In *Popular Culture in Late Imperial China*, ed. David Johnson, Andrew J. Nathan, and Evelyn S. Rawski, 255–91. Berkeley: University of California Press.

Noguchi Tetsurō. 1986. *Mindai byakurenkyōshi no kenkyū* [Research into the History of the White Lotus Teachings of the Ming Period]. Tōkyō: Yū sankaku shuppan.

Qin Baoqi. 1988. *Qing qianqi Tiandihui yanjiu* [Research into the Heaven and Earth

Gathering during the early Qing period]. Beijing: Zhongguo renmin daxue chubanshe.

Qingdai nongmin zhanzheng ziliao xuanbian [A Selection of Sources on Qing Period Peasants' Wars], vol. 6. 1990. Beijing: Zhongguo renmin daxue chubanshe.

Qingzhongqi wusheng bailianjiao qiyi ziliao [Sources on the White Lotus Rebellion in Five Provinces during the Middle Qing]. 1981. Suzhou: Jiangsu renmin chubanshe.

Ren Fang 1925. *Shuyi ji* [Record accounting of strange affairs]. In the *Shuoka* encyclopedia. Shanghai: Shanghai wenming Shuju. Reprint edition.

Sasaki Masaya. 1970. *Shinmatsu no himitsu kessha* [Secret Societies during the Late Qing]. Tōkyō: Gannandō shoten.

Satō Kimihiko. 1983. "Shindai Byakurenkyō no shiteki tenkai: Hakka kyō no sho hanran" [The historical development of the White Lotus Teachings during the Qing period: The uprisings by the eight trigrams teachings]. In *Zoku chūgoku minshū hanran no sekai* [The World of Chinese Popular Rebellions, Continued], 75–183. Tōkyō: Saiko shoin.

Schafer, Edward H. 1965. "The Origin of an Era." *Journal of the American Oriental Society* 85: 543–50.

Schipper, Kristofer. 1982. *Le corps taoïste*. Paris: Fayard.

Schlegel, Gustave. 1866. *The Hung League or Heaven and Earth League*. Batavia: Lange & Co.

Seidel, Anna. 1969–1970. "The Image of the Perfect Ruler in Early Taoist Messianism: Lao-tzu and Li Hung." *History of Religions* 9, nos. 2 & 3: 216–47.

————. 1983. "Imperial Treasures and Taoist Sacraments—Taoist Roots in the Apocrypha." In *Tantric and Taoist Studies in Honour of R. A. Stein II*, ed. Michel Strickmann. Brussels: Institut Belge des Hautes Etudes Chinoises.

————. 1984. "Le sûtra merveilleux du Ling-pao suprême, traitant de Lao Tseu qui convertit les barbares [The marvellous sutra of the supreme Lingbao, treating Laozi, who connected the barbarians]. In *Contributions aux études de Touen Houang*, [Contributions to research on Dunhuang], Vol. 3, ed. Michel Soymié, 305–52. Paris: Ecole Française d'Extrême Orient.

Shiliao congbian IX. Qingdai dang'an shiliao congbian [Collection of Archival Sources on the Qing Period]. 1983. Beijing: Zhonghua shuju.

Shiliao xunkan tian-series [Ten-daily Publication of Historical Sources]. 1930. Beijing: Shenwumen fashoushi.

Smith, Richard J. 1991. *Fortune-tellers and Philosophers; Divination in Traditional Chinese Society*. Boulder, Colo.: Westview Press.

Sun Guangxian. 1981. *Beimeng suoyan* [Desultory Notes from Yunmeng in the North]. Shanghai: Shanghai guji chubanshe.

Suzuki Chūsei. 1982. "Shinchō chūki ni okeru minkan shūkyō kessha to sono sennen ōkoku undō e no keikō" [Popular religious groups and their tendencies towards millenarianism during the mid Qing period]. In *Sennenōkokuteki minshū undō no kenkyū* [Research into Millenarian Popular Movements], ed. Suzuki Chūsei, 151–350. Tōkyō: Tōkyō daigaku shuppankai.

Tai, Hui-Tam Ho. 1983. *Millenarianism and Peasant Politics in Vietnam*. Cambridge: Harvard University Press.

Ter Haar, B. J. 1992. *The White Lotus Teachings in Chinese Religious History*. Leiden: E. J. Brill.

Tiandihui [Heaven and Earth Society]. 1980–88. Vols. 1–7. Beijing: Zhongguo renmin daxue chubanshe.

Wagner, Rudolf. 1982. *Reenacting the Heavenly Vision: The Role of Religion in the Taiping Rebellion*. Berkeley: University of California Press.

Zhang Xingbo. 1980. "Tantan bailian jiao Xiangyang qiyijun de bugao yu kouhao"

[Some remarks on a proclamation and slogans of the Xiangyang rebel army of the White Lotus Teachings]. *Wenxian* 1980: 156–64.

Zhongguo erqiannian zhi yuyan [Two Thousand Years of Chinese Predictions]. 1970. Taipei: Daxin shuju.

Zhuang Jifa. 1981. *Qingdai tiandi hui yuanliukao* [An Investigation of the Origins of the Heaven and Earth Gathering]. Taipei: National Palace Museum.

Zürcher, Erik. 1982. " 'Prince Moonlight,' Messianism and Eschatology in Early Medieval Chinese Buddhism." *T'oung Pao* 68: 1–59.

7

Migration, Protection, and Racketeering: The Spread of the Tiandihui within China

Dian Murray

One of the longest-held and most widely circulated beliefs about the Tiandihui (Heaven and Earth Society) is that it was a "secret society" dating from the late Ming or early Qing dynasty. According to this view, the Tiandihui "secret society" was a clandestine political organization, created by members of the Chinese elite (either Ming loyalists, Han "nationalist" scholars, or members of the Zheng family of pirate-loyalists) for the specific purpose of "Overthrowing the Qing and restoring the Ming" dynasties (fanQing fuMing). This view of the Tiandihui as an anti-Manchu society was embraced by Sun Yat-sen and his colleagues in their endeavors to generate support for the anti-Qing uprisings of the late nineteenth and early twentieth centuries. In the period since the 1911 Revolution, scholarship on the Tiandihui has been largely devoted to searching out historical evidence in support of Sun's views. This perception of the Tiandihui as a nationalist political organization is still deeply cherished by scholars on both Taiwan and the Chinese mainland (Murray 1993, Chapter 4).

Archival evidence discovered on Taiwan and the Chinese mainland since the mid-1960s, however, indicates that the Tiandihui, in the period before the Opium War, was not primarily a political organization devoted to "Overthrowing the Qing and restoring the Ming" but rather a mutual aid society directly linked to the socioeconomic circumstances and migration patterns of China's lower classes.[1] An underlying cause of the Tiandihui's formation was the spectacular population increase of the early Qing period, which resulted in severe economic dislocation for those endangered by declining man–land ratios. Circumstances forced many who had lost their means of livelihood or who did not have access to land to migrate out of their indigenous communities to earn a living. Cut off from local support systems and socially isolated in unfamiliar territory, these individuals had little recourse but to make do among themselves. In southeast China, one of the most common strategies for those displaced from their villages was to create organizations of their own for self-protection. Brotherhoods of different surnames constituted the organizational means most directly at their disposal. Within this context, the Tiandihui emerged as but one of many such multi-surname, mutual aid brotherhoods that proliferated throughout the region. This chapter discusses the formation of the Tiandihui and the various social and economic functions it performed in local Chinese society.

Formation of the Tiandihui

According to the reconstruction of Tiandihui history by Chinese and Western archival scholars, a developmental stage, before the society's actual founding in the early 1760s, seems to have occurred when the individuals who would be instrumental in its formation left their homes in Zhangpu county, Fujian province, to seek their fortunes in Sichuan. While in Sichuan these men—Tixi (Zheng Kai, also known as Monk Wan or Monk Honger), Li Amin (alias Li Shaomin), Zhu Deyuan, and Tao Yuan—appear to have used their hometown connections to join with monk Ma Jiulong in forming an unnamed brotherhood of individuals with different surnames (Murray 1993, Chapter 1).[2]

But the real emergence of the Tiandihui as a named organization seems to have occurred after their return to Fujian sometime in 1761 or 1762. Among the group, Tixi is the individual most often credited with the actual founding. After a brief visit to Guangdong, he appears to have returned from Sichuan to Fujian, where he took up residence at the Goddess of Mercy temple in his native Gaoxi and recruited three fellow residents of Zhangpu county: Lu Mao, of Duxun township; his former friend from Sichuan, Li Amin of Xiaceng village; and Fang Quan from Gaoxilou village (*Tiandihui* 1980, vol. 1, 96–100; 110–12; 1988, vol. 7, 522–27). In acknowledging Tixi as their leader, these men became the first generation of Tiandihui "brothers" who, during the Qianlong period, spread the society throughout the remainder of Zhangpu and Pinghe counties, Fujian, and through their disciples, across the strait to Taiwan. Later, during the Jiaqing era, the Tiandihui spread rapidly throughout the remainder of South China, where the Taiwanese scholar Zhuang Jifa has linked its expansion and growth to the migration patterns of individuals from Fujian and Guangdong provinces (Murray 1993, Chapter 2; Zhuang, 1986, 1990a, 1990b).

Archival evidence suggests that a large percentage of the pre-Taiping Tiandihui groups was formed by individuals who were originally from places other than those in which their societies were founded. According to data prepared by Zhuang, a total of 39 Tiandihui (including associations that had adopted other names) were founded by men from Fujian between 1761 and 1816. Of these, 23 were founded in provinces other than Fujian and of the 16 formed within Fujian itself, none was established in the native place of its principal founder. Similarly, each of the 28 Tiandihui founded by individuals from

Guangdong between 1783 and 1816 was founded in a province other than Guangdong (Zhuang, 1990a, tables on 749–59 and 757–58).

Membership in such organizations was often composed of people from a variety of provinces, some of whom had already spent considerable portions of their lives assimilating to and residing in their host communities (one such example was Lin Shuangwen, who had moved as a child from Fujian to Taiwan). Others may have been newly arrived, while still others may have been native residents. For example, of the 46 men initiated into a Tiandihui in Guanyang county, Guangxi, in 1820 for whom native place data are available, 17 appear to have been from the villages of Guanyang county (Guangxi); 8 each from Hunan and Jiangxi provinces; 2 from Guangdong province; and 11 from Fujian province (5 from Tong'an and 6 from Quanzhou). As can readily be seen, in this instance individuals from places other than Guangxi outnumbered the natives by almost two to one (*Tiandihui* 1988, vol. 7, 378–80).

In no two cases, however, were migrant communities or the circumstances of individual migrants the same. Elements such as the degree of assimilation into or estrangement from new communities, the length of time in which the newcomers had been in residence, the nature of the residence—that is, whether it was of a settled or sojourning kind—and the specific circumstances of the communities themselves defined the needs that members endeavored to satisfy through the creation of voluntary associations. In the case of the Heaven and Earth Society, the organizational format of the *hui*, as Ownby suggests, was flexible enough to allow the Tiandihui to be readily adopted as a means to the ends discussed below.

The Tiandihui and Protection

Among the most important needs of Chinese sojourners, including peddler-merchants and seasonal laborers, were networks of protection and introduction as they endeavored to make their way in alien communities. The Tiandihui frequently seems to have functioned as a kind of a poor man's *huiguan,* or native place association, for China's déclassé migrants. *Huiguan,* according to Susan Naquin and Evelyn Rawski, provided meeting grounds, lodging, financial assistance, storage facilities, and sometimes even regulation of trade for financially stable members, who at some level shared a common native place. These individuals had recourse to the services of the *huiguan* while they were away from home. *Huiguan* also constituted relatively formal, corporate organizations that managed communal property acquired by the contributions or fees of their members. At the core of most *huiguan* organizations was a shrine to a patron deity, providing a "structure for collective celebrations and a symbol of the community" (Naquin and Rawski 1987, 48–49).

Obviously, the Tiandihui was far less incorporated and native place–specific than the *huiguan,* but just as the *huiguan* afforded a sense of community and protection to society's well-established sojourners, so did the Tiandihui hold out to its members at least some promise of community and fraternity. Initiations of new members provided occasions for collective celebrations. The various plaques or portraits of founder Monk Tixi or other deities, which graced most ceremonies, along with the incense burned before them, served as the organization's "sacred" core, before which new recruits swore their oaths of loyalty. Thereafter society "secrets," in the form of codes, mantras, or gestures whose purpose was to enable members to recognize one another even if they were personally unacquainted, were revealed. On some occasions, initiates were also presented with cloth or paper certificates, known as *huatie,* as tangible proof of their membership in palpable communities, which, at least in theory, could be summoned to their assistance in times of need.

This aim was most explicitly stated in the testimony of Yan Yan, chief propagator of the Tiandihui to Taiwan, who said in 1788:

> Originally, the reason for people's willingness to enter the society was that if you had a wedding or funeral, you could get financial help from the other society members; if you came to blows with someone, there were people who would help you. If you encountered robbers, as soon as they heard the secret code of their society, they would then bother you no further. (*Tiandihui* 1980, vol. 1, 110–12)

In this regard, Yan Yan seems to have been speaking for countless others whose major reason for having joined the Tiandihui was to avoid being insulted, bullied, or beaten up by potential adversaries. Eighty-three (or 42 percent) of 196 Tiandihui members whose reasons for having joined are cited in the documents of the First Historical Archives indicated mutual aid or protection as their primary motivations. Seventy-three (37 percent) mentioned resisting arrest or protection against violence. Throughout South China, protection against extortion by others was invariably the primary rationale given by leaders and followers alike for having formed societies of their own. (These statistics were provided by Professor Qin Baoqi of People's University in Beijing and are based primarily on the cases that appear in *Tiandihui* 1986–88, vols. 5–7.)

For those assimilating into nonnative communities, the need for protection included support networks (sometimes in the form of gangs) by individuals of a given region or ethnicity to defend themselves against rivals from another region or ethnic group. For example, Tiandihui of this type were often created on Taiwan by former residents of Zhangzhou, Fujian, as a means of standing up to transplanted former residents from the neighboring Quanzhou, Fujian (for an example, see the case of Xie Zhi and Zhang Biao below).

In 1804, immigrants from Guangdong to Guangxi created a Tiandihui to obtain revenge from a resident of Yishan county (Guangxi). Zhong Yamao, of Nanhai, Guangdong, worked as a hired laborer in the area of Shanglin and Yishan counties, Guangxi, where during the seventh month of 1804, he joined Zhong Hezhao (not a kinsman) in making his way to Yishan county to buy saltpeter privately from Song Qing, an official in charge of its handling. When Song Qing did not agree to the purchase, a quarrel broke out. Song Qing ultimately captured Zhong Hezhao and took him to the county authorities. Zhong Yamao escaped, and a few years later, in 1808, rejoined his friend, the former captive Zhong Hezhao. The two men again found themselves in Shanglin county, where they stayed at the store of a friend. There they conceived the idea of forming a Tiandihui to obtain revenge by robbing Song Qing's home and killing him. On JQ 13.6.6 (1808), thirty-one men set out for Song Qing's with a clearly articulated plan of attack. Song Qing himself escaped, but his home was robbed, and one of its residents was wounded in the fray that followed (*Tiandihui* 1988, vol. 7, 330–32).

The Tiandihui and Xiedou

In Chinese society, the line between protection and predation was always thin, and as Elizabeth Perry has already shown, protection strategies often contained within them the potential for predation (Perry 1980, 48–95). This was certainly the case with the Tiandihui as well, and among more established communities, Tiandihui organizations became effective vehicles for *xiedou:* collective violence in the form of armed struggle and local feuding that characterized much of South China throughout the late eighteenth and early nineteenth centuries.

Nearly everyone who has written about the Minnan-Yuedong region of China has mentioned feuds as one of the major problems of governance. Highly organized blood feuds ritualistically conducted out of temple headquarters involved lineages in cycles of hostility that sometimes continued for generations (Lamley 1981, 305–10; 1990, 262–66).

At the same time, Tiandihui organizations often facilitated subethnic strife as well. One case involves Zhou Dalai, a Hakka from Guangxi province, who was having a difficult time earning a living at Malai, in Guangnan prefecture, Yunnan. Upon hearing about the Tiandihui, Zhou recruited fellow immigrant Hakkas from Long'an, Guangxi, and Meitan and Zunyi, Guizhou, who were initiated into a society at Malai on JQ 16.7.8 (1811). During the ceremony, Zhou Dalai stated that because the members were all Hakkas, they needed the Tiandihui for their mutual protection and to prevent their being taken advantage of by others (*Tiandihui* 1988, vol. 7, 464–68).

Similarly, as David Ownby's chapter has already shown, the creation of Lin Shuangwen's Tiandihui on Taiwan, before the rebellion in 1787, was a direct response to the *xiedou* of two brothers, Yang Guangxun and Yang Mashi, who had each formed societies *(hui)* in their battle to divide their father's property.

A few years later, Taiwan was also the site of a Tiandihui formed for the purpose of *xiedou* by Zhang Biao and Xie Zhi. Zhang Biao was a native of Zhangzhou who did not get along with his neighbors from Quanzhou and so formed a society for the purpose of revenge. In light of his many grudges against people from Quanzhou, Zhang decided to recruit individuals and found a society *(hui)*. On QL 56.7.28 (1791), Zhang Biao ran into his long-time acquaintance from Guangdong, Xie Zhi, and explained his situation. Xie responded by suggesting that he create a Tiandihui. When asked how to go about doing so, Xie explained:

> You must establish an incense altar and in front of the gods, sacrifice a chicken, drink its blood, and pass under the knives while saying the following oath to Heaven, "If one person experiences difficulty, everyone will come to his aid. If I break this oath, the knife will fall and destroy my body." Then the paper on which the oath is written is burned in front of the deity. You then drink wine and blood. When you encounter other members of the same society, extend three fingers of the left hand toward Heaven as a secret signal.

Zhang Biao was impressed, and thereupon the two men began recruiting initiates. After seven successful initiation ceremonies, however, Zhang Biao was arrested on the eve of his eighth, before he and his recruits had a chance to conduct any actual *xiedou* reprisals (*Tiandihui* 1986, vol. 5, 375–79). (For an additional example of *xiedou* strife leading to rebellion, see the account of the Tiandihui in Buluo, Guishan, and Yong'an counties below).

The Tiandihui and Entrepreneurship

Another element undergirding Tiandihui creation almost from the beginning was the idea of membership as a salable commodity that could be marketed by ambitious leaders. Such "sales" usually occurred in the form of initiation fees, paid by new recruits allegedly to cover the costs of their initiations. In reality, however, after the necessary paraphernalia—incense, paper, wine, and a sacrificial chicken—had been procured, the surplus funds provided leaders with quick sources of cash. Such entrepreneurial considerations were an important part of Tiandihui practices from the very beginning. On his deathbed, Tiandihui founder Tixi imparted the society's secrets to his ne'er-do-well son, Zheng Ji, as a means of enabling him to support himself through their further transmission. This motive is also referred to by Yan Yan, who spread the Tiandihui to Taiwan in 1786 and stated in his testimony that "if you were to transmit the sect to other people, you would also receive their payments of 'gratitude' " (*Tiandihui* 1980, vol. 1, 110–112).

Because the existence of the Tiandihui was not discovered by Qing authorities until after the Lin Shuangwen rebellion in 1788, the first specific example of how these fees worked dates only from 1787, when Lin Zhongyu, Yan Tuo, and Li Shui paid between 200 and 300 *wen* of copper cash apiece to join the society transmitted by Zhang Pu of Pinghe county, Fujian (*Tiandihui* 1987, vol. 6, 136–37). Ten years later, in 1797, individuals from Jianyang and Chongan, Fujian, were more explicitly described by government officials as having joined forces in forming a Tiandihui for the purpose of "swindling money" *(pianqian)* from recruits who paid 200–300 *wen* each for the privilege of joining (*Tiandihui* 1987, vol. 6, 139).

For two associations founded in 1800 and 1801, one leader in Nanjing, Fujian, netted more than 2,000 *wen* from a total of 24 members (83 *wen* per person), while in 1802, the second, Zhang Peichang and his ailing friend, took in 5,900 *wen* from 24 recruits (246 *wen* per person) (*Tiandihui* 1987, vol. 6, 153, 158). By 1808, initiation fees of between 500 *wen* of cash and one or two *yuan* of foreign silver were increasingly common (*Tiandihui* 1987, vol. 6, 179).

This practice seems to have become especially refined in Guangxi, where, during the seventh month of 1810, Tiandihui leaders collected initiation fees amounting to 5,400 *wen* for incense, chicken, wine, and paper that cost only 3,400 *wen*, thus leaving them with a profit of 2,000 *wen* to divide among themselves (*Tiandihui* 1988, vol. 7, 306). Similarly, during the second month of 1806, Huang Shike formed another association in Guangxi. He and his companions charged prospective members 1,200 *wen* apiece and found themselves with 9,000 *wen* to divide after subtracting the initiation expenses of 26 new members (*Tiandihui* 1988, vol. 7, 333).

Entrepreneurial sophistication ultimately extended to marketing the rights to society leadership as well as membership. In Jiangxi province, red paper or cloth *huatie,* certifying Tiandihui membership and authorizing their bearers to found societies of their own, were presented only to initiates who had paid large sums to join. For example, when Zhou Dabin, a peddler from Huichang county, Fujian, formed his society in Jiangxi, recruits who paid him between two and five *yuan* of foreign silver received the all important *huatie.* However, when the recruiting endeavors of his principal subordinates yielded initiates who paid fees of only 400 or 500 *wen* each, Zhou abbreviated their ceremonies by transmitting only the secret sentences and not bothering to sacrifice a chicken, drink its blood, or hand out *huatie* (*Tiandihui* 1987, vol. 6, 301).

The Tiandihui and Crime

In addition to selling membership and protection, the entrepreneurial agendas of Tiandihui leaders often included founding societies to conduct robbery. Such motives were certainly an integral part of Tiandihui formation on both Taiwan and in Guangdong province during the late Qianlong and early Jiaqing periods and are well documented in early Tiandihui legal cases. Soon after the Tiandihui made its appearance in Guangdong, the province became the site of huge organizations such as that of Chen Linan, formed for the explicit purpose of committing robbery. Chen Linan joined the Tiandihui in his native Tong'an, Fujian, but later, because of poverty, moved to a village in Dongguan county, Guangdong, to seek employment as a hired laborer. When this strategy failed, Chen Linan decided to found a Tiandihui and thereby initiated seven men into his unit on JQ 6.1.24 (1801), in Dongguan. The understanding was that they would recruit additional members until their collective efforts yielded an organization large enough to conduct robbery.

Within a few days, their enterprise produced seventy-six recruits who gathered to form a general association with Chen as its leader. Chen was arrested before he actually had a chance to carry out his scheme, but his intentions were later realized by his subordinate, Chen Wenan. After lying low for a couple of years, Chen revived his predecessor's Tiandihui, and on JQ 8.3.19 (1803), the group robbed 1,676 silver *yuan*, 142 items of clothing, and 12 *shi* of rice from a local dwelling before setting it on fire. Thereupon fighting broke out, and several people were killed; Chen's followers were in the process of burning the corpses at the time of their arrest (*Tiandihui* 1987, vol. 6, 421–24, 446–450).

In late JQ 8 (1803), 39 of association leader Guan Nianzong's 96 members joined him in robbing 70 *yuan* worth of head ornaments and clothes, 1,263 *yuan* of silver, and 45,580 copper cash in Zengcheng county, Guangdong. Guan Nianzong himself was a resident of Zengcheng, who during the third lunar month of JQ 8 (1803), went in search of employment to nearby Dongguan, where he joined a Tiandihui. When the founder of Guan Nianzong's Tiandihui was arrested, Guan became frightened and thus returned to Zengcheng, where, after discussing his poverty with friends, he decided to found a Tiandihui of his own for the purpose of committing robbery (*Tiandihui* 1987, vol. 6, 452).

Robbery was also the motive behind the Tiandihui formed by Huang Mingcan of Xinning, Guangdong, during the fifth month of JQ 7 (1802). Six individuals paid 300 *wen* for the privilege of joining him and were in the process of recruiting additional members for a general association at the time of their arrest (*Tiandihui* 1987, vol. 6, 467). Likewise, robbery carried out at the home of Wang Damei in Qiongshan county (Hainan), Guangdong, during the fourth month of JQ 9 (1804), netted 40 *yuan* of silver and 3,000 *wen* of copper cash (*Tiandihui* 1987, vol. 6, 476). Robbery conducted in Guangxi on JQ 13.10.1 (1808), yielded each of its nine Tiandihui perpetrators a sum of 3 *qian* and 3 *fen* of silver, plus an additional 3,000 *wen* from the sale of stolen clothes, which was pocketed by the leader (*Tiandihui* 1987, vol. 7, 294).

The Tiandihui and Rebellion

In popular perception, the activity that is probably most closely associated with the Tiandihui is rebellion. In some cases, rebellion seems to have been a conscious organizational strategy of Tiandihui founders almost from the society's establishment, while in other instances, "rising up" seems to have been more the unintended consequence of protective or predatory strategies gone awry.

Lu Mao, leader of the first Tiandihui uprising, decided during the tenth month of QL 32 (1767), to create a brotherhood, as Qing officials described it, to engage in "criminal activities" *(jiemeng weifei)*. But on QL 21.10.18 (1767), when the first recruits gathered at his home to form a blood covenant before the gods, Lu Mao gave each a piece of cloth and announced that the plan was instead to rob the storehouse, treasury, and homes of the community pillars of Zhangpu county and use the proceeds to carry out an uprising *(jushi)*. As a part of their preparation, Lu Mao and the other leaders came up with Zhao Liangming, an alleged scion of the Song dynasty, to serve as the symbolic leader for their undertaking. Although 365 of Lu's followers participated in an uprising on QL 33.3.14 (1768), the insurrection was quickly quelled (*Tiandihui* 1988, vol. 7, 522–33).

Similar motives inspired the second Tiandihui uprising as well. Its leader, Li Amin (alias Li Shaomin), created a Tiandihui for the explicit purpose of collaborating with an alleged descendant of the Ming dynasty to rob the wealthy households of Xiaceng village (also in Zhangpu county) and "rise up." Word of the enterprise leaked out, however, and most of the organizers were arrested before they had a chance to act at all (*Tiandihui* 1987, vol. 7, 534–50).

Local feuding provided the impetus for the founding of the Tiandihui in Boluo county, which along with Guishan and Yong'an counties, became the site of the first Tiandihui uprising in Guangdong. Boluo had many immigrants from Zhangzhou, Fujian, who fought with the natives over water rights. Individuals on both sides formed societies for self-protection, and casualties resulted from their leaders' desire for revenge.

The insurrection was instigated by the head of the Increase Brothers Society (also pronounced "tiandihui") in Boluo county, Chen Lanjisi. Chen had worked for two years building his organization and by 1802 had a considerable number of men at his disposal. (The sources say more than 10,000, but the figure cannot be taken literally.) Buoyed by the prospect of success, Chen decided to raise the standard of rebellion and dispatched various lieutenants to obtain saltpeter and weapons. He also manufactured ten cloth flags with the slogan "*shuntian xingdao*" (obey Heaven and follow the way).

On JQ 7.8.8 (1802), Chen Lanjisi mustered his forces. Taking advantage of a temporary low in the county's troop contingents, the rebels launched their movement the following week with attacks on several villages, including Tuguawei, Liujiawei, Wunitang, Xianggang, and Longhuawei. Governor-general Ji Qing mobilized 550 troops under Li Hansheng and Hu Junhong, but because the soldiers had to be brought in from outside, this force was unable to counterattack immediately. The first major battle occurred later in the eighth month, when the rebels were attacked in their mountain fortress by Sun Quanmou from the west and Li Hansheng from the east. An army under General Huang Biao arrived later that month to precipitate a campaign in which Qing troops burned the rebels' wooden palisade and captured more than 300 men. Thereupon, Chen and some of the others retreated to Houshan.

In the next major battle, on JQ 7.9.6 (1802), Chen Lanjisi, with several thousand remaining supporters, made a stand at Luofu Mountain. When their stockades were broken, the rebels were forced to retreat. As the rebel army scattered, another 300 participants were apprehended. Two weeks later, the twenty-six-year-old leader himself was captured on the border between Boluo and Zengcheng counties, and the uprising ended.

While rebellion was raging in Boluo, trouble was also brewing in nearby Guishan county, where two local Tiandihui leaders, Chen Yanben and Cai Buyun, one a native and the other an immigrant from Fujian, decided to follow Chen Lanjisi's lead. On JQ 7.4.11 (1802), Chen Yaben visited Cai Buyun to confer about the possibility of forming a Tiandihui. Cai agreed, and the men recruited sixteen others to join their society.

Because their numbers were so few and others were afraid to join, staging a rebellion at that time was out of the question. Nevertheless, Chen and Cai clearly had this in mind when they proclaimed themselves "Great King" (da wang) and "Great Generalissimo" (da yuanshuai), respectively; designated other officials from the north, south, east, and west; and began manufacturing weapons and recruiting participants in the neighboring villages.

They gradually succeeded in attracting several hundred followers, enough to carry out robberies in such villages as Renshan, Baimanghua, and Pingsha, which were under the domain of the rival Ox Head Society (Niutouhui), a protective association organized by the local landlords and the well-to-do. The Ox Head Society, whose name derived from the fact that its members tilled their fields with oxen, added to its strength by hiring township braves (xiangyong) for its ongoing battle with the Tiandihui. On JQ 7.8.15 (1802), Chen Yaben and Cai Buyun launched an all-out attack in Ox Head territory. Word of the enterprise spread and the participants were quickly apprehended and executed (Qin, 1988, 301–2).

The Tiandihui uprising in Yong'an also grew out of quarrels with the Ox Head Society. In the late summer of JQ 7 (1802), Wen Dengyuan recruited five others, including Zeng Qinggao, to join a Tiandihui for mutual aid. The following month, news of its creation reached the head of Qingxi's local Ox Head Society, a national student named Lan. Aware of the uprising in Boluo and fearful that the Tiandihui in his own county would also rise up, Lan ordered the members of his society to capture the Tiandihui leader, Wen Dengyuan, and turn him over to county authorities. Shortly thereafter, Wen died in jail. Zeng Qinggao, Guan Yuelong, and the other Tiandihui members carried out reprisals with as many as 200 and sometimes 500 men against the members of the Ox Head Society.

A month later, after the Boluo uprising had been suppressed, one of its leaders made his way to Tianzizhan's Qingxi and encouraged Guan Yuelong, Zeng Qinggao, and Lai Dongbao to "rise up." The men agreed, and on JQ 7.9.26 (1802) issued their proclamation and divided their force for attacks on Qingxi, Huangtang, and Zhongpuwei. Governor-general Ji Qing dispatched provincial troops, and the first major battles occurred on JQ 7.10.2 and 7.10.4. The tide turned quickly, however, when on JQ 7.10.6 Sun Quanmou brought his 2,000-

man army within 30 *li* of the rebel headquarters and defeated Zheng Qinggao, who surrendered with a large contingent of the rebel force. Thereafter, the movement quickly collapsed, and the remainder of the participants were either captured or surrendered of their own accord. During the course of battle, Guan Yuelong did not forget student Lan's hand in the capture of the Tiandihui leader Wen Dengyuan and burned the homes of both Lan and a relative.

Not surprisingly, trouble continued in Yong'an well after the suppression of the rebellion as members of the local Ox Head Society continued to seek revenge, and the Tiandihui replied in kind. The stalemate continued until early in the following year, when Sun Quanmou arrived to command a newly recruited force. A major battle ensued. The rebels defended themselves primarily with stones and cannon, but in the end, were forced to retreat behind their defenses. From this point, their momentum quickly ebbed. As the Qing forces came at them from all sides, their movement fell apart, and they were easily defeated. Calm finally returned to Boluo, Guishan, and Yong'an counties (Qin 1988, 302–6).

In the view of Tiandihui leader Su Ye, "rebellion" was the result of robbery gone awry. In 1792, Su returned from Taiwan to his native Fujian and decided to form a Tiandihui for the purpose of attacking the homes of the wealthy. After realizing that word of his plan had reached government officials, Su, fearing that all was lost, nevertheless ordered his followers to "raise their standard," after which 150 of his men were promptly killed and 200 were arrested (*Tiandihui* 1986, vol. 5, 450–82).

Although rebellion was certainly an important Tiandihui activity during the late eighteenth and early nineteenth centuries, Ming restorationism, so long believed to have been at the center of the association's *raison d'être*, seems to have played a minor role at best. For the most part, these rebellions resulted from concerns which can hardly be called political, and to the extent that they utilized Ming trappings at all, they did so only in the traditional way of invoking legendary scions of previous dynasties as spiritual leaders. Before the nineteenth century, slogans that suggested "eliminating the Qing and reviving the Ming" had yet to appear in Tiandihui literature, and the familiar slogan "Overthrow the Qing and restore the Ming," which seems to have made its first appearance in connection with the Taiping Rebellion, was still several decades away.[3]

Conclusion

This chapter has portrayed the spread of the Tiandihui throughout South China as an outgrowth of migrant society. As new arrivals came into contact with the most marginalized residents of their host communities—individuals who themselves may have been either native residents or former immigrants now assimilated—the Tiandihui gradually made its way into more settled communities, where, as even this brief discussion indicates, it quickly became a vehicle for such activities as robbery, feuding, and rebellion. Thus the Tiandihui in its early phase assumed an organizational form that both resonated with and reflected the society from which it had emerged. At the same time, this society could be readily adapted to various local, community, and personal agendas.

Notes

1. Documents regarding the origins of the Tiandihui can be found in the Palace Memorial Archive (*Gongzhongdang*) of the National Palace Museum in Taipei and the Rescripted Memorial Collection (*Zhupi zouzhe*) and Grand Council Reference File (*Junjichu zouzhe lufu*) of the First Historical Archive in Beijing. Imperial responses to the phenomenon can be found in the Imperial Edict Record Book *(Shangyudang, fangben)*, which is available in both the National Palace Museum and the First Historical Archive. Most of the relevant documents from the First Historical Archive have been published in the seven-volume series entitled *Tiandihui*, which was compiled under the joint editorship of the Qing History Institute of People's University and the First Historical Archives. The series was published in Beijing between 1980 and 1988.

2. The Tiandihui did not come to the attention of Qing officials until February 1788, nearly thirty years after its alleged founding (*Tiandihui* 1980, vol. 1, 64–65). By that time, many of its leaders had died, and the memories of those who survived had clouded. The little historical information that survives is vague and imprecise. Nevertheless, the view presented here is reconstructed from a literal interpretation of the archival documents and the testimony of apprehended society members, and is regarded by the author as a plausible account of what may have happened. However, Barend J. ter Haar disagrees and has suggested that the early phase of Tiandihui development in Sichuan, referred to in the testimonies of Yan Yan and his counterparts, was not an actual historical phenomenon so much as the incorporation of myth into history. He thus cautions against taking this historical reconstruction too seriously (ter Haar, chapter 6).

3. By way of illustration, Hsu Wen-hsiung has written, "Although the society's [Tiandihui's] avowed political goal was believed to be 'oppose the Qing and restore the Ming,' only its 1853 revolt ever raised this slogan" explicitly (Hsu Wen-hsiung 1980, 97).

References

Hsu Wen-hsiung. 1980. "Frontier Social Organization and Social Disorder in Ch'ing Taiwan." In *China's Island Frontier*, ed. Ronald G. Knapp, 87–103. Honolulu: University Press of Hawaii.

Lamley, Harry. 1981. "Subethnic Rivalry in the Ch'ing Period." In *The Anthropology of Taiwanese Society*, ed. Emily M. Ahern and Hill Gates, 282–313. Stanford: Stanford University Press.

―――. 1990. "Lineage and Surname Feuds in Southern Fukien and Eastern Kwangtung Under the Ch'ing." In *Orthodoxy in Late Imperial China*, ed. Kwang-ching Liu, 255–78. Berkeley: University of California Press.

Murray, Dian. 1993. *The Origin of the Tiandihui (Heaven and Earth Society)*. Stanford: Stanford University Press.

Naquin, Susan, and Rawski, Evelyn. 1987. *Chinese Society in the Eighteenth Century*. New Haven: Yale University Press.

Perry, Elizabeth J. 1980. *Rebels and Revolutionaries in North China 1845–1945*. Stanford: Stanford University Press.

Qin Baoqi. 1988. *Qing qianqi Tiandihui yanjiu* (Research into the Tiandihui of the Early Qing). Beijing: Renmin daxue chubanshe.

Tiandihui. 1980–88. 7 vols. Compiled by Zhongguo renmin daxue Qingshi yanjiusuo (Qing History Institute of People's University) under the editorship of Qin Baoqi and Liu Meizhen and the First Historical Archives, Beijing, under Yu Bingkun and Li Shoujun.

Zhuang Jifa. 1986. "Qingdai shehui jingji bianqian yu mimi huidang de fazhan: Taiwan, Guangxi, Yun-Gui diqu de bijiao yanjiu" (A comparative study of the social and economic changes of the Qing dynasty and the development of secret societies: in Taiwan, Guangxi, Yunnan, and Guizhou). In *Jindai Zhongguo quyushi yantaohui lunwenji* (Collected Essays from Discussion on Present Day Regional Studies of China), 49–100. Taipei: Academia Sinica Institute of Modern History, August.

————. 1990a. "Qingdai Min-Yue diqu de renkou liudong yu mimi huidang de fazhan" (Qing dynasty migration of people from Fujian and Guangdong and the development of secret societies). In *Jindai Zhongguo chuqi lishi yantao huilun wenji* (Collected Essays from the Symposium on China's Early Modern History), 737–73. Taipei: Academia Sinica.

————. 1990b. "Qingdai Huguang diqu de renkou liudong yu mimi huidang de fazhan" (The Migration in the Huguang region during the Qing dynasty and the development of secret societies). *Danjiang shixue* (Danjiang Historical Studies) November 2: 149–76.

8

Brotherhoods, Secret Societies, and the Law in Qing-Dynasty China

Robert J. Antony

While most scholarship on Chinese brotherhoods and secret societies focuses on questions of their origins and activities, little research has been done on the Qing government's response. What exactly did the state do to try to eliminate or curb these illegal associations? From the state's perspective, members of such groups were merely rebels and outlaws deserving of punishment for their crimes according to the established laws. Whenever these illegal societies became involved in large-scale uprisings, the army was called out to quell the disturbances; since these were rare occasions, however, military solutions were inappropriate in most cases. Instead, the state relied heavily on legal controls, promulgating numerous harsh laws to deal specifically with sworn brotherhoods and secret societies. Even military campaigns had to be coupled with regular legal procedures. All those who were arrested had to stand trial and face punishment, which, for many, meant death or exile.

This chapter examines the evolution of state views of brotherhoods and secret societies from the seventeenth through the early nineteenth centuries by looking at changes in various substatutes of the Qing Code *(Da Qing lüli)* used in adjudicating cases against members of these associations. The body of Qing law was organic and thus constantly evolved to meet new needs and conditions. Although changes in the laws presumably followed changing popular practices, the relationship between legal images of clandestine organizations and their actual practices is too complex to be treated in this chapter, which focuses on law and its implementation. The laws, as well as the actual criminal case records, point out important shifts in the government's perception of brotherhoods and secret societies: early in the dynasty the state viewed them principally as heterodox and seditious organizations dangerous to the well-being of the realm, but by the end of the eighteenth century they had also come to be viewed as predacious criminal associations deeply involved in organized crime and banditry.

We can discern three distinct stages in the evolution of Qing laws on brother-hoods and secret societies. Before 1671 the laws appeared in the code under the rubric of miscellaneous crimes *(zafan)*. That year an important change occurred —the substatute banning sworn brotherhoods was now included in a revised edition of the code under the statute on plotting rebellion *(moupan)*. The last significant change came in 1811 with the promulgation of a special substatute on Guangdong river bandits and sworn brotherhoods, which was included under the statute on robbery *(qiangdao)*.

In establishing its laws, the state differentiated among the various kinds of sworn brotherhoods, because distinguishing between the types of brotherhoods was a crucial factor in determining punishments. By the mid-eighteenth century, the laws recognized three major types of sworn brotherhoods concurrently in existence in South China: simple brotherhoods, blood oath brotherhoods, and secret societies.[1] The simple and blood oath brotherhoods were the first types to appear in the Qing laws. The former were characterized by informal organiza-tional structures and uncomplicated initiation ceremonies. What distinguished them from other types of brotherhoods was the absence of blood oaths and of the burning of petitions. The only "ritual" to symbolize the solidarity of the group was the mutual pledge of brotherhood among all members, which was often performed in a temple or before the image of a deity. Blood oath brotherhoods had more formal initiation ceremonies and rituals, which included the drinking of wine mixed with blood (either the blood of each member or that of a chicken) and the burning of petitions as offerings to the gods.

Secret societies were the third major type of sworn brotherhood. Although the best known of these associations was the Heaven and Earth Society (Tiandihui), there were also many related and unrelated societies using a wide variety of names. Unlike the simpler forms of brotherhoods described above, secret socie-ties usually adopted names for themselves and had more formal initiation cere-monies and elaborate rituals. In a word, they were a more complex form of the blood oath brotherhood. The most important distinguishing feature of secret societies was the initiation ceremony, which included not only blood oaths and the burning of petitions, but also the transmission of society secrets and legends. These elaborate, esoteric rituals, as well as secret hand signals and argot, and (particularly in the case of the Heaven and Earth Society and its affiliates) the use of written materials (manuals, banners, seals, oaths, certificates, and so on) set secret societies apart from other types of brotherhoods. In the case of the Heaven and Earth Society, at least, members swore to maintain absolute secrecy about their organization, even from their parents and wives (see Cai 1989, 1–2, 25–42).

As early as the late Ming dynasty, South China had become one of the most unruly regions in the empire, and it remained extremely troublesome and diffi-cult to control throughout the succeeding Qing dynasty. Given the mounting population pressure and increased commercialization during the early and mid-Qing periods, as David Ownby explains in chapter 2, economic relationships became more competitive and people more contentious in the southern provinces. One result was an upsurge of all sorts of social disturbances, in addition to the clandestine activities of sworn brotherhoods and secret societies, endemic feuds, brigandage, piracy, and smuggling also plagued the region. As these illegal activities and social disorders steadily intensified during the last half of the eighteenth century, the government responded with increasingly draconian measures, particularly the more frequent use of capital punishment (see Antony forthcoming; and Lamley 1990, 274–75). The evolution of Qing laws discussed in this chapter must be understood in this broader context.

This discussion proceeds chronologically by examining the origins, contents, and usage of each of the major substatutes banning sworn brotherhoods and secret societies from the early Qing period to 1811, when the last major law on the subject was promulgated. By analyzing Qing legal codes, legal treatises, and actual criminal case records we can arrive at a more balanced picture of the theory and practice of the law. Through an examination of both the laws and the actual sentencing practices, this chapter addresses three important interrelated questions. First, how did the Qing state view sworn brotherhoods and secret societies? Second, how did these views change over time? And third, what do these views tell us about the nature of the laws as well as of the brotherhoods they tried to suppress?

Early Laws against Brotherhoods, 1646–1725

The Qing was the first dynasty to codify laws prohibiting sworn brotherhoods and secret societies. Earlier dynastic codes had no laws interdicting brotherhoods, nor did the first Qing Code of 1646, which was largely a copy of the previous Ming Code. Although there was no mention of sworn brotherhoods in the actual code of 1646, the Yongzheng edition of the *Collected Institutes of the Qing Dynasty* (Da Qing huidian) included a regulation dating from the early Shunzhi reign, which punished anyone for joining a "multi-surnamed sworn brotherhood" with a flogging of one hundred strokes. In another regulation of 1661, joining a blood oath brotherhood in which members burned petitions to deities became a capital offense (DQHD 1732, vol. 194, 36a).

In the early Kangxi reign, the laws began to take definite shape after several memorials were submitted to the throne by the Board of Punishments between 1664 and 1668. First, anyone joining a simple brotherhood without blood oaths would be punished with one hundred strokes of the heavy bamboo. Second, anyone joining a brotherhood with blood oaths would receive a sentence of capital punishment to be reviewed at the autumn assizes.[2] The new regulations became law in a 1668 substatute and appeared in an edition of the law code called *Da Qing lü xinli* the following year (DQHD 1732, vol. 194, 36a; and He 1984, 248). Although these laws remained somewhat vague, the legal distinctions made at this time between "simple" and "blood oath" brotherhoods remained a fundamental principle in determining punishment throughout the Qing period. A 1671 substatute, now included under the statute on plotting rebellion *(moupan)*, made matters more precise. It clearly stated:

> Those who join brotherhoods having blood oaths, no matter how many persons be involved, shall be sentenced in accordance with the statute concerning attempted rebellion *(moupan weixing)*. The leaders shall be sentenced to strangulation after the assizes, and followers to life exile of 3,000 *li*, and one hundred strokes of the heavy bamboo. As for those who join a brotherhood that has no blood oaths, the leaders shall be sentenced to three years' penal servitude and one hundred strokes of the heavy bamboo, and followers only to one hundred strokes.

Only two years later, an amendment provided that in cases of simple brotherhoods the principals would be punished with one hundred blows and followers with eighty blows of the heavy bamboo (DQHD, 1732, vol. 194, 36a-b). This revised version, with some minor changes in wording, was later adopted as a substatute in 1725, and it appeared as such in the Qianlong edition of the *Da Qing lüli* of 1740 (HDSL 1818, vol. 617, 10a; and He 1984, 249).

The motivation behind the early Qing legislation against sworn brotherhoods remains somewhat mysterious. During the early Qing period, before the Manchus had fully consolidated their authority over all of China in the 1680s, the activities of sworn brotherhoods appear to have been relatively low-key and generally apolitical. While there were several "Ming loyalist" rebellions against Qing rule, the role that sworn brotherhoods played in them is by no means clear (Qin 1988, 109–11). Apparently, the Qing court was also unclear about brotherhood activities and therefore at first proscribed them under the rubric of miscellaneous crimes. But, given the rebellious climate and the general uneasiness of the times, the alien Manchu rulers were wary of all sorts of social organizations formed among the Han Chinese majority. Not only were sworn brotherhoods outlawed, but, for example, so were certain literary societies in 1660 (Xu 1986, vol. 8, 3626). It was not until 1671, more than a quarter of a century after the founding of the dynasty, however, that the law proscribing sworn brotherhoods was removed from the miscellaneous crimes category of the law code and placed under the statute on plotting rebellions.

The Substatute of 1764

When the name Heaven and Earth Society (Tiandihui) first appeared in South China in the early 1760s,[3] it was just one of many other secret societies flourishing in the region during this period. As Ownby points out in chapter 2, all sorts of brotherhoods and lower-class associations proliferated in South China at the time. Their proliferation resulted, in large measure, from socioeconomic factors combined with the state's inability to exert effective control over local society in the region. Beginning in the 1720s, some brotherhoods, apparently for the first time, started adopting names for themselves, as well as more elaborate rituals and secret argot, perhaps in part as a response to state prosecution. In Fujian province, which had the greatest number of these early secret societies, there were the Father and Mother Society (Fumuhui), Iron Whip Society (Tiebianhui), the Peach Garden Society (Taoyuanhui), the One Cash Society (Yiqianhui), Iron Ruler Society (Tiechihui), the God of War Society (Guandihui), the Small Knives Society (Xiaodaohui), and others. Local officials also uncovered the Father and Mother Society in Huizhou and Chaozhou prefectures in Guangdong, the Iron Ruler Society in Anhui, and the God of War Society in Jiangxi. Table 8.1 provides a chronological list of the names and locations of more than forty brotherhoods and secret societies in South China from the early Qing period through 1811, together with the substatutes discussed in this article. This list is meant to be illustrative, not exhaustive; it does not include brotherhoods without names.

The Father and Mother Society was one of the secret societies that emerged in South China between 1720 and 1764. According to Qing archival records, it originated earlier than, and independently of, the more famous Heaven and Earth Society. The earliest evidence of the Father and Mother Society comes from Zhuluo county in Taiwan, where it was formed as a mutual aid and bereavement association. On YZ 4.5.5 (1726), a man named Cai Yin gathered twelve followers and initiated them into his society. Two years later his organization had grown to twenty-one members, and on YZ 6.3.18 (1728), on the birthday of a local fertility deity known as Zhusheng Niangniang, they all met at a friend's house to swear oaths of brotherhood. On neither occasion did members of Cai's society admit to taking blood oaths. Cai was chosen as "elder brother," and Shi Yi, second in rank, was designated "younger brother." As part of the ceremonies, Cai bestowed on Shi a robe, a summer hat, and a pair of stockings.

In the meantime, in another Zhuluo village, Chen Bin and Tang Wan had also formed a Father and Mother Society in early YZ 6 (1728), with twenty-three members. The initiation ceremony, while similar to the one used at Cai's 1728 meeting, included a blood oath. In addition, each member had to pay one silver tael, which was put into a common fund to defray the funeral expenses of the deceased parents of members. This was why they took the name Father and Mother Society (GZDYZ, 1978, vol. 11, 67–69).

In the fourth month of YZ 6 (1728), local officials uncovered Chen's society and hastened to break it up. Shortly afterward Cai and his followers were also arrested and brought to trial. In reporting these two cases to the throne, the Fujian governor-general, Gao Qizhuo, chose to sidestep the above-mentioned 1725 law and instead recommended even harsher punishment for the most grievous offenders. Perhaps recalling the recent Zhu Yigui uprising of 1721, which also involved a clandestine brotherhood, Gao pointed out that the Taiwanese were habitually forming brotherhoods that stirred up local unrest. Even apparently innocuous associations like the Father and Mother Society he considered a

Table 8.1

Brotherhoods, Secret Societies, and Qing Laws to 1811

Year	Society	Place	Law
early Shunzhi			sworn brotherhoods
1661			blood-oath brotherhoods
1668			simple and blood-oath brotherhoods
1671			simple and blood-oath brotherhoods
1673			simple brotherhoods
1720	Nandouhui	Fujian	
1720	Beidouhui	Fujian	
1725			simple and blood-oath brotherhoods
1726–28	Fumuhui	Taiwan	
1728	Tiebianhui	Fujian	
1729	Taoyuanhui	Fujian	
1729	Zilonghui	Taiwan	
1729	Yiqianhui	Fujian	
1731	Fumuhui	Guangdong	
1735	Tiechihui	Anhui	
1736	Guandihui	Fujian	
1737	Tiebianhui	Fujian	
1742	Xiaodaohui	Fujian Guangdong	
1745–48	Tiechihui	Fujian	
1747	Bianqianhui	Fujian	
1747–48	Guandihui	Jiangxi	
1748	Fumuhui	Fujian	
1748	Beidihui	Fujian	
1750–53	Tiechihui	Fujian	
1753	Fumuhui	Guangdong	
1761–1811	Tiandihui*	Fujian Guangdong	
1764			Fujian secret societies
1772–83	Xiaodaohui	Taiwan	
1774			simple and blood-oath brotherhoods
1784–1811	Tiandihui*	Taiwan	
1786	Leigonghui	Taiwan	
1787	Yaqianhui	Guangdong Guangxi	
1789	Youhui	Taiwan	
1791	Tianganghui	Jiangxi	
1792			Taiwan Tiandihui
1794	Xiaodaohui	Taiwan	
1795	Wushuntang	Guangdong	
1798	Xiaozihui	Guangdong	

Table 8.1 *(continued)*

Year	Society	Place	Law
1800	Gongheyihui	Guangdong	
1800	Xiaodaohui	Taiwan	
1802	Niutouhui	Guangdong	
1802	Heyihui	Fujian	
1802	Xiaodaohui	Taiwan	
1803	Shuangdaohui	Fujian	
1803	Renyihui	Fujian	
1803			simple and blood-oath brotherhoods
1805	Baizihui	Fujian	
1805–11	Tiandihui*	Jiangxi	
1807	Huazihui	Fujian	
1807	Longhuahui	Guangxi	
1808	Chuanzihui	Fujian	
1808	Biangianhui	Jiangxi	
1808–9	Honglianhui	Jiangxi Guangdong	
1808–11	Tiandihui*	Guangxi	
1809	Taipinghui	Guangdong	
1811	Baizihui	Fujian	
1811	Shouyihui	Guangdong	
1811			simple and blood-oath brotherhoods
1811			Fujian-Guangdong Tiandihui
1811			Guangdong bandits and secret societies

*Includes branch societies such as Increase Younger Brothers Society, Sandianhui, Sanhehui, etc.
Sources: GZD (54174), QL 53.5.30; Lian (1989, 121–36); Sasaki (1970, 167, 184, 241, 244); SLJJ, 558–63; SYDFB, JQ 11.1.27; WJD (83), JQ 15.4.7; and Zhuang (1990, 111–20).

source of social disorder and a threat to law and order. As a warning to others that the government would not deal lightly with any such cases, Gao urged that the leaders Chen Bin, Tang Wan, and Cai Yin be brutally put to death by flogging *(libi zhangxia),* a highly unusual form of capital punishment in the Qing period. Although most of the remaining prisoners were sentenced according to the 1725 substatute, those members of Cai's society who had participated in the two initiations in 1726 and 1728 also received additional sentences of wearing the cangue in their home villages. The emperor concurred with Gao's draconian recommendation and the sentences were carried out forthwith (GZDYZ 1978, vol. 11, 69–70; and Zhuang 1990, 144).

With the proliferation of brotherhoods and secret societies throughout South China at this time, officials had to learn to deal with them more routinely. This was the situation in Fujian when its governor, Dingchan, memorialized the throne in late 1764 to detail the need for a new law. He complained that the people of Fujian were wicked and violent, and that they had the evil custom of "forming secret societies" *(jiehui shudang)* to engage in armed frays and resistance to officials. He noted that such associations had lately been on the increase and were somewhat different from other sworn brotherhoods in that these societies adopted names, organized clandestinely, and used secret cant or signs to recognize members. Even worse, from the governor's perspective, was the fact that corrupt officials, underlings, and soldiers not only neglected their duties but actually colluded with society villains.

There were, Dingchan continued, no laws dealing specifically with these secret societies. Whenever such cases came before the courts, they were adjudicated with reference to the 1725 substatute which distinguished only between simple and blood oath brotherhoods. It made no provisions for societies that stirred up local disorders or opposed officials, nor did it take into consideration how many people were involved. Furthermore, since it was difficult to prove that a given society used blood oaths, he believed that convicted wrongdoers often got off with the much lighter penalty of bambooing instead of capital punishment.[4] The governor therefore recommended that a new law be enacted against these secret societies in which the taking of blood oaths could not be proven and that in all cases the severity of punishment be proportional to the number of people involved (GZDQL 1984, vol. 22, 804).

The Qianlong emperor turned this matter over to the Board of Punishments for deliberation, and within a month it had agreed to the need for the addition of a new substatute. First, the new law reiterated the provisions of the earlier 1725 substatute on blood oath brotherhoods, but also it provided a stiffer penalty of decapitation after the assizes for convicted leaders of blood oath brotherhoods that engaged in local feuds and/or resisted officials. For followers the penalty was strangulation after the assizes. Next, it specifically dealt with members of secret societies in Fujian province, who used secret hand signals and argot and mistreated local villagers (and who presumably could not be proven to have taken blood oaths). In such cases, the new substatute stated that arrested wrongdoers were to be prosecuted according to the law on "vicious scoundrels" *(xiong'e guntu),* which prescribed military exile to the farthest malarial regions of South China for leaders, and one degree less for followers. The new law, however, did not follow up on Dingchan's suggestion to adjudicate cases on the basis of the number of people involved; that would come in a later substatute (discussed below). People who had been tricked into joining such associations were to receive lighter penalties of one hundred strokes of the heavy bamboo and made to wear the cangue for two months.

This law also provided that whenever soldiers and yamen runners were discovered belonging to these secret societies, they were in all cases to receive the same punishment as the principals. Other provisions of the law provided penalties for village headmen, local constables, and civil and military officers who neglected their duties in bringing these cases to justice. Finally, the law allowed an exception: villagers who assembled only to make offerings to the deities and then immediately dispersed would not be punished (HDSL 1818, vol. 617, 11a-b; Huang 1847, vol. 53, 141-b; and Xue 1970, vol. 3, 562–63).

Let us illustrate this law in action by examining a typical case. In 1783 local officials in Zhanghua county, Taiwan, apprehended thirty-three members of the Small Knives Society (Xiaodaohui).[5] A decade earlier, in 1772, a betel nut seller named Lin Da, having been insulted and bullied by a band of local soldiers, had rounded up seventeen acquaintances to form an association for self-protection. Promising to come to one another's aid in the event of further trouble with soldiers, each man carried a small knife, thus the appellation Small Knives Society. The official records do not mention whether or not members took blood oaths or used secret hand signals. Over the next decade the Small Knives Society continued to grow in the Zhanghua area. Then between 1780 and 1782, insults turned to armed violence between society members and soldiers. Alarmed by reports of several deaths, the government stepped in to stop the fighting and arrested several suspects. Nine society members received the death penalty for involvement in armed frays, considered a more serious crime than simply joining a secret society. Based on the above-mentioned 1764 substatute, the others also received stiffer penalties: fourteen leaders had their penalties of military exile increased to deportation to Ili to become the slaves of soldiers, and ten followers had their penalties of penal servitude increased to military exile in the malarial regions of the south (Lian 1989, 134–35; SLJJ, 563; Zhuang 1990, 150).

In reviewing similar cases, the higher authorities in Beijing often increased penalties because they believed the lighter sentences were insufficient in expiating the crime.[6] Such increases in penalties were also part of a broader hard-line policy implemented by the government in the last half of the eighteenth century to combat the general disorders in South China caused by local feuds, piracy, banditry, and brotherhood/secret society activities (Lamley 1990, 274–75).

The Substatute of 1774

The Chen Agao case of 1773 in Jieyang county, Guangdong, precipitated the next important modification of the laws a year later. Originally, Chen had been arrested, tried, and provisionally sentenced by the provincial court to strangulation after the assizes as leader of a blood oath brotherhood, and had been returned to the Jieyang jail to await review of his case in Beijing. Before the case reached the imperial capital, however, Lin Ayu and several sworn brothers climbed over the city wall "in the dead of night" to rescue Chen from jail. Chen's would-be saviors were spotted by a constable who sounded an alarm, and Lin and his men were apprehended and also thrown into jail.

An imperial edict, commenting on this case, noted just how serious the matter was and pointed out the need for a revision in the laws on brotherhoods. Lin Ayu's crime of attempting to break Chen out of jail was absolutely reprehensible, and he was to be severely punished. On the emperor's command, he was summarily beheaded, and his head then exposed in public as a clear warning to others. As for the instigator of this whole affair, the edict continued, Chen Agao had originally received too light a sentence. Had he been executed immediately after his trial, then Lin and his men would not have had the chance to break into the city to attempt to rescue their friend. What was more, Chen's brotherhood had involved more than forty members, and Chen himself was only twenty-two years old *(sui)*, much younger than most of the other members.[7] The emperor ordered the Board of Punishments to deliberate and propose a new substatute to handle such cases in the future (GZDQL 1984, vol. 34, 223–29; Huang 1847, vol. 53, 15a–16a; SYDCB, QL 39.1.22).

The new law that the Board proposed made two important changes in the earlier 1725 substatute. Penalties would be fixed first, according to the number of people involved in the association, and second, according to whether or not the leaders were chosen without regard to the principles of age (or seniority), that is to say, if leadership was invested in a youth.

Let me summarize this long and complicated substatute. (1) If blood oath brotherhoods contained fewer than twenty men, then the case was to be handled according to the 1725 law mentioned above (that is, leaders sentenced to strangulation after the assizes, and followers to life exile of 3,000 *li* and one hundred blows of the heavy bamboo). (2) If such an association involved twenty or more men, then the leaders were to be sentenced to imminent *(lijue)* strangulation,[8] and followers to military exile in the farthest malarial regions of South China. (3) As for simple brotherhoods, if they had forty or more members, then the leaders should be sentenced to strangulation after the assizes, and followers to one degree less. (4) If the brotherhood numbered between twenty and forty men, then the leaders should be sentenced to life exile of 3,000 *li* and one hundred strokes of the heavy bamboo, and followers one degree less. (5) If there were fewer than twenty members, the penalty would be reduced to one hundred blows of the heavy bamboo and the wearing of the cangue for two months for leaders, and one degree less for followers. (6) However, in the case of simple brotherhoods of forty or more members who did not abide by the principles of age and invested leadership in a youth, the leaders should be punished with imminent strangulation, and followers to military exile in the farthest malarial areas of the south (HDSL 1818, vol. 617, 10a–b; and Xue 1970, vol. 3, 561–64).

This new law, however, made no provision for the handling of cases involving simple brotherhoods with fewer than forty members whose leadership was invested in a youth. When Governor Qin Cheng'en of Jiangxi province was confronted with such a case he adjudged by using analogy *(bijiao)*.[9] Zhou Jizi, who belonged to a simple brotherhood with only thirty-two members, was chosen as "elder brother" in spite of his youth. Since thirty-two was less than forty, Governor Qin reckoned that Zhou should receive a reduced sentence by one degree, and so he was sentenced to strangulation after the assizes. In reviewing this case, the Board of Punishments agreed with Qin's logic, and it added this provision to the law in 1803 (Huang 1847, vol. 80, 13a–15a). Henceforth, in such cases leaders were to receive sentences of strangulation after the assizes, and followers to 3,000 *li* life exile and one hundred blows of the heavy bamboo (HDSL 1818, vol. 617, 10b–11a). This substatute of 1774, as revised in 1803, remained the standard law for adjudicating all cases involving simple and blood oath brotherhoods. In 1811, and again in 1812 and 1825 (with some minor changes), the government modified the law by combining it with the earlier 1764 substatute on Fujian secret societies (HDSL 1899, vol. 779, 14b–17b).

In early 1811, Han Feng, acting governor-general of Guangdong, memorialized the throne about a case involving a Xin'an county brotherhood called the Observe Righteousness Society (Shouyihui). Chen Bingjun, the leader, had gathered twenty-five followers among his kinsmen and friends in order to engage in local feuding. In sentencing his prisoners, Han applied the 1774 substatute as revised in 1803, dealing with simple brotherhoods of fewer than forty members who invested leadership in a youth. According to the law, Chen should have been sentenced to strangulation after the assizes, and his followers one degree less. But as Han pointed out, not only did Chen and the others have the audacity to break the law by forming a brotherhood, but they also prepared weapons and associated with bandits in committing violent robberies, armed frays, and resisting arrest. Chen therefore deserved more severe punishment in order to serve as a warning to others not to get involved in illegal associations.

Han Feng requested an imperial decree for Chen's immediate execution, and the emperor approved the request on JQ 16.3.16 (1811). Five followers also received heavier penalties (by one degree) of military exile of 2,000 *li,* because they either had helped to recruit members into the society or, in one case, had written extortion letters. All the other convicted offenders received the normal penalty as followers of 3,000 *li* life exile, and one hundred blows of the heavy bamboo (STJY, DG 6, 27a–28a).

If in some cases the sentences could be increased, in other cases they could be decreased. Jiang Zefang, for example, formed a simple brotherhood in Qujiang county, Guangdong, in the third month of DG 5, which consisted of fewer than forty members. For his crime he should have been sentenced, according to the 1774 substatute as revised in 1803, to strangulation after the assizes because Jiang was chosen leader without regard to age. Since he had voluntarily surrendered to the local authorities, however, his sentence was reduced in compliance with another law by one degree to life exile of 3,000 *li,* the same penalty as his thirty-one followers had received. Among these wrongdoers, two men who claimed that their mothers were aged widows had their sentences commuted in accord with yet another law to wearing the cangue and were allowed to return home so that they could care for their mothers.[10] Finally, two other men who had been coerced into joining the brotherhood received lighter sentences of one hundred blows of the heavy bamboo, according to a "catch-all" statute dealing with violating imperial decrees (Zhu 1832, vol. 15, 55a–59b).[11]

The Substatute of 1792

The third important refinement of the law came in 1792, soon after the suppression of the Lin Shuangwen rebellion (1787–88) in Taiwan. This had been the first major uprising led by members of the Heaven and Earth Society (see Ownby 1989, and chapter 2 in this volume). The new law, however, was not prompted directly by the rebellion, but rather by the efforts of Chen Tan, Zhang Biao, Xie Zhi, and others in Taiwan in 1790 and 1791 to revive Lin's old society after it had been suppressed by the authorities (Huang 1847, vol. 53, 17b–18a).[12] This was the first law to name a specific secret society. According to this substatute:

> Those criminals in Taiwan who clandestinely band together to revive the name Heaven and Earth Society in order to commit robberies and resist arrest shall be sentenced to imminent decapitation if they were the leaders, or had recruited other members, or had voluntarily joined with the intention to commit robbery. Others who had not recruited members or who had been tricked or coerced into joining, yet were dishonest, shall be sentenced to imminent strangulation.

This law was meant to be a temporary measure, for it stated that it was to remain in effect only until such time that the Heaven and Earth Societies no longer prevailed in Taiwan (HDSL 1818, vol. 617, 15a-b).

Yet the Heaven and Earth societies did not go away. Despite the efforts of the Qing state to eradicate them, they continued to spread throughout South China in the decades before the Taiping Rebellion. As secret societies were uncovered in other areas outside Taiwan, provincial officials also began applying this 1792 law to their cases.[13] In 1811 this substatute was revised to include Fujian and Guangdong provinces, as well as to provide leniency to those society members who were "ordinarily not bandits," and who had joined for only a short time. They were to be sentenced to deportation to Xinjiang to work as slaves at putting new lands under cultivation. Although this substatute, like the one of 1792, was meant to be only a temporary measure, it remained a part of the legal code until the end of the dynasty (HDSL 1818, vol. 617, 15a; and Xue 1970, vol. 3, 565–66).

The case of Xu Zhang and thirteen of his followers who were apprehended in Jiayi county in Taiwan illustrates the use of this substatute. In the summer of JQ 3 (1798), he and two friends decided to form a brotherhood with the intention of committing robbery. Because the name Heaven and Earth Society was too well known they took the name Small Knives Society instead, since each man would carry a small knife for self-protection. Xu and his friends then went about recruiting more members. They gathered a total of eighteen men, and on JQ 3.7.8 (1798), they were all initiated. Xu was chosen as elder brother. But before they could act, the authorities discovered their plans and soon afterward arrested Xu and eleven others. Since the authorities considered the Small Knives Society to be no different from the Heaven and Earth Society (both had similar initiation ceremonies and secret cant), they were all sentenced according to the 1792 substatute on the Tiandihui to imminent decapitation. The officials, however, considered their crime so grave that they were taken out to the market and summarily executed right after the trial (*Tiandihui* 1987, vol. 6, 86–88).

Later, in the fourth month of JQ 4 (1798), officials apprehended and tried Hu Fanpo and Zhang Zhan, both members of Xu Zhang's Small Knives Society. Since Hu Fanpo not only had voluntarily joined the association but also had recruited other members, he was sentenced to imminent decapitation according to the aforementioned 1792 substatute. Zhang Zhan, who had been cajoled into joining by Hu, and had not helped to recruit others, was sentenced according to the same law to imminent strangulation (*Tiandihui* 1987, vol. 6, 89–90).

The Special Guangdong Substatute of 1811

In 1811 another substatute appeared that was specifically aimed against Guangdong river bandits operating in gangs of forty or more men, and sworn brotherhoods of less than forty men that engaged in a variety of predacious crimes. Songyun, the governor-general of Guangdong, prompted the promulgation of this substatute in a memorial written in the third month of JQ 16, in which he described the lawless conditions in the province (Huang 1847, vol. 80, 99b–100a).[14] The new law provided that in cases where criminals (1) had wounded victims during the commission of their crime; (2) had injured officers of the law while resisting arrest; (3) had disguised themselves as officials or soldiers in order to commit crimes; (4) had been at-large for two or three years before their arrest; or (5) had been involved in three or more robberies, then in all such cases the guilty offenders would be summarily decapitated (according to a judicial procedure known as "summary execution by royal mandate," *wangming xianxing zhengfa*[15]) and their severed heads publicly exposed. Unlike the other laws discussed above, this law applied to all types of brotherhoods, including simple brotherhoods, blood oath brotherhoods, and secret societies. The law made no distinctions. Significantly, too, this substatute broadened the basis for capital punishment, not distinguishing between leaders and followers. All those found guilty under the provisions of this law were summarily executed. This law was also special because it only applied to crimes in Guangdong province (HDSL 1899, vol. 784, 13a-b).

Following the 1811 promulgation of the special substatute on bandits and brotherhoods operating in Guangdong, that province witnessed a definite shift in the pattern of prosecutions. Thereafter, according to the available evidence from palace memorials, the majority of cases on brotherhoods, and many of those involving the Tiandihui and other secret societies, were adjudicated with reference to this new law. The reasons are not difficult to find. First, a large percentage of the prosecuted cases on brotherhoods and secret societies also involved banditry; second, this law provided generally stiffer and more expedient penalties—summary decapitation and exposure of the head—for convicted wrongdoers. Of course, those cases not concerning banditry were still handled according to the previously mentioned laws on sworn brotherhoods and secret societies, or other appropriate laws.

Typical examples of how this 1811 law operated are the cases of Liang Yajin and Huang Yaying. Each man had organized a brotherhood in Nanhai county, near the provincial capital of Canton, in 1813 and 1814 respectively. In Liang's case, it was uncovered at his trial that he had also been involved in several thefts and robberies. Huang, however, had only formed a brotherhood consisting of twenty-two members, in which he was chosen leader without regard to age. He had not participated in any other crimes. In deciding the case, the provincial officials sentenced Liang to summary decapitation and exposure of the head in accordance with the 1811 Guangdong substatute. But Huang was sentenced to strangulation after the assizes according to the 1803 substatute on brotherhoods, because being a leader of a brotherhood had been his only crime (WJD, JQ 19.4.3).

In another case, a notorious bandit named Zheng Dashisi was sentenced to summary execution in accordance with the 1811 Guangdong substatute. Zheng had been involved in at least four robberies between 1803 and 1813. In the eleventh month of JQ 8 (1803), he joined an Increase Younger Brothers Society (although written with different characters, it is also pronounced *Tiandihui*) in Zengcheng county, and soon became one of its leaders. Later, in the twelfth month of JQ 16 (1812), he joined another sworn brotherhood, in Shunde county. In determining Zheng's sentence, the provincial authorities cited several laws he had violated: one, because he was a follower in a brotherhood the penalty was military exile to the malarial regions of South China (1774 substatute); two, as a leader in forming a secret society the penalty was imminent decapitation (1792 substatute); and three, for committing over three robberies the penalty was summary decapitation and exposure of the head (1811 Guangdong substatute). The court sentenced Zheng with the summary execution, the harshest and most expeditious sentence applicable in this case (GZD [19261], JQ 20.7.6).

Observations and Conclusions

By 1811 all the main features of the laws concerning sworn brotherhoods and secret societies had been established. The state dealt with these clandestine associations harshly but in different ways. The general trend had been toward the promulgation of increasingly harsh laws and more frequent use of capital punishment, particularly summary executions. These harsher measures, however, must be understood as part of an overall hard-line policy adopted by the government at this time to combat the mounting social disorders caused not only by brotherhoods and secret societies but also by local feuds, banditry and piracy.

In meting out punishments, the Qing Code made clear distinctions between simple brotherhoods, blood oath brotherhoods, and secret societies. The laws dealing with simple brotherhoods were the most complicated. Based on the substatutes enacted in 1774 and 1803, penalties for leaders of simple brotherhoods ranged from one hundred blows of the heavy bamboo to imminent strangulation, depending on the number of members involved and whether or not leadership was invested in a youth. For blood oath brotherhoods, the same substatutes provided penalties of either strangulation after the assizes or imminent strangulation, depending on the number of members involved.

The substatute of 1764 (later modified in 1811, 1812, and 1825) was the first law specifically to ban secret societies. According to this law, the leaders were sentenced to military exile to the farthest malarial regions in South China. Later leaders of the secret society known as the Heaven and Earth Society were treated even more harshly under the law. According to the substatute of 1792, and later revised in 1811, leaders were to be punished with imminent decapitation. Finally, in another substatute of 1811, one that dealt specifically with certain predacious crimes in Guangdong province, both leaders and followers in either brotherhoods or secret societies were equally punished with summary decapitation and exposure of the head. Figure 8.1 outlines the regular penalties inflicted upon convicted leaders of brotherhoods and secret societies. For clarity and convenience, it is arranged by penalties (from light to heavy).

Although the laws regarding sworn brotherhoods and secret societies were clear and precise, especially after 1725, the few case studies mentioned in this chapter demonstrate that seldom was the letter of the law followed in actual practice. Since it was an axiom in Qing law that the punishment must fit the crime, there was a good deal of flexibility in meting out punishments. The laws were more like guidelines to decide cases rather than straitjackets. Punishments were often either decreased or increased depending on the specific circumstances involved in each individual case. As a general rule, the heavier penalties were applied whenever appropriate. Although in one case, as we noted, sentences of life exile were commuted to wearing the cangue so that the wrongdoers could remain at home to care for their aged mothers, in most cases penalties were increased—for instance, from life exile to military exile, or from strangulation after the assizes to imminent strangulation—because the authorities believed that the lighter sentence did not fit the magnitude of the offense.

Ringleaders were treated especially harshly. Because the state considered brotherhoods and secret societies dangerous seditious associations, and threats to the stability and well-being of society, officials often invoked extraordinary legal procedures in order to expedite the punishment of leaders. Convicted leaders

Figure 8.1. Penalties for Convicted Brotherhood and Secret Society Leaders

---

100 Blows of the Heavy Bamboo
Simple brotherhoods with fewer than 20 members

3,000-li Exile
Simple brotherhoods with 20–40 members

Military Exile to Farthest Malarial Regions
Fujian secret societies (vaguely defined)

Strangulation after the Assizes
Simple brotherhoods with 40 or more members
Simple brotherhoods with fewer than 40 members
and leadership invested in a youth
Blood oath brotherhoods with fewer than 20 members

Imminent Strangulation
Simple brotherhoods with 40 or more members
and leadership invested in a youth
Blood oath brotherhoods with more than 40 members

Imminent Decapitation
Secret societies (namely, the Tiandihui)

Summary Decapitation and Exposure of the Head
Guangdong brotherhoods and secret societies
engaged in various predacious crimes

Source: HDSL 1899, vol. 779, 13a–19b; vol. 784, 13a–b.

routinely had their sentences of imminent strangulation or decapitation changed to summary execution, officials explaining that it would be unwise to delay carrying out the sentences.

This study of the evolution of Qing laws interdicting sworn brotherhoods and secret societies also reveals something about their general evolutionary process from simple to more complex forms of association. The earliest laws of 1646 to 1671 show that the state was aware that elementary forms of sworn brotherhoods had existed at the very start of the dynasty (and in fact, as other contributions in this volume show, much earlier). Within a century of Qing rule, as the substatute of 1764 indicates, officials in South China had uncovered the more complex forms of brotherhoods we refer to as secret societies. Thereafter, as all types of sworn brotherhoods expanded throughout the south over the next half-century, the laws became more and more complex, as did the brotherhoods and secret societies.

Here we may even hypothesize that the government crackdowns played an important role in causing many societies to develop ever more complex structures and organizations in order to avoid detection and prosecution. In other words, the originally simple brotherhoods may have developed into more complicated secret societies, adopting esoteric rituals, secret hand signals and argot, out of necessity for self-protection and self-preservation in the face of official repression.[16] After the promulgation of several laws in the early Qing, for instance, many simple and blood oath brotherhoods began adopting names, organizing in secret, and developing secret cant and rituals. We also know from archival evidence that after the stern suppression during and immediately after the Lin Shuangwen rebellion, many of the Heaven and Earth societies became even more clandestine and began adopting various names in order to keep from being uncovered and prosecuted by the authorities.[17]

As rulers of an alien conquest dynasty, the Manchus were very concerned about social organizations among the Han Chinese majority, especially those formed by the "ignorant masses" (yumin), which showed potential for stirring up disturbances, or even worse, rebellions. Yet, during the first several decades of Qing rule, the court remained unclear and even ambivalent about sworn brotherhoods, merely classifying them in the miscellaneous category of the law code. What early Qing officials found most repugnant was the heterodox nature of these associations. Although members of brotherhoods did not regard themselves in this way, officials viewed them as a threat to the foundations of state and society, as well as being injurious to social customs and morality.

The state found it reprehensible that brotherhoods and secret societies disregarded the accepted Confucian standards of behavior and social relationships. This was implicit in the language of the early laws, which described sworn brotherhoods as jiebai dixiong, that is, as creating an unnatural, disordered relationship of younger brother to older brother (dixiong). From the orthodox view, the natural relationship was older brother to younger brother (xiongdi). This point was made more explicit in the substatutes of 1774 and 1803, which (in part) denounced multisurname brotherhoods that invested leadership in a youth without regard for age or seniority. Such a state of affairs clearly violated Confucian notions of propriety (li), those innate and universal rules of behavior regulating human relationships according to one's rank, age, and sex. When the Heaven and Earth Society was first uncovered by officials in the 1780s, it was referred to as a heterodox sect (xiejiao) (Tiandihui 1980, vol. 1, 83). While later officials ceased to identify South China's secret societies as religious sects, nevertheless they continued to be regarded as dangerous heterodox and seditious associations. From the perspective of the state, sworn brotherhoods and secret societies formed perverse relationships between unrelated people that were considered contrary to the natural order of things and subversive of society.

After 1671 the laws proscribing simple and blood oath brotherhoods, and later, secret societies, were included in the Qing Code under the statute or plotting rebellion. Thereafter, forming or joining a sworn brotherhood became a more serious crime because plotting rebellions was one of the Ten Abominations *(shi e)*, crimes so offensive and heinous in traditional China that they were unpardonable. What the state found most threatening about the societies was their potential for fomenting rebellion mainly because of their ritual solidarity and their ability to attract and mobilize the most alienated and disgruntled segments of Chinese society (see Smith 1983, 78, 154).

From the state's perspective, such clandestine organizations were arranged in a hierarchy of dissidence: from simple to blood oath brotherhoods to secret societies as their potential for causing disturbances progressively increased. Those associations with pseudo-religious blood oath pacts were especially disturbing. "The religious bond formed by the ritual of letting blood and burning a written oath and a membership list," according to C. K. Yang, "added strength to an organization by invoking the witness and sanction of the supernatural, and the law took full cognizance of this" (Yang 1961, 206). The secret societies posed even greater threats, for members not only took blood oaths but also shared in more elaborate, esoteric rituals and rites that bound them together in absolute secrecy. The secrecy of such "closed associations" easily aroused official suspicions and fears, and was taken as proof in itself of their sinister intentions to undermine established authority and public morality.[18]

Then in 1811 the Qing court promulgated a new law against brotherhoods that engaged in banditry and other criminal activities in Guangdong province. This particular substatute represented an important conceptual shift on the part of Qing officialdom because it was included not under the statute on plotting rebellions but rather, for the first time, under the statute on robbery *(qiangdao)*. Although previously the substatutes of 1764 and 1792, had (at least in part) condemned secret societies for certain criminal activities related to banditry, nevertheless the focus and primary assumption underlying those laws were that secret societies were clandestine organizations that aimed to overthrow the government.[19] This special 1811 substatute, however, was specifically aimed against banditry in Guangdong, not rebellion or sedition. Governor-General Songyun, the memorialist who had proposed the adoption of this substatute, made this point clear when he explained the need to include brotherhoods in this law because it was very common in Guangdong for sworn brotherhoods to engage in robbery and other violent crimes (WJD, JQ 16.4.18).

Laws were meant to serve as important ideological instruments of the state, and were enacted, in large measure, to protect the state's own interest by assuring its longevity through the creation of a society that was controllable and orderly. Unfortunately for the state, the Qing legal system never worked this effectively. As noted in this and other chapters in this volume, over the course of the eighteenth and early nineteenth centuries illegal associations flourished and expanded throughout South China. Legal controls, and even the use of increasingly draconian punishments, were unable to curb their spread and influence in local society. Indeed, crime and social disorders did not diminish but continued to grow and swell over the next several decades before the tumultuous explosion of the Taiping Rebellion in the 1850s. One censor expressed his sense of help-lessness and impending disaster when he reported to the throne in 1835 that lawlessness had gotten so far out of hand in the southern provinces that there was virtually nothing that the government could do to remedy the situation (*Canton Press* 1835, 100). In this respect the malfunctioning of the legal system in its efforts to curb and control clandestine associations was but an early manifesta-tion of the deeper troubles that lay just ahead.

Notes

An earlier version of this chapter was presented at the annual meeting of the Association for Asian Studies in 1989. The author thanks Wen-hsiung Hsu, Harry Lamley, Joanna Waley-Cohen, and Zhuang Jifa for their helpful comments and suggestions. Research for this chapter was supported by grants from the Fulbright-Hays Faculty Research Abroad Program, the National Endowment for the Humanities, the Committee for Scholarly Com-munications with China, and Western Kentucky University.

1. These three types of sworn brotherhoods are discussed in detail in my forthcoming book, *Bandits, Brotherhoods, and Qing Law in Guangdong, South China, 1760–1840*. See also David Ownby's discussion of blood oath fictive brotherhoods in this volume.

2. Although the laws of 1661 and 1668 were vague on the precise form of capital punishment (using only the generic term *zhengfa*) to be imposed in blood oath brother-hood cases, nevertheless, in view of later developments, it most likely meant strangulation after the assizes. The autumn assizes, which were held annually in Beijing before the Three High Courts, provided judicial reviews for certain capital cases, which were then reclassified into one of several categories (e.g., *qingshi*, which meant that the offender deserved capital punishment, or *huanjue*, which meant that the decision would be deferred until the following year). On the Qing autumn assizes see Meijer (1984).

3. Although the origins of the Tiandihui remain a controversial topic among Chinese scholars, extant archival sources indicate that it was most likely founded in 1761 by a monk named Tixi from Gaoxi village in the Yunxiao area of southern Fujian. Qin (1988), Cai (1989), and He (1984) represent various Chinese views on the scholarly debate; in English see Dian Murray (1993), and her chapter in this volume.

4. My own study of Guangdong sworn brotherhoods between 1760–1840 confirms Governor Dingchan's contention that it was difficult to prosecute alleged blood oath brotherhoods successfully. Among the 54 brotherhood cases (excluding secret societies) that I have investigated, only three were reported as having blood oaths. (See Antony, forthcoming.)

5. On the activities of the Small Knives Society see Zhuang (1974–75).

6. Examples of other cases that cite this 1764 substatute and also impose increases in penalties are in *Tiandihui* (1980, vol. 1, 120–23; 170–75; 1986, vol. 5, 367–73), and Zhu (1832, vol. 15, 37a–40b).

7. Barend ter Haar also points out in chapter 6 that a common feature in China's messianic traditions was the youth of leaders and saviors.

8. I use the term "imminent" rather than the conventional "immediate" to describe the *lijue* executions, e.g., imminent strangulation and imminent decapitation. To describe the executions as "immediate" is a misnomer because they were never carried out im-mediately, but rather had to await the approval of the emperor, which could take months. A more appropriate meaning of the term "*lijue*" is "imminent" because the sentence was impending and almost certain to be carried out after approval was received from the

emperor. For a general discussion on these types of execution, see Bodde and Morris (1967, 92–93, 134).

9. Chen (1970) provides a good introduction to the use of analogy in Qing law.

10. Wrongdoers who voluntarily surrendered to authorities or who had aged parents often had their sentences reduced. A brief discussion of such cases of leniency, and the laws for handling these cases, is found in Alabaster (1899, 103–6).

11. On the "catch-all" statute, see Bodde and Morris (1967, 178).

12. These and several other important criminal cases leading up to the enactment of this substatute are in *Tiandihui* (1986, vol. 5, 375–98). See also the discussion in Qin (1988, 277–79).

13. See, for example, the Heaven and Earth Society case of 1801 in Xinning county, Guangdong. Two of the leaders were sentenced to imminent decapitation and another man to imminent strangulation in accordance with the 1792 law, and 39 other followers received reduced sentences of deportation to Ula, Manchuria, a modification in the law that received official sanction as a substatute in 1811 (GZD [6782], JQ 6.11.28). In 1805 an imperial edict ordered that all society bandits *(huifei)* from Fujian and Guangdong who received sentences of deportation to Manchuria should henceforth be sent to Xinjiang (Huang 1847, vol. 80, 18b–19a).

14. The origins of this substatute are treated at length in Antony (1990, 38–45).

15. Normally all capital cases had to have the approval of the emperor before execution could be carried out. The *wangming* summary executions (which were done in the name of the sovereign) bypassed time-consuming procedures so that executions were carried out right after trial (normally at the provincial level). In such cases the presiding official would memorialize the case to the throne and at the same time carry out the execution (Na 1982, 230–34).

16. I do not mean to imply here that simple brotherhoods as a type disappeared as the victims of evolutionary processes, for in fact they continued to flourish throughout the Qing period.

17. We know that this ploy worked on at least one occasion in the early Daoguang reign, when more than a hundred members of two Sanhehui (Triad) societies were arrested in eastern Guangdong. From archival evidence it is clear that this group was a branch of the Tiandihui, but the officials who handled this case, apparently ignorant of the fact, prosecuted the case using the earlier 1774 substatute, not the 1792 substatute on the Tiandihui. See Zhu 1832, vol. 15, 55a–59b.

18. For cross-cultural comparison, this same point has previously been made by E. E. Evans-Pritchard (1931), Georg Simmel (1950), and J. M. Roberts (1974) in their studies of secret societies.

19. Although this new Guangdong substatute of 1811 was included under the robbery statute, earlier as well as later substatutes still remained under the statute on plotting rebellion. On those laws promulgated after 1811 see Zhuang (1990, 157–61).

References

Alabaster, Ernest. 1899. *Notes and Commentaries on Chinese Criminal Law*. London: Luzac & Co.

Antony, Robert. Forthcoming. *Bandits, Brotherhoods, and Qing Law in Guangdong, South China, 1760–1840*.

_____. 1990. "The Problem of Banditry and Bandit Suppression in Kwangtung, South China, 1780–1840." *Criminal Justice History* 11: 31–53.

Bodde, Derk and Clarence Morris. 1967. *Law in Imperial China*. Cambridge: Harvard University Press.

Cai Shaoqing. 1989. *Zhongguo mimi shehui* [Chinese secret societies]. Hangzhou: Zhejiang renmin chubanshe.

Canton Press 1 (December 5, 1835).

Chen, Fu-mei Chang. 1970. "On Analogy in Ch'ing Law." *Harvard Journal of Asiatic Studies* 30: 212–24.

Da Qing huidian (Collected institutes of the Qing) (DQHD). 1732.

Evans-Prichard, E. E. 1931. "Mami, Azande Secret Society." *Sudan Notes and Records* 14: 108–48.

Gongzhongdang (unpublished palace memorial archives) (GZD). National Palace Museum, Taibei.

Gongzhongdang Qianlong chao zouzhe (Palace Memorials of the Qianlong Reign) (GZDQL). 1984. Taibei: National Palace Museum.

Gongzhongdang Yongzheng chao zouzhe (Palace Memorials of the Yongzheng Reign) (GZDYZ). 1978. Taibei: National Palace Museum.

He Zhiqing. 1984. "Lun Tiandihui de qiyuan" (On the origin of the Heaven and Earth Society). *Qingshi luncong* 5: 239–72.

Huang Entong, comp. 1847. *Da Qing lüli anyu* (Notes on the Qing Code).

Lamley, Harry. 1990. "Lineage and Surname Feuds in Southern Fukien and Eastern Kwangtung under the Ch'ing." In *Orthodoxy in Late Imperial China*, ed. K. C. Liu, 255–78. Berkeley: University of California Press.

Lian Lichang. 1989. *Fujian mimi shehui* (Secret Societies of Fujian). Fuzhou: Fujian renmin chubanshe.

Meijer, M. J. 1984. "The Autumn Assizes in Ch'ing Law." *T'oung Pao* 70: 1–17.

Murray, Dian. 1993. *The Origin of the Tiandihui (Heaven and Earth Society)*. Stanford: Stanford University Press.

Na Silu. 1982. *Qingdai zhouxian yamen shenpan zhidu* (The Local Government Judicial System in the Qing Period). Taibei: Wenshizhi.

Ownby, David. 1989. "Communal Violence in Eighteenth Century Southeast China: The Background to the Lin Shuangwen Uprising of 1787." Ph.D. diss., Harvard University.

Qin Baoqi. 1988. *Qing qianqi Tiandihui yanjiu* (A Study of the Heaven and Earth Society in the Early Qing). Beijing: Zhongguo renmin daxue chubanshe.

Qinding da Qing huidian shili (Imperially Endorsed Supplement to the Collected Institutes of the Qing) (HDSL). 1818.

Qinding da Qing huidian shili (Imperially Endorsed Supplement to the Collected Institutes of the Qing) (HDSL). 1899.

Qing shilu jingji shi ziliao (Source Materials on Economic History from the Qing Veritable Records) (SLJJ). 1989. Beijing: Beijing daxue chubanshe, vol. 3 *xia*.

Roberts, J. M. 1974. *The Mythology of the Secret Societies*. St. Albans.

Sasaki Masaya. 1970. *Shinmatsu no himitsu kessha shiryo kessha: zempen, tenchikai no seritsu* (Secret Societies of the Late Qing: First Part, the Establishment of the Heaven and Earth Society). Tokyo.

Shuotie jiyao (Collected Board of Punishments memorandum) (STJY). Rare Books Collection, Fu Sinian Library, Academia Sinica, Taibei.

Simmel, Georg. 1950. *The Sociology of Georg Simmel*. Kurt Wolff, ed. Glencoe, Ill: The Free Press.

Smith, Richard. 1983. *China's Cultural Heritage: The Ch'ing Dynasty, 1644–1912*. Boulder, Colo.: Westview Press.

Shangyudang changben (Imperial edict record books, long version) (SYDCG). National Palace Museum, Taibei.

Shangyudang fangben (Imperial edict record books, square version) (SYDFB). National Palace Museum, Taibei.

Tiandihui (Heaven and Earth Society). 1980–88. Beijing: Zhongguo renmin daxue chubanshe, 7 vols.

Waijidang (Outer court record books) (WJD). First Historical Archives, Beijing.

Xu Ke, comp. 1986. *Qing bai leichao* (Unofficial sources on the Qing arranged by categories). Beijing: Zhonghua chubanshe. (Originally published in Shanghai, 1917.)

Xue Yunsheng. 1970. *Duli cunyi* (Concentration on Doubtful Matters while Perusing the Substatutes). Punctuated and edited by Huang Jingjia. Taibei: Chinese Materials and Research Aids Service Center, 5 vols. (Originally published in Beijing, 1905.)

Yang, C. K. 1961. *Religion in Chinese Society*. Berkeley: University of California Press.

Zhu Yun, comp. 1832. *Yuedong cheng'an chubian* (Leading Cases from Guangdong). Canton.

Zhuang Jifa. 1974–75. "Taiwan Xiaodaohui yuanliukao" (A study of the origins of the Small Knives Society in Taiwan). *Shihuo yuekan fukan* 4, no. 7: 293–303.

_____. 1990. "Cong Qing dai lüli de xiuding kan mimi huidang de qiyuan ji qi fazhan" (A look at the origins and development of secret societies from the changes in Qing laws). *Guoli Taiwan Shifan Daxue lishi xuebao* 18: 107–68.

9

Epilogue: Ritual Process Reconsidered

Jean DeBernardi

The studies in this volume depart radically from earlier scholarship on Chinese "sworn brotherhoods" in many salutary respects. First, the search for the historical "origins" of these groups (usually attributed to political opposition to Manchu rule) has been replaced by the search for cultural sources for the tradition, sources often found in the social life and ritual forms of Southern Chinese communities. However, in contrast with earlier scholars fascinated with the parallels between Triad ritual practice and that of European Freemasonry (Schlegel 1866; Ward and Stirling 1925; Wynne 1941), most of these authors do not consider ritual the primary focus of analysis. Rather, they view ritual practice in functional terms as a means of bonding a group's members together. Second, these authors challenge earlier scholars who assumed that secret societies like the Triads were long-enduring corporate groups with branches in many areas of Asia. The new studies characterize these groups as forms of social organization that (in the apt words of Heidhues) were both "ephemeral" and "indestructible," formed when Chinese required an organizational structure to achieve their goals. Finally, and perhaps most important, these new analyses link the organization of sworn brotherhoods and the pursuit of economic goals.

This epilogue offers commentary on these new interpretations, together with a reconsideration of the functions of the elaborate ritual process of the kongsi and the *hui*. While earlier scholars may have overestimated the political agenda of the Triads, or expressed an almost obsessive concern with decoding the meanings of its arcane rituals, contemporary social historians have emphasized the importance of the socioeconomic dimension of the secret societies to the neglect of those very political and ritual dimensions. I will here consider the functions of ritual process in Chinese society in light of the ritual practices of the kongsis and *hui* of the nineteenth-century Straits Settlements. I will argue below that the form of political authority established in the secret societies had as basis for its legitimacy a compelling hegemony forged in a ritual practice that recreated the City of Willows in the jungles of Malaya, and imagined an empire in the sworn brotherhood of the "family of Hong." The British colonial rulers of the Straits Settlements initially reinforced the power of these groups by using the secret societies to govern the Chinese community indirectly, only to outlaw the societies in 1890 as a dangerous "empire within the empire."

The case studies in this volume explore the range of institutions referred to as secret societies and provide insight into their diverse organizational forms. Heidhues, for example, delineates the organizational structure of kongsis and *hui* on the economic frontier of nineteenth-century West Borneo and Bangka, which were then part of the Dutch East Indies. Some scholars and colonial administrators appear to have termed both forms of organization "secret societies." However, kongsis were essentially shareholding operations (idealized by de Groot as egalitarian oligarchic republics), while *hui* or Triad groups were associated with both political goals and uprisings. Nonetheless, kongsis and *hui* shared many features, including leadership structure, rites of initiation, and worship of the God of War. Heidhues concludes that both groups constituted forms of sworn brotherhood that drew on a common fund of rites and traditions to form groups for mutual aid. Kongsis were primarily economic enterprises, rooted in the gold and tin mines; *hui* by contrast were both "ephemeral" and "indestructible," in that they were (according to her argument) an organizational strategy rather than an enduring organizational structure. *Hui* (or "secret societies") were not devoted primarily to violence, but rather arose as a "response to a provocation and served to organize and strengthen that response."

The indestructibility of the *hui* resulted in part from the fact that Chinese maintained such organizations even in periods when their potential for self-defense was not actively invoked. For example, Cheng reports that secret societies continue to exist in Kulim, West Malaysia, despite being outlawed. He observes that "although the majority of the Chinese community claim to have no connection with these secret societies, informal and indirect ties do exist and can easily be strengthened should the need arise" (Cheng 1969, 77).

While kongsis and *hui* waxed and waned in importance, they perpetuated themselves by managing collective property that in turn provided a site for meetings and the celebration of collective events. In 1879, the British Protector of Chinese reported that the Triad (as British colonial officials termed the complex of societies under discussion in this volume) had considerable property investments and held their meetings in a "superior building":

> In the British Colony of the Straits Settlements . . . each [Triad] Lodge has a substantial *"Hui-Kuan"* or Meeting-house; and at Singapore, the Grand Lodge possesses a very superior building at Rochore, where, twice a year (on the 25th of the 1st and on the 25th of the 7th moons), the "five ancestors" are worshipped, and feasts, with theatricals, are held in their honour, by the . . . nine branches of the "Ghee Hin" Society. (Pickering 1879, 2)

The extent of these collective holdings was impressive in nineteenth-century Pinang: when the Suppression of Dangerous Societies Act of 1890 dissolved the secret societies of the Straits Settlements (both kongsis and *hui*), the value of the Pinang Ghee Hin properties was appraised at $300,000 (CO273/159). The groups were allowed to maintain temples, but were forced to sell other properties, and the Pinang secret societies ultimately paid proceeds of over $100,000 into the Supreme Court.[1] To put these figures into relative perspective, the starting salary for a cadet in the Chinese Protectorate Office at that time was $2,400 per annum (CO273 306 of July 4, 1888).

In contrast with the situation in Southeast Asia, Triad groups in southern China were reported to be associated with the socially marginal. Drawing on the Qing archives, Murray argues that the Tiandihui emerged in conditions of economic dislocation and that the group had many dimensions as a socioeconomic institution. Among these dimensions she includes the desire to profit from performing a management role in the group (or as she states it, swindling money by charging initiation fees) and selling protection. She also suggests that robbery was a motive behind the formation of certain groups and links them as well to the conduct of "collective violence in the form of armed struggle and local feuding." By comparison with the secret societies in Taiwan or Malaysia, these groups appear relatively alienated from the larger society. At the same time, the ostensibly less marginal *hui* and kongsis of the Straits Settlements were also implicated in feuding and theft. Indeed, when Republican leader Sun Yat-sen sought financial support from the Singapore secret societies in 1906, they reportedly raised funds for the revolution through robbery (Blythe 1969, 279).

One might question whether the social alienation described by Murray was typical for secret societies in China. The groups best documented were those judged in violation of Qing law, and the image of marginality and "alienation" may well have been fostered by the Qing officials who criminalized these groups. Antony notes that from the perspective of the Qing government, members of sworn brotherhoods were stigmatized as mere "rebels and outlaws." However, the Qing legal code singled out a common form of social organization for harsh treatment, denouncing multisurname brotherhoods with un-Confucian forms of leadership as unacceptably heterodox and potentially subversive. Evidently, the Qing state would admit no competitors.

In his discussion of *hui* in Taiwan, Ownby expands on the theme that the formation of sworn brotherhoods was a useful organizational strategy for mobile non-elite members of southern Chinese society. These groups proliferated on Taiwan's rough-and-ready frontier, but remained useful in the competitive atmosphere that followed the closing of the frontier as well. Ultimately, they came into conflict with the state. The Lin Shuangwen rebellion clearly reveals several of the themes elaborated in all these chapters. First, people formed groups in response to conflict, which in this instance was between two brothers who disputed property rights. Second, the groups were "fairly embedded in local society," and here the Taiwanese case appears to resemble the Southeast Asian case. The economic dimension of these groups was critical, and as economic groups *hui* played an important role in local politics (even when they were not engaged with the national politics of the Qing dynasty).

Trocki's analysis also emphasizes the economic dimension of these groups, and indeed he has argued persuasively in *Opium and Empire* (1991) that "sworn brotherhoods" were basic to the economic order of nineteenth-century Singapore. Kongsis were formed in Southeast Asia not as alternative forms of social organization for a marginal fringe of unsettled drifters (as the Qing government would have it). Rather, sworn brotherhoods were the only available basis for social organization for the male immigrants to this region, and they performed many social functions for their members (see also Freedman 1960). In Trocki's words, "kongsis undertook social, economic, military, and even religious functions for the immigrants. They were armed, organized brotherhoods of economic adventurers and, in that respect, not so different from the Europeans they encountered in the region" (1991, 27). As he notes above, the Chinese were able to migrate in large numbers and set up successful communities in part because they carried the kongsi with them as a social and economic institution.

An earlier generation of scholars paid close attention to Triad ritual texts, but tended to read into the myth-history of the Triads an account of actual historical events and to overemphasize their antidynastic program. Ter Haar reasserts the importance of this textual tradition, and rereads the texts in light of their messianic themes and symbolism. In contrast to the other authors in this volume, he argues that the Triads did indeed have an antidynastic aspect, but interprets Triad opposition to the Qing in light of a worldview that regarded barbarian invasion as an eschatological disaster. Ter Haar infers from the textual evidence that Triad rituals culled their beliefs from a long-standing messianic tradition that anticipated a Luminous King who would rescue the people from such disasters and suggests that anti-Manchu sentiment was the result of messianic beliefs rather than their cause. Ter Haar's insights do not integrate readily with interpretations of secret societies that emphasize the socioeconomic functions of these groups rather than their messianic aspirations. Since both aspects coexist, we must take a closer look at the relationship between myth, ritual, and social practice.

The case of the Chinese Kapitan Yap Ah Loy suggests that myth and history could be interwoven uniquely through the use of shared cultural forms (see also Carstens 1988). Carstens details the career of Yap, who progressed from penniless immigrant to pig trader, fighter, tin miner, and community leader (considered by many to be the founder of Kuala Lumpur). Although he also enjoyed success as an entrepreneur, his leadership derived not from birth or wealth but from his military prowess and his ability to manipulate symbols skillfully to legitimate his authority. For example, Kapitan Yap sponsored Kuala Lumpur's first temple, one that deified not the God of War or the Goddess of Mercy but rather Kapitan Shin—the very kapitan whom Yap Ah Loy had served in his youth as a fighter. Carstens reads the deification of Kapitan Shin as an ideological act, a symbolic assertion of the existence of a "continuum of power and legitimacy between strongmen kapitans in this world and their counterparts in the next."

The refocusing of analytical emphasis in these chapters provides fresh insight into secret societies as early modern social institutions, but to some extent the ritual and ideological dimensions of the secret societies remain a puzzle. This puzzle results in part from a perspective that equates ritual practice with a sacred reality incompatible with the profane world of profits and self-defense (DeBernardi 1991). So, for example, Trocki (who tends to regard religion as epiphenomenal) suggests that a kongsi fulfilled "social, economic, military, and even religious functions" (implicitly segregating the religious), and Murray regards the entrepreneurship of Tiandihui teachers as evidence of their lack of sincerity with respect to spiritual matters. Chinese religious culture itself had social, economic, and military functions, and Carstens's study of the life and times of Yap Ah Loy demonstrates how tightly interwoven these dimensions of social life were for the Chinese in colonial Malaya. In kongsis and *hui*, ritual practice was a fundamental aspect of lived and practical consciousness, and the social historian should seek to interpret that practice in order to fully comprehend kongsis and *hui* as social institutions.

In the remainder of this epilogue, I will discuss the relationship between ritual practice and the activities of the secret societies (including self-defense, self-rule, economic entrepreneurship, and predation). Although these groups had overtly practical (and often illegal) goals, they also sponsored the performance of complex allegorical rituals, and the heady mix of myth and ritual in an often predatory tradition is remarkable. Because the British colonial response to these groups offers a unique perspective on the political and ideological dimensions of the secret societies, I will also discuss the fate of secret society ritual practice under British colonial rule in the Straits Settlements and Malaya, focusing on the period from 1786 to 1890.

Ritual Process: An Overview

To some extent, it is misleading to call Chinese popular religious culture "religion" at all. Many scholars adopt a Durkheimian perspective and locate "religion" in the set-apart realm of the sacred, but for Chinese the sacred and the secular are not separate (see also DeBernardi 1991). We also tend to conceive of religion as institutionalized orthodoxy, and although such institutions exist in Chinese society, popular religious practice is a syncretic blend of the "three religions": Daoism, Confucianism, and Buddhism. In Malaysia and elsewhere, people say that they "worship/respect gods" (Hokkien *bai anggong*; *bai sin*) rather than professing commitment to a sect or congregation. Yang described this form of religion as "diffused," characterized as having a "theology, rituals, and organization intimately merged with the concepts and structure of secular institutions and other aspects of the social order" (Yang 1970, 20).

The Chinese term translated as "ritual" (*li*) also means "etiquette" or "propriety," and Chinese ritual performances are frequently expressions and confirmations of social hierarchy. Confucians were aware that they could employ ritual performance to exact deference and obedience, and the logic of their preference for rule through ritual rather than rule through law and verbal command is well summarized by Pocock:

> Command entails disobedience, not because human personalities are recalcitrant, but because the nature of command is verbal and intellectual; instructing the penny to show only one side, we remind it that it has two. And because *fa* [laws] are verbal, they entail punishments; if you command a man to do something and, understanding your command, he does the contrary, you have no recourse left but to use force upon him. But since rituals are non-verbal, they have no contraries. They can therefore be used to produce harmony of wills and actions without provoking recalcitrance; if a man finds himself playing his appointed role in *li* [ritual] . . . in harmony with others, it no more occurs to him than it occurs to a dancer to move to a different rhythm than that being played by the orchestra. (Pocock 1964, 6)

Rituals do have contraries, although one usually has to stage a different ritual to make the point.

The observation, however, is apt: ritual is above all a social choreography. As patterned social interaction, ritual is a powerful medium with which to construct and display social hierarchy and distinction (Kertzer 1988). Consequently, in many societies, religious culture provides powerful political tools with which to maintain a sense of cultural order. Purcell is not alone in observing that "the medium which is as efficacious as anything in keeping the [Malaysian] Chinese together as a community is the cement of ritual" (Purcell 1948, 130).

Anthropologists have analyzed the role of ritual in indexing social status (Tambiah 1985) and expressing status pride (Geertz 1980). Ritual practice also establishes a legitimate moral community and circumscribes its boundaries. Indeed, the Confucian ideology that saw ritual as a means of regulating the social order resembles the social theory of structural–functional anthropologist Radcliffe-Brown, who observed that:

> an orderly social life amongst human beings depends upon the presence in the minds of the members of a society of certain sentiments, which control the behavior of the individual in his relation to others. Rites can be seen to be the regulated symbolic expressions of certain sentiments. Rites can therefore be shown to have a specific social function when, and to the extent that, they have for their effect to regulate, maintain and transmit from one generation to another sentiments on which the constitution of the society depends. (Radcliffe-Brown 1945, 157)

He follows up this classically Durkheimian statement by noting that the theory was not new, but cites the writings of "the philosophers of ancient China" (rather than Durkheim) to demonstrate his point. Indeed, he sums up his argument with a sentence from the *Book of Rites*: "Ceremonies are the bond that holds the multitudes together, and if the bond be removed, those multitudes fall into confusion" (Radcliffe-Brown 1945, 159).

The ritual process of contemporary secret societies separates insiders—the initiates—from outsiders and guarantees the social legitimacy of society leadership. Chinese religious culture also inculcates a moral code that is expressed vividly in a rhetoric of praise and blame. In contemporary Pinang, the histories of the gods extol the social and moral worth of the deities and condemn the moral depravity of their opponents. The rhetoric of virtue and vice, however, is not necessarily uniform for all members of the community, and different groups will seek different patron deities (see also DeBernardi 1987). Blythe also noted that he found "ritual variations and deviations" in Malaysian Chinese secret societies (though he apologetically omitted analysis of this reportedly copious data from his politically oriented study of secret societies [Blythe 1969, xiii]). In contemporary secret societies, this "ritual variation and deviation" is meaningful and indeed linked to the character of the groups and their members.[2]

As one example of an identifiable social group giving symbolic meaning to a particular deity, take worship of the "Inconstant Ghost," a deity who possesses spirit mediums in Pinang. As one of four assistants to the King of Hell, the Inconstant Ghost is placated by all during the Hungry Ghosts Festival, but he is regarded as an appropriate patron deity for the socially marginal, who offer him worship in spirit-medium cults identified as secret societies. The history of this "god" is morally ambivalent, since he was an unfilial son who frightened his mother, causing her to commit suicide by jumping into the family well. Repentent, he died of grief and remorse, and the Lord of Heaven rewarded his belated filiality by appointing him to a bureaucratic posting in hell. In retelling the story of the Inconstant Ghost, Pinang Chinese add that he has a "good heart," and that gamblers and prostitutes worship him (DeBernardi 1994).

Some researchers might regard ritual practice as a mystification of power or a mask for domination. In the case of the Chinese secret societies discussed in this volume, ritual is perhaps best understood not as the mask of domination but as the very face of power. As argued below, in the ritual performances observed by Pickering and Schlegel, secret society leaders were possessed by the founders of the Tiandihui, and they themselves became embodiments of the gods. My ethnographic evidence suggests that important collective decisions were made in consultation with such "gods" as they possessed spirit mediums. This process of consultation solved a leadership problem for an essentially egalitarian gathering, since the "god," who occupied the center of the temple space and employed dramatic symbols evocative of imperial authority (flags, imperial seals, dragon-embroidered imperial yellow costumes) articulated a consensus for the group.

The leadership of the secret society brotherhoods was thus autocratic and hierarchical, and Trocki and Wang's suggestion that the groups were founded on egalitarian principles and were perhaps even incipient democracies may be called into question (see Trocki in this volume).

Ritual Process in the Nineteenth-Century Southeast Asian Triad

In nineteenth-century Malaya and the Straits Settlements, Chinese secret societies (called the Triad or Heaven and Earth Society) performed elaborate initiation rituals that drew symbolic elements from Confucianism, Daoism, and Buddhism. New immigrants were compelled to undergo this ritual, in which the vanguard in response to the questions of the master narrated an imaginary journey, putting the "new horses" through a rite of passage that transformed them into members (and soldiers) of the family of Hong. They took an oath to follow the social rules of the group and later would be taught secret signs and society slang. The leaders of the group were highly visible in the ritual performance, and their power thereby given further validation (Blythe 1969; Pickering 1878, 1879; Schlegel 1866; Stanton 1899; Ward and Stirling 1925).

Collins has argued that political actors use ritual to form solidary groups and that the use of ritual allows them to manipulate "emotional solidarity as well as the lines of group identification to the advantage of some and the disadvantage of others." In his view these actors compete for control of the means of "ritual production" in order to gain control over a potent "means of emotional production" (Collins 1988, 117). The ritual process inculcates "sentiments" (as Radcliffe-Brown might have said), including sentiments of respect toward the paternalistic leaders of these groups. In so doing, it becomes a source of social power as well as a potent form of ideological control. As a means of emotional production, ritual (like its close relative, politics) derives much of its impact from spectacle and "the ordering force of display, regard, and drama" (Geertz 1980, 121). Chinese leaders had face in the community as the result of acts that earned them the respect of their followers (see Carstens in this volume), but also as the result of their participation in rituals that gave them public visibility. Ritual performance arranges people in space and time and generates both the experience of community and dramatic images of authority. The ritual process lends itself to the construction of charismatic centers—centers that might be as temporary as a tent and a stage or as permanent as an elegantly decorated temple.[3]

While the written record for secret societies includes many ritual handbooks, few eyewitness accounts of actual ritual performances exist. One of the few is offered by Pickering (1878, 1879), the Protector of Chinese in the Straits Settlements and Malaya from 1877 until 1889. As he reports, the initiation rituals of the Triads (which were said to be held in mountains or jungle clearings, but more often held in urban meeting houses) were impressive displays that both introduced newcomers to the leadership of the lodge and demanded commitment from them. New members were sponsored by officers of the group, who ideally ensured that the new recruits did not break the 36 articles of the society's oath in the three years after the initiation ceremony (Pickering 1879, 6). The ritual master orchestrated the event, while holders of three offices (vanguard, red baton [or executioner], and grass sandals) performed in the initiation rituals as "generals."

Two major actors in the ritual performance were the master *(xiansheng)* and the vanguard *(xianfeng)*. In the ritual performance, the vanguard identified himself as "General Tianyou Hong of the Gaoxi [High Mountain Stream] Temple." The genealogical tablet displayed by one Triad group honored General Tianyou Hong together with the master (identified as Chen Jinnan) as the two "Great Founders" of the Gaoxi Temple, the temple in which the Triad was originally established (Schlegel 1866, 22–23). In the Triad history recounted by Schlegel, Master Chen Jinnan is described as a former officer of the Board of War and member of Hanlin College who lost his job because of intrigue and traveled about under the pretense of teaching philosophical doctrines (1866, 14); Tianyou Hong (whose name literally means "Heaven Protects Hong") is described simply as the "bravest of all" (Schlegel 1866, 17). These two together form the classic alliance of literary and military prowess.

Pickering described as a dramatic apex the stage in the ritual in which the vanguard performed the 333-line catechism of the Ghee Hin, detailing an allegorical journey in response to the questions of the master. Pickering noted that "it is really astonishing to hear a clever *Sien Hong* [vanguard] give every answer and verse correctly, without referring to a Book, or requiring any assistance from the Master, who has the Ritual before him on the altar" (Pickering 1879, 15).

According to Pickering, the generals were set apart from the initiates by their dress and role. For example, at each performance of the initiation ceremony, the "Grass Sandals" acting as generals wore new white costumes, red turbans, and "straw shoes laced over white stockings, something in the style of the pictures of Italian bandits," while the master wore a "suit of clothes and a turban of pure white" (Pickering 1879, 11). Others played the roles of individuals encountered in the allegorical journey described by the vanguard: the "Red Boy," armed with a spear, with rouged face and a circular frame as a halo, guarded the "Fiery Valley," while another Triad member impersonated the fruit-seller in the "Market of Universal Peace" (Pickering 1879, 13). In the ritual performance, the identities of the main actors were submerged in those of their ritual characters, and I speculate that a British observer would see a dramatic enactment where a Chinese participant would see trance possession.

In the Triad, military prowess (as well as political authority) had spiritual and magical dimensions. The Triad tradition claimed the militant monks of the Shaolin Temple of Fujian as its legendary founders, and in the initiation ceremony, General Tianyou Hong stated that he had learned military art at the Shaolin Temple, beginning his studies with the "art of boxing of the Hong-brethren" (Schlegel 1866, 65).[4] Worship of the God of War was central to Triad ritual, and Triad officials, identified to the initiates as generals, were also possessed by masters of military arts.[5]

Ritual performance made heroic gods of the leaders of a Triad Lodge. At the same time, the ritual performance of texts and oaths (which even in oral performance carried the authority of the written word) created a social contract among all members of the "family of Hong." In *The Elementary Forms of the Religious Life*, Durkheim argued that the social contract was inscribed in language, and here religion has an "empire over intellect," as he phrased it (Durkheim 1912, 486). The sworn brotherhoods used language and ritual together to demarcate social boundaries, separating insiders from outsiders, friends from enemies. The vocabulary, for example, of Triad initiation ceremonies exalted virtues—loyalty, filiality, honesty—and initiators administered oaths to guarantee their fulfillment. Members swore neither to steal from one another, nor to cheat one another, nor to covet one another's wives. The groups devised secret signs that allowed members who were strangers to identify themselves to one another in public. By contrast, stealing from nonmembers was legitimate, and the rich slang of the Triads attests to the range of predatory activities allowed, ranging from piracy and theft to murder—but only against outsiders (Schlegel 1866, 230–34; Ward and Stirling 1925, vol. 1, 128–81).

In one secret society that I studied during the course of my ethnographic research, the spirit medium used a slang in trance in which insiders were "friends," but the government was a wicked opponent: members of his group interpreted the term "thief–child" to mean "detective," and accepted his labeling of the police as "wicked" and "evil." The negative labels applied by members of the larger society to those involved in predation were thus turned back on the forces of "law and order." The authority of the god who allegedly possessed this spirit medium dramatically underscored the legitimacy of these judgments (DeBernardi 1987).

In considering the relationship between Chinese religious culture and power, Ahern (1981) argued that the ritual process is a "learning game" for the political order. She observed that relationships between Chinese and their gods were parallel in etiquette to relationships between citizens and their rulers, and concluded that religion was a learning game that taught strategies for approaching the politically prominent. In general, studies of Chinese popular religion have assumed that the political was to be equated with the political order of traditional China, ruled by an emperor and a civil bureaucracy. By this reading, the persistence of Chinese religious idioms based on the traditional order is a charming anachronism, even when modern idioms slip into the religious discourse. (For example, Wolf reports that in Taiwan, worshippers of the protective Earth God, Tudigong, whose responsibilities include escorting the souls of the dead to the underworld and keeping order among the ghosts, imagine him as a "policeman who wears a uniform" [Wolf 1974, 138–39]).

By focusing on interpretation of the religious idiom rather than on use in social context, these scholars have failed to convey the full sense of such religious practices. Secret societies appropriate the symbols of empire into the ritual domain in order to imagine communities that are themselves replications (albeit in miniature) of the state. Some researchers recognize this appropriation when they study "secret societies" or counterhegemonic groups, but they often interpreted it much as the imperial government would interpret—as a potentially seditious utilization of symbols of legitimate rule. However, the leadership of these groups employed ritual forms to exact deference from members of the group (who regarded Triad officers as gods within the frame of the initiation ceremony), thereby ensuring hegemony within.

Pickering's biographer observes that ritual process of the secret societies was in part responsible for Chinese success in establishing an "empire within the empire" in the Straits Settlements:

> The [secret society] novitiates were subjected to an impressive, prolonged, complicated, and awe-inspiring ordeal which left them in no doubt about what they were committing themselves to and the seriousness of the commitment. The Government made no such formal and effective claim on an immigrant's loyalty. (Jackson 1965, 76)

Exact figures will never be known, but the extent of their influence can be glimpsed in Pickering's 1876 estimate that 60 percent of the Chinese in the Straits Settlements and the "native states" (i.e., Malaya) were secret society members, and that the remaining 40 percent of the population were "subject to their influences" (Pickering 1876, 440).

A War of Competing Colonialisms

The history of interaction between the British and the Chinese in the nineteenth century provides an illuminating perspective on the secret societies. From the British perspective, the secret societies posed a genuine threat to law and order: they were unquestionably involved in theft and piracy as well as feuding. At the same time, the secret societies posed an additional political threat, and the British deemed them an "empire within the empire." Nonetheless, they were tolerated and indeed employed in a form of indirect rule in the Straits Settlements (as if their headmen were tribal chiefs) until their abolition in 1890 (Lee 1991).

When the British established a settlement in Pinang in 1786, they found that the Chinese workers whom they brought in almost immediately formed "combinations." In 1794, Francis Light, the founder of the British settlement on Pinang, observed that the Chinese were:

> A valuable acquisition, but speaking a language which no other people understand, they are able to form parties and combinations in a most secret manner against any

regulation of government which they disapprove, and were they as brave as intelligent they would be dangerous subjects, but their want of courage will make them bear many impositions before they rebel. They are indefatigable in the pursuit of money. (cited in Purcell 1948, 40)

Their alleged "secrecy" was to a great extent the product of a communication barrier. Remarkably, until Pickering arrived in Singapore in 1872 to serve as Chinese interpreter, no European officer in the service of the Straits Settlements could speak Chinese (Jackson 1965, 18).[6] In 1888, the year preceding his retirement, Pickering noted that "[t]he turbulent, conceited, and alien masses of the Chinese inhabiting and entering the Straits Settlements and the Native States, are understood by at most four or five officials of the Colony" (CO273/154, vol. 4, 361).

In the first twenty years after the British established a settlement in Pinang, there was in fact no code of law in effect, and one British colonial officer in the Straits Settlements observed: "In matters of succession, personal status, contract, and perhaps tort also, as many systems of law were in force as there were nationalities in the Island" (Maxwell 1859, 34). The British adopted a policy of indirect rule and relied on Chinese headmen (who were invariably secret society headmen) to control their followers (see Carstens and Trocki in this volume; Wong 1964).

In justifying the adoption of this policy, the British argued that the European ideal of rule by law or contract could not be implemented because it collided with a Chinese notion of "personal government." A member of the Chinese Protectorate commented:

> In governing Asiatics the great secret of success is, personal government untrammelled by the technicalities of British law. We have had to give way on this question of technicalities already. In the matter of Chinese Secret Societies—in such everyday affairs as Chinese marriages—we have had to give way ... and dispense with useless technicalities. (Dennys, cited in Weld 1884, 82)

Indirect rule was a practical necessity for the British.

In the mid-nineteenth century, colonial administrators expressed the fear that they were competing with the Chinese secret society headmen not only for control of the Chinese population but also for authority over the Malay population. The British learned in 1854 that Melakan Malays were joining the Ghee Hin and worshipping Chinese gods. In 1859 the British were tipped off to an initiation ceremony held in the home of the local Malay chief. The police found several Malay chiefs and a "Melakan Chinese of respectable connections" in attendance, as well as nearly a hundred Malays and Chinese. They also found considerable firearms and "a Chinese altar and Joss lighted up, to which both Malays and Chinese indiscriminately made obeisance" (Blythe 1969, 103). They were alarmed to learn that Melakan Malays "dreaded the Hoeys more than the

Law" and had joined Chinese secret societies for their own protection (Blythe 1969, 105). The local chiefs *(Penghulus)* who joined were tried for joining an "unlawful assembly," and the colonial governor warned the Malays against being misled by the "false words of designing foreigners" who had no attachment to the country (Blythe 1969, 104).

A degree of control over the secret societies was established in the Straits Settlements with the passing in 1869 of the Dangerous Societies Suppression Ordinance, which required every society to register, to advise the police of all meetings, and to permit any magistrate, justice of the peace, or police officer to attend them (Jackson 1965, 49). However, the Chinese continued to prefer to settle matters within their own communities, and they frequently resisted British attempts at regulation. For example, in Singapore in 1876 the rumor was circulated that the British were going to establish a monopoly over the postal service that handled remittances to China. Chinese were alert to the possibility that a monopoly might lead to higher costs, and two secret societies instigated wide spread rioting, including an attack on the police station (Blythe 1969, 201–7). Trocki suggests that battles such as the Post Office riots approached a form of class conflict, and argues that the kongsis functioned as "agents of the popular will" in a native Chinese form of democracy (Trocki 1991, 222). While the democratic nature of these groups may be questioned, they undoubtedly were a powerful force in shaping and expressing the popular will of the Chinese community.

In essence, the British were unable to enforce their rule on the Chinese of Singapore. From the perspective of the Dutch East Indies (where the societies were illegal), Schlegel ascerbically noted that "Singapore . . . owes the unruliness of her Chinese population to the defects in her own government" (Schlegel 1866, xl). Ten years later, Pickering critically observed that "one indispensible requisite of good government is knowledge of the people to be governed; for the last fifty years we have been content to go on in almost total ignorance of the language, habits and feelings of a great, and at any rate the most important part, of the population of our colonies in the Far East" (Pickering 1876, 439–40).

When Pickering arrived in Singapore in 1872 to serve as Chinese interpreter, he discovered that the registration of societies was in fact a farce, and he noted as well that many of the emigrant Chinese, unaware of the colonial government, went to the secret societies when they had problems. And in 1876, the year of the Post Office riots, he concluded that "by the workings of the secret societies the larger and more dangerous portion of the Chinese community is ruled, not by our laws, but by the will of the headmen" (Pickering 1876, 440).

In 1877, Pickering was appointed to a newly created post as "the Protector of Chinese," and his ability to speak Chinese reportedly won him the respect of the Chinese community. Lee notes that Pickering also succeeded in projecting an image of himself as an "authoritarian figure in the Chinese manner . . . a good mandarin, meting out justice firmly and fairly." The Chinese recognized this by addressing him with the title *Tai Jin*, or "great man," a title normally reserved for the mandarin (Lee 1991, 274). Kynnersley observed that the immigrant Chinese

> has no respect for red-haired governors, or for the race of barbarians who perform the dirty work of government for his benefit. For the *Tai Jin* [i.e., Pickering], who has taken the trouble to learn his language, and dwells in a Chinese house hung with mystic scrolls, he has some regard, especially when later he finds that he carries banishment warrants about him. (Kynnersley 1893, 4)

Pickering set about governing the Chinese and, to the displeasure of colonial magistrates, began to mediate disputes for members of the Chinese community. Pickering frequently settled matters according to Chinese custom, requiring the person judged wrong to present his apology to the other party with the gift of a pair of red candles and a piece of red cloth. Pickering was also presented with red candles as a token of respect, and it was reported that Pickering's Protectorate Office walls were soon covered with pairs of candles wrapped in red paper (Jackson 1965, 79).

As mentioned above, in the early days of the Chinese Protectorate, Pickering observed a five-hour secret society initiation ceremony in which 70 new members were admitted to a lodge in Singapore. He described this ceremony in an article in which he also proposed that the British continue to rule the Chinese of the colony (characterized here as the "scum of the Empire") through the secret societies. He argued that British law was inexplicable to the Chinese who was "accustomed from infancy to lean upon, or to dread, some superior and ever present power, either in the shape of his government, his clan, or the village elders." Reversing his earlier opinion that "recognition of the Hoeys, or Heaven and Earth Societies, is a disgrace to our government" (Pickering 1876, 440), he concluded: "I can see no other way of ruling Chinese, than by recognizing the secret societies, and by immediately commencing the training of a competent staff of officials, conversant with the Chinese language, and mode of thought, to supervise and control them" (Pickering 1879, 10). Pickering employed evolutionism to justify rule through the secret societies rather than through British law, suggesting that the socially advanced British love of freedom had developed over a thousand years at the expense of great personal sacrifices and could not be exported to Asia in a matter of decades (Pickering 1879, 10).

Pickering's description of the Triad initiation ceremony illustrates the mixed progress made by the Protectorate. For Pickering's benefit, the master modified the oaths administered to the initiates, addressing them as follows:

> Many of our oaths and ceremonies are needless, and obsolete, as under the British government there is no necessity for some of the rules, and the laws of this country do not allow us to carry out others; the ritual is however retained for old custom's sake.

The real benefits you will receive by joining our Society are, that if outsiders oppress you, or in case you get into trouble, on application to the Headmen, they will in minor cases take you to the Registrars of Secret Societies, the Inspector General of Police, and the Protector of Chinese, who will certainly assist you to obtain redress; in serious cases, we will assist you towards procuring Legal advice. (Pickering 1879, 9)

However, Pickering complains that in the course of the event the "generals" lapsed into colloquial Hokkien, referring to the British as "red-haired barbarians" and to the police inspectors as "big dogs" (this even though Pickering strongly discountenanced use of these terms). He observed that the candidates had difficulty understanding the more respectful Chinese terms and noted that the effort to do so "seemed to be an even more severe ordeal than the drawn swords under which they had to pass" (Pickering 1879, 17).

Impressed with the ritual practice of the secret societies, Pickering himself took steps to increase the visibility of the British colonial government by initiating a secular process for greeting new immigrants and advising them of their rights under British colonial rule. Pickering reported that the object of this new system of control was "to bring the newly arrived Chinese into immediate contact with the Government and to make them feel that there is the power both to protect them and keep them in order" (quoted in Jackson 1965, 68–69).

In this period, the British noted their lack of success in instilling the Chinese with respect for British rule. Pickering is reported to have said that "even the Straits-born Chinese care more for a Mandarin's button that for a King's crown" (CO273/154, vol. 4 [July–September 1888], 86). Frederick Weld, who was governor of the Straits Settlements in the early 1880s, observed that

capacity for governing is a characteristic of our race, and it is wonderful to see in a country like the Straits, a handful of Englishmen and Europeans, a large and rich Chinese community, tens of thousands of Chinese of the lowest coolie class, Arab and Parsee merchants, Malays of all ranks, and a sprinkling of all nationalities, living together in wonderful peace and contentment. It always seems to me that the common Chinese feeling is that we—an eccentric race— were created to govern and look after them, as a groom looks after a horse, whilst they were created to get rich and enjoy the good things of the earth. Be my theory true or not, the fact remains that the general purity and high tone of our service is a main secret of our remarkable influence over the Malay races, an influence that cannot be approached by that of any other nation. (Weld 1884, 46–47)

In Weld's view, the Chinese recognized British fitness for the task of ruling, but they regarded the British as mere "grooms" to the prosperous Chinese horse. The British colonial rulers not infrequently accused the Chinese of ingratitude, and of benefiting from British laissez–faire policies while refusing to act as loyal citizens.

For example, in 1887 the Pinang Chinese protested the enactment of a Burials Ordinance that would restrict the areas in which they could establish burial grounds, as well as forcing them to disinter previous burials so that a district magistrate's house could be built on an elevation in Balik Pulau. Koh Seang Tat, an English-educated opium revenue farmer, addressed an eloquent defense of Chinese rights to the governor and published this defense in the *Penang Gazette*.[7] In this article, a member of the very population that colonial officers had deemed unable to live by the British code of law cited Enlightenment political ideals and Roman law in defense of Chinese rights to maintain their burial grounds.[8] W. E. Maxwell responded to the Pinang protests by implying that the protesters were "Chinese who have, by residence in the Straits, learned to think lightly of authority" (CO273/151 28 September 1887). The tart response from Pinang once again asserted Chinese rights:

> Enlightenment, consequent on liberal education and contact or intercourse with civilized people, encourages loyal subjects and citizens to act as their brethren in civilized countries, in contending for their rights and privileges when they are deemed to be encroached on, or threatened, by any legislative measure. This liberty or freedom is allowable, you will admit, to the highly privileged and favored of men, the British subjects, at the helm of whose affairs and interests in Pinang you are temporarily residing. (CO273/151, October 3, 1887)

Far from indifferent to the business of government, the Chinese claimed the rights and privileges of British subjects. The incipient Straits Chinese middle class, formed by British colonial rule, was beginning to claim a voice (and herein lies a new story [see Lee 1991, 287–92]).

The controversial practice of ruling the Chinese through the secret societies was ultimately overturned. Colonial officials argued that the Chinese had formed a dangerous "empire within the empire," and spurred by events, they moved to outlaw these groups. Jackson sums up the problem succinctly:

> The Chinese formed an *imperium in imperio*. The innate feeling of superiority and racial separateness that characterized them in their relationships with foreigners, and ignorance of their language and customs among the rest of the population, and the fact that they regarded themselves as temporary residents with no loyalty to the place, seeking only to make a fortune and return to their villages in China, were strong predisposing factors. . . . But the main reason was that the powerful Chinese secret societies, which were sworn brotherhoods, had enrolled a very large part of them and took upon themselves many of the normal functions of government in what amounted to an unmistakable though not necessarily unfriendly disregard of the official administration. (Jackson 1965, 17)

The situation might be described as one of competing colonialisms: feelings of superiority, racial separateness, and the state of being temporary residents characterized British sojourners as well as Chinese.

The British colonial rulers criminalized the societies, and the groups together with their impressive initiation rituals became illegal in the Straits Settlements in 1890. In the heated debates that led to their suppression, the key argument was that the secret societies were an "empire within the empire." However, the decision to outlaw the societies was made only after the attempt to control Chinese gambling led to a power struggle between the Chinese Protectorate and the police (many of whom were suspected of complicity with the secret societies).

In 1887 a Chinese carpenter flung an axehead at Pickering in his Protectorate office (Jackson 1965, 106), inflicting physical damage that sent Pickering into an early retirement. The British punished the entire Chinese community for this act of violence, withdrawing permission for mounting of the Hungry Ghosts Festival. In response, an anonymous Chinese wrote a letter to Powell in which he accused six leaders of the Ghee Hok secret society of instigating the attack (and requested permission to hold the festival "so that the neglected spirits will not be deprived of their whole year's food by the wicked action of one man" [CO273/153, vol. 3, 239 of June 1888, 13–15]). The headman and four officeholders (who were also suspected of involvement with gambling) were ultimately banished from Singapore (Jackson 1965, 108). The British quickly implemented a policy of complete suppression and brought the period of indirect rule to an abrupt end (see Lee 1991, 134–54). As Trocki suggests, the policy was an attack on "the internal power structure of Chinese society," with the goal of establishing more effective control over the Chinese (Trocki 1991, 178).

The Ghee Hin contributed a lengthy memorial to the debate that preceded the suppression:

> Your memorialists venture to call attention to the fact that if under the former Registration acts certain control was allowed to the headmen of these Societies, the exercise of which might have given rise to the allegations that they claimed an "imperium in imperio," on the other hand grave responsibility was cast on them—a responsibility as to the use and exercise of which they appeal with confidence to the fact, and which has been successfully used in the preservations of order and the safety of the State. (CO273/159, April 15, 1889, 570).

In an eloquent statement, Fairfield, an upper division clerk in the Colonial Office in London, commented that unless the secret societies were replaced by another institution, the abolition of secret societies would "pulverize" Chinese society and "break it up into its individual atoms." He predicted that abolition would be unsuccessful, merely intensifying the secrecy of the groups (CO273/158 77, February 25, 1889).

Rather than enacting laws to punish criminals, the British ultimately outlawed a form of social organization, and in so doing Fairfield estimated that they made "100,000 into Misdemeanants" (CO273/158 77, February 25, 1889). The suppression of secret societies denied them legitimacy and public presence, since the societies no longer had access to visibility in the Straits Settlements through the performance of the initiation rituals (though they continued to sponsor other events such as the Hungry Ghosts and Chinggay festivals [Trocki 1991, 181]). In Pinang and Singapore, the societies sold their meeting houses, and the headmen handed over their insignia, registers, and seals to the British (CO276/22 1891 *Interim Report on the Suppression of Dangerous Societies*, 1083). In 1889 the new Protector of Chinese witnessed not an initiation ritual but a ritual of dissolution: the headmen of "the six Triad branches made formal renunciation by the burning of the original diplomas which constituted them part of the mother organization—the Gi Hin [Ghee Hin]" (CO276/21 *Chinese Protectorate Report for 1889*, 846). In the battle for empire over intellect, the British counted themselves victors.

One might ask whether the British rulers in truth succeeded in their goals. Wynne suggests that many societies, rather than dissolving themselves, merely changed form, chameleonlike. He cites evidence that secret societies posed as clan associations (Wynne 1941, 408), renamed themselves "societies" *(she)*, or chose "retirement for a space within the folds of a local temple" (Wynne 1941, 396–97). During the period after World War II known as the Emergency, the secret societies were again active in Malaya and the Straits Settlements, and the British suspected them of fomenting a range of anticolonial activities. In this period, British scholars metaphorically construed the secret societies as a disease of the Chinese body politic that had not been "cured" by British rule. Thus, in reviewing the history of the secret societies, Purcell noted that the 1870 system of registration "did not cure this ulcer on society" (1948, 164). Blythe, who had been Secretary for Chinese Affairs in Malaya during the Emergency, observed that even after their suppression in 1890, "the secret society virus [later termed by him a 'cancer'] continued to infect the Chinese community" (Blythe 1969, 7). He concluded that brotherhoods like the Triads were virtually impossible to eradicate through legislation because of the depth of their "historical, traditional, ritualistic background" (Blythe 1969, 11).

Conclusion

In this war of competing colonialisms, two forms of government coexisted, each with its own notions of propriety and justice. If politics is a struggle by, with, and over "the means of emotional production" (Collins 1988, 117), then clearly the British did not feel that they controlled those means vis-à-vis the Chinese. The British felt great frustration over their inability to instill respect for their rule into members of the Chinese community and were vexed that the Chinese were not impressed by the "high tone" of their service. Pickering noted that "[t]hey only acknowledge our superiority in brute force and ferocity, and a certain amount of skill in what they deem the manual labour of engineering, and the fabrication of arms" (1876, 445).[9]

Scholars who have studied the Chinese secret societies have often viewed them as forms of resistance to the state. The ideology of the Triads indeed invites such an interpretation, since the myth-history of the group enjoins members to "overthrow the Qing and restore the Ming." The secret societies of colonial Malaya, however, were not created in opposition to the state. Rather, they recreated a political order in a Chinese image that satisfied the needs of the Chinese for a legitimate authority structure. This authority structure, like that of the Chinese state, used the pomp and display of ritual process to reveal hierarchies and sacralize the group and its leaders. The structure was oppositional only in its premises, since the secret societies represented themselves as totalities.

Both British and Qing rulers responded to the presence of these "empires within the empire" by outlawing the secret societies. Legal measures banned the ritual performances that gave secret society leaders social power, and their members' entry into a moral community. In so doing, both states attempted to deny their subjects a form of social organization that bound unrelated individuals together in cohesive social groups. However, British and Qing legal measures failed to eradicate the sworn brotherhoods, perhaps because these rulers themselves had failed to establish "empire over intellect."

Notes

Earlier versions of this chapter were presented at the 1991 meetings of the Association for Asian Studies, at the Southeast Asian Summer Studies Institute at Cornell University, and at the History Colloquium at the National University of Singapore. I would like to thank the Southeast Asia Center at Cornell University, the American Philosophical Society, and the Southeast Asia Council of the Association for Asian Studies for funding for research on Chinese popular religious culture under British colonial rule in the Straits Settlements. John Badgley, David Chng, Paul Kratoska, Norman Parmer, and O. W. Wolters provided guidance in the use of nineteenth-century documents for this project; for critical advice, I thank Sharon Carstens, Stephen Kent, Carl Trocki, and the editors of this volume.

1. CO276/22 1891 *Interim Report on the Suppression of Dangerous Societies*, 1083.
2. For discussion of the social meaning of variation in Chinese ritual, see also Bell (1989); Freedman (1974); Sangren (1987); Weller (1987); and Wolf (1974).
3. The Chinese temple, like the palace, represented cosmic totality in microcosmic form. The center defined an axis around which the four quarters were oriented; the symbolism of center and periphery was joined by a symbolism of elevation, in which "above" and "below" (represented by altars) defined Heaven and Hell. For discussions of the symbolism and importance of sacred centers in East and Southeast Asian polities, see Geertz (1980); Granet (1922); Heine-Geldern (1942); Mus (1935); Tambiah (1976); and Wheatley (1967; 1971).
4. The Triads claimed the Shaolin temple of Fuzhou, Fujian, as their point of origin. However, the historical legend describing the events that led to the founding of the Triads appears to have been inspired by a Tang dynasty account of events involving the Shaolin temple of Henan province (Wynne 1941, 116).
5. Contemporary martial artists (and Malaysian Chinese spirit mediums) trace their martial arts tradition back to the Boddhidharma, who is the founder of Chan (Zen) Buddhism as well as the originator of Shaolin Temple Boxing (P'ng and Draeger 1979). In

contemporary Chinese communities, the gods who possess spirit mediums often are martial artist gods—the God of War, the "Baby" God (Lo Qia), the Monkey—and in trance demonstrate their invulnerability to pain in intimidating performances (DeBernardi 1987). One form of magic that spirit mediums in trance offer is invulnerability magic, which allegedly fortifies those who fight, and the spirit mediums themselves are regarded as "omniscient, impervious to pain and invulnerable" while in trance (Shaw 1973, 101).

6. Missionaries to this region, by contrast, were committed to mastering Chinese. Denied access to China (where teaching the Chinese language to foreigners was illegal), the London Missionary Society established its primary mission in Melaka in 1815 (Lovett 1899, 429), and an outpost in Pinang in 1820 (436).

7. Koh Seang Tat, *Penang Gazette* October 14, 1887 (enclosure in CO273/151).

8. See also Yeoh (1991) for a detailed consideration of the impact of the Burials Ordinance on the Chinese community of Singapore.

9. Purcell also concluded that "[t]he Chinese are most impressed by the European lack of propriety: the Europeans are most impressed by the Chinese industry and love of lucre" (1948, 55).

References

Official Records

The records cited may be found in the archives of the Public Records Office in Kew Gardens (London), England. Series CO273 contains correspondence between the governor of the Straits Settlements and the secretary of state for the colonies for the period from 1867 to 1914; series CO276 contains the Government Gazette and includes the annual reports of the Chinese Protectorate.

Books and Articles

Ahern, Emily Martin. 1981. *Chinese Ritual and Politics*. Cambridge: Cambridge University Press.

Bell, Catherine. 1989. " Religion and Chinese Culture: Toward an Assessment of 'Popular Religion.' " *History of Religions* 29, no. 1:35–57.

Blythe, Wilfred. 1969. *The Impact of Chinese Secret Societies in Malaya*. London: Oxford University Press.

Carstens, Sharon A. 1988. "From Myth to History: Yap Ah Loy and the Heroic Past of Chinese Malaysians." *Journal of Southeast Asian Studies* 19, no. 2:185–208.

Cheng, Lim-Keah. 1969. "The Chinese Community in Kulim Town: A Case-Study of Chinese Social, Economic, Cultural, and Political Activities in West Malaysia." M.A. thesis, University of Wellington, Victoria.

Collins, Randall. 1988. "The Durkheimian Tradition in Conflict Sociology." In *Durkheimian Sociology: Cultural Studies*, ed. Jeffrey C. Alexander, 107–28. Cambridge: Cambridge University Press.

DeBernardi, Jean. 1987. "The God of War and the Vagabond Buddha." *Modern China* 13, no. 3: 310–32.

———. 1991. "Space and Time in Chinese Religious Culture." *History of Religion* 31, no. 3: 247–68.

———. 1994. "Tasting the Water." In *The Dialogic Emergence of Culture*, ed. Bruce Mannheim and Dennis Tedlock. Urbana: University of Illinois Press.

Durkheim, Emile. 1912. *Les Formes élémentaires de la vie religieuse: le système totemique en Australie.* Translated in 1915 and reprinted in 1965 as *The Elementary Forms of the Religious Life,* trans. Joseph Ward Swain. New York: Free Press.

Freedman, Maurice. 1960. "Immigrants and Associations: Chinese in Nineteenth-Century Singapore." Reprinted in 1967 in *Immigrants and Associations,* ed. L. A. Fallers, 17–48. The Hague: Mouton.

————. 1974. "On the Sociological Study of Chinese Religion." In *Religion and Ritual in Chinese Society,* ed. Arthur P. Wolf, 19–41. Stanford: Stanford University Press.

Geertz, Clifford. 1980. *Negara: The Theatre-State in Nineteenth Century Bali.* Princeton: Princeton University Press.

Granet, Marcel. 1922. *La Religion des Chinois.* Paris: Presses Universitaires de France. Translated and reprinted in 1975 as *The Religion of the Chinese People,* trans. Maurice Freedman. New York: Harper & Row.

Heine-Geldern, Robert. 1942. "Conceptions of State and Kingship in Southeast Asia." Reprinted in 1956 as Cornell University Southeast Asia Program Data Paper no. 18.

Jackson, R. N. 1965. *Pickering: Protector of Chinese.* Kuala Lumpur: Oxford University Press.

Kertzer, David I. 1988. *Ritual, Politics, and Power.* New Haven: Yale University Press.

Kynnersley, C. W. S. 1893. "The Prevention and Repression of Crime." Reprinted in 1913 in *Noctes Orientales: Being a Selection of Essays Read Before the Straits Philosophical Society Between the Years 1893 and 1910,* 1–25. Singapore: Kelly & Walsh.

Lee, Edwin. 1991. *The British as Rulers.* Singapore: Singapore University Press.

Lovett, Richard. 1899. *The History of the London Missionary Society, 1795–1895,* vols. 1 & 2. London: Oxford University Press.

Maxwell, P. Benson. 1859. "The Law of England in Penang, Malacca, and Singapore." *Logan's Journal* n.s. vol. 3. Singapore. Reprinted in 1970. Nendeln/Liechtenstein: Kraus–Thomson.

Mus, Paul. 1935. *Barabadur.* Hanoi: Imprimerie d'Extrême Orient.

Pickering, W. A. 1876. "The Chinese in the Straits of Malacca." *Fraser's Magazine* n.s. 14 (October):438–45.

————. 1878, 1879. "Chinese Secret Societies and Their Origin." *Journal of the Straits Branch of the Royal Asiatic Society* 1:63–84; 3:1–18.

P'ng, Chye Khim, and Donn F. Draeger. 1979. *Shaolin: An Introduction to Lohan Fighting Techniques.* Rutland, Vt.: Charles E. Tuttle.

Pocock, J. G. A. 1964. "Ritual, Language, Power: An Essay on the Apparent Political Meanings of Ancient Chinese Philosophy." *Political Science* 16, no. 1: 3–31.

Purcell, Victor. 1948. *The Chinese in Malaya.* Reprinted in 1967. Kuala Lumpur: Oxford University Press.

Radcliffe-Brown, A. R. 1945. "Religion and Society." Reprinted in 1952 in *Structure and Function in Primitive Society,* 153–177. London: Cohen and West.

Sangren, Steven P. 1987. *History and Magical Power in a Chinese Community.* Stanford: Stanford University Press.

Schlegel, Gustave. 1866. *Thian Ti Hwui, The Hung League or Heaven-Earth-League: A Secret Society with the Chinese in China and India.* Reprinted in 1991. Scotland: Tynron Press.

Shaw, William. 1973. "Aspects of Spirit Mediumship, Trance and Ecstasy in Peninsular Malaysia." *Federations Museum Journal* n.s. 18:71–176. Kuala Lumpur: Museums Department.

Stanton, William. 1899. *The Triad Society, or Heaven and Earth Association.* Reprinted in 1900. Hong Kong: Kelly & Walsh.

Tambiah, Stanley Jeyaraja. 1976. *World Conqueror, World Renouncer.* Cambridge: Cambridge University Press.

————. 1985. "A Performative Approach to Ritual." In *Culture, Thought, and Social Action: An Anthropological Perspective*, 123–66. Cambridge: Harvard University Press.

Trocki, Carl A. 1991. *Opium and Empire: Chinese Society in Colonial Singapore*. Ithaca: Cornell University Press.

Ward, J. S. M. and W. G. Stirling. 1925. *The Hung Society, or the Society of Heaven and Earth*, vols. 1–3. Reprinted in 1977. Taipei: Southern Materials Center.

Weld, Sir Frederick A. 1884. "The Straits Settlements and British Malaya." Reprinted in 1983 in *Honourable Intentions: Talks on the British Empire Delivered at the Royal Colonial Institute*, ed. Paul Kratoska. Singapore: Oxford University Press.

Weller, Robert P. 1987. *Unities and Diversities in Chinese Religion*. Seattle: University of Washington Press.

Wheatley, Paul. 1967. *City as Symbol*. London: H. K. Lewis.

————. 1971. *Pivot of the Four Quarters: A Preliminary Enquiry into the Origins and Character of the Ancient Chinese City*. Chicago: Aldine.

Wolf, Arthur P. 1974. "Gods, Ghosts, and Ancestors." In *Religion and Ritual in Chinese Society*, ed. A. P. Wolf, 131–82. Stanford: Stanford University Press.

Wong, Choon Sang. 1964. *A Gallery of Chinese Kapitans*. Singapore: Ministry of Culture.

Wynne, M. L. 1941. *Triad and Tabut: A Survey of the Origin and Diffusion of Chinese and Mohamedan Secret Societies in the Malay Peninsula A.D. 1800–1935*. Singapore: Government Printing Office.

Yang, C. K. 1970. *Religion in Chinese Society*. Berkeley: University of California Press.

Yeoh, Brenda S. A. 1991. "The Control of 'Sacred' Space: Conflicts over the Chinese Burial Grounds in Colonial Singapore, 1880–1930." *Journal of Southeast Asian Studies* 22, no. 2:282–311.

Glossary

Unless otherwise indicated, all glossary terms are rendered in Mandarin. To the extent possible, we have identified the derivation of non-Mandarin terms in parentheses following the entries. H = Hakka; M = Southern Min, or Hokkien; T = Teochiu.

ba	霸
bai angong (M)	拜红公
bai sin (M)	拜神
Baiding	百钉
bashiyuan hui	八十元会
baxianhui	八仙会
biaohui	标会
bijiao	比较
chanpingwang	铲平王
Chen Jinnan	陈近南
cheng	城
chifuhui	吃福会
Chong Chong	张昌

chushe	锄社
Da Qing huidian	大清会典
Da Qing lü xinli	大清律新例
Da Qing lüli	大清律例
Dabogong	大伯公
Dabu	大埔
ding	订
dixiong	弟兄
duiji hui	堆积会
erbaiyuan hui	二百元会
fa	法
Fang Dahong	方大洪
fang	房
fashe	法社
fei	匪
fen	分
fenghua ting	凤花亭
Fo-Sjoen (H)	和顺
Fumuhui	父母会
fun si ka (H)	份子家
Gaoxi	高溪
Gaozhou	高州

Ghee Hin (M)	义兴
Ghee Hok (M)	义福
Guandi	关帝
Guandihui	关帝会
Guanshenghui	关圣会
Hai San	海山
Han Shantong	韩山童
haohan	好汉
hetong	合同
Hiu Siew (H)	邱秀
Hong Dasui	洪大岁
Hong Erfang	洪二房
Hong Litao	洪李桃
hong (vast, flood, Tiandihui surname)	洪
hong (red)	红
hongbaihui	红白会
honglishe	红礼社
hongmaohui	红帽会
Hongwu	洪武
huanjue	缓决
huatie	花帖
hui	会

huifei	会匪
huiguan	会馆
huishou	会首
Huizhou	惠州
hun (M)	分
hunjiahui	婚嫁会
ji shi	继室
jia	家
jianmin	奸民
jiansheng	监生
Jiayingzhou	嘉应州
jiayin	甲寅
jiazi	甲子
jie	结
jiebai dixiong	结拜弟兄
jiehui shudang	结会树党
jiemeng weifei	结盟为匪
jieyi	结义
jijinhui	集金会
jiu	九
junzihui	君子会
jushi	举是

kangchu	港主
kangkar	港脚
kanqinghui	看青会
Kapthai (M)	申太
Keng Tek Hoey (M)	庆德会
khie (M)	旗
Kioe Liong (M, H)	九龙
Kok Kang Keown (H)	郭庚娇
kongsi	公司
Kwan Teck Hui (T)	建德会
Lanfang	兰芳
Leigonghui	雷公会
Leizhou	雷州
Li Dexian	李德先
Li Hong	李弘
Li Jiukui	李九葵
Li Kaihua	李开花
Li Mei	李枚
Li Quanr	李犬儿
Li Taohong	李桃红
Li Zicheng	李自成
li (ritual)	礼

li (unit of distance)　　　里

Li/li (surname, peach)　　李

libi zhangxia　　　　　立毙杖下

lijue　　　　　　　　　立决

Lin Shuangwen　　　　林双文

lin　　　　　　　　　　邻

Lin'er　　　　　　　　林儿

Liu Bowen　　　　　　刘伯温

Liu　　　　　　　　　刘

Liu Futong　　　　　　刘福通

Liu Ji　　　　　　　　刘基

Liu Ngim Kong (H)　　刘壬光

Liu Xigour　　　　　　刘喜狗儿

Liu Zhaokui　　　　　刘照魁

liu　　　　　　　　　　柳

Liucheng　　　　　　　柳城

Lo Fong Pak (H)　　　罗芳伯

Luo Ping　　　　　　　罗平

Ma Chaozhu　　　　　马朝柱

mao　　　　　　　　　卯

Maxi　　　　　　　　马溪

meng　　　　　　　　盟

ming	明
mingjun	明君
mingwang	明王
mingzhu	明主
mou	亩
moupan	谋叛
moupan weixing	谋叛未行
mudou	木斗
muli doushi zhi tianxia	木立斗世知天下
muyang cheng	木杨城
Ngee Ann Kun (T)	义安郡
Ngee Heng (T), Ngee Hin (H), Ghee Hin (M)	义兴
Niu Ba	牛八
nu	奴
peng	朋
qian	钱
qiangdao	强盗
qianhui	钱会
qie	妾
qinghui (invite to enter society)	请会
qinghui (sentiments society)	情会

Qingminghui	清明会
qingshi	情实
qishi	起是
qixianhui	七贤会
qixinghui	七星会
ri	日
Sam Tjam Foei (H)	三点会
Samthiaokioe (H)	三条沟
san ba nian yi	三八廿一
Sandianhui	三点会
Sanhehui	三合会
Shaobingge	烧饼歌
Shaolin	少林
she	社
shehui	赊会
Sheng Ming Li	盛明利
shenghui	圣会
shenminghui	神明会
shenxian	神仙
shi e	十恶
shi (unit of measure)	石
shi (oath)	誓

Shouyihui	守义会
shubaoshe	书报社
shuguan	书馆
shuntian	顺天
shuntian xingdao	顺天行道
Si Sen Ta (H)	四仙大
Sien Hong (M)	先锋
sinkeh (M), sinhak (H)	新客
sui	岁
sujiang	俗讲
Taijin (M)	大人
taiping	太平
tao	桃
taoli	桃李
Taoyuanhui	桃园会
taozishu chushi	桃子树出世
Taukeh	头家
Thai Sen Ta (H)	太仙大
Thaikong (H)	大港
thang (H)	厅
Tiandihui (Heaven and Earth Society)	天地会
Tiandihui (Increase Younger Brothers Society)	添弟会

tianming	天命
tianyu daoxing	天与道行
Tianyun	天运
Tiebianhui	铁鞭会
Tiechihui	铁尺会
Tiko, Thaiko (H)	大哥
Toapekong (M)	大伯公
tongyangxi	童养媳
tuanlian	团练
Tudigong	土地公
tuhao	土豪
Wan Tiqi	万提起
Wan Tuxi	万涂喜
wangdao	王道
wangming xianxing zhengfa	王命先行正法
weitian cheng yunshi	为天承运是
wen	文
wu dian er shi yi	五点二十一
wu shi er	五十二
wufang	五房
wugongjing	五公经
wuhuhui	五虎会

wuzonghui	五总会
Xian Si Shi Ye Miao	仙四师爷庙
Xianfeng	先锋
xiang (township)	乡
xiang (incense)	香
xianghui	香会
xiangyong	乡勇
xiangyue	乡约
xiansheng	先生
xiantao	仙桃
xiantong	仙童
xiao mingwang	小明王
Xiaodaohui	小刀会
Xiaoyihui	孝义会
xiaozhu	小主
xiedou	械斗
xiejiao	邪教
xilufan	西鲁番
xing (seh)	姓
xinghan mieman	兴汉灭满
xiong'e guntu	凶恶棍徒
xiongdi	兄弟

xishe	喜社
yang	杨
Yangzhou	阳州
yaohui	摇会
Yap A Loy (H) (Ye De Lai)	叶亚来（叶德来）
Yap Ah Shak (H)	叶亚石
Yap Si (H)	叶四
Yep Siong-yoen (H)	叶湘
yi	邑
Yiguan dao	一贯道
yin	寅
yinhui	银会
yinqian yaohui	银钱摇会
Yiqianhui	一钱会
yishe	邑社
youzhu	幼主
yuan	圆
yue (moon)	月
yue (compact, bond)	约
yueguang tongzi	月光童子
yufohui	浴佛会
yumin	愚民

zafan	杂犯
zangqinshe	葬亲社
zha	札
zhafu	札付
zhaihui	斋会
Zhang	张
Zhang Zhengmo	张正谟
Zhao	赵
zhen	镇
Zheng Chenggong	郑成功
zhengfa	正法
zhenming tianzi	真明天子
zhenzhu	真主
zhiji	知己
Zhu Dingyuan	朱鼎元
Zhu Hongde	朱洪德
Zhu Hongjin	朱洪锦
Zhu Hongtao	朱红桃
Zhu Hongzhu	朱红竹
Zhu Hongzong	竹红宗
Zhu Jiutao	朱九桃
Zhu	朱

Zhu Yuanzhang	朱元璋
zhu	主
zi	字

Index